DAILY LIFE IN

THE AMERICAN WEST

D0082018

Recent Titles in
The Greenwood Press Daily Life Through History Series

DAILY LIFE IN

THE AMERICAN WEST

JASON E. PIERCE

The Greenwood Press Daily Life Through History Series

GREENWOOD

An Imprint of ABC-CLIO, LLC
Santa Barbara, California • Denver, Colorado

Library of Congress Cataloging-in-Publication Data

Names: Pierce, Jason (Jason Eric), author.
Title: Daily life in the American West / Jason E. Pierce.
Description: [Santa Barbara, California] : Greenwood, [2022] |
Series: The Greenwood Press daily life through history series |
   Includes bibliographical references and index.
Identifiers: LCCN 2022001350 (print) | LCCN 2022001351
   (ebook) | ISBN 9781440876196 (hardcover) |
   ISBN 9781440876202 (ebook)
Subjects: LCSH: Frontier and pioneer life—West (U.S.) | West
   (U.S.)—Social life and customs—19th century. | West
   (U.S.)—History—19th century.
Classification: LCC F596 .P53 2022 (print) | LCC F596 (ebook) |
   DDC 978—dc23/eng/20220114
LC record available at https://lccn.loc.gov/2022001350
LC ebook record available at https://lccn.loc.gov/2022001351

ISBN: 978-1-4408-7619-6 (print)
      978-1-4408-7620-2 (ebook)

26 25 24 23 22   1 2 3 4 5

This book is also available as an eBook.

Greenwood
An Imprint of ABC-CLIO, LLC

ABC-CLIO, LLC
147 Castilian Drive
Santa Barbara, California 93117
www.abc-clio.com

This book is printed on acid-free paper ∞

Manufactured in the United States of America

CONTENTS

PREFACE

"Eastward I go only by force," Henry David Thoreau famously said, "but westward I go free." It is a famous line that has aged into cliché, the kind of thing that ends up emblazoned on posters of gorgeous Western landscapes: snowcapped peaks; stark, ruddy deserts; or the molten globe of a setting sun sinking into the Pacific. Indeed, that is exactly what it has become, and you can download wallpapers for your personal computer from a website called "Quote Fancy" with the line emblazoned on it.

Less well known is the essay in which that line appears. The essay in question, "Walking," appeared in *The Atlantic* in June 1862, a month after Thoreau's death. In it, Thoreau celebrated the benefits of "sauntering," casually strolling for hours wherever one felt compelled to go, but "Walking" was no mere advice column on the mental and physical benefits of a good walk. It was also a rumination on the importance of open spaces. Thoreau groused, "Nowadays almost all man's improvements, so called, as the building of houses and the cutting down of the forest and of all large trees, simply deform the landscape, and make it more and more tame and cheap" (Thoreau 1862). The only region as yet untainted by excessive civilization, Thoreau believed, was the West. Even from Massachusetts, the American philosopher could feel the pull of the West when he left his house on his daily walks, and he believed it spoke to something universal in the American spirit. "I should not lay so much stress on this fact [of going west], if I did not believe that something like this is the prevailing tendency of my country-men," he observed. "I must walk toward Oregon, and not toward Europe. And that way the nation is moving, and I may say that mankind progress from east to west" (Thoreau 1862). For Thoreau, and he believed his countrymen as well, going west meant becoming more uniquely American.

Thoreau would not live to see the West fully settled, and perhaps, for him, it was just as well. A mere seven years after his death, the completion of the first transcontinental railroad tethered the nation together, making the once arduous and dangerous crossing of the continent a comparatively easy affair. A bit more than 15 years after that, in 1886, Geronimo and a few dozen other Chiricahua Apache surrendered at Skeleton Canyon, in the Arizona Territory, mark-ing an end to the centuries of conflict between whites and Indian peoples, a finale with the tragic exception of one bitter coda that would occur on a December morning in 1890.

Indeed, by the 1880s, the wildest days of the Wild West had already lapsed into memory and, increasingly, mythology. Towns and cities sprang up; railroads crisscrossed the region; mines poured fourth tons of gold, silver, copper, and coal; and the West's wild places, its crenelated canyons, towering mountains, and sinu-ous rivers that so captivated Thoreau's imagination had been over-run by miners, lumberjacks, and engineers bent on transforming the region to make it serve the interests of an increasingly powerful industrial nation. The West would never again be as seemingly pris-tine, but people like Thoreau—and a bit later Theodore Roosevelt, John Muir, and others—would have an effect on Americans as well, convincing them that there was something to be said for leaving some places alone, leaving wildlands as part of the nation's inheri-tance. Conservation, the belief that resources should be used and managed wisely, and preservation, the desire to leave some places without obvious signs of human interference, both found support at the turn of the last century, and the West offered most of the best remaining land for such reforms. Theodore Roosevelt, the first president to have spent much time in the West, championed these efforts, setting aside more land as national parks, national monu-ments, and national forests than all presidents before or since, and the vast majority lay in the West.

The West lived on, as well, in the imaginations of all Americans and even among peoples in other nations. By the late 19th century, Americans, especially young Americans, consumed the various dime novels that recounted the (generally exaggerated) exploits of Western heroes and outlaws like Buffalo Bill, Billy the Kid, and Calamity Jane. The transition of these mass-market heroes to film and radio proved remarkably easy, and by the mid-20th century, celluloid cowboys rode to glory every night of the week on big screens and flickering home television sets. Americans, even in an age of industrial conveniences like air-conditioning, TV dinners, and automobiles, could imagine themselves confronting danger on the edges of an always vanishing Western frontier. Many believed, as Frederick Jackson Turner had asserted in 1893, that the frontier was the place where Americans became truly American.

As early as the dawn of the 19th century, Americans already felt these impulses in the marrow of their bones. Westward expansion provided a sense of mission. As the newspaperman John O'Sullivan declared in the 1840s with his evocative phrase "Manifest Destiny," God himself saw the Americans as His new chosen people, destined to spread Christianity, democracy, and American civilization to the very shores of the Pacific. This sense of mission inspired Americans as they made their way alongside creaking wagons over the Oregon Trail. It added a unique flavor to the religious beliefs of the Mormons, who felt themselves caught up in the romance of westward expansion while reenacting biblical tropes of enduring prosecution and exodus in order to reach the promised land.

The settlement of the West and its incorporation into the nation certainly had romance and adventure, but it was less the unalloyed success that writers, scholars, and mythmakers like Roosevelt, Turner, and the novelist Owen Wister imagined. Certainly, its settlement added wealth to the coffers of the nation, helping propel the United States to greatness. But there were losers too, people whose lifeways vanished in the conquest. In the Southwest, many Mexican Americans saw their land swindled from them by unscrupulous lawyers, government officials, and sometimes even Anglo sons-in-law who married into wealthy families only to steal the land for themselves. No people, however, lost more than the American Indians of the West. While they would make a concerted effort to resist, as the United States grew ever larger and more powerful, their defeat became inevitable. Despite the desperation of a religious revival movement known as the Ghost Dance, there could be no going back to the world of the past. Ironically, the very people who conquered and dispossessed the Indians would come to celebrate Indian resistance as part of the American story, and Indian leaders such as Crazy Horse, Sitting Bull, and Geronimo became household names.

A century and a half after Thoreau's famous essay, the second episode of season six of *The X-Files* took the idea of going west quite literally. First aired on November 15, 1998, the episode sees the hero, FBI agent Fox Mulder (played by David Duchovny), racing westward across Nevada and California with a wanted man named Patrick Crump (Brian Cranston) writhing in pain in the backseat of a stolen station wagon. Mulder's partner, agent Dana Scully (Gillian Anderson), discovers that the excruciating pain, centered in Crump's ear, is the result of a secret government radio array whose waves, she explains during a cell phone conversation, "somehow match the resonant frequency of the human skull . . . and somehow exert a rising pressure on the labyrinth of the inner ear, in a sense shattering it." The pain subsides so long as Crump and Mulder hurtle to the west. In reply, Mulder notes, "But with constant movement somehow ameliorating that pressure making it bearable. But why only westward movement?" Scully can only speculate as they hatch a plan to meet at the end of the highway to try and save Crump's life by relieving the pressure in his ear with an emergency surgery. However, as Mulder pulls into a parking spot overlooking the Pacific Ocean to meet his partner, a telltale splatter of blood on the car's window shows they are too late (Fandom n.d.).

The fantastic nature of the episode works in part because of the deep cultural predilection to go west (perhaps answering Mulder's question in the process) and is perhaps a tongue-in-cheek reference to Frederick Jackson Turner's assertion that western expansion could serve as a pressure release for population growth by episode writer Vince Gilligan. The episode ends with Agent Mulder looking distraught as he stands on the edge of the West at the literal end of the road.

Encapsulated in these cultural artifacts, separated by a century and half, are Americans' views of the West and, not inconsequentially, of themselves. The optimism of the 19th century has given way to a sense of inevitable loss, a West that is not inexhaustible and unending. More than any other region of the nation, the West is the place where we let our imaginations flourish, and part of that is imagining who we are. The conquest of the West and the invention of Americans occurred together and have been fused ever since. Part imagined world and part a real but wondrous place, the West has a hold on the American consciousness that will endure for as long as the nation itself endures.

Jason Pierce

San Angelo, Texas, 2021

ACKNOWLEDGMENTS

After a bit more than 15 years of teaching, I have been fortunate to have scores of enthusiastic students, students who have taught me that we as people enjoy stories. Indeed, humans, so far as we know, are the only storytelling animal. Stories are powerful things. They tell us much about ourselves; our hopes, fears, and dreams are encapsulated in the stories we tell. Stories are also how we empathize with people who differ from us, how we understand our common humanity across time, space, language, and culture. While history is often about great sweeping changes (the rise and fall of empires, the struggle for rights, or titanic bloody conflicts), it is also found in the small, the ordinary, and the everyday. Having taught numerous sections of the history of the American West over the years, I have had the opportunity to include some amazing stories in my classes. Most of those are now found in the pages of this book.

Thus, I would like to thank ABC-CLIO for giving me the opportunity to compile some of my favorite stories into a book that tries to relate the wonderous and the mundane, the well known and the obscure, that shaped and created one of the most unique and inescapably romantic regions in the world. At ABC-CLIO, my thanks especially go to Erin Ryan, for her editorial and stylistic insights on the manuscript and for her patience with the deadlines as well.

I would also like to thank all the storytellers who have shaped my love of the West, professional influences such as Arnoldo De León, Elliott West, Bill Lang, Robert Bunting, and Duane A. Smith, the latter the first bona fide historian I ever encountered in my mother's Western Mining class at Fort Lewis College in the 1980s. Dr. Smith knew how to spin a yarn that kept an elementary school kid's attention during a field trip to Silverton, Colorado. More personally, I would like to thank my mother and her father for instilling a love of storytelling and the West in me from the very beginning.

Finally, I would like to acknowledge my sons, Cyrus and Darius, and my kind and generous wife, Mondie, for the stories we create as a family, adding our own thin skeins to the tapestry of the human experience.

INTRODUCTION

Hoping to capitalize on the incandescent fervor of the California gold rush, John C. Frémont's publisher rushed out a revised version of the report of his Western expeditions in 1853. By the early 1850s, Frémont had become a celebrity of sorts, and the reports of his expeditions (spruced up by the talented pen of his wife, Jessie) had become unlikely best sellers due to their relative accuracy when compared to some of the more fanciful guidebooks on the market. While Frémont's text remained appropriately sedate in its prose, the included advertisement for the new edition did not. It began in almost messianic tones: "The dreams of the visionary have 'come to pass!' [*sic*] the El Dorado of the 'fathers' looms, in all its virgin freshness and beauty, before the eyes of their children! The 'set time' for the Golden age, the advent of which has been looked for and longed for during many centuries of iron wrongs and hardships has fully come." No longer a prosaic explanation of geography and resources, Frémont's report bordered on the prophetic. The promised land for the new Israelites, as Americans increasingly thought of themselves, lay out in the hazy West, goading them into converting wilderness into garden: "In the sunny clime of the south west—in Upper California—may be found the modern Canaan, a land 'flowing with milk and honey,' its mountains studded and its rivers lined and choked, with gold!" (Frémont 1853).

America's destiny lay in the West; its rise to greatness, rivaling any-thing in scripture or antiquity, seemed assured. Americans gained confidence from this belief in themselves as the new chosen people of God. America would look west, and the frontier seemed endless.

Going west, therefore, was not merely a move; it was a cultural experience, one Americans knew they were participating in even as they were doing it. Anglo-Americans, African Americans, recent European immigrants, and eventually the Chinese and Japanese, all carried their hopes and aspirations into the West. The Oregon Trail experience, for example, was freighted with notions of national pride, patriotism, and a desire to see the United States expand to the Pacific. Participating in this once-in-a-lifetime experience prompted many to keep diaries and send letters to family back in the East and Midwest. Like the bass line in a song, this belief in being part of something bigger than oneself lingered on the periphery of consciousness, taking various phrases over the decades, but most notably that of "Manifest Destiny."

Grandiose pronouncements by editors and politicians could only occupy one so much. Settlers would not only have to come to terms with their hopes but also the steely-eyed reality of the West as vast, isolated, and often arid. Overcoming these challenges—challenges as enormous as changing the course of rivers and as personal as learning to bake bread at 10,000 feet above sea level—shaped and transformed both its settlers and the West in numerous and sometimes surprising ways.

To be sure, these mostly Anglo-American settlers did not encounter, as they often believed, virgin lands; indeed, thriving cultures had occupied the region for thousands of years, their cultures firmly planted in the thin Western soils. These earlier peoples had likewise grappled with the capricious nature of the West, facing its blizzards and its droughts and forging unique societies and cultures in all the region's varied environments. American Indians and Mexican Americans had their own histories of conquests and conflicts, and they too harbored hopes and aspirations. But their ways of life, their very existence, soon became threatened by these newcomers in their tens of thousands. They would resist, but it would be too little to stem the tide.

This book, *Daily Life in the American West*, recounts those grand sweeping changes of conquest and settlement that occurred in the West over the course of the 19th century, but it also looks at the more mundane, the more ordinary, to see how these various peoples learned to live in the West.

Chapter 1, "Domestic Life of American Indians in the American West," begins with life among the Indians of the West at the dawn of their contact with Europeans. It looks at how American Indian peoples, especially in the Southwest, conceived of their world and shaped their natural environment to meet their needs. For example, the Pueblo peoples of New Mexico farmed along the life-giving waters of the Rio Grande for centuries. The arrival of the Spanish, in many ways, disrupted their way of life, but in the end, both would have to adapt to coexist and survive in the region.

The Spanish entrada also set in motion profound changes. Some of these changes, like the introduction of European diseases such as smallpox, presented unimaginable threats, but others brought opportunity. The most significant opportunity for many American Indian peoples came with the introduction of the horse. In a few short decades, Indian peoples like the Kiowa, Comanche, Cheyenne, and Lakota reinvented themselves to be peoples of the Plains. Hunting buffalo provided a seemingly inexhaustible and reliable source of food, and the fleet horses enabled humans, for the first time, to follow the herds from place to place. The resulting cultures became world famous, the very avatars of how peoples around the world would conceive of American Indians. The first chapter explores how these peoples reinvented themselves, but chapter 7 will narrate their efforts to preserve their cultures in the face of a massive industrial enemy in the United States.

Chapter 2, "Domestic Life on the Overland Trails," follows the experiences of emigrants to Oregon and California. These were mobile communities, Midwestern farm towns on wheels, traversing a scenic but dangerously unfamiliar country. Daily life, while similar in many ways to the life they left behind, adapted to the trail experience, falling into the rhythms of footsteps and creaking wagons. Overland emigrants carried their values and beliefs as much as their clothing and tools with them into the West. This experience filled with them with a sense of mission and national pride.

Chapter 3, "Domestic Life on the Mining Frontier," looks at daily life on the mining frontier. No other industry contributed so rapidly to the Anglo-American conquest of the West. The temperate climate and good soils of the Oregon Country coaxed a few thousand farmers to relocate from the Midwest to the Willamette Valley, but the 1848 discovery of gold in the foothills of the Sierra Nevada mountains caused one of the most rapid and momentous migrations of people in human history. In 1849 alone, over 100,000 people gravitated to California from all points of the globe. Less than two years after the territory had been added to the nation, thanks to the Treaty of Guadalupe Hidalgo that ended the Mexican-American War, California applied for statehood. Subsequent discoveries in Oregon, Colorado, South Dakota, and nearly every Western territory would see similar rushes. Overnight towns, composed almost entirely of men, sprouted up along streams and hillsides. Some prospered, their mines proving profitable, but most fizzled out and disappeared almost as quickly and they had appeared.

Mining discoveries, however, brought their own issues. For Indian peoples, the discovery of gold meant the arrival of scores of miners and often soldiers and diplomats eager to push them off their ancestral lands in the name of progress. Mining also scarred the land, denuded the available timber, and diverted streams or filled them with tons of sludge and sediment that killed fish for miles downstream. Flash floods became more common, and as the industry developed, the mouths of underground mines spewed forth waters carrying heavy metals. While very few mines are still in operation in the West, long-abandoned mines continue to pour forth their poisoned waters, a toxic legacy that endures to this day.

Chapters 4 and 5, "Economic Life in the American West" and "Political Life in the American West," respectively, analyze the economic and political transformation of the West. The spread of capitalism in industries such as mining, the railroads, and the cattle industry fundamentally changed the region. Similarly, the acquisition of the West came at something of an inopportune time for the young nation. The 1803 purchase of the Louisiana Territory opened up numerous possibilities for the fledgling United States, and Americans proved eager to explore and eventually settle it. The fundamental question, which became more contentious in the decades to come, was what that settlement would look like. Would the new territories in Louisiana and those acquired after the Mexican-American War be settled only by free white Americans, or would Southerners move west with thousands of slaves? The resulting debate over the expansion of the "peculiar institution" of slavery would be the catalyst for the Civil War.

Chapter 6, "Religious Life in the American West," explores religious attitudes in the region, particularly those of Plains Indians, such as the Lakota, and one of the West's most iconic and misunderstood peoples, the Mormons. Harried and persecuted for their beliefs, the Mormons eventually found their promised land in the Salt Lake Valley, seeing their own story as an echo of the struggles of the Israelites to find their chosen land. Despite what Americans thought at the time, the Mormon experience was indelibly American, their exodus part of a larger narrative of expansion and reinvention in the West.

Chapter 7, "The Indian Wars and the Transformation of Daily Life for American Indians" covers the decades of Plains Indian people's resistance to American expansion, and the profound changes to daily life that stemmed from the conflict over territory and resources. This period saw the defeat of all American Indian peoples and their relocation to reservations where they struggled to survive and maintain their identity.

Chapter 8, "Intellectual Life and the Myth of the West," deals with the mythic West. No other region of the nation is so firmly entrenched in our collective imagination as the West. Indeed, in the later 19th century, a variety of authors, artists, and promoters churned out novels, paintings, and popular entertainments like Buffalo Bill Cody's Wild West show that played up the romance of the West. So popular were these "dime novels," paintings, and shows that they created a ready-made plot for early movies and later television programs. By the 1950s, heroic cowboys swaggered across the big screen and the television sets of millions of Americans. Even today, the Western endures—changed, but the outlines are still there—in popular programs such as *The Mandalorian*, a Western set on the Outer Rim (the frontier) of the Star Wars galaxy.

Finally, the epilogue, "The Future of the West," reflects on the past and ponders what the future of the West will look like. The region, always harsher than the more temperate parts of the nation, is facing incredibly challenging issues, largely the result of climate change and the ways in which we have structured our technological civilization. The future of the West, a region synonymous with open spaces, individuality, and freedom, may depend on that least Western of attributes: cooperation.

TIMELINE

50,000–20,000 years ago
Humans arrive in the Americas, possibly following a coastal migration route. Little is known about these early cultures.

13,500 years ago
The Clovis culture emerges, leaving their distinctive spearpoints scattered around the Americas. They are the first identifiable culture. Clovis peoples, named for a site discovered in the 1930s near Clovis, New Mexico, hunted big game, such as the American mastodon.

11,500 years ago
The Holocene period begins. Earth warms, and the ice age ends. Many large animals disappear, likely due to a warming climate and, at least in part, predation by humans.

10,000 years ago
Corn (or maize) is probably first cultivated in modern Mexico. Corn, beans, and squash, often called the "Three Sisters," are cultivated across many areas in Central and North America. Other domesticated crops proliferate in the Americas as well, including potatoes and cocoa. However, there are comparatively few domesticated animals.

Before AD 1492
Agriculture leads to the creation of many powerful sedentary civilizations, including the Inca in South America, the Maya and Aztec in Central America, and the Ancestral Pueblo peoples of the American Southwest. At least 60 million people lived in the Americas.

1492   Christopher Columbus makes his first expedition to the New World and mistakenly believes he has reached Asia.

1513   The Spanish Balboa expedition crosses Panama and reaches the Pacific Ocean. The Spanish realize they are not in Asia but rather in a New World.

1528–1536   A band of Spaniards, remnants of the failed Narváez expedition to Florida, come ashore on the Texas coast. Among them are Álvar Núñez Cabeza de Vaca and Estevanico, an African slave. The surviving members immerse themselves in Indian culture until they are able to return to Spanish territory in Northern Mexico in 1536. Apparently, the survivors tell of a kingdom of rich cities known as Cíbola.

1540   The expedition of Francisco Vázquez de Coronado heads north from Mexico, eventually traveling through Arizona, New Mexico, Texas, Oklahoma, and Kansas in search of the Seven Golden Cities of Cíbola. He returns empty-handed but claims these new territories for Spain. He also brings the first horses into what would become the West.

1542   Juan Cabrillo, a Portuguese captain employed by Spain, sails along the coast of California.

1598   Juan de Oñate arrives with a large expedition to colonize and Christianize New Mexico for Spain. Missions are built to convert the Indians, and local Indian peoples provide (willingly or not) labor to build churches, supply *presidios* (military bases), and enrich the *encomenderos*, owners of large estates.

1680   Pueblo Indian peoples in New Mexico grow angry at Spanish greed and the imprisonment of several religious leaders for "witchcraft." They stage a shocking and well-planned revolt against Spanish rule, killing numerous Spaniards and forcing the Spanish out of New Mexico. The tumult frees many horses, which are soon adopted by other Indian peoples.

1692   Diego de Vargas reconquers New Mexico. By 1700, a stable and largely peaceful accommodation is reached. The Pueblo Indians and Spaniards need each other, and both are increasingly threatened by the *bárbaros*, tribes of mounted Indians from the plains that include the Apache and the Comanche.

1680–1700   The Apache, Comanche, and other Indians of Texas and the Southern Plains acquire the horse. In the coming decades, the horse will spread across the West. Horses transform many Indian cultures, allowing for the pursuit of bison as a food source year-round and enabling trading and raiding over vast distances.

1716   Spaniards establish the first missions in Texas.

1730s   French fur trappers begin to probe the Missouri River, establishing a presence among the Mandan peoples of the upper Missouri River.

1758   The Comanche destroy the Mission Santa Cruz de San Sabá, on the San Saba River in central Texas. Its destruction illustrates the precarious position of Spanish settlements in Texas.

1763   The British victory in the French and Indian War removes the French from North America, but many French settlers and fur trappers remain.

1769   Father Junípero Serra establishes missions in southern California to convert local Indians. Many, however, die from mistreatment and disease.

1778   British captain James Cook explores Washington and British Columbia. He establishes the sea otter fur trade by selling skins in China. Soon, British and American ships are visiting Indian villages to trade for skins and furs.

1792   American captain Robert Gray discovers the Columbia River and helps establish American claims to the Pacific Northwest.

1803   The United States purchases the Louisiana Territory from the French for $15 million.

1804–1806   The Lewis and Clark Expedition explores the northern Louisiana Territory and winters on the Pacific coast, near the mouth of the Columbia River.

1806–1807   Zebulon Pike leads an expedition into Colorado and is captured by the Spanish, who take him deep into Mexico before returning him to Louisiana. Pike is not impressed with the terrain he passes through and helps convince Americans that it is in fact a desert unsuitable for agriculture or settlement.

1811   John Jacob Astor's American Fur Company establishes Astoria, Oregon. Returning trappers blaze a trail that will eventually become the Oregon Trail.

1821   Spain grants Moses Austin a contract to bring settlers into their northern territory of Texas. His son, Stephen F. Austin, will take over the contract after his father's death. By 1830,

	about 7,000 Americans are living in the Mexican state of Coahuila y Tejas.
1836	The Texas Revolution establishes Texas as an independent nation.
1836	Marcus and Narcissa Whitman and Henry and Eliza Spalding cross overland to establish missions among the Cayuse and Nez Percé Indians in the Pacific Northwest. Their success inspires settlers to venture to the "Oregon Country."
1845	The United States annexes Texas, angering Mexico.
1846–1848	The Mexican-American War takes place.
1848	James Marshall discovers gold at Sutter's Mill in central California.
1848	The Treaty of Guadalupe Hidalgo cedes half of Mexico to the United States, including California.
1849	News of the discovery of gold attracts more than 100,000 "forty-niners" to California.
1850	The Compromise of 1850 brings California into the Union as a free state.
1858	Gold is discovered in Colorado.
1859	Oregon is admitted to the Union as a free state.
1861–1865	The U.S. Civil War takes place. The expansion of slavery in the West brought about war, but very few battles are fought in the West.
1862	Congress passes the Homestead Act, making Western lands easily affordable to settlers, and the Pacific Railway Act, which outlines plans for a transcontinental railroad.
1862	The Dakota War takes place in Minnesota. Dozens of settlers are killed, prompting reprisals from the U.S. military and volunteers. After cursory trials, 38 Dakota men are executed in a mass hanging at the town of Mankato, Minnesota.
1864	Colorado volunteers massacre a peaceful village of Cheyenne and Arapaho Indians at Sand Creek, killing as many as 500 people. Angered, Plains Indians retaliate across the West.
1866	Red Cloud's War between the Lakota and the U.S. Army takes place.

1867	The Medicine Lodge Treaty ends the violence on the Southern Plains for a time.
1868	The Treaty of Fort Laramie promises the Lakota a vast reservation in the territories of Montana, Wyoming, and Dakota that includes the sacred Black Hills.
1869	The Union Pacific and Central Pacific Railroads meet at Promontory Point, Utah, completing the nation's first transcontinental railroad line.
1874	Prompted by rumors of gold, George Armstrong Custer leads an expedition into the Black Hills, setting off a gold rush and violating the terms of the Treaty of Fort Laramie.
1874–1875	The Red River War ends with Quanah Parker's surrender in June 1875, and Indian resistance on the Southern Plains largely ceases.
1876	The U.S. Army launches a campaign against the Lakota Sioux. Custer and all the men directly under his command are killed in a failed attack on the Lakota and Cheyenne village at Little Bighorn River.
1877	After a winter of privation and hardship, the Lakota leader Crazy Horse and nearly 900 followers surrender at Fort Robinson, Nebraska.
	War erupts between the U.S. military and the peaceful Nez Percé. Joseph and Looking Glass lead a daring escape to Canada through Idaho, Wyoming, and Montana but are defeated in October less than 40 miles from the border.
1886	The Chiricahua Apache leader Geronimo and his followers surrender at Skeleton Canyon, in southeastern Arizona. Indian resistance essentially ends in the West as Indian peoples are forced onto reservations.
1887	The Dawes Allotment Act is passed. Designed to convert collectively owned reservations into private landholdings, the act is intended to help Indian peoples adapt to the modern world. Instead, it ends up taking more land away from Indian peoples.
1890	The vision of a Paiute prophet, Wovoka, spreads across the West. The Ghost Dance ceremony promises to restore the lost bison and end the control of whites. In December, the Ghost Dance leads to a tragic massacre of peaceful Lakota at Wounded Knee Creek.

1893   The historian Frederick Jackson Turner delivers his famous essay "The Significance of the Frontier in American History" at the Chicago World's Fair. His claim that the frontier experience is now over causes shock and dismay for Americans.

1896   The Klondike gold rush, the last of the major gold rushes, begins.

1898   The Spanish-American War takes place. Soldiers from Western forts, especially African American "buffalo soldiers," do much of the fighting in the war.

1905   The U.S. Forest Service is created during the Theodore Roosevelt presidency, with Gifford Pinchot as its first head.

1906   The San Francisco earthquake burns much of the city, killing thousands.

1914   Despite the opposition of John Muir, construction of the controversial Hetch Hetchy dam begins, providing water for San Francisco but flooding a beautiful mountain valley inside Yosemite National Park.

1917   The United States enters World War I.

1922   The Colorado River Compact is created to share the water of the Colorado River between seven Western states.

1929   The Great Depression begins.

1932   Franklin Delano Roosevelt, who promises the American people a "New Deal," is elected president. Soon, Westerners are employed by a variety of government agencies, such as the Civilian Conservation Corps.

1941   The Grand Coulee Dam in Washington—one of dozens of large dams built in the West—is completed.

1941–1945   World War II takes place. Defense spending, migration, and other factors related to the war dramatically change the West. California, in particular, grows rapidly.

1942   Japanese Americans along the Pacific coast are forced into internment camps, most in the Intermountain West. The majority lose their homes and businesses during the internment period.

1962   Pete Seibert founds Vail Ski Resort in central Colorado, as skiing and other forms of recreation have become increasingly popular and lucrative. By the 1980s and 1990s, many Western towns have transitioned to a tourism-based economy, as mining and other traditional industries have declined.

1945– present Western cities grow dramatically, making the region more politically powerful. Postwar politicians from the West include conservatives such as Barry Goldwater, Richard Nixon, and Ronald Reagan. In the 1960s to 1980s, rural residents complain about federal regulations, especially environmental regulations, and stage protests and revolts known as the "Sagebrush Rebellion." In recent decades, California, Oregon, Washington, New Mexico, and Colorado have been trending toward more socially liberal policies.

1998– present Drought conditions persist across the region, especially in the Colorado River Basin, on which 40 million people depend for their water.

GLOSSARY

Allotment: The process of breaking up Indian reservations into privately held small farms as part of the 1887 Dawes Act.

Annexation: The addition of an independent territory into another territory. In 1845, the United States annexed Texas, adding it as a state.

Aridity: The lack of readily available water, a major feature of life in the American West.

Bárbaros: The Spanish term for the fearsome mounted Indians that terrorized settlements in the 1700s.

Blotaunka: The Lakota name for a leader assigned war powers.

Book of Mormon: The sacred book of members of the Church of Jesus Christ of Latter-day Saints, recounting the settlement of the New World and Jesus's visit to the Indians.

Brucellosis: A parasitic bacterial infection that infects the lungs of cattle and bison.

Chuck wagon: A mobile kitchen mounted on a wagon that fed cowboys during a cattle drive.

Comancheros: Hispanic professional traders from New Mexico who exchanged foodstuffs and manufactured goods with Plains Indians for buffalo hides and skins.

Commodification: The process of taking something, a beaver pelt, for example, and transforming it into a commodity that can be bought or sold.

Counting coup: A display of extreme bravery by Plains Indians warriors in which an individual physically touches an enemy without killing the enemy.

Diné: The proper name for the Navajo Indians of the Four Corners area, literally meaning "the people."

Encomenderos: Spaniards given land and dominion over Indian peoples.

Engages: Fur trappers who worked for the large trading companies on salary.

Free-Soilers: People who wanted to outlaw slavery in the territories of the West.

Hard rock mining: Extracting valuable minerals, like gold, from buried rock, often by following mineral-bearing veins deep underground.

Hocoka: The arena in which Lakota peoples participate in the Sun Dance ceremony.

Kachinas or Kachina dancers: Dancers who wear masks and embody sacred entities while leading important ceremonies in Pueblo cultures.

Kinaalda: The coming of age ceremony for Navajo girls.

Kivas: Circular, often underground, religious structures found in Pueblo Indian villages.

Lamanites: In Mormon beliefs, the Lamanites are the descendants of Laman, who rebelled against the authority of Nephi. Mormons believe the Lamanites became the modern American Indians.

Mano: A stone used to grind grains, especially corn, into flour.

Megafauna: The collective name for the exceptionally large animals of the late Pleistocene period, including the American mastodon and woolly mammoth.

Millennium: The belief among many Christian groups that if humanity perfected itself, the Second Coming of Christ would occur.

Nauvoo: Onetime Mormon capital city on the banks of the Mississippi River in Illinois. It was abandoned in 1846 as Mormons relocated to Utah, away from religious persecution.

Neophyte: A recent convert to Catholicism.

Numunu: The Comanche name for themselves, translated, as was typical, to mean "the people."

Olla: Pottery water jug traditionally used by the Pueblo peoples.

Paleo-Indians: Prehistoric Indian peoples of the late Pleistocene period, including cultures such as the Clovis and Folsom.

Placer mining: The mining of gold that has collected in streams and rivers from years of gradual erosion.

Pleistocene: The period in Earth's history from 2.6 million to 11,700 years ago, coinciding with the ice ages.

Pneumoconiosis or "black lung": A disease afflicting coal miners caused by long exposure to coal dust that gradually damages and destroys the lungs.

Potlatch: A ceremony, practiced by Indians in the Pacific Northwest and Canada, in which wealthy tribal leaders distributed gifts to other members of the tribe. These gifts shared property and created networks of reciprocity among the members.

Presidio: The Spanish name for a military outpost or base.

Public domain: Land owned and managed by the federal government in the name of the American people.

Repartimiento: A system of forced labor that replaced the encomienda system. Technically, Indians provided only temporary or seasonal labor under the repartimiento system.

Shaman: A religious figure, sometimes called a medicine man, who acts as a bridge between Indian peoples and the forces of the universe, often by performing sacred ceremonies.

Silicosis: An often fatal lung disease caused by inhaling silicate dust. Over time, the silica gradually hardens the lungs, making them less pliable and breathing more difficult. Many cases were caused by early hydraulic drills.

Stampede: The uncontrolled flight of a herd of terrified cattle.

Sun Dance: The most important religious ceremony for many Plains Indian peoples. It was designed to get assistance from the forces of the universe through ritualistic dancing and symbolic sacrifice as forms of veneration.

Tiospaye: Large groups of related extended Lakota families.

Travois: Wooden poles that Plains Indians tied to their horses that enabled them to load and transfer their tipis and other belongings from camp to camp.

Vaquero: The Spanish term for "cowboy."

Wakantanka: The Lakota name for the creative force of the universe, sometimes also called "the Great Spirit," though not in the Christian form of an all-powerful human-like God.

Wakiconza: An important Lakota leadership position whereby an individual acts as a judge and important leader for the village.

Wasichus: The Lakota word for "white man."

Wi wanyang wacipi: The "Sun Gazing Dance," the Lakota name for the Sun Dance ceremony.

Wicasa wakan: The Lakota name for a shaman or medicine man.

Wicotipi: Smaller groups of closely related Lakota peoples.

Wotawe: A medicine bag in which the Lakota kept items that were believed to convey spiritual power.

1

DOMESTIC LIFE OF AMERICAN INDIANS IN THE AMERICAN WEST

DOMESTIC LIFE AND PALEO-INDIANS

In 1982, a team of surveyors from the Texas Department of Transportation, laying out a new road along the banks of Brushy Creek north of Austin, stumbled across the grave of a young woman. Although remarkably preserved, the grave was not of recent vintage. An archaeological team excavated the site and concluded that the young woman had died sometime around 11,000 years ago. Soon dubbed "Leanne," for the nearby town of Leander, her grave became one of the oldest and most complete Paleo-Indian burials ever found.

Little is known about Leanne—even the year is only the roughest of estimates—but this much is known: someone loved her, someone who would miss the young woman (aged somewhere between 18 and 30 years old at the time of her death), someone who knew that burying her would be the last thing they could ever do for her.

That someone carefully placed her in her final resting place, digging, likely with a stick, a grave deep enough for her. Next, they gently placed her on her right side, her right hand under her head as if she were sleeping. They drew her legs close to her chest, the ending of life so much like the beginning. Beside her they placed a worn *mano*, a grinding stone used to make flour. Perhaps, she could use it wherever she was going. Around her neck she wore a shark's tooth necklace, but only the tooth would be found, the cord long since moldered to dust. Where she got it and from whom, like everything else, is a mystery. Perhaps, she acquired it through trade with coastal peoples, or maybe a loved one gave it as a gift. Around her, they may have wrapped a hide covering. Perhaps, there were several family members and friends to bid her farewell, and they likely said words over her in a language, like her real name, lost to time. They covered her with a limestone slab, to protect her and mark her grave, and there she lay (Texas beyond History n.d.).

As the discovery of Leanne's grave illustrates, the New World, despite the claims of Europeans, was anything but new. People had called the Americas home for at least 20,000 years, and possibly far longer. These "Indians," as Christopher Columbus mistakenly called them, had colonized deserts, mountains, jungles, and the icy wastes of the Arctic. Virtually the entire hemisphere had felt the footsteps of humanity a dozen millennia before the first Europeans waded ashore.

The first peoples to arrive in the Americas may have made their way along the coasts, hunting, fishing, and gathering edible plants as they went, but around 13,500 years ago, a new group of Paleo-Indians arrived, Leanne's people, the Clovis people. Named for sites excavated in 1932 near Clovis, New Mexico, the Clovis people left an indelible impression on the historical record as the first distinctive culture in the Americas. Their culture flourished across the Americas, but many of the best sites have been found on the Great Plains of New Mexico and Texas. Little endures from their time, however. We do not know, for example, what kind of dwellings they constructed, but we do know from their large spearpoints that they hunted a variety of megafauna (large animals), such as the American mastodon and woolly mammoth. For centuries, the Clovis people must have enjoyed the bounty of the Americas, with its varied plants and animals, but the ice slowly lost its hold on the planet as the climate warmed. The last of the ice ages ended around 12,000 years ago, not long after the arrival of the Clovis people.

The gradually warming planet and predation by humans likely contributed to the extinction of many of the large animals of the late Pleistocene. The mammoths and mastodons, giant cave bears and saber tooth tigers, and many other gargantuan mammals disappeared at the beginning of the Holocene period, about 12,000 years ago. One animal, the ancestor of the modern horse, survived this extinction event by taking the land bridge into Asia, before the rising oceans closed the route. So, while horses vanished from the Americas (only to return with the Spanish in the 1500s), they did exceedingly well on the plains of Central Asia.

The disappearance of many of the large game animals forced Paleo-Indian peoples to change their survival strategies. Hunting continued, of course, but deer, elk, and bison were increasingly found on the menu in place of the larger megafauna. Gathering also remained important, but around 10,000 years ago, plants began to be consciously cultivated.

Agriculture, which would spread across the Americas, likely first began with maize (often called corn) in central Mexico. Maize, along with beans and squash, proved popular with a wide variety of American Indian peoples. These three crops, or "three sisters," could be found from Massachusetts to Mexico and everywhere in between. The trio worked in harmony, with beans adding nitrogen to the soil to the benefit of nitrogen-hungry maize. Conversely, bean vines benefited from spiraling up the rigid cornstalks, and squash plants spread horizontally, crowding out weeds. Humans, for their part, had access to carbohydrates from the maize, protein from the beans, and vitamin C from the squash.

Agriculture provided a reliable food source, and agricultural production led to some Indian peoples choosing to remain in one locale year around, helping to create sedentary civilizations. Farming also allowed fewer people to raise more food for an entire group, enabling a wider division of labor. The labor of everyone would no longer be required to produce food, and this agricultural surplus could free up some people to pursue other occupations. A small group of farmers could, therefore, support artisans and craftspeople as well as religious specialists who could divine the will of the gods. Over time, these societies, especially in Central and South America, became larger, wealthier, and increasingly sophisticated. Groups like the Inca, Maya, and Aztec erected impressive temples and created cities as large and beautiful as any in the world.

Compared to the grandeur of South and Central American civilizations, precontact North America can appear oddly lacking in large sedentary civilizations, but for a time, such civilizations did flourish in North America. Along the Mississippi River and its tributaries, the "Mound Builders," or Mississippians, built villages.

Temples were often erected on artificial earthen mounds that lorded over the surrounding villages. The largest of these, the city of Cahokia, across the Mississippi from modern St. Louis, Missouri, boasted the largest population of any city in North America with roughly 15,000 residents at its peak. At its center stood the imposing Monks Mound (named for the Catholic monks who later used the site). At the top of the mound, the "Great Sun," a kind of chief/priest, divined the secrets of the universe.

In the desert Southwest, the ancestors of the modern Pueblo Indians of New Mexico built large agrarian villages on the Colorado Plateau, a relatively cold and dry expanse of land with few reliable sources of water. And in southern New Mexico and Arizona, the villages of the Mogollon peoples sheltered thousands of residents. Unlike the great civilizations to the south, all of these sedentary civilizations vanished before the arrival of Europeans, likely due to terrible droughts that made it hard to sustain large populations. The abandoned mounds and empty dwellings remained, giving rise to tales of spirits and wild speculation about the identity of the vanished people.

The most impressive ruins in North America are surely the Ancestral Pueblo ruins of the Colorado Plateau, and those in Mesa Verde National Park are the most impressive of all, constructed as they are in sandstone alcoves hundreds of feet long. Abandoned in the late AD 1200s, and largely undisturbed until their rediscovery in the late 19th century, the ruins attract hundreds of thousands of visitors each year, drawn by the beauty and mystery of this "lost civilization."

The Ancestral Pueblo peoples of Mesa Verde successfully farmed in an area of unpredictable precipitation for hundreds of years, often making efficient use of what water became available through clever catchment and irrigation systems. The spectacular cliff dwellings that today attract tourists from around the world, however, were a relatively late development, built in the two centuries between AD 1150 and 1350, a period dubbed Pueblo III by archaeologists. Constructed in often inaccessible and defensible positions, these cliff dwellings offered shelter, reliable water from nearby springs, and protection from attack. From these alcoves, farmers, mostly men, ascended up treacherous trails to their mesa-top fields. Indeed, in places, the visitor can still see the hand- and toeholds cut into the sandstone.

Maize, beans, and squash were the staple crops, supplemented by hunting for deer and elk. Domesticated turkeys, as well, provided food and feathers for garments. Women probably worked collectively to grind corn into cornmeal, prepare meals, and watch children. Religious life centered around the *kivas*, subterranean circular structures where male societies conducted secret rituals. During significant times, like solstices, the Kachinas arrived to lead the people in important ceremonies. These ancestral spirits, inhabiting the bodies of men, appeared adorned in fearsome wooden masks. These rituals often took the form of dances, designed to attract the attention of deities and bring about benevolent change, such as bringing rain to a parched land.

Legends and myths functioned to provide lessons and rules of behavior, but in a very real way, mythic events were not relegated to stories from long ago; rather, mythic events remained vital and alive, with contemporary events echoing the acts of heroic characters in the mythic past. For the Ancestral Puebloans and their descendants, time did not flow in a linear way. Instead, they envisioned time as cyclical, and the behavior of living individuals was reminiscent of the behavior of mythical figures of the past.

Societies are tethered together by their rules, rituals, and rites of passage, and the Ancestral Puebloans were no different. Rituals began at birth. For example, on the fourth day (four being an important symbolic number for Puebloan peoples) of life, a shaman would take the child and present it to the rising sun, bestowing upon it a name. As children matured, they were expected to learn the important skills they would need in life. Boys, for example, would learn about hunting, warfare, and how to perform rain ceremonies. Girls learned to make pottery, heal the sick, and cook. Sharing knowledge with the young required young boys and girls to reciprocate by laboring for their elders. Girls would cook and grind corn into meal, and boys would hunt and tend to the fields. The fruits of their labor would then be given to their elders in a sign of respect. Gift giving similarly functioned to bind people together, creating webs of reciprocal networks. This even extended to the animal world. Sacred cornmeal, for example, might be offered as a gift to a deer they had killed in the hunt as a sign of respect for the sacrifice of the animal's life to sustain their lives and to allow for future successful hunts.

Marriage also represented an important rite of passage, marking the transition from being a young person to being a full adult. Girls married around age 17 and boys around 19. While young people could marry for love, it was expected that a prospective husband would give gifts to his future in-laws, but the gifts would be provided by his parents. A son who had not fulfilled his obligation to labor for his parents would not receive gifts and thus would not be able to marry. If a son was given gifts, these would be presented to his future in-laws, and four days later, they would reciprocate, giving gifts of equal value to his family. In this way, the marriage was agreed to by both the groom's and the bride's families. More gifts were given at the ceremony itself. The bride's gifts included domestic articles, such as a *mano* and an *olla* (a pottery water jug). These signified her role as the preparer of food to support her spouse and children. The husband, meanwhile, received a bow, shield, and war club to signify his duty to protect his wife and children and to hunt to provide for them.

These marriages—much to the dismay of later Catholic priests who settled in the villages of the Pueblo peoples in New Mexico— could be ended at any time by either spouse deciding to leave the arrangement. Particularly successful heads of household could attain great wealth (perhaps through unusual success in hunting or skill as a shaman, warrior, or bringer of rain). Less successful adults and young people would be beholden to him through the giving of gifts they could not repay. Men would repay this through labor, and women often became wives to the successful individual. Polygamy was common among these important individuals, but it reflected a desire to care for all members of society, with widows and orphans, for example, often incorporated into these wealthier households.

While the Pueblo peoples had personal property, society frowned upon conspicuous displays of wealth. Property was also not solely under the control of one person. Women, for example, owned the household, the sacred fetishes that held great spiritual power, and the seeds for planting maize. This ownership gave elder women, who controlled this wealth, great power and respect. Elder men, likewise, governed the pueblo, determining the proper course of action to take.

After thriving for centuries, the Ancestral Puebloans of the Colorado Plateau would be compelled to move, as their civilization began to struggle with unprecedented changes. Archaeologists think a number of things may have conspired to make their way of life untenable: climate change and drought, competition for dwindling resources, a growing population, and conflict. A terrible "super drought" gripped the area in the mid-13th century and lasted for decades. Crop productivity certainly suffered, and large populations struggled to feed their people. Overhunting of animals like deer also became a problem, and indeed the drought must have had a devastating effect on animals as well.

As food resources declined, societal conflict certainly increased. The increasingly fortified architecture of the cliff dwellings suggests a need to defend one's community from attack, but whether these enemies came from other tribes arriving in the area or from some faction within their society is unknown. Finally, around AD 1280, the Ancestral Puebloans abandoned the Colorado Plateau entirely, relocating to more predictable sources of water, especially in the Rio Grande Valley of New Mexico. The river's more predictable waters irrigated fields of maize, beans, squash, and chilies. It was here where the diverse and largely independent Pueblo peoples would encounter the Spanish when they arrived in the 1540s.

By the early 1400s, Indian peoples had adapted to life in a variety of different environments. Hunters and gatherers continued to occupy vast regions of the West. The Paiute people, for example, managed to survive in the difficult Great Basin Desert. In the Pacific Northwest, the area's boundless resources made for relative wealth, which chiefs shared in elaborate potlatch ceremonies. Yearly salmon runs also attracted numerous tribes at places like Celilo Falls, on the Columbia River. Meanwhile, the Karankawa of Texas found all they needed along the swampy margins of the Gulf Coast. Diversity of cultures, languages, and survival strategies made the West a varied and amazing place unlike any other on the planet, but change was coming.

DAILY LIFE FOR INDIAN PEOPLES AT THE DAWN OF CONTACT

Shortly after dawn on November 6, 1528, a small raft washed ashore on the Gulf Coast in a place that would one day be called Texas. Glad to be in sight of land, the exhausted men jumped from the raft and "began to crawl out on all fours," according to the expedition's de facto leader, Álvar Núñez Cabeza de Vaca. Wet, tired, and hungry, these would-be conquerors represented the last survivors of the failed Florida expedition of Panfilo de Narváez. Once proud conquistadors, this ragtag bunch of starving men was in no position to conquer anything; in fact, the expedition had become a desperate struggle to survive. Despite the help of local Indians, Cabeza de Vaca's men sickened and died. By 1529, an expedition that had begun two years earlier with 500 men had dwindled to 15. Ironically, the conquerors became the conquered, as the Spanish ended up as slaves to local Indians. Finally, only four men remained: Cabeza de Vaca, Alonso del Castillo Maldonado, Andrés Dorantes de Carranza, and Dorantes's African slave, Estevanico.

Unlike European slavery, American Indian slavery was a less permanent condition. If slaves proved their loyalty to their captors, earned their trust, or demonstrated great skill in healing or war, they could advance above the status of slave. Eventually, the strange foreigners developed reputations as healers, employing an amalgam of native and Christian practices. Freed from slavery and relying on their growing renown as healers to provide for them, the quartet embarked on an ambitious plan to walk from somewhere in Texas to Mexico City. Encountering a tribe called the Avavares, for example, the Spaniards were presented with prickly pear cactus fruits (an important food for many tribes in Texas and Northern Mexico) "because they had heard of us and of how we cured people and of the marvels our Lord worked through us," Cabeza de Vaca explained (Cabeza de Vaca 2002, 55). Their ordeal ended in 1536 when a group of Spanish slave raiders near Culiacan apprehended them and returned them to Mexico City, a sinuous journey of perhaps 2,000 miles from where they began in Texas.

Cabeza de Vaca and his compatriots had experienced indigenous cultures in a way few Europeans ever would, giving them insight into a world the Europeans would never really understand. Cabeza de Vaca, in particular, came away convinced that the Spanish should treat the Indians better and meet them on their terms. It was an insight few others would share, for few people were interested in hearing about the cultures of the Indians, but all were eager to learn whether the survivors had seen any kingdoms as wealthy as those of the Aztecs Hernán Cortés had conquered in 1520. Shortly after their return, a story began to circulate that claimed a fabulous kingdom, whose seven cities had streets that were paved with gold, did in fact exist to the north.

In 1539, Marcos de Niza led a small expedition to search for the seven cities of Cíbola. Guiding de Niza's expedition was the unfortunate slave Estevanico, who was either sold or lent by his master, Dorantes, to the expedition. Estevanico, acting as a warm-up act for de Niza, went from village to village, informing them of the arrival of the powerful Spanish and the need for Indians to submit to their authority. Several villages, hoping to avoid a conflict, promised to provide food and fuel to the Spaniards, but Estevanico eventually encountered the fiercely independent pueblo of Zuni in modern northeastern Arizona. Angered at Estevanico's demands, the

Zuni killed him, forcing de Niza to retreat to Mexico in fear of his life. Upon returning to Mexico, de Niza claimed that he had seen golden cities from a distance. Whether he was simply mistaken or an inveterate liar is unknown, but certainly his report only added to the excitement that an undiscovered empire of great wealth lay waiting to be conquered.

Francisco Vázquez de Coronado's two-year expedition into the Southwest, from 1540 to 1542, would be the largest and best-supported effort to find these cities of gold. While his efforts would prove futile, his mistreatment of the Pueblo Indians would leave behind a bitter memory for the Indians of the Rio Grande Valley. Coronado, seeing himself as a conqueror, felt justified in appropriating food to feed his roughly 2,000 men (and a few women) and an even larger number of horses and cattle. Such numbers put a sudden and unsustainable strain on the Rio Grande pueblos' limited reserves. Angered, the men from Tiguex pueblo (on the banks of the Rio Grande near modern-day Bernalillo, New Mexico) decided to lessen the strain on their land by killing several dozen of Coronado's horses. In retaliation, the conquistador's men set fire to the village and burned the leaders at the stake.

Aghast at this cruelty, the Puebloans concocted a plan to maroon the Spaniards on the trackless expanse of the Great Plains. They convinced Coronado that a wealthy city named Quivara did in fact exist, far to the northeast. To guide them, they appointed a Pueblo Indian the Spaniards nicknamed "El Turco," or "The Turk" (on account of his large crooked nose, which apparently reminded them of the impressive protuberances of the Turks). In reality, the Turk intended to abandon the Spanish on the Great Plains, leaving them to wander until they died. He carried out the plan, leading the expedition away from the Rio Grande and across eastern New Mexico, the Texas Panhandle, and as far north as Kansas. Eventually, however, the Spaniards realized they had been duped, and in anger they executed the Turk. Before his execution, he supposedly confessed that he had been tasked with getting the Spaniards "lost on the plains . . . so that, lacking food and supplies, the horses would die" and any survivors fortunate enough to return to New Mexico would be weak and easy to kill (Coronado 2005, 319). The plan had almost worked as the exhausted expedition made its way back to the Rio Grande before returning to Mexico.

Coronado had imagined himself returning to Mexico as a conquering hero, another Cortés or Pizzaro; instead, he returned a failure. To the north, there were no villages with streets paved with gold bricks. They mostly found only the vast emptiness of deserts, mountains, and plains, with the pueblos of the Rio Grande Valley offering scant respite. Worse, Coronado explained in his report, the isolation of "the settlements along [the Rio Grande] are not [such] as to allow [Spaniards] to settle [here] because they are more than four hundred leagues from the Mar del Norte [Pacific Ocean] and more than two hundred from the [Mar] del Sur [probably the Gulf of Mexico]" (Coronado 2005, 319). Isolated and poor (at least by the Spanish conception of wealth), the pueblos possessed nothing worth taking—a fact that worked in their favor. So complete was Coronado's failure that Spaniards would not return to New Mexico for over half a century.

In 1598, Juan de Oñate led the Spanish back to New Mexico, and unlike the Coronado expedition, these Spaniards intended to stay. The lands of the Pueblos would become a province of New Spain, and the Spanish, like Oñate, would become *encomenderos*, essentially feudal lords, who would control the Pueblos, forcing them to perform work that would enrich the lords. In exchange, the *encomendero* would provide protection for the residents of the village and instruction in Christianity, so their souls could be saved from eternal damnation. For a time, the Pueblos endured these conditions. The Spanish occupation, after all, introduced horses, cattle, and sheep. New foods, like rice; augmented older crops; and wonderous material goods made of steel and cloth transformed daily life. Firearms, and Spanish soldiers, also helped prevent the periodic raids on villages from Apache, Navajo, and other nomadic tribes, who saw the settled villages as easy targets. Within a few decades, however, the Spanish had begun to wear out their welcome.

The uneasy coexistence between the Pueblo Indians and the Spanish began to collapse in 1675, when a new governor, Juan Francisco Treviño, arrived in the provincial capital of Santa Fe. Eager to see Catholicism take hold, the governor decided to round up "idolaters." To the Pueblo peoples, however, these "idolaters" were revered spiritual leaders and practitioners of traditional religious ceremonies.

Although the Pueblo Indians lived in much the same fashion, there were extensive linguistic and cultural differences among the dozens of scattered villages, and the Tewas near Santa Fe proved to be the most vociferous in their opposition to Spanish control. Despite warnings of growing Tewa anger, Treviño went ahead with his plan to suppress native religious traditions. His soldiers rounded up 47 religious leaders for practicing "witchcraft," as native ceremonies appeared to the Spanish priests. The Spanish sentenced four to death and promised to whip and enslave the rest. Only the arrival of a contingent of roughly 70-armed Tewa men prevented the sentences from being carried out. Realizing the danger of the situation, the governor released the prisoners, but events had been set in motion that could not be revoked, for among the released prisoners was a Tewa spiritual leader named Po'pay.

The crackdown on the shamans, or spiritual leaders, allowed long-simmering antipathies to bubble to the surface: the persecution of religious leaders, the unjust system of forced labor, and the appearance of deadly and mysterious diseases that decimated Pueblo communities. Led by Po'pay, the Tewas began to plot an uprising. Po'pay, worried about being arrested again, fled his home pueblo of San Juan and took refuge at the isolated northern pueblo of Taos. From Taos, he sent runners out to coordinate the attack. Scattered across hundreds of square miles, the Pueblos had rarely acted as a unified group, but now, with a common enemy, they prepared to unleash a carefully planned, multifronted assault on Spanish control and authority.

On the morning of August 10, 1680, Captain Francisco de Anaya Almazán and a small detachment of soldiers stood watching over a herd of horses grazing near the pueblo of Santa Clara. Without warning, Almazán's men came under attack from a band of men from the village. The Tewas killed two Spaniards in the attack, and the rest fled to nearby Santa Fe. Unfortunately, Almazán's hacienda lay in the path of the angry Tewas, who fell upon his family, murdering everyone on the ranch, including his wife and infant child, who were both found dead in a nearby field. This first salvo caught the Spanish completely by surprise, but the uprising soon gathered momentum. Angry mobs burned the impressive church east of Santa Fe in the pueblo of Pecos. The Spanish buildings of Santa Fe were occupied by Indians. In the chaos and bloodshed, Spaniards abandoned horses and other domesticated animals that quickly went feral, a seemingly minor occurrence with profound long-term consequences.

With few soldiers to defend them, the Spaniards could do little to protect themselves against neighbors turned into enemies. Nearly 400 Spaniards perished in the fighting, and the remaining 2,000 or so fled south to El Paso with little more than their lives. The assailants had particular antipathy for the Spanish priests, killing 21 of the 33 priests in the province. So thorough and complete was the victory that for 12 years, the Spanish stayed away. Never before, or since, had Indian peoples so completely defeated a European power, and for 12 years the Pueblos resumed life as it had once been—only now with the new things the Spanish had brought with them to add to their civilization.

When the Spanish did return, they returned somewhat chastened. The exploitative *encomendia* system was replaced by a less demanding labor requirement called the *repartimiento*, which, in theory, only allowed for temporary or seasonal forced labor. Just as important, the priests decided to turn a blind eye to traditional religious practices, and most Pueblo peoples soon practiced both Catholicism and their traditional beliefs. Violence continued for the next several years, including a second less successful revolt in 1696. Within the pueblos, factions emerged, either for or against the Spanish. These disputes often divided communities and led to cycles of murder and revenge. These debates grew so divisive in the pueblo of Pecos, for example, that it was eventually abandoned. Slowly, though, a new peace emerged.

By the early 1700s, daily life in Santa Fe and the surrounding pueblos had settled into a fairly stable pattern. Isolated and largely ignored by the larger Spanish empire, New Mexicans relied on their own labor to survive. Agriculture, fed by the benevolent waters of the Rio Grande, created a green ribbon in an otherwise harsh landscape, and herds of sheep and cattle grazed in mountain pastures. Spaniards and Pueblos coexisted and intermarried, their lifeways intermingling to create a unique culture. The adobe Catholic cathedrals located at the center of Pueblo Indian villages became symbolic of this amalgamated culture. Indeed, only the increasingly terrifying raids of the *bárbaros*, or barbarian Indians, disrupted the relative peace and security of life along the Rio Grande. Sometimes the raiders had been Apache or Navajo, but increasingly, they came from a terrifying new tribe of horse-riding Indians known as the Comanche.

By the 1700s, New Mexico's missions were a model for subsequent settlements in Texas and California. Generally staffed by Franciscan monks, a mission functioned as both church and colonial outpost. Each mission was largely self-sufficient, with a labor force composed of local Indians who would be "civilized" through this labor and the lessons in Christianity taught by the monks. To ensure security, a *presidio*, or military base, was often located near the mission. As in New Mexico, however, the missions in Texas and California were often isolated and largely ignored by the king and high-ranking officials, who found Mexico and South America to be far richer and more profitable.

The biggest problem the mission model faced came from the Spaniards themselves: disease. For example, the Pueblo population shrank in the first half of the 1600s from an estimated 60,000 to about 30,000 due to disease, drought, and raiding. California's missions proved even deadlier. The concentration of previously dispersed Indians with little resistance to European diseases around the California missions created a perfect environment for the transmission of deadly pathogens. Poor sanitation made the situation even worse. The Indian population between the missions of San Diego and San Francisco plummeted from 72,000 to 18,000 within a few years of the arrival of Franciscan missionaries.

Buffeted by raids from the increasingly powerful Comanche, Texas and New Mexico held little appeal for Spanish settlers, and California fared little better. For the Spanish, their northern territories were, at best, mere buffer zones to protect their more lucrative holdings farther south from hostile Indians, meddling Frenchmen, opportunistic Englishmen, and by the early 1800s a new group, the expansionistic Americans.

DAILY LIFE OF THE PLAINS INDIANS IN THE 18TH AND 19TH CENTURIES

As a boy, Long Arrow had been adopted by Good Running. Years later, and grown to manhood, he sought to repay his adopted father for his kindness. Long Arrow asked his father what he wanted. The old man replied that a strange animal, as fast as a deer but able to carry heavier burdens than the dog, lived in a lake with the spirit people. Long Arrow vowed to bring back this wonderous animal and set out to find the lake. Finding the lake proved easier than getting down to the bottom, but Long Arrow recruited a friendly spirit who agreed to guide him to the home of the animals and their owner, an aged grandfather spirit. The young spirit told Long Arrow that if he caught a glimpse of the old man's feet, then the grandfather spirit would be obligated to grant Long Arrow's wish.

For three days, Long Arrow lived in the home of the aged spirit, and each day he tried unsuccessfully to see the man's feet, which remained hidden under a long, black robe. On the fourth day, he finally caught a glimpse of the man's feet and discovered they were in fact hooves like those of the strange animal, the Elk Dog. Compelled by Long Arrow's discovery, the old man had no choice but to comply with Long Arrow's demands. He gave the young man three gifts: a length of the magic rope that allowed the old man to catch and restrain the Elk Dogs, a rainbow belt that explained the sacred songs and dances for keeping the strange beasts, and a herd of the magical animals. In this way, the Blackfeet became people of the horse.

The adoption of the horse by the Blackfeet, Lakota Sioux, Crow, Kiowa, Nez Percé, and others changed everything for these peoples, but perhaps no Indian tribe so totally reinvented themselves around the horse as the *Numunu*, or Comanche as they came to be known. Once peoples of the mountains, the Comanche came out onto the plains through passes over the Sangre de Christo Mountains of Colorado and New Mexico, spilling out onto the forbiddingly vast grasslands sometime around 1700. They first appear in the historical record in 1706, a passing, seemingly insignificant reference in a Spanish report. Within a few years, other Indians, like the Apache and Jumano of Texas, gave way before their invasion, and the Spanish came to fear and respect these new horsemen of the plains.

The horses the Comanche had acquired descended from Spanish stock, many turned loose during the tumult of the 1680 Pueblo Revolt. These sturdy, compact horses had the deserts of Spain and North Africa in their blood, bred to survive heat and drought and able to subsist entirely on grass. Horses took to the semiarid Southern Plains with ease and opened a new world to the Comanche. Humans, of course, cannot eat grass, and there are few edible plants for humans to consume on the plains. However, bison and horses could access the energy of the plains by eating the nutritious grasses. Horses, in turn, converted this to energy, and people could harness that energy to follow the bison herds from the backs of their mounts. Bison, living in herds so vast they were beyond counting, also turned grass into energy and were accessible to the Comanche as meat. Compared to life in the Rockies, the Southern Plains seemed a source of inexhaustible and predictable bounty—so long as the Comanche had horses to ride and bison to hunt.

Horses, however, offered advantages beyond bison hunting. With the ability to travel great distances relatively quickly, horses enabled the Comanche to peacefully trade with or violently raid settlements from Santa Fe to San Antonio and deep into Mexico. Moreover, trading and raiding provided necessary items that the

Comanche could not get otherwise. First, an all-meat diet, while high in protein, lacked many important vitamins and carbohydrates. Trading bison meat and hides with the agricultural peoples provided the Comanche with maize, beans, squash, and other foods that made up for the nutritional deficiencies in their diet. Trade, often with French traders and later a group of professional, mostly New Mexican, traveling salesmen called Comancheros, also garnered foodstuffs, tobacco, coffee, and a variety of manufactured goods, including firearms and gunpowder.

While the Comanche certainly traded a great deal, they remained committed to raids, and they often raided peoples with whom they had previously traded peacefully. In addition to supplies and horses, raiding also brought another important element into the Comanche world: slaves.

Comanche slavery became a vital survival strategy, as the tribe, like all Indian peoples, suffered in the face of European diseases, most notably smallpox. With an empire that stretched from San Antonio, Texas, to southern Colorado to maintain, the Comanche needed to expand their population at the same time disease was decimating them. The solution lay in raiding villages for slaves. These slaves could fill the void left by the deaths of their people, and though the Comanche did not know it, Spanish and, later, Anglo-American captives also likely had some resistance to the imported diseases that ravaged the plains. Children born from non-Indian female captives may have inherited resistance to some European diseases.

Unsurprisingly, women (whose reproductive capacity could augment population) and children were the most likely to be taken captive. Children, unlike adults, had an easier time adapting to a new language and culture. In the fall of 1719, for example, New Mexico governor Antonio Valverde led a military expedition against the Comanche in the Arkansas valley. Along the route, they encountered terrified Apache who reported that the Comanche had "killed many of their nation and carried off their women and children [as] captives until they no longer knew where to go to live in safety" (Hämäläinen 2008, 32). In addition to providing new people who could be assimilated into their society, slaves could also be ransomed back to their people in exchange for trade goods. Slavery, therefore, served several necessary functions, and this reality, compounded by a culture that rewarded young men for daring campaigns of violence, created powerful inducements for continued raiding. In time, the sudden appearance of Comanche raiders became a familiar and terrible possibility for other Indians, Spaniards, Mexicans, and, finally, Anglo-Texans. Scores of victims would be carried off in these raids, facing an uncertain and terrifying future.

One such unfortunate soul was an 11-year-old German American boy named Herman Lehmann, who was taken captive in 1870 while playing near his home in Loyal Valley, Texas. He and his younger brother, Willie (who soon escaped and made his way home), became captives of the Apache. Stripped naked and tied to a horse, Lehmann had suddenly been expelled from everything he knew. "Imagine," he explained decades later, "the sufferings of a child who had up to a day or two before been tenderly cared for by a kind father, loved by a devoted mother, cut off from all hope of recovery, not knowing but that each moment was to be the last, his face blistered by the scorching sun, the skin peeled off his back and breast. . . . Could the sufferings of Job have been greater?" (Lehmann 1993, 9). Yet, he found a home among the Apache and soon came to love Carnoviste, the man who had captured him, as a father.

As the years wore on, Lehmann loathed the idea of returning to his family so much that he left the Apache to take up refuge among the more militant Comanche. When this finally became untenable, Lehmann reluctantly decided to return to his family. Now a grown man, he faced a world he did not understand and only vaguely remembered. Indeed, returning to Anglo-American society often proved difficult for former captives.

THE CENTRAL ROLE OF THE BISON IN DAILY DOMESTIC LIFE

Long before Herman Lehmann's capture in the twilight years of Plains Indian independence, many Indian peoples had been attracted to seemingly infinite monotony of the plains by an apparently endless supply of bison. This new lifestyle was enabled by the horse, but it was impossible without the bison.

Long ago, Paleo-Indians had hunted bison on foot, and sometimes, in particularly advantageous situations, they successfully drove herds over cliffs and thus acquired a great deal of food with little risk. The practice continued for thousands of years. Meriwether Lewis was likely the first Anglo-American to see the results of a "buffalo jump," writing in 1805 from Montana, "Today we passed . . . the remains of . . . many mangled carcasses of Buffalow [*sic*] which had been driven over a precipice of 120 feet by the Indians and perished" (Bergon 1995, 141). Indian peoples also hunted bison on foot, often disguised in hides taken in previous hunts, when herds of the animals appeared near their homes. Without the fleet horse, however, Indian peoples could not pursue the mobile bison herds year-round.

The American bison is an impressive animal. At roughly 2,000 pounds, bulls (male bison) are the largest land animals in North America, but they are surprisingly fast, attaining speeds of up to 35 miles an hour. Nor are bison solely sprinters, for they can maintain rapid speeds for hours. Herds of thousands of bison thundering across the plains must have been an awesome sight. Francis Parkman, who went west in 1846, shortly after graduating from Harvard, described the innumerable bison (or buffalo as the animals are typically, though inaccurately, called). He observed, "At noon the whole plain before us was alive with thousands of buffalo—bulls, cows, and calves—all moving rapidly as we drew near; and far-off beyond the river the swelling prairie was darkened with them to the very horizon" (Parkman 1891, 362). William Clark, decades earlier, likewise marveled at the size of a herd next to the Missouri River, writing in his journal, "I do not think I exaggerate when I estimate the number of Buffaloe which could be compre[hend]ed at one view to amount to 3000" (Bergon 1995, 49). Estimates vary for the number of bison in the early 19th century, but most likely, at least 40 million of the wooly creatures wandered North America at the time.

Hunting bison from horseback became the preferred method for Plains peoples, but such hunting required skill and bravery on the part of both the rider and the horse. Parkman described the hunting of the bison in great detail, and while certainly not as skilled as an Indian hunter, he still managed to accomplish the task. He wrote, "There are two methods commonly practised [*sic*] [for hunting] bison—'running' and 'approaching.' The chase on horseback, which goes by the name of 'running,' is the more violent and dashing mode of the two. Indeed, in all of American wild sports this is the wildest. Once among the buffalo, the hunter, unless long use has made him familiar with the situation, dashes forward in utter recklessness and self-abandonment" (Parkman 1891, 360). The hunter's mind is focused solely on the task of bringing down the powerful brute, preparing for the fatal shot, the rider "drops the rein and abandons his horse to his furious career; he levels his gun, the report sounds faint amid the thunder of the buffalo; and when his wounded enemy leaps in vain fury upon him, his heart

The acquisition of the horse in the late seventeenth century enabled many American Indian peoples to hunt bison full-time, radically changing how they lived. (Rare Book Division, The New York Public Library. "Indianische Bisonjagd. Indiens chassant le bison. Indians hunting the bison." New York Public Library Digital Collections. Accessed January 4, 2022. https://digitalcollections.nypl.org/items/510d47da-c455-a3d9-e040-e00a18064a99)

thrills with a feeling like the fierce delight of the battlefield" (Parkman 1891, 360). An experienced hunter could kill half a dozen buffalo in such manner over the course of a hunt, Parkman claimed, and the best could even reload the cumbersome single-shot muzzleloaders on the gallop; but Parkman acknowledged this to be the biggest problem faced by would-be bison hunters.

Plenty-coups, a Crow elder interviewed by the anthropologist Frank Bird Linderman in the early 20th century, explained that his people had little use for muzzleloaders when hunting bison, preferring the old-fashioned but more effective bow and arrow. He explained, "The bow was the best of weapons for running the buffalo. Even the old-time white men, who had only the muzzle-loading guns, were quick to adopt the bow and arrow in running a buffalo. But a powerful arm and a strong wrist are necessary to send an arrow deep into a buffalo. I have often seen them driven through [the buffalo]" (Linderman 2002, 9).

The horse proved as crucial as a bow and arrow (or, later, improved firearms) in the running of buffalo. Ordinary horses were of little use in bison running. Horses became status symbols and sources of wealth among Indian peoples, commodities that could be traded, but every Indian hunter had one preferred horse for the task of hunting bison. There were several requirements for a good buffalo horse. It had to be fast and with good endurance, but also intelligent and brave. A good buffalo horse helped separate a bison from the rest of the herd, and it knew to steer its rider close to the bison for the kill shot. But the best horses also knew to be wary of the bison and its sword-sharp horns.

Pretty-shield, another Crow elder, also spoke to Linderman of her childhood when her people still roamed the plains, and she told of her father's prized possession: his buckskin-colored buffalo horse. One day, as often happened, her people decided to move camp, packing up their tipis and loading them on travois (wooden frames lashed to the sides of horses that dragged behind them). Her father's buffalo horse was never used for such drudgery, and after some convincing, Pretty-shield's father agreed to let her ride the well-trained horse to the next campsite to "give him something to do." Unfortunately, during the day's ride, the Crow passed a herd of bison. Seeing the herd, Pretty-shield decided to rope a calf to show off in front of her friends, and so she plunged into the herd. She described what happened next:

> He [the horse] noticed that I seemed to want a calf, and picked one out for me, a good fat one, too. I threw my rope, but missed. The buckskin [horse] kept right on after that same calf, as though no other one would do. Before I knew what was happening I was in the running herd, my horse going like the wind after that calf, dodging in and out among hundreds of buffalo cows and males, with no thought of letting his choice get away. I dropped my rope, luckily a short one, to hold onto my saddle. I could have touched that calf with my hand, any time, but now I did not want it. Disgusted because I did not shoot, the buckskin horse struck the calf with his front hoof, knocking it down, and jumping over it to save himself from falling. (Linderman 1978, 94)

Paralyzed by fear, and gripping the saddle with all her strength, she could do nothing but hold on until her father, mounted on another horse, managed to catch them and lead them away from the rumbling herd. Her father, angry and bemused, scolded her,

"This horse has more sense than you have. . . . He saw that if any meat was going to be killed he would have to do the killing himself." From the vantage point of old age, Pretty-shield concluded with a laugh, "Running buffalo was a man's business, anyhow" (Linderman 1978, 95).

While hunting buffalo tended to be a man's business, the processing of the animal was decidedly women's work. Dressing the skins and drying the meat were both laborious activities. The artist George Catlin, who spent time in the 1830s visiting Indian peoples in the West, described the process Lakota Sioux women employed to tan the hides to make leather. First, the hide was stretched out "either on a frame or on the ground, and after it has remained some three or four days, with the brains of the buffalo or elk spread over the fleshy side, they grain it with a sort of adze or chisel, made of a piece of buffalo bone" (Catlin 1870, 60). Next, women dug holes in the ground and smoked the hides in small tents over the fire. The resulting garments, Catlin claimed, "made of these skins may be worn repeatedly in the rain, and will always dry perfectly soft—a quality which, I believe, does not yet belong to dressed skins from the civilized countries" (Catlin 1870, 60). Women also dried the meat, cutting thin slices and hanging them on wooden racks in the sun.

Indeed, observers were always quick to comment on the endless drudgery Plains Indian women endured: processing hides, drying meat, cooking, putting up the lodge, taking care of children, and so on. "It is proverbial in the civilized world that 'the poor Indian woman has to do all the hard work.' Don't believe this," Catlin cautioned, "for it is not exactly so. She labours [*sic*] very hard and constantly, it is true. She does most of the drudgery about the village and wigwam, and is seen transporting heavy loads, &c." Catlin acknowledged, "This all looks to the passer-by as the slavish compulsion of her cruel husband, who is often seen lying at his ease, and smoking his pipe" (Catlin 1870, 61). However, the men also had duties to perform for the village, Catlin noted, embarking on potentially dangerous hunts to provide food, and, of course, men had to defend the village from the possibility of enemy attack. Scouts constantly patrolled the perimeter of the camp.

Nevertheless, women did indeed have a lot to do, and women who kept clean and orderly lodges or tipis were respected. Pretty-shield admired Kills-good, the only wife of Long-horse, a revered Crow leader, for her fastidiousness with upkeeping her tipi. Kills-good's lodge was nicer than those of other women; its "poles were taller, its lodge-skin whiter and cleaner, its lining, beautifully painted, reaching all around it. Its back rests, three of them, were made with head-and-tail robes; and always Kills-good burned a little sweet-grass, or sweet-sage, so that her lodge smelled nice." Beautiful and tall, with a kind heart, Kills-good was the model of a Crow woman. "I tried hard to be like her, even after I grew up and had children of my own," Pretty-shield explained (Linderman 1978, 32–33). Men appreciated the work of women, and among the Crow, one sign of a man's love for his wife could be found in the care a man took in brushing and braiding his woman's hair. Pretty-shield noted that "Long-horse kept [Kills-good's hair] looking as though it had just been combed. One could always tell when a man loved his woman by her hair" (Linderman 1978, 33).

A good hunter could easily provide for a large family, but the labor of butchering a 2,000-pound animal and the ancillary tasks that created, such as tanning hides and sewing clothing, meant that women's labor could be unending. One solution was to have women work together, often as wives of a single hunter. Polygamy, thus, became common among many Plains Indian societies. This likely came as a result of moving onto the plains and hunting bison. The Lakota, for example, did not practice polygamy when they lived in the forests of the Midwest, but as they moved onto the plains, the practice developed quickly. Given that a mounted warrior could kill several bison in one hunt but the processing of that animal could take far longer, polygamy made sense. A warrior often married several sisters from the same family, as in the case of Pretty-shield. Pretty-shield's father had promised her to a young warrior named Goes-ahead when she was only 13, but she was not married to him until she turned 16. Although she knew her prospective husband, she did not love with him. Only after marriage did she fall in love with him, "because he loved me and was always kind. Young women did not then fall in love and get married to please themselves as they do now. They listened to their fathers, married the men selected for them, and this, I believe, is the best way," she explained to Frank B. Linderman in the 1930s (Linderman 1978, 130). Pretty-shield, however, was Goes-ahead's second wife, having already married her older sister, and later he would marry her younger sister as well. Although her older sister proved unfaithful to Goes-ahead, Pretty-shield and her younger sister, Two-scalps, seemed content in the arrangement. "We got along well together. I helped her all I could, and she helped me" (Linderman 1978, 132). Indeed, Goes-ahead not only provided for his three wives and Pretty-shield's children (only she had children), but he also provided food for his in-laws until their deaths, a sign of his goodness as much as his hunting prowess.

Skill at hunting and warfare typically defined a young man's worth and status. Developing the skills required for both thus began at an early age. Black Elk, a Lakota medicine man, recalled being a boy in 1866. All the boys played war games and dreamed about the day they too could go to battle, especially against the hated *Wasichus*, the Lakota name for white men. Young boys, like himself, pelted each other with dirt clods, but "the big boys played the game called Throwing-Them-Off-Their-Horses, which is a battle all but the killing; and sometimes they got hurt." Black Elk recalled that two lines of boys, mounted on horses, would charge into each other at full gallop, their horses screaming, snorting, and kicking up clouds of dust, "and the riders would seize each other, wrestling until one side had lost all its men, for those who fell upon the ground were counted dead" (Neihardt 1979, 15).

Plenty-coups and his fellow Crow boys, the bitter enemies of Black Elk's Lakota, engaged in very similar activities. For example, young men were trained to raid enemy villages by practicing on their own village. Instead of stealing horses, however, these aspiring warriors were tasked with pilfering meat. Painted gray and wearing wolf skins, like grown warriors, they began their mission. Before the raid, Plenty-coups recalled their teacher admonishing them: "Now be Wolves! Go carefully. Beware of the old women." Unfortunately for Plenty-coups, a vigilant old woman proved to be his undoing. He found a rack of meat drying in the village and tried to creep up to it as quietly as possible, but a woman saw him and grabbed him. Dragging him to the creek next to the village, she washed the mud from his face to reveal his identity. Recognizing him, the old woman gave him a chunk of meat, but Plenty-coups had failed. "I could not say I stole it, because my face was clean," he lamented (Linderman 2002, 11–12).

The daily composition and size of a Plains Indian village varied with the seasons. For example, during the Sun Dance in June, the various Lakota clans came together for the most important ceremony of the year, which doubled as a social occasion. Here young people could find potential spouses (marrying within one's clan being strictly taboo), and people could renew friendships across the entire Lakota nation. The warm temperatures and availability of food made it possible for large villages to form for several weeks, but in the winter, these large villages dispersed into extended family groups often composed of only a dozen lodges. Dispersing their populations across a wide area made it easier to find food and shelter, whereas feeding a larger concentrated group would have been impossible.

The children, however, were always among their extended family members: parents, siblings, grandparents, cousins, aunts, and uncles. Aunts and uncles, in particular, played important roles in the raising of children. Lakota uncles, for example, often took their nephews on hunts, instructed them in the arts of war, and generally did as much or more to prepare them for life as their fathers. Girls, meanwhile, assisted their mothers, aunts, and other women in the work that was necessary for survival, learning skills that they would then employ when they married. But it was not all work for Plains Indian children.

Children had considerable free time and were generally left to their own devices, roaming in packs and exploring the world around the village with little supervision. In the winter, sledding was a popular activity; the sleds were fashioned from hard pieces of rawhide. Boys, unsurprisingly, played games designed to prepare themselves for war, pelting each other with snowballs or dirt clods, depending on the season. Girls, likewise, played with dolls and made scaled-down tipis. Pretty-shield explained, "Several of us girls made ourselves a play-village with our tiny tepees. Of course, our children were dolls, and our horses dogs, and yet we managed to make our village look very real" (Linderman 1978, 28).

Preparing for adulthood, though, could be anything but child's play. On one occasion, Plenty-coups and other boys were brought forward to test their bravery before a cornered and wounded male bison. His grandfather commanded the boys to "get down from your horses, you men." He continued, "A cool head, with quick feet, may strike the bull on the root of his tail with a bow. The young man who strikes, and is himself not hurt, may count coup" (Linderman 2002, 16). Counting coup proved one's manhood perhaps better than any other single exploit. For adult men, counting coup involved touching an enemy and retreating from that enemy unharmed, a far more difficult prospect than merely killing an enemy. Those who accomplished such tasks had demonstrated great prowess in battle and may have even showcased a great spiritual power that protected them from harm.

For these boys, the wounded bison played the antagonist, and counting coup on it would separate them from their peers. But confronting a wounded bull was fraught with danger. Not yet nine years old, Plenty-coups volunteered to try his luck. Dismounting, he approached the wounded animal. "The bull saw me, a human being afoot! He seemed to know that now he might kill, and he began to paw the ground and bellow as I walked carefully around him," Plenty-coups recalled (Linderman 2002, 16). He succeeded in touching the bison with his bow, but the angry animal charged him. The other men and other boys looked on as, at the last moment, Plenty-coups darted to one side, and the bull missed him. He had proven his bravery.

No society can survive without the addition of new lives, making women's reproductive ability critical to all. Women's power to create new life often echoed myths of creation of the universe in many Indian societies, and many Indian peoples had important rituals built around fertility. For example, the relationship between women's bodies and survival helped account for the importance placed on slavery by the Comanche; one way to increase the population was to steal women from other peoples. Sometimes birth was accompanied by important rituals, as in the naming ceremony held on the fourth day among Pueblo peoples or the burying of a male baby's umbilical cord in a cornfield to signify his future role as a producer.

Ceremonies often marked important life events, including puberty and, for girls, the beginning of menstruation. *Kinaalda*, the coming of age ceremony for Navajo girls, is one such ritual. Lasting over four days, the girl is symbolically refashioned into a woman as if she were composed of clay. She dresses in her finest clothes and eats nothing but a kind of gruel and water. On the fourth day, she bathes, and her hair is dried with sacred cornmeal. Next, she dresses and runs to the east while a medicine man, or shaman, chants sacred songs. Now considered a woman, she and her attendees share a cake made of cornmeal and feast in her honor.

As for the proper way of delivering newborns into the world, Pretty-shield explained the process for her Crow people to Frank B. Linderman. First, a special lodge was erected for the expectant mother. A wise midwife was then hired to assist in the delivery. In Pretty-shield's case, her father offered her midwife, Old Left-hand, several fine robes and one of his best horses for payment. Inside the tipi, a buffalo blanket was spread, along with other robes, and two poles were driven into the ground. The poles would be for Pretty-shield to grasp while pushing. She told Linderman, "Crow women do not lie down when their babies are born, nor even afterward" (Linderman 1978, 146). Next, Old Left-hand buried four coals around the lodge in strategic places. As she stepped over the coals, she felt the baby coming, and grabbing the stakes, she began to push. Soon her first child, Pine-fire, came into the world.

Shortly after birth, the new mother returned to her work, now with a swaddled baby in tow. For the first month, however, women only did light activities, taking short steps and drinking nothing save for cold water. If riding a horse was necessary, the woman tied her legs together above the knees. At around six months, the baby would be placed in a cradleboard, and the mother could complete most any activity with the baby securely held in place, as the Shoshone woman Sacagawea memorably demonstrated to Lewis and Clark during their trip to the Pacific and back.

ON THE CUSP OF GREAT CHANGES

The influence of Europeans in the West—Frenchmen, Spaniards, and Englishmen—had been felt for centuries by the dawning of the 19th century. Their arrival brought both hardship (disease and conquest) and opportunity in the form of a connection to the global market. Trade brought new and valuable additions to Indian cultures across the West. Iron tools, beads, and manufactured cloth, to name the most obvious, enlarged the material world of Indians and made their lives much easier. For example, how much easier was it to chop down a tree with an iron axe rather than one made of stone? Of all the new things the Europeans brought, surely the horse had the biggest effect on Indian cultures, transforming many Indian peoples, such as the Lakota, Crow, and Comanche, into lords of the plains.

For all of the material gain and the ease of domestic life, the arrival of Europeans also brought problems. Traders often employed alcohol to lubricate trade relations with Indian peoples, and alcohol, by being consumed quickly, forced Indian peoples to increase their harvesting of furs to acquire more alcohol. This trade was far different from gaining a durable iron pot or axe that would last for years. Worst of all, however, were the alien diseases that spread across the Indian world. A continent-wide smallpox epidemic erupted in the 1770s that followed well-established trading networks. In New Mexico, more than 5,000 people died of smallpox in 1780–1781. Smallpox and a terrible drought afflicted the Hopi in modern Arizona and may have killed over 90 percent of the population, reducing them from over 7,000 residents to only 798 in the years between 1775 and 1780.

Entire villages disappeared before the onslaught of smallpox. Lewis and Clark, for example, noted that among the Mahar (Omaha) Indians, "the ravages of the Small Pox (which Swept off 400 men & Womin [*sic*] & children in perpopotion [*sic*]) has reduced this nation not exceeding 300 men and left them to the insults of their weaker neighbors" (Bergon 1995, 28–29). Unfortunately, this scourge, and numerous others, would revisit with deadly frequency. Pretty-shield's father died of it "and more than a hundred others, in one moon. . . . I had it myself. A wise-one named Sharp-shin healed me." She explained to Frank Linderman, "This bad-sickness came to us from the Shoshones. We were in our winter camp when it came. We did not know what sickness it was. We did not scatter, as we ought to have done, and bad-sickness got into every lodge before we knew its power" (Linderman 1978, 45).

Smallpox reached all the way to the Pacific, spread either via overland trade networks connecting different Indian tribes or per-haps by European or American ships that visited coastal villages. The Englishman Nathaniel Portlock was surprised to see so few Tlingit Indians in the area around Sitka, Alaska, when he visited in 1787. He "observed the oldest of the men to be very much marked with the small-pox, as was a girl who appeared to be about four-teen years old" (Calloway 2003, 422). All across the West, countless Indian peoples perished, many long before their people had ever seen a white man. Smallpox, of course, originated in the Old World, a terrible harbinger of the years of sorrow that lay ahead for Indian peoples.

2

DOMESTIC LIFE ON THE OVERLAND TRAILS

INTO THE WEST

The overland trails, especially the Oregon-California Trail, are iconic in American history. Movies, books, and a popular, but difficult, 1980s video game all recounted the adventure of the trail. Artists created monumental paintings of the trail experience on massive canvases meant to convey the enormity of the West, most notably Albert Bierstadt's 1869 *Emigrants Crossing the Plains*, with its covered wagons and horsemen, flanked by imposing rock walls and ancient twisted trees, pushing inexorably into the ruddy setting sun. The covered wagon itself became a symbol of American progress and Manifest Destiny, and covered wagons still feature prominently in historic sites related to the trails, including on the symbol of the Oregon National Historic Trail. One can even "glamp" (luxury camping, a portmanteau for "glamorous camping") in a covered wagon near Yosemite National Park for only $179 a night, according to *Travel + Leisure* magazine (Romano 2018).

While we remember and romanticize the overland trail experience today, emigrants to Oregon and other destinations were keenly aware of the novelty of their experience—plucked from the daily chores of farm life, they embarked on a grand once-in-a-lifetime

Albert Bierstadt's 1869 painting *Emigrants Crossing the Plains* captured the romance and sense of mission that many Oregon Trail emigrants felt as they made their way West. Trail life, however, could be anything but romantic. (Library of Congress)

adventure—and subsequently a large number kept diaries, sent letters to loved ones, or wrote memoirs detailing their experiences later in life. Journeying west meant bettering their lives and helping expand the culture, values, and power of their nation. In effect, the vanguards of Manifest Destiny, the first emigrants in the 1840s to Oregon and California, entered territories that were still not yet the exclusive domain of the United States. Many felt this patriotic zeal and sense of national pride, even on the trail. Independence Rock, jutting out of the surrounding scrubland in southern Wyoming, became a common place of reverie. The name itself came from the belief that a wagon train should reach the rock by the Fourth of July if they hoped to arrive in Oregon or California before the snows came to the mountains. Winfield Scott Ebey felt a sense of national pride at Independence Rock on July 4, 1854. He wrote, "Crowds of emigrants got to the Rock, to spend Independence Day, and the loud reports of fire arms throughout the day, testifies that this is the birth Day [*sic*] of American Freedom; & that although here in the wilds of the Rocky Mountains, a thousand miles from our home we are Yet [*sic*] American Citizens a part of that great family who have inherited Freedom from our Ancestors" (Ebey 1997, 103).

A MESSAGE FROM THE WEST

Americans hit the shore of the Atlantic and seemed keen on heading west right from the very beginning, but the settlement of the Trans-Mississippi West really could not become a possibility until 1803 with the Louisiana Purchase. Even after the acquisition of the Louisiana Territory, settlement did not accelerate until the 1830s, and then only after an amazing incident in 1831.

On October 17, 1803, President Thomas Jefferson went before Congress in his Third Annual Message to press for the ratification of the Louisiana Purchase. To say that Jefferson and the American public were excited about adding not just New Orleans but all of the vast territory of Louisiana to the nation would be an understatement. Jefferson envisioned the Louisiana Purchase as a defining moment in the nation's history with profound social and economic consequences for the young nation. As he explained to the nation's lawmakers, the Louisiana Territory's "climate and extent, promise in due season important aids to our treasury, an ample provision for our posterity, and a wide-spread field for the blessings of freedom and equal laws" (Jefferson 1803). The next step, as Jefferson explained, would be to ascertain what lay beyond the known, and thus he would send expeditions to sketch out the blank areas on the map. One of these expeditions, the 1804–1806 expedition of Meriwether Lewis and William Clark, set off a series of events that would hasten the transformation of the West. While Jefferson predicted that these new lands would soon brim with settlers, initial reports from explorers painted a relatively negative picture of the newly acquired lands. The impetus for Anglo-American settlement would not come for several decades and from a very different origin.

In late 1831, three Nez Percé and one Flathead Indian, all from the Pacific Northwest, appeared in St. Louis, Missouri, in the company of an employee of the American Fur Company. They met with William Clark (of Lewis and Clark fame and at the time superintendent for Indian affairs for the U.S. government), and their arrival generally caused a sensation. Apparently, they had come to learn more about the white man's religion and to cement ties between their people and the United States that had first been created during Lewis and Clark's visit two decades earlier. Unfortunately, two of the men died from disease in the city and a third on the return voyage up the Missouri River. The fourth was killed by the Blackfeet Indians after joining his fellow Nez Percé on a bison hunt. Word of their visit and experiences, however, made it back to the Nez Percé in the Pacific Northwest.

Among Anglo-Americans, the tale of their visit spread thanks to the efforts of a man named William Walker. Walker, a devout Methodist and part Wyandot Indian, had visited St. Louis to help the Wyandot locate good lands for their removal to the West as part of the Indian removal project of President Jackson's administration then underway. While in St. Louis, Walker heard the tale from William Clark. He wrote his friend G. P. Disoway, "Gen. C[lark] related to me the object of their mission, and, my dear friend, it is impossible for me to describe to you my feelings while listening to his narrative." He continued, "It appeared that some white man had penetrated into their country, and happened to be a spectator at one of their religious ceremonies. . . . He informed them that their mode of worshipping the supreme Being was radically wrong, and instead of being acceptable and pleasing, it was displeasing to him; he also informed them that the white people away toward the rising of the sun had been put in possession of the true mode of worshipping the great Spirit." After hearing this, Walker claimed, they elected four men to go to St. Louis and meet with William Clark to see if this was true. Clark met with them and explained that what they had heard was true, but "poor fellows, they were not all permitted to return home to their people with the intelligence," for two died in the city, and the fate of the others was unknown. He concluded, "If they died on their way home, peace be to their names! They died inquirers after the truth" (Walker 1833). Indeed, in Walker's recounting, the story of the quartet of Indians became a tale of a people in the wilderness crying out for salvation. His letter soon found its way into the pages of the *Christian Advocate and Journal and Zion's Herald* in early 1833, a paper dedicated to American Methodist issues, and ignited calls to send missionaries to the West.

As was often the case in such Indian pleas for conversion, religion probably was not the only motivation. Lewis and Clark's appearance among them years earlier had created the basis of an alliance, and clearly the Nez Percé saw economic and military assistance as potential by-products of encouraging American missionaries to settle among them. Whatever the motivations, the stratagem had worked, and missionary efforts were hastily assembled back east. Jason and Daniel Lee would be the first to arrive in 1834, but they would settle in the Willamette Valley of Oregon and not among the Nez Percé to the east. However, plans were being put in motion to send missionaries to the Nez Percé and other Indian peoples on the Columbia Plateau. In 1836, two newly married Presbyterian missionary couples made their way to the Nez Percé and Cayuse Indians. Marcus and Narcissa Whitman settled among the Cayuse, and Henry and Eliza Spaulding set up their mission among the Nez Percé. Despite a flush of initial optimism, the missions proved largely unsuccessful, or at least unsuccessful in their goal of converting Indians.

By another measure, their journey proved prophetic. The missionaries ascended to the top of the South Pass in southern Wyoming on July 4, 1836, crossing the Continental Divide at a far easier pass than that of Lewis and Clark. The South Pass had been used by Indians for thousands of years, and fur trappers later learned of the route. But Eliza and Narcissa had the distinction of being the first white women to ever cross the Continental Divide. This route, and their success, illustrated the ease by which other women could similarly follow suit. Entire families could successfully traverse the mountains, making an overland trip to the Pacific coast feasible.

As the years went on, it became apparent that the missions were not succeeding; there were few genuine converts to show for the effort and expense. By the 1840s, however, the Whitmans' mission in the Walla Walla Valley had become a common stop for Oregon Trail emigrants, who could count on the mission to provide food and assistance should they need it, and many did. Largely rejected by the Indians, the Whitmans pondered whether God really wanted them to convert the Indians, or did He have another motive entirely? Marcus, for example, observed, "It has been distinctly my feeling that we are not to measure the sphere of our action & hope of usefulness by the few natives of this country" (Jeffrey 1994, 172–173). Their shift in focus, however, alienated the Cayuse they had been sent to convert and would eventually lead to tragedy.

TO OREGON!

Following the success of the Whitmans and Spaldings in crossing the mountains and setting up missions (which doubled as semiautonomous farms), and with increasingly florid descriptions of Oregon and especially the Willamette Valley finding their way into print, more Americans began to endure the hazardous journey across the continent. Nathaniel Wyeth was among them. Wyeth wanted to accomplish several important goals when it came to the Oregon Country. First, he wanted to set up a fur company to rival the British Hudson's Bay Company, and second, he hoped to help convince Americans to claim the Oregon Country for the United States and not let it remain the possession of the British. In the first, he failed, but in the second, he largely succeeded in encouraging Americans to head for the Willamette Valley. For example, he wrote in his journal that the Willamette Valley offered an ideal location for small farmers. A few Canadians, he explained, had settled in the valley and in the first year were able to raise hogs, cattle, and horses. They also reaped substantial crops of "wheat, barely [sic], potatoes, turnips, cabages [sic], corn, punkins [sic], mellons." The valley floor offered both open land and excellent stands of timber and in the distance, on both the east and west, lay rolling hills. The valley's bottomland, he explained, was composed of "uniform soil extremely rich equal to the best of the Missouri lands." He continued, "I have never seen country of equal beauty except the Kansas country and I doubt not will one day sustain a large population" (Wyeth 1983).

Even better, these fertile lands were cheap, much cheaper than good farmland in the Midwest. Add to that descriptions of a beneficent climate; mild, wet winters; no severe thunderstorms or tornadoes; and, perhaps best of all, no malaria and Oregon's call proved irresistible to many. To spur immigration to Oregon, the newly formed Oregon Provisional Government passed a land law that gave 320 acres to male heads of household and another 320 acres to the wife of a male head of household out of the territory's public domain. The 640-acre limit represented the most generous amount ever offered by the federal government (far better than the 160 acres promised under the 1862 Homestead Act), and the fertility of the available lands surely made this an enticing opportunity. Even after the 1850 Oregon Donation Land Law limited the size of claims to 320 acres, the amount still encouraged settlers to relocate, and relocate they did. They only problem lay in actually getting there.

The cost of the journey proved to be the first hurdle faced by would-be Oregon settlers. Purchasing a wagon, four oxen, and the required goods often exceeded the means of many would-be emigrants. These items alone generally cost $400, a considerable amount. Several hundred dollars more would be needed to begin the process of building a house, clearing fields, and so on. By many estimates, a family needed somewhere between $500 and $1,000 to make the trip and get set up in the first year. Poor families could never acquire so large a sum, so middle-class families from the farming regions of the Midwest composed the vast majority of

Oregon settlers. Thus equipped, families crammed as many of their possessions as they could manage into wagons that typically only had about 40 square feet of space in them (just slightly larger than the dimensions for a medium-sized U-Haul rental pickup truck's 36.92 square feet). Required to transport hundreds of pounds of food and supplies, the emigrants had to be judicious in their choices. All along the trail, especially near obstacles like Windlass Hill in Nebraska, heavy trunks and other furniture lay scattered about and cast off on the plains, their status as heirlooms and vessels for memories sacrificed to necessity. Carrying one's belongings in small overloaded wagons required most of the family to walk to lighten the load for the family's oxen. The oxen, their powerful shoulders straining against their harnesses, could only move the wagon at a walking pace in the best of circumstances, making it easy for travelers to keep up.

Perhaps even more daunting than the planning and the cost was the actual journey itself. While the route over the South Pass had been "discovered" by trappers with the American Fur Company in 1812, and Eliza Spalding and Narcissa Whitman had proven that women could make the journey in 1836, large parties of families did not set out until the 1840s, often after having read John C. Frémont's best-selling report of his experiences in the region. The *Daily Missouri Republican*, after reading Frémont's account, declared the journey to be "little more than a pleasure excursion, requiring scarcely as much preparation as a journey from St. Louis to Philadelphia thirty-five years ago" (Faragher 1979, 7). Such nonchalant underestimations often proved fatal.

Emigrants faced a journey of almost 2,000 miles, climbing over mountains, fording rivers, and crossing vast plains and parched deserts. They hoped to make 20 miles a day, but many only managed 10 or 15 miles for their day's effort. Starting in late March or April, they hoped to arrive in Oregon (or California, depending on their destination) by October or early November—starting any later than that and the delay, as the Donner party discovered, might prove fatal.

Travelers typically envisioned the journey as a series of legs. The first leg, across the rolling plains in the verdure of spring, took them from Independence, Missouri, to Fort Kearny, on the Platte River, a distance of 320 miles. Parties making good time would reach Fort Kearny by late May. Next, the wagons steadily climbed toward Fort Laramie, still following for a time the North Platte River, passing such landmarks as Courthouse Rock, Chimney Rock, and Scott's

Bluff. Trees had petered out by this time, and the June heat could be unbearable. They completed this second 300-mile leg when they arrived at Fort Laramie. Another roughly 300-mile section took them past Independence Rock, through the Devil's Gate on the Sweetwater River just beyond, and finally over the 8,000-foot summit of South Pass.

The journey continued on to Fort Bridger. Mormon emigrants turned south to Salt Lake City, the new Zion of their faith, but most others headed north to Fort Hall. The wagons had now covered 1,200 miles since Missouri, and the August days grew noticeably shorter. Exhausted people and animals, often with battered wagons, pushed on inexorably west to reach Fort Hall. From there, those heading to California turned southwesterly, and those destined for Oregon headed northwesterly for 175 miles of rough trail toward Fort Boise. The California route promised vast alkali deserts and a climb over the Sierra Nevada mountains. The route to Oregon was no better, and for both trails, the greatest challenges still lay ahead. Oregon's Blue Mountains broke both wagons and spirits, then it was across the dry plains of eastern Oregon, with the snowcapped summit of Mount Hood rising in the West. Finally, they arrived at the Dalles, where series of giant rapids on the Columbia River awaited them. Emigrants could decide to load their wagons on rafts here for the last hundred miles through the Columbia River Gorge, a potentially deadly descent, or skirt around the southern shoulder of Mount Hood on the rugged Barlow Trail. Either route brought them, finally, to the Willamette Valley in Oregon. Travelers bound for the goldfields of California had equally difficult terrain to cross, especially the ascent over the Sierra Nevada mountains. Between the 1840s and 1870s, somewhere between a quarter million and a half million emigrants made their way across the overland trails, and for many, the journey, regardless of age, proved to be one of the most memorable experiences of their lives.

DAILY LIFE ON THE OREGON TRAIL

Despite the novelty of six months of walking, daily life on the Oregon Trail in many ways mirrored the settled life that bookended the experience. The overland trail experience was generally a family affair. To be sure, the peak gold rush years between 1849 and 1852 were an exception, as tens of thousands of men sought their fortunes in the California goldfields, typically leaving wives and children behind for what they hoped would be a short but profitable sojourn in the mines. Officials at Fort Laramie kept a census of emigrants, and in June 1850, they noted that 99 children, 119 women, and 17,443 men had passed by the fort en route to the Pacific. Such was the goldfield mania. Once the gold fever broke, the numbers returned to something closer to gender parity.

On the trail, men, women, and children continued to do the things they had always done, and Victorian ideas of gender accompanied them west. Men and boys tended to the ox teams and performed physical tasks such as fording streams and maneuvering wagons over obstacles. Men provided security for the party and attempted to hunt to supplement their families' food supply. They also made most decisions on course and navigation, when to stop and when to go, and, indeed, men typically made the decision to migrate in the first place, sometimes against their wife's wishes.

Men's work, therefore, involved activity during the day, and they measured their success in miles completed and obstacles conquered. Except for possibly guard duty or looking for lost stock, men did little activity in the mornings or evenings. This was the time when women had to do the most work (after completing the day's travel, often on foot).

As soon as the wagons stopped for the evening, women's labor began. First came hauling water to drink and cook with and then gathering firewood, a task that sometimes fell to children but never to the men. Cooking the evening meal over an open fire was followed by cleaning and putting away the crockery. Finally, women brought out the bedding and made beds for the family in the wagon. In addition to these daily tasks, the women and girls kept watch over smaller children, assisted as midwives, and cared for the sick and injured. In short, women were always working. Mollie Sanford, crossing the plains in 1860, asked sarcastically about resting on Sundays, "Rest? Where is the rest for us [women]?" (West 1992).

With no doctors or hospitals for hundreds of miles, women provided medical care for their parties. A surprisingly high number of women set out for Oregon pregnant and gave birth while on the trail. While the prospect of giving birth with no physician or hospital nearby seems unimaginable today, it apparently did not deter women or their families from setting out on the trail. Certainly, back home, women often gave birth with only the aid of fellow women and did not see the need for a physician to be present. If a family did not have other women to help with labor, husbands often rode along the trail looking for other families with a woman willing to assist.

Such was the story told by Merritt Kellogg. Kellogg described how a rider suddenly appeared in their camp, explaining that a young wife was in labor and that she was the only woman in a party of 10 men. Kellogg noted that the plight of the young woman "touched my wife's heart and she said, 'I am lame and ought not to go, but that woman needs help.' She then slipped on a pair of my trousers under her dress, then mounted the mule man-fashion, and galloped away with the man." With her help, the young woman gave birth to healthy baby, and "all the pay my wife received was the thanks of the couple, who, like ourselves were travelling without money. She also had the satisfaction that a person feels in doing for others as they would like others to do for them under similar circumstances" (Faragher 1979, 141–142).

Women tended the sick and injured, and there were a lot of sick and injured on the trails. Accidents occurred with regularity. Men managed to accidentally shoot themselves in hunting adventures gone awry or even when pulling their weapons out of trunks by the barrel. The seats of wagons were fixed to the front, and occasionally people dozed off, lost their balance, and fell beneath the wagon wheels. Catherine Sager "had become so accustomed to getting in and out of the wagon as to lose all fear, and would get out on the tongue [of the wagon] and leap clear of the wheel without putting Father to the trouble of stopping the team." One afternoon, however, "the hem of my dress caught on an axle-handle, precipitating me under the wheels both of which passed over me, badly crushing my left leg, before Father could stop the wagon" (Schlissel 1982, 39). Of course, the Sagers' misfortunes had only just begun.

Wagons often had to cross rivers, some big enough that the men spent precious time building makeshift rafts to float them across. Dangerous stream crossings made drowning a real possibility. Elizabeth Stewart Warner, in a letter back to family and friends describing the journey to Oregon, described a terrible ferry accident at St. Joseph, Missouri. She watched as the ferry her family was waiting to catch caught a submerged snag in the river, spilling the passengers into water. She wrote that the sinking "drowned 7 men. A woman was standing on the bank, she said to mother, do you see that man with the red warmer on well that is my husband and while she spoke the boat struck and went down and she had to stand within call of him and see him drowned" (Schlissel 1982, 92).

Even snakebites could injure and kill. Catherine Haun wrote in her diary, "To add to the horrors of the surroundings one man was bitten on the ankle by a venomous snake. Although every available rimidy [*sic*] was tried upon the wound, his limb had to be amputated with the aid of a common hacksaw. Fortunately, for him, he had a good, brave wife along who helped and cheered him into health and usefulness" (Schlissel 1982, 178). Haun noted that despite missing a leg, the man continued to be useful, mending shoes and fixing wagons as needed by her party. She concluded, "He was one of the most cheery members of the company and told good stories and sang at the campfire, putting to shame some of the able bodied who were given to complaining or selfishness" (Schlissel 1982, 178).

Emigrants often crossed the trail filled with apprehension about Indian attacks. Occasionally, attacks did occur, as Jane Gould Tortillott described in her diary entry from August 9, 1862. She wrote, "In a short time the word came back [to her party] that a train six miles on had been attacked by the Indians, and some killed" (Schlissel 1982, 224). For days afterward, the nervous train contended with sporadic fire from Indians. While some attacks did occur, the numbers of Indians killed by white emigrants was greater than the reverse. Historian John Unruh found that between 1840 and 1860, the number of Indians killed by whites was 426, and the number of whites killed by Indians was 362 (Unruh 1993, 185). Moreover, the majority of attacks did not occur on the Great Plains as one would imagine, given the reputation of Indians like the Lakota Sioux, but instead west of the South Pass. Needless to say, 362 killed out of an estimated 500,000 who crossed the trail is statistically insignificant.

Still, emigrants lived in fear of attack. Catherine Haun's party expected attacks at any moment along the Platte River: "Had they [hostile Indians] cared to attack us from the heights above we could have made no effective defense. After the possible massacre had been accomplished their booty would have been our money, clothing, food and traveling paraphernalia—and worse still those of our women who had been unfortunate enough to have escaped death" (Schlissel 1982, 178). The fate worse than death that Haun implies would be to be raped by the savage Indians. Such an attack, however, existed only in her imagination.

In reality, Indian peoples routinely assisted the emigrants. Some Indians ran ferries to help emigrants cross rivers, and many others offered to barter food or clothing for manufactured items or goods like tobacco. Lydia Allen Rudd, for example, traded some hardtack for berries from the Snake Indians, and a few days later, she wrote, "I traded an apron today for a pair of moccasins of the indians [*sic*]" (Schlissel 1982, 193). Despite the help given, emigrants routinely complained about the Indians. Sometimes they appeared in camps unannounced, hoping to barter, and on many occasions, emigrants woke to discover small items, like combs or frying pans, had been stolen in the night—the culprits likely being young men or boys who sought to demonstrate their bravery and cunning by taking an item from the passing emigrants.

Contrary to the popular imagination (then and now), hostile Indian encounters were exceedingly rare, but terrible killers did lurk along the trail who would claim thousands of victims. These killers went by many names "camp fever," "the bloody flux," "scarlet fever," "ague," and "mountain fever," to name a few. We know these by different names: cholera, dysentery, malaria, Rocky Mountain spotted fever, typhus, and measles. Disease represented the greatest peril on the trail.

Some diseases, like malaria and Rocky Mountain spotted fever, were carried by insects. Malaria, for example, spread from infected mosquitoes, and while malaria-carrying mosquitoes did not thrive in the West, the disease could be carried for decades in one's body. Relapses were common, especially under the exhaustion and privations caused by the relentless labor of the trail. Rocky Mountain spotted fever, however, was spread by ticks indigenous to the Rockies. Dysentery, also known as the "bloody flux," and cholera primarily spread through contact with polluted water sources. In many places on the trail, thousands of people and animals had to use the same limited water sources. Once a spring was contaminated, all subsequent travelers would be exposed to possible infection when they stopped to get water, making the transmission of these diseases almost inevitable. Of all the diseases, cholera probably killed the most, with outbreaks traveling the trail every year from 1849 to 1852, the peak years of the California gold rush (in fact, cholera epidemics spread all around the globe in these years).

In a world without physicians, fighting the myriad diseases of trail life once again fell to women. Without effective medications, there was little they could do, but they tried nonetheless. Lydia Allen Rudd, heading to Oregon in 1852, noted the effects of cholera on May 11, 1852, writing, "Our men are not any of them very well this morning. We passed another grave to day which was made this morning. The board stated that he died of cholera" (Schlissel 1982, 189). The party's men continued to suffer, and on the May 14, they "passed four men diging [*sic*] a grave. They were packers. The man that had died was taken sick yesterday noon and died last night. They called it the cholera morbus" (Schlissel 1982, 189–190). The next weeks brought a steady passage of fresh graves and companies of the dying. Rudd's party found an ill man beside the road on June 6. "We doctored him what we could but he was to [*sic*] far gone." Worse, the members of her own party began to die. On the June 11, they left behind a member of their party, who soon died. Within a fortnight, several others passed as well. On June 23, Rudd wrote, "Mr. Girtman died last night about 11 o'clock. He has left a wife without any relatives. . . . Sickness and death in the states is hard but nothing to be compared with it on the plains" (Schlissel 1982, 192).

Graves popped up with regularity, like grim mile markers, but worse than graves were the bodies themselves. Survivors struggled to dig graves in the hard soil, yet another unremitting task to complete in the hot, exhausting sun, and often the diggers only managed a shallow trench. Many of the gravediggers were themselves not healthy, and always in the back of their minds lingered the knowledge that they needed to keep going to make it to their destination before the snows blocked the passage west—delaying too long over the dead might cause others to suffer later. Wolves and other scavengers often dug into the shallow graves and feasted on the bodies. Bones lay scattered about these disturbed graves. The Stewart sisters, for example, decided to play near their evening's campsite only to stumble upon the exhumed skull of a woman, a comb still affixed to her hair. As Louise Clappe (heading to California with her physician husband) noted in a letter to her sister, the trail was "this boundless city of the dead" (quoted in West 1992). Death, already a part of daily life in Victorian times, became an ever-present companion on the trails. One party's misfortune and plight, however, stood above all others, becoming a symbol of the horrors of the overland trail, a cautionary tale for other travelers, and finally a story of heroism and survival.

THE DONNER PARTY

On April 15, 1846, a party of almost three dozen people from the Donner and Reed families set off from Springfield, Illinois, bound for the promised land of California, some 2,000 or so miles away, in a total of nine wagons. Sarah Hanley Keyes, the oldest member of the party at around 70, was the mother of Margaret Reed. Thomas Keyes Reed and Eliza Poor Donner represented the youngest members at only three years of age. The Reeds and Donners, like many of the emigrants, were comfortably middle class and moved in the best Springfield social circles. James Reed, for example, counted a young lawyer named Abraham Lincoln among his personal friends, and he may have even attempted to persuade Lincoln to come to California with his family.

The financial fortunes of the two families, despite appearance, did differ. Reed, more flamboyant and status conscious, flirted with bankruptcy and hoped California would change his fortunes; the Donners, conversely, had ample funds, including the princely sum of $10,000 in cash sewn inside the layers of a quilt. But the allure of California attracted them equally. They did have some advantages over many emigrants, however, in that they were able to bring three wagons for each family. Two carried supplies, and the third had been transformed into a rolling house. The wagon for Grandma Keyes, already in failing health when they set out, even featured a heavy iron cookstove and furnishings typical of a comfortable sitting room. So opulent was the wagon that 11-year-old Virginia Reed dubbed it the "Pioneer Prairie Palace."

To help with the wagons, oxen, and cattle, George Donner placed an advertisement in the Springfield, Illinois, *Gazette* in search of hired hands, asking, "Who wants to go to California without costing them anything? As many as eight young men of good character who can drive an ox team will be accommodated. Come, boys, you can have as much land as you want without costing you anything." Almost half a dozen young men in their twenties joined on to the expedition, eager to work their way to California and financial success.

The first roughly three weeks' travel from Springfield, Illinois, to Independence, Missouri, passed without incident. After resting for a few days, the party set out on May 12, 1846—a bit later than the typical mid-April start. Tamzene Donner took the opportunity to send a letter to her sister Elizabeth Poor in Massachusetts. "We go to California, to the bay of Francisco. It is a four month trip. . . . I am willing to go & have no doubt it will be an advantage to our children & to us. I came here last evening and start tomorrow morning on the long journey" (Wallis 2017, 58). Spring rains turned the route to mud, and the oxen pushed through mud almost to their chests. May 29 brought the first death. Sarah Keyes succumbed to tuberculosis, and the family stopped to bury her. That evening, in the bed her grandmother had died in that morning, young Patty Reed asked God to "watch over and protect dear Grandmother, and don't let the Indians dig her up" (Wallis 2017, 88). Grandma Keyes was the first death, but hers would not be the last.

The Donner party, having joined up with a larger expedition of wagons, made decent time along the Platte River. Buffalo proved plentiful, and the few Indians they encountered were friendly. Tamzene Donner wrote in a June 16 letter, "Indeed, if I do not experience something far worse that I have yet done, I shall say the trouble is all in getting started" (Wallis 2017, 112). As the wagons continued their steady progress toward Fort Laramie, things seemed to be going well. A fateful decision would change everything.

Jacob Donner and James Reed had poured over the contents of Lansford W. Hastings's guidebook *The Emigrants' Guide to Oregon and California*. Hastings had marketed the book as the definitive guide to the trails, and he claimed to have found a better route to California that went south of Salt Lake City, through the Wasatch Mountains, and then out onto the arid salt flats before finally rejoining the regular California Trail along the Humboldt River. Hastings claimed this route would save a month of travel, but he had never taken the route—in fact, no one had. At Fort Bernard, the party met James Clyman, an experienced mountain man who had served with James Reed in the Blackhawk War back in Illinois. As fate would have it, he was returning from California and had, until recently, traveled with Hastings and found him to be untrustworthy. Clyman warned James Reed and Jacob and George Donner against the Hastings Cutoff. "I told him [Reed] to take the regular wagon track [via Fort Hall] and never leave it—it is barely possible to get through if you follow it and it may be impossible if you don't" (Wallis 2017, 132). Reed ignored Clyman's advice, a decision that would prove disastrous. Only Tamzene Donner seemed suspicious of Hastings's route, but on the morning of July 20, the Donner and Reed party split off from a larger train and set off on the Hastings Cutoff.

After purchasing goods at Fort Bridger and allowing both man and beast time to recover, the Donner party, now numbering some 74 men, women, and children, entered the unknown on July 31. They hoped to reach California by mid-September, long before storms locked the mountains in snow. Instead, the route over the Wasatch Mountains that Hastings had proposed was almost impossible. Another party had made it through before them, guided by Hastings himself, but even he admitted it was too rugged in a note he fastened to some sagebrush recommending an alternative route. The Donner party pressed on, hacking another route through the

Wasatch, and they finally emerged out of the imposing range. The route that Hastings claimed should take but a few days had taken them almost three weeks of exhaustive effort. A few days brought them to Hope Springs. Attached to a piece of wood was another note from Hastings, but bits had flaked off and blown away. They collected what they could, and Tamzene Donner assembled the fragments into a message: "2 days—2 nights—hard driving—desert—reach water" (Wallis 2017, 167). Ahead lay the barren salt flats, a landscape as inhospitable as any on earth and utterly devoid of vegetation and fresh water.

By early October, they reached the Humboldt River, rejoining the main trail to California. Already a month behind schedule, they still had the ascent and descent of the Sierra Nevada mountains ahead of them. They could see the V-shaped flocks of geese flying south and feel the chill in the morning air as fall made its presence felt. The party splintered, with the Donners going ahead and the Reeds and others falling behind. They had sent some men up the trail to reach California and return with needed supplies.

Nerves were fraying, slights growing into grudges, and finally, on October 5, James Reed ended up in an altercation with a man named John Snyder. The furious Snyder assaulted Reed with a bullwhip. Reed's wife, Margret, threw herself between them, but Snyder rained several blows down on her. James Reed pulled out his knife and fatally stabbed Snyder in the chest. That evening, the men in the party debated Reed's fate and decided to banish him from the party, giving him only a horse and the clothes on his back. He would have no food to eat or weapons to defend himself. Reed had no choice but to leave his family behind. However, his daughter Virginia managed to sneak him some food, his rifle and pistols, and some ammunition. He would have to ride on by himself with no knowledge of the fate of his family.

By the third week of October, the ragged party had reached the Truckee Meadows at the foot of the Sierra Nevada mountains. James Reed and a companion, Walter Herron, meanwhile, had made it over the mountains but were perilously close to starvation. They still had found no one able to provide them with assistance. After a few days more, the exhausted, famished men found a party heading to California. Among them was Charles Stanton, one of the men from the Donner party who had ridden ahead to Sutter's Mill for help. He was now returning with several mules and supplies for the beleaguered train. Reed continued to Sutter's Mill, and

Stanton headed east with Luis and Salvador, two Miwok Indians John Sutter had provided (although Sutter called them "cowboys," he controlled several hundred Miwoks in a kind of quasi slavery). Stanton found the Donner and Reed wagons scattered along the train and distributed what he had brought. It seemed that the worst might be over as the brittle wagons and bedraggled emigrants made their way toward the pass over the Sierra Nevada mountains at Donner Summit, later named for the unfortunate train. Once over the pass, they would gradually descend out of the mountains and the threat of snow. Just as it seemed the ordeal would finally end, the weather turned. On October 16, the first snow fell. More storms followed in short order, and soon the parties, spread out in several locations, were hopelessly snowbound—and only a few miles from the summit of the pass and what would have been salvation.

Unable to climb the pass in deep snow, the trapped emigrants set about building cabins. With few other options for food, the families slaughtered their oxen, the animals that had brought them so far. First, they ate the meat, and then they boiled the bones and hides. Eventually, they had nothing left, and the dying began. In mid-December, a group of 15 (10 men and 5 women) of the strongest remaining members donned makeshift snowshoes and set out for help, including Stanton and the Miwok Indians. By this point, the snowdrifts exceeded 20 feet in many places.

The group of 15, dubbed the "Forlorn Hope," for their unlikely chance of success, took enough rations to keep them alive for the six days they thought would be necessary to reach settlements, but the six days passed with the group still trapped in the mountains. Charles Stanton was the first of the trekkers to die. He had made it to Sutter's Fort and returned with food, despite the fact that he had no relatives in the party. By all accounts a hero, he ultimately paid for his heroism and selflessness with his life. A few days later, Patrick Dolan, Antonio (a hired man), and the teenaged Lem Murphy all died. With nothing else to eat, the survivors decided to cannibalize the three dead men. A few days after that, William Foster murdered the two Miwoks, despite the protestations of William Eddy. Once again, they ate the dead—only Eddy refusing the grisly meal. Finally, the dwindling group managed to find an Indian village. The Indians fed them and guided them to a settlement of whites in Bear Valley. The ordeal had taken them 33 days, with all five women surviving and only two of the men, Eddy and Foster. Eddy wrote a letter and sent it to Sutter's Mill, where the plight of the stranded train elicited calls for a rescue. Two parties were hastily put together, one led by Aquilla Glover, who had known the Donners and Reeds back in Illinois, and the other by James Reed himself.

As Reed's and Glover's teams pushed through the snow, the number of the living in the snowbound camps was dwindling, as starvation had begun to take its toll. Just before the Forlorn Hope set off, James Donner died, his brother George at his side; then Sam Shoemaker, James Smith, and Joseph Reinhardt passed in quick succession, all three young and single men. Others followed, and like the members of the Forlorn Hope, many had no choice but to eat the dead to stay alive.

Glover's rescue team arrived on February 18, 1847. Approaching the almost totally buried cabins, Glover's men shouted out, and several heads appeared above the snow. Dan Rhoads, one of the rescuers, recalled, "They were gaunt with famine and I never can forget the horrible ghastly sight they presented. The first woman spoke in a hollow voice very much agitated & said, 'Are you men from California or do you come from heaven?'" (Wallis 2017, 291). Glover and his men had only brought what they could carry, and even much of that they had left behind in caches. They could help, but they could not alleviate the suffering. They could, however, take some survivors over the mountains. Margret Reed agreed to go, even though it meant leaving two of her children behind. Patty, her nine-year-old daughter, would have to care for her three-year-old brother in Margret's absence. The Breens, who had survived better than most because they did have some supplies left, sent their sons Edward and Simon. Many others stayed behind, including Tamzene Donner, who would not abandon her ailing husband, George.

Reed's party arrived and then a third led by Eddy and Foster, and slowly they evacuated the survivors over the Sierras. A few remained, including Tamzene Donner, who continued to refuse to leave her husband's side, even after her children were saved. By the time the fourth party arrived, George Donner was dead, carefully wrapped in a sheet, and Tamzene had vanished. Many suspected that Lewis Keseberg, the last survivor rescued, had murdered her and consumed her body, but no evidence of the crime remained. Keseberg had clearly eaten the dead (as had others), but he denied killing Tamzene. He would, however, be vilified for his alleged actions for decades.

The army showed up the following summer and burned the cabins and collected the remains. The grisly site of the terrible ordeal then returned to nature. The memory of the Donner party endured, however, and became a stark reminder of what could happen in the harsh terrain of the West.

CHILDHOOD ON THE TRAIL

Children, of course, helped the family in a variety of ways while on the trail. They gathered firewood, fetched water, and helped herd the cattle that often accompanied families west. Older children, especially girls, took care of younger children, and sometimes they had to take on adult tasks, like driving the wagon, if a parent fell ill or died on the trail. For example, when Joseph and Ester Lyman took a supposed cutoff on their way to Oregon, they became lost. Joseph decided to ride back down the trail, leaving his ill wife and family in the care of his son Luther. Similarly, the Pringle family ran out of food in the Cascades in the fall of 1846 with winter setting in (the same time, incidentally, that the Donner party was finding itself trapped to the south in the Sierras). Octavius Pringle, a boy of 14, took the family's only surviving horse and set off over the mountains in search of help. For three days, he rode through the frigid Oregon rain. Finally, he found a settlement and rested for the night. The following day, he set off with flour and a bushel of peas for his starving family. When he made it back, his father noted in his diary that it was "the happiest day to us for many days" (West 1989, 94–95). Entrusting a family's survival to a young teenager in the midst of a fearsome wilderness spoke volumes about the role of children in helping a family survive the ordeal of the trails.

The overland trail experience could be disorienting and monotonous as well. Little Jane fell asleep in the back of the family wagon and awoke when it stopped for the day. Looking around, she started crying. Her older brother asked why she was so distraught, to which she replied, "Oh we will never get to Oregon if we come back and camp in the same place every night." Her brother assured her that despite the uniformity of the landscape, they had in fact traveled many miles to a new camp (West 1989, 33). The featureless flatness terrified children accustomed to a world bounded by trees. Nighttime was also frightening because of the distant cries of wolves and coyotes, which sometimes proved to be not distant enough. Worse, the heat of the day often created powerful thunderstorms that swept across the plains overnight. Huddled together in a small wagon, lightning illuminating everything around them in brilliantly brief flashes while thunder growled and horses and oxen gave voice to their fear, proved almost unbearable for some children.

Children also feared getting lost, and some did in fact, requiring adults to try and locate them. One 12-year-old got lost gathering firewood and spent an uncomfortable and scary night alone on the plains until he was found by a passing horseman. Perhaps most of all, the children worried about the danger of Indians, conditioned as they had been from their earliest memories by tales of Indian "savagery." Thus, when children saw Indians, they usually tried to hide in the wagons or behind the parents, but more adventurous children sometimes traded items with passing Indians. A few even came to appreciate the help Indians sometimes provided emigrant families. Elisha Brooks and his mother set out to reach his father in California but were abandoned on the plains by their hired teamster. The family continued on, and when they grew desperate, they had to trade with the Sioux, who helped them. Elisha concluded the Sioux were "not so bad as they were painted" (West 1989, 36).

Children, like young Patty Reed lamenting her grandmother's death, also experienced death at a young age on the overland trails. While the overall death rate was only a bit higher than life back home, the graves of white emigrants and the funerary platforms of Indians dotting the trail spoke of its omnipresence. Animal carcasses littered the trail in various states of decay. Wolves often dug up the shallow graves, so passersby would find body parts strewn about. Hastily erected crosses often bore the names of deceased children. The deaths of loved ones on the trail only made the fear and pain worse, and, as in the case of the Sager children, sometimes children lost both parents. One traveler came across a girl of 10 and her 12-year-old brother next to their wagon. Their parent's bodies were inside the wagon, dead from cholera. They had been abandoned by their wagon train, until the traveler took them and caught up with their former companions, forcing them to take in the orphans.

Thoughts of their own mortality also influenced these young people, and some in fact had to confront the prospect of their own deaths at terribly early ages. One girl, dying of "mountain fever," begged her mother to "dig her grave six feet deep for she did not want the wolves to dig her up and eat her." She instructed them to "pile a lot of rocks on her Grave after they had covered it up right." Her mother forced the party to stop and properly bury her, honoring her last request (West 1989, 42).

Children, though aware of the hardships and death, proved resilient, and for many of them, the trail offered excitement and adventure. Children found time to enjoy being children. Each day, when the wagons stopped, they bolted out and began exploring the area around the campsite. J. Goldsborough Bruff, arriving at the end of the trail in California, saw the children "laying and playing on the green sward, happily unconscious of the troubles of others" (West 1989, 101). During one of the earliest organized crossings on the Oregon Trail in 1841, some of the boys in the party came across the bloated carcass of a dead ox. Somehow, the boys realized that they could bounce on the swollen paunch of the animal like a trampoline, and each took turns in the activity. Finally, Andy, one of the older boys, decided to see how high he could bounce off the ox trampoline by getting a running start. He sprinted toward the target, jumped, and coming down with all the force he could muster promptly plunged into the rotting carcass up to his waist. With some difficulty, and no doubt copious laughter, the other children managed to extract the goo-covered boy.

Children, unlike adults, marveled at the tiny details around them: colored stones, plants, snakeskins, and whatever else they found. While adults grew tired of the endless days of pushing their animals and themselves for distant Oregon and California, children saw each day as a chance at a new adventure.

By the 1870s, overland travel had become obsolete. Rail lines spread out across the West, and in 1869, the completion of the nation's first transcontinental railroad reduced the six-month journey and its attendant sorrows to a few days jostling across the West from the relative comfort of a train car. The memory of the overland experience, however, would never be forgotten by those who had completed the journey, and their experiences would be woven into the narrative of American resolve, vigor, and progress for generations to come. While time would add a veneer of romance to the trip, many felt like an 1852 traveler who wrote, "To enjoy such a trip along with such a crowd of emigration, a man must be able to endure heat like a Salamander, mud and water like a muskrat, dust like a toad, and labor like a Jackass" (Unruh 1993, 414).

3

DOMESTIC LIFE ON THE MINING FRONTIER

SETTLING INTO THE WEST

The hardship and privation of frontier life did not end with a successful passage over the overland trails. Indeed, many early towns barely deserved to be called towns when first erected, and this was especially true of mining camps, which seemingly appeared overnight and often vanished just as quickly. The West, contrary to the popular imagination of isolated dwellings, was largely an urban frontier. In most places, settlers congregated in towns, often with miles of open spaces separating one town from the next. These urban environments, somewhat ironically, suffered some of the same problems of sanitation and crime that larger cities in the East endured. Certainly, many settlers did not live in the West's cities. Ranches could be isolated, and tens of thousands took up land claims, or purchased land, in places like the Dakotas in the hope of establishing their own farms on which to support themselves. Life on a farm on the Great Plains could indeed be isolating, but even here, farmers still found themselves tied to the larger market economy, their success dependent on the railroad as much as the vagaries of weather. Nor did they typically come alone. Immigrant groups, especially, often settled in the West en masse, with dozens of residents of the old country plopped down onto land on the plains, creating instant towns with names that reflected their places of origin: New Ulm, Minnesota, or New Braunfels, Texas.

The discovery of gold in California (and subsequently in other Western locales) proved to be the engine driving Western settlement. While some farmers had made the treacherous crossing of the plains and Rockies to reach the agrarian paradise of Oregon, their numbers paled in comparison to the tremendous and unprecedented migration of people to California.

DAILY LIFE IN THE MINING CAMPS

The California gold rush would prove to be one of the most important events in the 19th century, a globally transformative event that reshuffled wealth, people, and power around the globe, but it began innocuously enough in the gurgling waters of the American River where it meandered through a bucolic valley of rolling hills in central California.

Johan Sutter, or John Sutter, as he is remembered today, had immigrated to the United States in 1834, eventually setting in Missouri and working as trader on the Santa Fe Trail, but he wanted more than the meager prosperity he had achieved and decided to try Mexican California. In 1838, he crossed the Oregon Trail to Fort Vancouver and eventually made his way by ship to California. The following year, with the permission of the provincial governor of California, he settled along the Sacramento River east of San Francisco (then called Yerba Buena). The grant he received made him virtually king of his domain and gave him authority over the local Indians, who would essentially be treated as serfs.

Sutter built his home, Sutter's Fort, on the American River and soon became prosperous. He raised acres of wheat, ran thousands of cattle, developed a fruit orchard, and even had two acres of roses he lovingly cultivated. He had also developed a reputation for helping (and charging) the increasing number of Americans who came by his fort to settle in California. Even the change in government from Mexico to the United States did not alter his fortunes, for he had been just as careful to establish friendly relations with the Americans, hedging his bets in case of a change in rule. Still eager to make more money, and realizing that the hordes of Americans would need wood for businesses and houses, Sutter decided it would be advantageous to also go into the lumber business. This would supply the needs of his estate and enable him to sell lumber to newly arrived Americans. To do this, he needed to build a sawmill, so he hired a carpenter named James Marshall to build it for him. He hoped to ride this swelling tide of American emigration to the very pinnacle of society, but the tide would soon drown his hopes.

On the morning of January 24, 1848, a mere week before the signing of the Treaty of Guadalupe Hidalgo gave the United States formal ownership of California, Marshall was inspecting the nearly completed mill. The sawmill ran on the power of water that was diverted from the river into a millrace, a ditch barely wider than a man could jump. The diverted current spun a waterwheel, which created the mechanical energy to power the saws of the mill. As Marshall walked along the millrace, he noticed a metallic shine glittering among the dirt. On closer inspection, he discovered flakes of gold. He took the samples to Sutter, who confirmed that Marshall had indeed found gold.

Sutter and Marshall did their best to keep the discovery secret, but such a secret cannot be kept for long. Ironically, this discovery bankrupted Sutter, as gold seekers trampled his land, tore down his fences, shot his cattle, and destroyed everything he had built. He would spend the rest of his life trying fruitlessly to get compensation for his lost fortune from the federal government. James Marshall did little better. Sutter's sawmill soon collapsed as the sawyers and lumberjacks abandoned the mill to hunt gold. Marshall also tried to file several mining claims, but he was not able to secure the proper rights to these. He died in 1885 in a dilapidated cabin, virtually penniless. His discovery of gold, however, had set off a global frenzy.

Sutter's own employees divulged the discovery in March 1848. The *Californian* newspaper printed the first story soon thereafter, and on March 25, Sam Brannan, an enterprising Mormon newspaperman and entrepreneur, published the story of the gold discovery in his paper, the *California Star*—but only after buying up all available shovels, picks, and other tools, which his mercantile store then resold at tremendous markups.

While 1849 is remembered for the influx of American (and other) "forty-niners," those would-be gold seekers (or Argonauts as they were often called) living in California in 1848, had a distinct advantage. By late summer, San Francisco was virtually abandoned, and most of the crews of ships that happened to be anchored in the harbor when news of the discovery arrived disappeared into the mountains. Mexicans and Chileans were also comparatively close and able to reach the goldfields in a few weeks. In comparison, news of the strike would not reach the East Coast of the United States until late fall. Federal officials, however, worried that a large influx of foreign miners would take their gold home with them and therefore out of the U.S. economy. Thus, federal officials hoped to see American miners get access to goldfields as quickly as possible.

In late September, the *New York Daily Herald* published a dispatch, dated June 1, detailing the excitement of the discovery: "Three-fourths of the houses in San Francisco are actually vacated; even lawyers have closed their books, and taken passage, with a spade and wooden dish, to make fortunes by washing out gold from the sands of the Sacramento" (*New York Daily Herald* 1848).

Another report from Mr. Larkin, the U.S. consul at Monterey, found its way into the pages of the *Baltimore Commercial Journal*, which editorialized that local "merchants find it profitable specu-lation to send cargoes of biscuits, flour, &c. round to the Pacific coast," as all farming activity had been abandoned in favor of min-ing. Larkin observed that reports of the discovery had been accu-rate and that "it is supposed that the banks and bottoms of all these small streams contain vast quantities of gold." Larkin himself had visited an embryonic gold camp, writing,

> The place I visited was about a league in extent; on this were about fifty tents; many have not even this covering. At one tent, belonging to eight single men, I remained two or three days. These men had two machines made in a day, from 80 to 100 feet, inch boards, and very roughly put together. Their form was something like a child's cradle, without the ends; at one end there was a moveable sieve or rack to wash down the dirt, and shake off the stones. Holes were made in the bottom of the machine to catch the gold this wash stopped, and this was scrapped out hourly. These two machines gathered each day I was present three-fourths to one pound each, being three to four ounces of gold per man. (Larkin 1848)

Even President Polk felt a tinge of gold fever and expressed it in his State of the Union address on December 5, 1848, a few months before he left office. He explained to the members of Congress, "The accounts of the abundance of gold in that territory are of such an extraordinary character as would scarcely command belief were they not corroborated by the authentic reports of officers in the public service who have visited the mineral district and derived the facts which they detail from personal observation." Developing these reserves would be beneficial to the entire nation, and Polk explained to the gathered members of Congress that it was critical that the nation "speedily and fully avail ourselves of the undeveloped wealth of these mines, [therefore] it is deemed of vast importance that a branch of the Mint of the United States be authorized to be established at your present session in California. . . . A branch mint of the United States at the great commercial depot on the west coast would convert into our own coin not only the gold derived from our own rich mines, but also the bullion and specie which our commerce may bring from the whole west coast of Central and South America" (Polk 1848). Having expanded U.S. dominion to the Pacific, Polk was already envisioning more for his nation.

While Polk's enthusiasm was surely warranted, it was hardly necessary given the throngs of would-be prospectors heading to California by land and sea. The numbers staggered the imagination. In 1849 alone, some 100,000 people arrived in California from all points on the globe. Roughly two-thirds were American citizens, but miners came from Chile, Mexico, Ireland, Australia, France, England, and, most conspicuously, China. Those hailing from the Midwest tended to come overland, following the established Oregon Trail before turning southwest to California. Those closer to port cities like New York tended to go by boat, and foreign miners, naturally, arrived by boat.

Argonauts from South America, Australia, and China actually had it easier than those on the East Coast or in Europe. A New York to San Francisco trip via ship consumed some six months, but faster clipper ships could make the trip in three to four months. These faster ships, however, lacked much space for cargo, and travelers often had little more than some extra clothes, some bedding, and maybe a few small tools for mining. The rest would be purchased upon arrival in California—at grossly inflated prices. Some aspiring miners saved time by crossing the Isthmus of Panama, which cut out the passage around South America but required a treacherous journey through the jungles and their attendant dangers, most notably a variety of diseases, such as malaria. Any method of travel, however, promised months of tedium, hardship, and peril.

The early days of the California gold rush (and of most subsequent gold rushes elsewhere in the West) began with placer mining. Gold is formed in pockets and veins of molten magma that cools slowly, deep in the earth. The pieces of gold are often embedded inside a matrix of quartz, the result of this process of cooling. Over time, these gold-bearing quartz veins, in some places, become exposed to the elements. Water erosion slowly and inexorably wears down the stubborn quartz, freeing the particles of gold from their crystalline prisons and sweeping them down the mountains in streams and rivers. As a metal, gold is nearly as dense as lead, and in places where the current of a stream slows, the heavy gold particles settle on the bottom. Sandbars, for example, became ideal locations for finding gold deposits. Nature, therefore, had done most of the mining for the miners—all that remained was finding a place where nature had made a deposit. Thus, placer mining did not require a great deal of geological knowledge or tools beyond shovels, picks, and a few other basic instruments. Unlike later underground mines, which would require an army of miners and a huge outlay of capital to develop, the California gold rush and other placer rushes promised riches to anyone with a strong back and enough money to get to the diggings.

To locate a possible site, prospectors might have used the famous gold pan, which resembled a metal pie pan in shape and size. Scooping some sediment from a stream into the pan, the prospector carefully washed the lighter material out of the pan with water while swirling the pan, causing the heavier metals to settle at the bottom. After a few minutes of work, if the site proved fruitful, the miner might see some flecks or even nuggets of gold mixed in with black sand called magnetite, a magnetic iron ore that weighs roughly the same as gold.

While a gold pan might be used to reveal a good location to start mining, laboriously cleaning one pan at a time was a tremendously slow and inefficient way to mine. So, miners turned to other methods, such as the "gold rocker" previously described by Consul Larkin, or increasingly the sluice box. A sluice box resembled a long wooden trough, like a horse trough, but at regular intervals, a piece of wood was affixed to the bottom to create a raised ridge or rifle. The purpose of the ridge was to trap the heavy gold behind it. Once completed, water was diverted into the sluice box from a nearby stream. Miners then shoveled sandy material into the sluice box and let gravity and water do the work of removing the lighter material and leaving the heavier gold behind. Every few hours or so, the miners shut off the water and cleaned out the collected material from behind the rifles, which hopefully contained gold. To ensure that no lightweight gold dust escaped them, miners often placed chunks of moss at the outlet of the sluice box, using the moss as a filter to trap the tiny particles of valuable gold.

Eventually, miners introduced hydraulic mining, using high-pressure water jets that resembled firehoses, to wash entire hillsides into giant sluice boxes. Such large-scale mining could make less gold-rich deposits profitable by efficiently washing vast quantities of dirt and rock to get at small traces of gold. The loose sediment, however, continued downstream, and the once clear and free-flowing rivers became choked with mud, killing fish and polluting the water. The Scotsman J. D. Borthwick described the damage such operations had wreaked on the natural environment at Hangtown (Placerville), California. Once gold had been so plentiful that men had pried nuggets from the soil with Bowie knives, he explained,

> But those days had passed, and now the whole surface of the surrounding country showed the amount of real, hard work which had been done. The beds of the numerous ravines which wrinkle the faces of the hills, the bed of the creek, all the little flats alongside of it, were a confused mass of heaps of dirt and piles of stones lying around the innumerable holes, about six feet square and five or six feet deep, from which they had been thrown out. The original course of the creek was completely obliterated, its waters being distributed into numberless little ditches, and from them conducted into the "long toms" [sluice boxes] of the miners through canvass hoses, looking like immensely long slimy sea-serpents. (Borthwick 1857, 113–114)

By the 1870s, farmers and townspeople along the Sacramento River were experiencing frequent floods. The buildup of sediment washed down by the hydraulic miners had effectively made the rivers shallower and more prone to flooding, and once navigable rivers had become impassible for all but the smallest boats. Towns like Sacramento and Marysville built levees to protect homes and businesses from flooding. Further, the sediment-laden waters could no longer be used for human or animal consumption by communities downstream. Farmers demanded the passage of laws to protect their land and livelihoods from damage caused by upstream miners. Finally, in 1884, farmers won a major victory over the miners in the *Woodruff v. North Bloomfield et al.* case. In one of the earliest court cases involving environmental quality, the court issued a permanent injunction against the dumping of sediment and gravel into rivers, effectively dooming the hydraulic mining industry in California.

Miners often advanced into the mountains faster than the niceties of civilization. Law enforcement and legal systems, for example, often proved nonexistent in the early days of a mining discovery, so miners created their owns laws and even court systems. A key component of coexistence in the mining camps was the right to file a mining claim. A claim gave a miner, or group of miners, exclusive rights to extract gold from a particular site. These claims varied in size but were generally not more than a hundred feet or so, large enough to encompass, for example, a small sandbar. Once claimed, the miner could extract all the gold on the claim, but if abandoned, other miners could come in and take control of the claim. Adjudicating conflicting claims and other transgressions generally fell to "miner's courts," hastily convened legal proceedings that decided issues with speed more than deliberation. Serious crimes often led to hangings, and minor offenses resulted in corporal punishment or banishment from a mining claim.

Dreams of golden riches pulled tens of thousands into the mountains, but life in gold camps offered few luxuries. Camps began as little more than enclaves of tents erected on sites deemed most convenient—comfort was secondary to access to the goldfields. Groups of men, often family or friends who had come to the gold rush together, lived in these tents and shared the household duties of cooking and cleaning and the cost of items like food. These tent-mates formed a strange economic unit of perhaps half a dozen men, all living under the same roof, such as it was. Domestic chores would have been tasks for women, but with no women around, men had no choice but to cook and clean when not occupied in the placer diggings.

In time, tents might be replaced with wooden cabins and then frame buildings, if the diggings proved to be sufficiently profitable and enduring. The camp might grow into an actual town, but just as likely, the gold might play out. Then rumors of a better, newer site somewhere else would prompt an exodus and leave the site virtually abandoned. Such was the capricious nature of mining camps.

Food and supplies commanded extravagant prices that resulted from the prohibitive cost of shipping goods by sea and over roads that were little more than trails. Moreover, a captive audience of hungry miners, many with sudden wealth, created a situation where merchants could expect to reap high profits. In truth, the easiest path to wealth lay in "mining the miners," by offering them goods and services that ranged from food and tools to entertainment and female companionship. Gambling halls and armies of professional gamblers also did their best to reallocate the miner's hard-earned gold.

J. D. Borthwick described how some miners lost a week's worth of work in a few hours at the gaming tables. Sundays brought the miners, who had been scattered around Hangtown on their various claims, into town to refresh supplies and entertain themselves. Borthwick observed, "The gamblers on Sundays reaped a rich harvest; their tables thronged with crowds of miners, betting eagerly, and of course losing their money. Many men came in, Sunday after Sunday, and gambled off all the gold they had dug during the week, having to get credit at a store for their next week's provisions, and returning to their diggings to work for six days in getting more gold, which would all be transferred the next Sunday to the gamblers, in the vain hope of recovering what had already been lost" (Borthwick 1857, 119).

WOMEN IN THE MINING CAMPS

Men constituted the overwhelming majority of residents in a mining camp. J. D. Borthwick, for example, described a "ball" in which there were no women present at all. "It was a strange sight to see," he explained, "a party of long-bearded men, in heavy boots and flannel shirts, going through all the steps and figures of the dance with so much spirit, and often with a great deal of grace, hearty enjoyment depicted on their dried-up sunburned faces" (Borthwick 1857, 320). To make each dancer's role clear, Borthwick noted, some men wore large squares of bright fabric to denote their role as ladies in the dancing.

Mark Twain, who wrote of his experiences in the mining camps of California and Nevada in his book *Roughing It*, claimed, with only a little exaggeration, that the composition of the California goldfields was unlike that of any other in history. "For observe," he wrote, "it was an assemblage of two hundred thousand *young* [italics in original] men—not simpering, dainty, kid-gloved weaklings, but stalwart, muscular, dauntless young braves, brimful of push and energy, and royally endowed with every attribute that goes to make up a peerless and magnificent manhood" (Twain 1962, 309).

The appearance of a woman in the mining camps caused widespread excitement. Twain claimed, in fact, that he and scores of men once waited in line in Star City, California, to peek inside a cabin where at a newly arrived woman lived. After waiting for half an hour, he put his eye to the crack, "and there she was, with one arm akimbo, and tossing flapjacks in a frying pan with the other. And she was one hundred and sixty-five years old, and hadn't a tooth in her head." Twain joked, "Being in a calmer mood, now, I voluntarily knock off a hundred from that" (Twain 1962, 311–312)." While prone to comic exaggeration, Twain certainly drew from the reality of mining camps as spaces composed almost entirely of men. But women sometimes did take up residence in mining camps, and among the most insightful was a newlywed named Louise Amelia Knapp Smith Clappe, or, as she is remembered by the nom de plume she used to sign a series of vivid letters she sent to her sister back East, Dame Shirley.

Dame Shirley came to Rich Bar, a ramshackle mining camp on the Feather River, in 1851 with her husband, Fayette Clappe. Fayette, a doctor by profession, suffered from the lingering and often debilitating effects of malaria, or the *ague*, as it was then called. He sought a better climate in California and hoped to make money as a physician in the gold camps. Fortunately, for posterity's sake he brought along his clever and perceptive wife, whose letters to her sister were published in *Pioneer* magazine a few years later. Young, adventurous, and with a good sense of humor, Louise came to appreciate the rough and hardscrabble life of the mining camps, a shocking thing for a young and proper physician's wife. On seeing Rich Bar for the first time, she left a description that could stand in for any of the hundreds of mining camps that dotted the West, from California to South Dakota to Alaska. She wrote, "Through the middle of Rich Bar runs the street, thickly planted with about forty tenements, among which figure round tents, square tents, plank hovels, log cabins, etc., the residences varying in elegance and convenience from the palatial splendor of 'The Empire' [hotel] down to a 'local habitation' formed of pine boughs and covered with old calico shirts" (Shirley 1922). Lest one get the impression that the Empire Hotel was in fact "palatial," she had described it in her previous letter as follows: "The Empire is the only two-story building in town, and absolutely has a live 'upstairs.' Here you will find two or three glass windows, an unknown luxury in all the other dwellings. It is built of planks of the roughest possible description. The roof, of course, is covered with canvas, which also forms the entire front of the house, on which is painted, in immense capitals, the following imposing letters: 'THE EMPIRE!'" (Shirley 1922).

Nor could Dame Shirley expect much female companionship, she claimed, from the few examples to be found in Rich Bar. The owners of the Empire Hotel, where the young couple stayed on their arrival, had arrived from the Midwest a few years earlier. But the journey and lifestyle had been hard, Shirley observed, "Mrs. B. is a gentle and amiable looking woman, about 25 years of age. She is an example of the terrible wear and tear to the complexion in crossing the plains, hers having become, through exposure at that time, of a dark and permanent yellow, anything but becoming." Worse Shirley could not fathom the inner workings of Mrs. B.'s heart, writing with great disapproval that "I will give you a key to her character, which will exhibit it better than weeks of description. She took a nursing babe, eight months old, from her bosom, and left it with two other children, almost infants, to cross the plains in search of gold!" (Shirley 1922). Already Mrs. B. had another newborn, whose plaintive cries woke the Empire's boarders at all hours of the night.

In addition to Mrs. B., there were three other women in Rich Bar. Shirley informed her sister, "One is called 'the Indiana Girl,' from the name of her pa's hotel, though it must be confessed that the sweet name of girl seems sadly incongruous when applied to such a gigantic piece of humanity." She continued, "This gentle creature wears the thickest kind of miner's boots, and has the dainty habit of wiping the dishes with her apron! Last spring, she walked to this place, and packed fifty pounds of flour on her back down that awful hill, the snow being five feet deep at the time" (Shirley 1922). Of her female companions, Shirley joked, "Splendid material for social parties this winter, are they not?" (Shirley 1922). The difficulty of life in the mines became apparent scarcely a week later when Mrs. B. fell ill and died.

In Rich Bar, like other mining camps, women proved exceptional, but even for these rare creatures, life remained hard. Dame Shirley, of course, cooked and cleaned for her husband, struggling at times to find enough food, especially in the winter. She wrote to her sister of the privations brought on by the closure of the pack trails from snow and ice, writing, "Everyone upon the river has been out of butter, onions, and potatoes. . . . Ham, mackerel, and bread, with occasionally a treat of the precious butter, have been literally our only food for a long time" (Shirley 1922).

As a physician's wife, Shirley had it comparatively easy; other women worked much harder. Mining, unsurprisingly, fell under the purview of men, the hard physical labor of excavating gold from the earth being the epitome of "men's work," but women worked nearly as hard in nonmining occupations. Some owned boardinghouses and restaurants. Others took in washing or put sewing skills to use, mending and making clothing. Then, of course, women also found themselves pulled into the trade of prostitution.

Dame Shirley, in her first letter to her sister, claimed that the Empire Hotel in Rich Bar had originally been built by "a company of gamblers as a residence for two of those unfortunates [prostitutes] who make a trade—a thing of barter—of the holiest passion, when sanctified by love, that ever thrills the wayward heart of poor humanity." Yet, she continued,

> To the lasting honor of miners be it written, the speculation proved a decided failure. Yes! These thousand men, many of whom had been for years absent from the softening amenities of female society, and the sweet restraining influences of pure womanhood—these husbands of fair young wives kneeling daily at the altars of their holy homes to pray for the far-off ones—these sons of gray-haired mothers, majestic in their sanctified old age—these brothers of virginal sisters, white and saintlike as the lilies of their own gardens—looked only with contempt or pity upon these, oh! so earnestly to be compassionated creatures. (Shirley 1922)

Within a few weeks the owners of the Empire sold out and took their fallen women with them, driven away, Shirley claimed, by public opinion—although in that same letter, recall that Shirley mentioned the activities of the upstairs as "lively," which could be a euphemism for prostitution, so perhaps the men were not so chaste as she claimed. Regardless of the morality of the men of Rich Bar, almost all mining camps welcomed the "soiled doves."

William Perkins, a Canadian working the southern goldfields in California, objected to a brothel populated entirely by French women in the town of Sonora, California. France had a long-established tradition of legal prostitution in cities such as Paris, and given the profitability of California's mines and the overwhelming male population, the arrival of French prostitutes was not surprising. The ladies served drinks, worked the gambling tables, and generally worked to free the miners of their wealth. Perkins remarked, "Artificial in the extreme, [the French woman] adapts her manners, as she does her dress, to circumstances. . . . [S]he is a lady, a gambler, a coquette, a fury, a bachante [*sic*] and a prude by turns . . . for money to the Frenchwoman is the real object of her adoration, and to acquire it there is nothing she won't do" (quoted in Johnson 2000, 77). Perkins seemed disappointed with the artificiality of the entire spectacle, but, after all, prostitutes sold the illusion of companionship as much as sex.

Brothels dotted the Western landscape, and, often the proprietors were men, but not always. In Helena, Montana, for example, women dominated the sex trade, not just as prostitutes but also as madams. Josephine Hensley, known as "Chicago Jo," owned most of the city's brothels and turned a handsome profit. Individual "ladies of the evening" earned between $179 and $339 a month, compared to perhaps $65 a month that a woman might make as a salesgirl (White 1991, 305). The experience of Josephine Hensley was exceptional, but others also found economic success and even something akin to local celebrity by running brothels. Such a case was on display when a new bride first arrived in Telluride, Colorado, in the early 1900s. Harriet Fish Backus stepped off the train in the town high in the San Juan Mountains and set out to stretch her legs after several days of traveling to meet her new husband. On a crisp morning, she walked through town, its "streets appeared strangely deserted and silent. Then I saw a hearse approaching slowly followed by two lines of men marching sedately. A funeral, undoubtedly, of a prominent member of the community. . . . Thus, the men of Telluride paid homage and said farewell to the leading madam of their underworld, in her way the town's best known citizen" (Backus 1969, 10).

Few women would amass large fortunes, but prostitution offered the best hope to support oneself for women with few other skills. Frank Crampton, a miner in the early 20th century, described how Estelle, the local madam in Kingman, Arizona, entered the trade. She explained to Crampton that she had come west with a musical troupe "that played one-week stands in towns and camps, wherever there was an 'opera house.'" From town to town, they toured, performing popular plays and musicals of the day. "Everything was going fine," she explained, "until the manager skipped out with the troupe's money and the blonde who played the juvenile parts. The men of the cast scattered and left the girls to shift for themselves in the only business in which they could earn enough money" (Crampton 1956, 117–118). Indeed, few women willingly entered the sex trade; many found themselves pulled in after suffering setbacks, such as the death of a husband or spousal abandonment. A woman often remained in the profession until she was able to save enough to leave (as Estelle and her girls were trying to do) or until she had succeeded in marrying a man who did not hold her previous career against her.

Life certainly must have been difficult for prostitutes. Venereal diseases and unwanted pregnancies would have been common issues, and prostitutes often faced abuse from pimps and customers. This abuse was probably worse for independent prostitutes, who had neither pimps nor the protection of brothels. Indeed, brothels probably offered the best protection for the West's "soiled doves" and perhaps fostered a sense of community and camaraderie with coworkers. Unfortunately, very few records of what life was like for prostitutes exist. Most accounts, like those of William Perkins, were written by men, and often in disparaging terms for their audience's consumption. Court records and newspaper accounts reveal a bit about the issues these women faced, but given the stigma surrounding their trade, no memoirs or reminiscences exist. When women were fortunate enough to leave the life of a prostitute behind, they typically let the past remain in the past.

The image of a California gold miner is surely that of a burly, bearded white man leading a loaded mule in search of riches—and a number of men fit the profile—but the California gold rush attracted people from all over the world. Thus, a "typical" miner could be a white American, or an African American, or a Mexican, Chilean, Australian, Englishman, or German. A large number of miners also hailed from China, and no group was more conspicuous or mistreated than the Chinese.

When historians discuss why groups of people choose to leave their lives and families behind to venture to another country, they usually discuss "push/pull" factors, the reasons pulling people to a new place and the conditions that are pushing them out of their home countries. For all gold seekers, the pull was obvious and undeniable: a chance at attaining unimaginable wealth or at the very least an opportunity to improve one's financial condition. Certainly, the Chinese men who came to the goldfields hoped to—if not strike it rich—at least find enough gold to alter the fortunes for their families back in China. Few, at least at first, hoped to stay in the United States. Instead, they hoped to spend a few months or years collecting gold before returning home with enough to help their families thrive.

Many factors, however, conspired to push these young Chinese men from their homelands. In the mid-19th century, China faced a tsunami of difficulties. First, foreign nations, such as Great Britain, had insinuated themselves into China and demanded concessions from the Chinese government. A key issue was access to Chinese markets for English products, most importantly the addictive drug opium. Opium, grown in the British colony of India for very little, would then be shipped to China and sold to Chinese customers. The sale of opium transformed the trade relationship between Great Britain and China. Previously, the British and other Europeans had to offer hard currency (gold or silver) to acquire Chinese tea, porcelain, or silk—all highly desirable goods in the West. This trade enriched China, but at the expense of European nations. The advent of the opium trade changed that. By addicting an estimated

30 million Chinese people to the drug, the British completely reversed their trade deficit. Invariably, other nations and individuals, including U.S. entrepreneurs, also entered the opium business.

China attempted to stop this corrosive trade, only to end up losing a war to the British in 1842. The treaty to end the war forced the Chinese government to accept terms that essentially enabled the trade to continue. Buffeted by the incursion of foreigners, the Chinese government began to unravel. Further, as the authority of the central government declined, individual warlords filled the power vacuum, conscripting peasants into their armies and taking food from farmers. A series of famines made an already desperate situation worse. All of these factors combined meant that a young Chinese peasant had few opportunities to support his family and little hope for a better life. Going to the "Gold Mountain," as the Chinese came to call California, offered a chance to change the fate of one's family.

How, though, could one get to the Gold Mountain? Unsurprisingly, the majority of would-be Chinese miners hailed from provinces close to the ocean, such as Guangdong Province. For those deeper in the hinterlands, the journey to a port city alone proved prohibitive. For the scores of impoverished Chinese men dreaming of gold in the mountains, booking passage on a steamship presented the first of many obstacles. Most young men lacked the money to purchase a ticket and had to rely on credit brokers. While this enabled individuals to book passage on the ship, the outrageous interest rates made the tickets even more expensive, so the miners were often forced to pay some of their profits back to these brokers. Once reaching San Francisco, many Chinese again turned to credit to purchase food, tools, and passage to the goldfields. Chinese merchants loaned the money (at predictably high interest rates). Thus, before ever sinking a shovel into the ground, these impoverished miners had already sunk themselves deep into debt. Paying off this debt could take months or even years.

Their eventual arrival at the goldfields, however, did not represent the end of their trials and travails. Indeed, this often marked the beginning of more hardship and suffering. Despite the gold rush being an international affair, access to the best sites was anything but egalitarian. Anglo-Americans, Europeans, and others of European descent (like Australians) monopolized the best spots. Latino miners, for example, were often forcibly removed from mining claims, and both Latinos and Chinese were forced to pay a "Foreign Miner's Tax," passed in 1850, that charged a $20 per month fee for the right to mine. Ironically, many Latino miners charged this "foreign" tax were native-born Californians now made strangers in their homeland. White miners from foreign countries were exempt from the tax. The message was clear: the goldfields belonged to whites only.

The Chinese, however, found a way around this discrimination. Barred from working the most lucrative claims, they instead mined in areas abandoned by other miners. Placer mining, of course, was an effort in diminishing returns. When first discovered, a rich sandbar, or similar site, could produce a fortune every day; but as days and weeks went by, the site would eventually be cleaned of gold, and less and less would be produced. At this time, word often reached the diggings that somewhere, perhaps a few drainages over, miners had found a newer and better site. Seemingly overnight, the "played out" site would be abandoned as the miners hustled to make it to the newer diggings before other miners beat them to it. The Chinese realized that they would face little opposition by working abandoned claims in areas that had already been mined out. In the words of one local Amador County newspaper, a group of Chinese miners mined a creek near the town of Jackson that had been "worked over at least a dozen times," and yet enough gold remained that the miners collectively pulled "from $2.50 to $8 per day" from the cold waters, not enough to entice a crew of Anglo miners but more than enough for the frugal Chinese to earn a living (quoted in Johnson 2000, 243–244).

Eking out a living on the margins of society, therefore, appeared a useful and necessary strategy, one that would allow the Chinese to work in peace. However, they soon found themselves unwelcome and unwanted at every turn. The arrival of Chinese miners who worked abandoned claims made them harbingers of economic ruin for local communities. Eager to have their mining camps and towns appear solvent and profitable, local merchants and other business owners often went to extremes to keep Chinese miners out of their towns, as their arrival signaled to other miners that the area's riches had already been exhausted. Local businessmen and what miners remained, therefore, often turned on the Chinese, beating them, killing them, and driving them out of town. In May 1852, the miners of Columbia, California, formed a vigilance committee to force the Chinese from their area. Later that same year, a group of roughly 60 miners attacked Chinese working the old diggings at Mormon Bar on the American River. These angry Anglo miners brought a brass band with them to play as they ransacked the

Chinese camp, destroying their tents and equipment and severely beating the Chinese miners in what surely must be the strangest musical performance in California history. In time, such violence against the Chinese became commonplace, and all across the West, in places like Denver, Seattle, and even Laramie, Wyoming, scores of Chinese were murdered at the hands of angry mobs. But they refused to give up, and many continued to work claims across the region.

Chinese miners had to be adaptable and mobile, and thus they employed less efficient but more portable tools, preferring, for example, the gold rocker to the sluice box because a gold rocker could be easily moved if they faced eviction from an area with little notice. The vast majority of miners toiled for little gain, perhaps earning enough to make ends meet and keep going. For the Chinese, discrimination only added to the difficulties inherent in wresting wealth from the earth. For most Chinese miners, the Gold Mountain turned into a land of disappointment. As one Chinese miner lamented, "I have walked to the very ends of the earth, a dusty, windy journey. I've toiled and I'm worn out, all for a miserable lot. Nothing is ideal when I'm down and out" (Hom 1992, 99). Despite the hardships and injustices, some achieved their dream of building up a nest egg and returning home, and still others remained, eventually being pulled into other enterprises when mining did not produce the desired results.

While there would never be another world-changing California gold strike, placer gold rushes continued across the West in places such as Gold Beach, Oregon, in 1852; Colorado in 1858; Virginia City, Montana, in 1863; the Black Hills in 1874; and finally, the last and most remote of all, the Klondike gold rush of 1897. Each of these rekindled dreams of wealth. Like California before them, most prospectors only made enough to get by and nowhere near enough to become rich. However, the mining industry had changed, with "poor man's" placer diggings increasingly giving way to expensive industrial mining, or hard rock mining, as it came to be known.

The poet Robert Service (famous for his poems about the Yukon gold rush and later World War I) noted this change from the independent miner to the age of industrial-scale mining in his poem "The Prospector." In the poem, an aging, largely unsuccessful, miner revisits a now abandoned boomtown, which is silent except for the solitary clamorous toiling of a mammoth gold dredge, a huge machine that resembled a steamboat that could scoop and efficiently wash copious amounts of soil to extract tiny flecks of gold.

The most reliable way to make money in mining camps came from providing services to miners. Here a group of "actresses" heads to the Klondike gold fields. While mining camps were overwhelmingly male, women could be found in a variety of professions, but most notoriously in the sex trade. Many women fell into prostitution as a last resort. (Library of Congress)

Such gold dredges could move tons of earth in a few minutes' time, doing more work in a short period than the independent prospectors could do in a season with sluice boxes and shovels. Thus, gold dredges could profitably work areas that had been mined before and abandoned. Service's prospector laments these changes as he watches the great machine: "I strolled up old Bonanza. The same old moon looked down; The same old landmarks seemed to yearn to me; But the cabins all were silent, and the flat, once like a town, was mighty still and lonesome-like to see. There were piles and piles of tailings where we toiled with pick and pan, and turning round a bend I heard a roar, and there a giant gold-ship of the very newest plan was tearing chunks of pay-dirt from the shore." Still, onward Service's lone prospector goes in search of fortune to feel the thrill from "when I picked the first big nuggets from my pan. It's still my dream, my dauntless dream, that drives me forth once more to seek and starve and suffer in the Vast" (Poetry Foundation n.d.). Fading into the past, the prospector continued on, but the industry itself had changed.

Unlike placer mining, which collected gold already eroded out of the parent rock, hard rock mining involved finding valuable veins of gold (or other metals) still encased in the mountains and then tunneling hundreds, sometimes thousands, of feet deep into the earth to extract the valuable mineral-bearing rock. To operate an underground mine required crews of dozens of experienced miners and a tremendous amount of equipment, including picks, shovels, drills, explosives, ore carts, ore buckets, steam engines, and elevators that would enable men and equipment to be raised and lowered throughout a mine. In other words, hard rock mining was a large-scale industrial operation that required financial resources far beyond the ordinary prospector. Unsurprisingly, large corporations came to dominate the mining industry, just as they had railroads and other industrial enterprises in the 19th century, and the miners, all dreams of wealth gone, became wage workers who were little different than their peers in factories and steel mills around the nation.

Underground mining represented the first step in the process of producing gold, silver, copper, or other metals. Chunks of mineral-laden rock, extracted in the deep of the mines, were loaded into mine carts and driven out of the depths of the mineshaft. From the mine, the ore-bearing rock was transported to a stamp mill, where giant hammers pulverized the rocks and steel rollers ground the chunks into a fine powder. Then, the ore, gold, or other valuable minerals were extracted from the worthless rock with chemicals (in the case of gold, mercury or cyanide performed this extraction) to form a pasty ball of material, called an *amalgam*, that would finally be sent to a smelter. The smelter heated the amalgam and burned off everything but the valuable metals, finally producing an ingot of almost 100 percent purity. The entire process required the skills of dozens of workers, and often a ton or more of earth was mined to produce a few ounces of gold or silver.

The daily life of a hard rock miner revolved around his shift, usually 8 to 10 hours underground. A mine operating 24 hours a day could send two or three shifts underground into the inky depths. For centuries, candles provided the best illumination, but in the mid-19th century, oil-wick lamps came into favor and around the turn of the last century carbide lanterns. Carbide lanterns used a chemical reaction between calcium carbide pellets and drops of water to produce acetylene gas. The gas would be lit on fire, and the result would be enough light to work by in the darkest of mines. Battery-powered electric lights provided miners' lighting needs by

1918. Each of these represented big advancements in the amount of light provided and was safer to use; open flames, like candles or oil-wick lamps, for example, proved exceedingly dangerous in underground coal mines where volatile gases could easily be ignited.

After descending into the mine, crews of hard rock miners made their way to the site of the day's work, the place where the vein was encased in surrounding rock. To get the vein of valuable quartz and gold free of the surrounding rock, the miners drilled holes into the face and packed the holes with explosives. Drilling was done by hand, either with one miner holding a metal drill bit in one hand and hitting it with a small sledgehammer (called a single jack drill, because a single miner, or Jack, could hold both the hammer and the drill) or a pair of miners using a double jack drill. In a double jack team, one miner held a long drill bit (about the size of a crowbar) and turned it as the other miner hammered on the end with a large two-handed sledgehammer. Each hit and twist pushed the bit a fraction deeper into the stubborn granite. Once several holes had been drilled to a depth of about a foot, they were packed with explosives (originally black powder but later dynamite) and detonated from a safe distance. Following the explosion, the miners would "muck" up the broken rock into ore cars, but miners always kept an eye out for unexploded charges—a shovel or pick hitting one would cause an explosion and kill the miner instantly. After muckers loaded the ore cart, a trammer took the filled ore carts away and left others to be filled, and the process of drilling, detonating, mucking, and tramming continued.

Single and double jack drilling eventually became obsolete with the introduction of power drills in the late 19th century. The power drillers, or machine men, were the highest-paid miners in the mine, for drilling holes properly required skill and stamina. According to David Lavender, who worked in the Camp Bird Mine in the San Juan Mountains of Colorado, "The drill runner must know the varying nature of every kind of stone, the proper angles, the number and depth of holes for a given surface, in order that he can get maximum breakage from each charge of dynamite." Thus, careful angles and patterns were carved into a rock face so that the charge would succeed in breaking up the granite face. The powerful drills, in confined spaces, produced an unearthly racket that filled "the narrow confines until it shakes your very bones. Compressed air fogs about you, shutting you off alone in a world of crashing noise and terrible power. It is no wonder that the machine man is looked up to by the muckers as king of the trade and that his skills and stamina—mental stamina to stand that unholy racket—command higher wages than any other job in the mine" (Lavender 1943, 43).

Power drills radically increased the efficiency of mining, but the new technology brought with it new hazards. The tremendous sound, even with ear protection (which many miners refused to wear so that they could hear warning shouts about cave-ins or other dangers), destroyed miners' hearing, but the greatest hazard lay in the clouds of pulverized rock, turned into silicate dust, that miners inhaled with every breath. Prolonged exposure to this silica dust actually made the miners' lungs less pliable and led to a condition called *silicosis*, which could slowly suffocate the miner. This problem was eventually alleviated by having drills shoot water to capture the dust before it could be sent airborne, but not before scores of miners died from having their lungs turn almost to stone.

Cave-ins represented a hazard that all miners faced, particularly in the soft rock coal mines. To help prevent cave-ins, miners had to timber the mine, which meant putting up wooden beams and posts to support the ceiling. Mines could also be exceeding hot, such as the fabulously rich Comstock silver mine in Virginia City, Nevada, where geothermal activity created temperatures that exceeded 100 degrees year-round and scalding water that could easily kill a miner. Most mines, however, were cooler, and many were wet. Miners could expect to spend their shifts soaked in chilly conditions.

Miners spent their entire shift underground. They ate their lunches in the shafts (it was slow and inefficient to take them back to the surface to eat), and when "nature called," a bucket would have to suffice as a toilet. Often a young miner, just learning the trade, would have to take care of these buckets and earned the title of "honeydipper." If a young miner proved his worth and willingness to do this most disgusting of work, he would earn the respect of older miners and eventually be allowed to work better jobs. Only when their shift ended would the miners finally leave the shaft and return to the surface. Physically demanding, dark, and dangerous, this was the daily life of a miner.

Today, a great deal of mining is done by machines, including the transport of workers and ore from the mines, but well into the 20th century, many mines employed mules to pull ore carts. David Lavender recalled that miners loved the mules they worked alongside, with the exception of one particularly mean mule who had a penchant for biting and kicking the miners. Needing him on an upper level, the crew decided it was easier to leave him inside the shaft instead of leading him back down to the barn each day (the trail down was narrow, and the ornery animal often tried to push his human master off the trail so he could run away). Unfortunately, a surprise blizzard closed off the trail, forcing the miners to leave the mule in the shaft alone. Each day, food and water were taken up to him via the elevator, but the elevator was too small to rescue him; so he spent the winter largely alone. Lavender recalled, "It was very dark inside that hole and very lonesome. No amount of braying would bring an answer, no tantrum break those soft chains of snow and blackness" (Lavender 1943, 41).

Left to reflect on his sins for half a year, the mule came to appreciate the daily appearance of miners, who he once abhorred. They left a carbide lamp burning for him, and when they disappeared back down the elevator shaft, "the last thing that met our ears was a low, heartbreaking bray, the saddest sound I have ever heard" (Lavender 1943, 41). Finally, Spring came to the mountains and the snow melted in the high country, opening the narrow trail to the shaft. Freed from his icy prison, the mule raced back and forth over the valley, "kicking his heels and shaking his head. Then down on the warm earth to roll before he leaped up again to run some more, as though he had to pack a lifetime of sun and air into those few minutes before darkness closed down again" (Lavender 1943, 42). Reformed now, the mule never returned to his wicked ways.

Hard rock mining was certainly wage work, but many of the positions, like drilling, required years of practice and very particular skills. Thus, as skilled workers, hard rock miners commanded fairly high wages, but miners in the coal mining industry did not possess such skills. Poorly paid and exceedingly dangerous, coal miners had a much more difficult life than their hard rock peers.

COAL MINING IN THE MOUNTAIN WEST

Coal remains an important fossil fuel today, powering many power plants across the United States, but its significance in the 19th century was much greater than today. Indeed, coal was the first fossil fuel to be exploited by humanity, and its harnessing released more energy more efficiently than burning biomass such as wood or peat. By the 1600s, the British Isles began to exploit their extensive coal reserves. Soon, English and Welsh miners probed ever deeper into the earth, reaching depths of 200 feet by the early 1700s, where they encountered flooding. To extract water from these mines, they needed a pump efficient enough to draw out the water. The Englishman Thomas Newcomen came up with an innovative invention to accomplish the task. In 1712, he designed and built a pump that burned coal to heat water and generate steam. The pressurized steam pushed up a piston, then the steam was cooled back to water and the piston plunged downward, creating a vacuum. This piston was attached to a rocker beam, and on the other end, a chain of buckets pulled water out of the mines. Newcomen's original "fire engine," as it was called, could extract 120 gallons a minute. The whole assembly slightly resembled the pumpjacks that tirelessly pull oil out of the ground today. While Newcomen's engine produced a modest 5.5 horsepower, it was nevertheless revolutionary. Now humanity was exploiting stored sunshine and, in conjunction with steam, putting it to new uses.

Toward the end of the 1700s, the Scottish inventor James Watt made a more efficient and smaller steam engine than Newcomen's. By the early 1800s, modified versions of Watt's steam engine were powering pumps, factories, and eventually ships and locomotives. Great Britain had 1,400 miles of railroad track, continental Europe 1,500, and the United States 4,600 by the 1840s. At the same time, steamships cut the voyage across the Atlantic from months to days. The steamship *Sirius* completed the first steam-powered crossing of the Atlantic in 1838, in 18 days and 10 hours, arriving in port a few hours before the *Great Western*, which completed the passage in only 15 days (Crosby 2007, 71–77). In the thousands of years of human development, people had never before moved faster than a fleet horse could carry them or the vicissitudes of the wind could push them.

Factories also relied on coal to power steam engines, and a burgeoning steel industry required coal in vast quantities because only coal could attain a temperature hot enough to melt iron and other metals. Indeed, by the late 1800s, Americans had come to depend on steel for a variety of products, as steel served many of the same functions then as plastics do today. By the end of the 19th century, Americans and Europeans sailed in steel-hulled steam-powered ships, ventured across continents in fire-breathing "iron horses," and erected buildings of previously unimaginable heights. But all of these achievements, to one degree or another, depended on coal.

Fortunately, the United States had coal reserves in seemingly inexhaustible abundance. Coalfields in the Appalachia, for example, fed the steel mills of Pennsylvania and the factories of the East Coast, but some of the best coal in the world lay out west, in Colorado, Utah, and Wyoming. From the very beginning, the coal mining industry differed greatly from hard rock mining. While valuable on an industrial scale, coal discoveries did not prompt mining rushes like gold mining had because coal was plentiful and cheap, measured in tons rather than ounces.

The nature of the mining also differed tremendously. While hard rock miners followed thin veins of mineral-filled quartz in whatever strange patterns they had formed, coal seams could be dozens of feet thick and run for thousands of feet. These huge seams often sat sandwiched between layers of sedimentary rock. Whereas hard rock miners relied on skills honed from years of working underground, coal miners had to do little more than pry the coal out of these seams with shovels, picks, prybars, explosives, and eventually powered drills. This made coal miners, in comparison to their hard rock brethren, essentially unskilled workers, and unskilled workers could be paid comparatively little for their work. Unsurprisingly, coal mines soon came to rely on immigrant labor, and on any given day, a Babel of foreign languages could be heard underground: Spanish, Greek, Italian, Russian, and Polish. This diversity made communication, both underground and aboveground, difficult, and it gave owners—often large corporations—even more power over their employees.

Coal mining also differed from hard rock mining in another important way: it was exceedingly dangerous.

Certainly, accidents happened in hard rock mines. Machinery killed men; rocks tumbled down shafts and fell from the ceilings, crushing unlucky miners; and the early power drills caused fatal silicosis. But the rock in which hard rock miners toiled was typically stout granite and unlikely to cave-in. Coal mines, however, presented an array of dangers that made the profession the most dangerous job in the United States—at a time when workers risked their lives in a variety of occupations. Between 1884 and 1912, 1,708 coal miners died in Colorado alone (Andrews 2008, 138).

Coal mines were laid out in orderly grids, almost like city streets, with a main artery leading outside. Coming off this artery were side streets called *side entries* and *rooms* where the coal miners worked, many of these operating at the same time in different locations. Some coal was left in place to form *pillars* to support the roof. Miners could add wooden supports to further prop up the ceiling to help prevent cave-ins. However, these wooden supports often came out of the miners' paychecks, so the more supports they installed, the less profit they made. Worse, miners were paid only for the coal they dug, so taking the time to install wooden supports meant they made less money. Thus, miners were incentivized to skimp on installing these timbers. Coal miners, despite working for companies, functioned as independent contractors, and in their rooms, they determined their workloads. They could work as hard as they wished, put in as many supports as they wanted, take breaks as they wanted, and so on because they were not paid hourly but by tonnage rates—essentially how much coal they could dig and load into mine carts during their shift.

As in hard rock mines, the first step in extraction began with drilling holes into the face, packing the holes with explosives, and then detonating the face. After the dust of the explosion settled, the miners, usually working in teams (often friends, brothers, or even fathers and sons), loaded the coal into ore carts pulled along rails by mules and later miniature locomotives. These individual carts were weighed on leaving the mine, and the weight was marked next to the names of the miners who had dug it. Then the carts made their way to either the coke plant (*coke* being a distilled form of coal that could be reheated in steel mills to attain the high temperatures required to melt iron ore) or loaded onto rail cars for transportation elsewhere (Andrews 2008, 125–129). Thus, miners engaged in a competition of sorts between their desire for more money and the physical limits of their bodies. The harder and faster (and more recklessly) they worked, the more money they could make. These remunerative desires could make a dangerous situation worse, for coal mines offered a litany of hazards for the unwary or unlucky.

Cave-ins represented a constant threat. The layers of coal and surrounding sedimentary rock, like sandstone and shale, were much softer than the granitic rock of hard rock mines. Huge chunks could break off from ceilings or walls without warning, crushing a man. Worse was the nature of coal itself, a material, after all, that was desirable because it was combustible. Coal developed as organic material buried for millions of years in an oxygen poor environment, and when exposed to air for the first time in countless centuries, it began to react. Methane gas could be released from fissures, flood the mines, and quickly overwhelm and kill any miners present. Without modern detection equipment, the miners learned to cultivate friendships with the mice that invariably infiltrated the diggings. The mice, which often became so tame they would eat out of the miners' hands, provided whimsical company, but they also succumbed to poisonous gases at lower levels than humans, acting as rodent versions of the more famous miner's canary.

While some mines were naturally more gassy than others, mining coal invariably kicked up clouds of coal dust that remained suspended in the air for hours. Miners inhaled this dust, and over time, many of them contracted the often fatal black lung disease, or *pneumoconiosis*. Tight mines, with sweating men and animals inside, also often used up much of the available oxygen, making for suffocating conditions. Carbon monoxide, colorless and odorless, could silently overwhelm miners, causing them to lose consciousness and suffocate. Worst of all, however, were the explosions. Mines with higher levels of methane, filled with floating coal dust, could explode instantaneously: a spark from a frayed electrical wire, an explosive charge blowing out instead of being limited to the rock face, or even a kind of spontaneous combustion without an apparent cause. Sprinkling, the technique of installing water hoses punctured with tiny holes, could tamp down the floating coal dust. But sprinkler systems cost companies money, and in many Western mines, like those in the southern Colorado coalfields, water was simply not available. Yet, in other mines, water could be a curse, and miners might be killed in a flood that swept through the shafts.

Deaths were common enough in the mines, but explosions could take the lives of dozens, sometimes hundreds, of miners in a flash. Such disasters became a common part of life in the coalfields. Colorado's first big mining disaster occurred in January 1884 at the Jokerville Mine, near Crested Butte, when 59 miners, some as young as 12, perished in an explosion. Two decades and roughly 200 miles farther west, in Utah, the Scofield disaster of May 1, 1900, proved the deadliest in the history of the Western mines. At 10:28 a.m., the No. 4 shaft of the Pleasant Valley Coal Company's Winter Quarters Mine detonated. One man near the mouth of the shaft was blown over 800 feet by the blast and killed. Inside, dozens died instantly in the massive explosion or soon succumbed to poisonous gases. Rescue workers pulled the living out of the mines and rushed them to the hospital in the nearby town of Scofield, but survivors were few—they mostly found bodies. The disaster cleared out the supply of coffins from Salt Lake City and required more to be sent from Denver. The Scofield disaster took the lives of 200 miners, making it the worst mining disaster in U.S. history at the time.

Miners and their families often placed the blame for disasters like those in Crested Butte and Scofield at the feet of the mining companies, arguing that the companies bore responsibility for creating the dangerous working conditions that led to miners' deaths. Working conditions proved to be a major source of anger, but miners and their families voiced other grievances that contributed to their growing resentment toward the owners of the coal mines. These varied from minor sources of irritation to profound violations of the rights of miners and their families. To understand these, it is imperative to look at how coal mines and the towns around them operated.

By the 1890s, coal mining companies had turned to building entire *company towns* that they owned. Previous to the 1890s, miners often erected their own small houses near the mines. Now, under the guise of benevolent paternalism (the belief that companies knew what was best for their employees), companies built entire model towns, landscapes that they completely controlled. Designed with input from doctors, architects, engineers, and early social workers, these company towns claimed to be morally and materially superior to the homes the miners cobbled together themselves. But they also made it easier for companies to supervise and therefore control their workers, preventing them from protesting or joining unions.

In company towns, the company owned the houses and rented them to the workers, making it easy to evict troublesome miners and their families. Typically, company towns included company stores that sold food and other mercantile goods to families. The prices in these stores tended to be higher than independent stores in towns some distance away because of the company's monopoly on trade within the confines of their community. Further, some companies went so far as to pay their employees in company scrip, money of a sort that was only good at the company store. Company stores also extended credit to miners' families. Some families, invariably, sank into debt, further eroding what little economic independence they had attained.

Colorado Fuel and Iron (CF&I), the most powerful company in the southern Colorado coalfields, created its own Sociological Department under Dr. Richard Corwin to plan its company towns and keep out the pernicious threat of union activism. To be fair, these towns did offer better quality houses and relatively cheap rent, access to services like medical care improved, and some even offered educational opportunities like English language classes. On balance, however, these benefits came at the expense of individual license and freedom and contributed to a belief that the companies had too much power over the lives of miners and their families. Nor did the creation of these company towns succeed in suppressing dissent.

Issues over pay, working conditions, hours, and the oppressive control of the company towns contributed to growing animosity toward the owners of the mines, particularly the Rockefeller-owned CF&I corporation. Angry miners turned to the United Mine Workers (UMW), the preeminent union for miners in the country, to help organize. In 1913, miners and their families took to the streets of Trinidad, Colorado, one of the two major towns in the southern Colorado coalfields, demanding recognition of unions.

Nationally, unions came to the fore following the Civil War in a variety of industries, but union activities typically received open hostility from corporations and generally from government officials as well. Joining a union, anywhere in any industry, was a confrontational action; joining a union in the corporate-controlled southern Colorado coalfields was tantamount to rebellion.

The UMW organized members in secret, recruiting miners to the union and trying to force out nonunion miners. If the majority of miners could be convinced to join the union in secret, then when they went public to demand improvements, they presented a united front. The strategies employed by union activists took industrial espionage to extreme levels, but, of course, so too did the corporate response to union organizing. Typically, the UMW worked to get a member, called the "Outside Man," hired in a corporate-controlled mine. The Outside Man worked alongside the other miners and surreptitiously recruited them to join the union, often holding secret meetings underground in the mines or in the surrounding hills, away from the prying eyes of corporate managers. Meanwhile, a second spy, the "Inside Man," also got hired on and soon became a model employee, earning the favor of management in the process. Claiming to despise the union, the Inside Man provided information on supposed union men to mine managers; in reality, he turned in the names of miners who had proven hostile to the union and the Outside Man's activities. If things went according to plan, the managers themselves purged the nonunion men, leaving behind only union supporters who could then push for union recognition or threaten a strike (Andrews 2008, 235).

Needless to say, CF&I and the other major coal companies, Victor-American and Rocky Mountain Fuel, responded with their own espionage operations, turning to private detective companies for security, policing, and infiltration services. In August 1913, the situation in the southern fields intensified after the murder of a union organizer, Gerald Lippiatt, by agents of the Baldwin-Felts Detective Agency. In mid-September, the UMW organized a convention in

Trinidad to decide in favor of a strike. A string of union leaders and supporters (including the fiery union activist Mother Jones) made their way to the podium and recounted the horrors faced by miners, the hardship and grief bore by the families of miners killed in mines, and the indifference of management and ownership. They concluded with a demand to strike. Delegates to the convention voted in favor of a strike that would begin on September 23, a mere week away. The great strike of 1913–1914 had begun (Andrews 2008, 235–238).

Strikes are, in essence, a battle of stamina. Each day a factory or mine is closed, the company loses money, but so do the workers. The winner will be the side that forces the other to give up first and make concessions. If the company relents and recognizes the union and its demands, the strikers win. However, if the company outlasts the strike, it wins, and the strikers lose and are forced out of the mines. The advantage to a large union like the UMW, with its 400,000 members in 1913, came from having its membership support strikers with funds set aside for just such a purpose. Payments from union dues helped strikers and their families make ends meet while the mines were closed. However, owners often countered by hiring replacement workers, or "scabs," as the strikers called them, to reopen the shuttered mines. If companies successfully brought in strikebreakers, they reopened the mines, and the strikes failed.

Companies had other assets at their disposal. CF&I had developed its own in-house detective agency, and the Baldwin-Felts Detective Agency (which had helped stop a strike in West Virginia) also found plenty of work to do. While the coal companies purged suspected union men from their company rosters, they also set about hiring thugs from cities like Denver and Kansas City who could be used as a private "police" force. Corporations also worked with sympathetic newspapers to get their official interpretation of events out to the public, arguing that the union members were outside agitators who had duped the largely ignorant immigrant miners into believing ridiculous stories about the advantages of unionism. Should these tactics not be enough, the companies had one final card to play: the governor and the national guard. In strikes around the nation, governors often sided with the companies and called in the national guard to protect strikebreakers and end the strikes.

To combat the introduction of strikebreakers, striking workers set up tent cities near the railroad stops that provided access to the mines. Tent cities sprang up at Aguilar, Rugby, Piedmont, Old Segundo, Tercio, Walsenburg, Forbes, Pictou, and Ludlow.

By late September 1913, miners had virtually stopped working in all the mines of southern Colorado. The families of miners packed up their belongings and left the company towns for the tent cities that would be home during the strike. Indeed, company guards often forcibly evicted the families of striking miners. In the town of Tabasco, according to one report, "mine guards hastened to the little huts where miners lived and threw their families and furniture into the street. Little children so ejected were hurt and several fights resulted" (quoted in Andrews 2008, 247). In overloaded wagons, the families made their way to the tent camps, with Ludlow soon growing to be the largest.

In camps, domestic life resumed as close to normal as possible. The union paid strikers on average about $6 a week, about half of their usual wages. Independent merchants (not tied to the company store system) opened stores in these tent camps and sold groceries to the strikers. Women continued in their duties of cooking, cleaning, and childcare with little change from their previous routines, except for the additional hardships caused by living in a tent as winter approached the foothills of the Southern Rockies. Children had time to play, weaving among the tents in packs, while unemployed miners clustered in groups around campfires and debated the proper course of action. The camps all had a central open area, a place for bands to play and union leaders to give speeches. The camps, like the closed mines, represented more than 20 nationalities. Mike Livoda, a union organizer, remembered, "In the evening I used to go out there a little ways from the camp, you know, and listen to music from those camps. They'd be singing in every language in the world in that tent colony, how those miners were unified and stuck together" (quoted in Andrews 2008, 252).

Over the cold winter months, episodes of violence between company guards and strikers led to the deaths of several people. As one federal investigator put it, "The strikers at the Ludlow tents are in a highly nervous condition," expecting an attack by company agents at any time (Andrews 2008, 255). Indeed, both sides had armed themselves in preparation for an attack. In late October, soldiers from the Colorado National Guard arrived. At first, it appeared that Colorado governor Elias Ammons and the guard would not take sides in the strike. He ordered the guard to enforce the peace, disarm both sides, close down saloons, and force company guards to remain on company property. However, he ordered them to allow nonunion workers to return to work but not to permit outside strikebreakers into the mines. Some strikers believed this to be an evenhanded approach, but the application of the governor's plan differed greatly from his words. While ostensibly there to keep the peace, the guard's presence would instead bring tragedy.

The guard proved to be anything but impartial. Guardsmen, for example, proved more fastidious about confiscating weapons from the strikers' camps and generally left the mine guards' stockpiles alone. Even more egregiously, the CF&I arranged to pay the guard's food and heating costs, effectively making them employees of the company. The commander of the guard, General John Chase, also augmented his forces by mustering in former sheriff's deputies, mine guards, and private detectives. Instead of an impartial force of trained soldiers, the Colorado Guard, in the words of historian Thomas G. Andrews, became "a force of men boasting a checkered history as criminals, counterinsurgents, and union busters" (Andrews 2008, 257).

The presence of guardsmen (despite being supplemented by CF&I money) drained the Colorado government's coffers, prompting Governor Ammons to remove the vast majority of soldiers from the strike zone in March 1914. By mid-April, the only guardsmen still in the area were the 34 men of Company B, under the command of Lieutenant Karl Linderfelt, and a slightly larger force from nearby Walsenburg. Nearly all of the rank-and-file guardsmen were drawing wages from the coal companies. With the sides clearly drawn, and rumors and paranoia rampant, both the strikers and the guard feared an all-out war.

War came to Ludlow on the morning of April 20, 1914. It began innocuously enough when Louis Tikas, a Greek miner who was the de facto leader of the Ludlow tent colony, met with Major Patrick Hamrock, the commander of the guard detachment. Hamrock had received a claim that an anti-union miner was being held against his will in the tent city and went to Tikas to clear up the matter. As the two men talked, armed strikers began to collect around them, and Hamrock's guardsmen nervously took up positions overlooking the camp, including at some machine gun emplacements. A single shot rang out, from which side will never be known, but that single shot detonated the peaceful morning. The militiamen opened fire with their machine guns, riddling the camp with bullets. The strikers, despite the efforts of the guard to disarm them, also had plenty of weaponry at their command and returned fire. The battle raged for hours, with one militiaman, Private Alfred Martin, killed and a 12-year-old boy among the dead. During the chaos, Lt. Linderfelt smashed Tikas in the face with a rifle butt and then had him shot in the back. The worst tragedy, however, did not occur until later that afternoon.

The strikers, of course, had long been aware of the threat posed by the presence of the guard and the ominous power of their machine gun emplacements. Ludlow was not a military encampment but rather a civilian community, and the strikers feared that in an attack, innocent women and children might be slaughtered. Anticipating such an eventuality, miners had dug underground rooms below some of the tents to give noncombatants a place to shelter from the fury of the bullets.

That afternoon, the militia advanced on the camp, still exchanging fire with strikers. Somehow a fire began in the tent city, and which group was responsible for starting it—like much else about that day—is unknown. Strikers claimed the guardsmen intentionally ignited the tents. Conversely, the leaders of the guard claimed a fire ignited caches of ammunition and gunpowder that the strikers had stored in the camp. What is known is that the canvas and wood tents quickly went up in flames, the fire consuming tent after tent. Under one of those burning tents, 11 children and 2 women were huddled, now with no way to escape from the smoke and fire above them. All 13 died from suffocation and burning. In total, some 25 people died in an attack that came to be called the Ludlow Massacre.

Rather than ending the conflict, the massacre unleashed open warfare across the southern Colorado coalfields. Many of the strikers had served in various militaries over the years. Many of the Greeks, for example, had seen action in the Balkans. Combined with their superior knowledge of the terrain, they soon unleashed an effective guerilla campaign across the region, blowing up mines, bridges, and even a dam. The violence leveled the company town of Forbes. Strikers also took out their anger on strikebreakers, mine managers, mine guards, and anyone whose loyalty lay with the companies. At least another three people died in the weeks following Ludlow (Andrews 2008, 273–279).

The events of the Colorado coalfields attracted national attention and finally federal intervention. In late April, President Woodrow Wilson, hoping to quell the violence, sent federal troops to restore order. The guerillas proved unwilling to attack federal troops and had perhaps grown weary of the fighting. Nine days after the attacks on Ludlow, the fighting finally stopped. The U.S. military, for its part, largely remained neutral and would not allow the company to import strikebreakers. However, it also would not interfere with individuals who wanted to return to the mines. Exploiting this loophole, the companies advertised nationally for workers and probably offered free train fare to the mines. Hundreds of new nonunion workers flooded into the area and took jobs in the mines, effectively ending the strike. By July 1914, CF&I's mines were already back to producing at 70 percent of their prestrike levels. The miners had lost (Andrews 2008, 282). John D. Rockefeller Jr., who led the company, which was a subsidiary of his father's Standard Oil, did offer his workers a company union instead of representation by the UMW. A company union, of course, had little power. There were some modest reforms to the company town system, but a company union did nothing to address the dangers of life underground or the exploitative nature of the coal mining industry. Congress eventually investigated the events surrounding the massacre, but no one was held to account.

While the events of the Ludlow Massacre and the coalfield war would not be replicated elsewhere, strikes in both hard rock and coal mining districts continued throughout the 20th century, and both industries remained dangerous, especially coal mining. For example, a fire at the Wilberg Mine, owned by the Utah Power and Light Company, erupted on the evening of December 19, 1984. The fire blocked the main entrance to the mine, and 28 people, including one female miner, were trapped and killed (Cocke n.d.).

THE LEGACY OF MINING IN THE WEST

No industry did more to develop the West, especially the Intermountain West, than mining. The California gold rush instantly transformed California, bringing statehood only two years after the discovery of gold. San Francisco blossomed into a major city, seemingly overnight. Mining did the same for Denver, Boise, and even Seattle, the latter benefiting tremendously from the discovery of gold in Alaska. Homages to these events are even enshrined in the names of local sports teams, such as the National Football League's San Francisco 49ers and the Denver Nuggets of the National Basketball Association. Smaller towns developed across the West and became regional hubs, like Telluride and Aspen in Colorado and Park City in Utah, places that would later be reborn as tourist

Gold discoveries created mining camps almost overnight. Miners quickly denuded the landscape near their claims, using trees for cabins and sluice boxes. Just as quickly as they appeared, however, camps could vanish as miners set off for better diggings. (Library of Congress)

towns and enclaves for the rich and beautiful. Many more boomed for a short time before becoming ghost towns, leaving behind rotting buildings and abandoned mines.

Mining also left another tangible but less celebratory legacy in the form of mine pollution. Mines in the Rockies, many of which have been abandoned for over a century, pour millions of gallons of mineral-laden water into the streams and rivers of the West. The few large mines that are still active also tend to be massive open pits that scar the land, and when abandoned, they sometimes fill with water, like the Berkley Pit near Butte, Montana. Great quantities of copper were once removed from the Berkley Pit, but now only a toxic lake, incapable of supporting life, remains. Coal mining, with coal still used to produce electricity, remained more prominent in the economy until very recently. Recent concerns over climate change, and the cost advantages of natural gas, have made coal a less attractive source for energy development, and the coal mining industry, like the hard rock industry before it, appears to be declining in importance in the United States. Without the mining industry, however, the West would never have become the modern and developed region of the country it is now.

4

ECONOMIC LIFE IN THE AMERICAN WEST

The discovery of gold in California radically accelerated the arrival of Western capitalism, but capitalism had been quietly shaping the West for decades.

American Indian peoples and the Europeans who came among them had decidedly different economic strategies. Indian peoples certainly understood the value of goods and articles of trade, but the acquisition of goods either served vital survival purposes or was designed to create an intricate web of interrelated networks of reciprocation that helped bind individuals to the larger society, like the Potlatch among the Pacific Northwest peoples. Accumulating wealth to demonstrate social status rarely occurred, and conspicuous consumption was generally seen as undesirable or even taboo. The Pueblo peoples of New Mexico, for example, thought such acquisition was a sign of an individual being a witch. Instead, generosity marked one as a truly benevolent person. Great economic changes, however, would come with the arrival of Europeans.

Probably the clearest economic transformation came with the advent of the fur trade. Europeans and Anglo-Americans placed great value on furs, in particular beaver. These furs, processed into clothing or expensive felt hats, were de rigueur for fashionable

Europeans. With demand for pelts high, it stood to reason that the more beaver one could harvest, the greater the profit. In exchange for furs, trappers offered goods to the Indians: cloth, tobacco, iron tools, guns and gunpowder, and, worst of all, alcohol.

Contrary to the popular image of the fur trapper, few actually trapped their animals themselves. Instead, they relied on Indian peoples to do the trapping. The idea of trapping or hunting far more animals than required for subsistence was an alien concept to many Indian peoples at first, but they quickly learned that more furs meant more trade goods. This transformation of living animals into abstract articles of trade is called *commodification*, and the commodification of New World animals would repeatedly prove environmentally disastrous. In time, it would also undermine the independence of Indian peoples who participated in the trade because they became dependent on goods (like gunpowder and alcohol) that they could not produce for themselves. Capitalism generated great fortunes for the owners of a few companies and became a useful tool of conquest more generally.

THE INTRUSION OF CAPITALISM AND
THE FUR TRADE

Contrary to the popular imagination of the buckskin clad trapper, the fur trade in the West actually began with sailors. In 1778, the English ship captain and explorer James Cook purchased 1,500 otter skins from Indians on Vancouver Island for a pittance, which he turned around and sold for a huge fortune in China. English and American sailors saw the potential of this trade and thus began to ply the waters of the Pacific Northwest. George Vancouver helped solidify British claims to the Pacific Northwest and established friendly trade relations with local Indian peoples in 1792. That same year, the American captain Robert Gray piloted his vessel, the *Columbia*, up the mouth of the river he would christen for his ship. More Americans followed, so many, in fact, that local tribes took to calling the Americans "Bostons," as the ships hailed from Boston or nearby ports in New England.

While the trade proved lucrative for both sides, the sailors also brought with them a variety of diseases that, predictability, took a toll on Indian populations. Fifteen years later, Lewis and Clark would notice the effects of disease on the populations near their winter home of Fort Clatsop on the Oregon coast: the captains saw ample evidence of past smallpox epidemics and venereal diseases, in particular. In 1806, William Clark noted the influence of small-pox on the Clatsop Indians, writing, "An old man who appeared of some note . . . brought forward a woman who was badly marked with the Small Pox and made signs that they all died with the disorder which marked her face" (Bergon 1995, 376–377). Clark judged the woman's age to be around 30, coinciding with the arrival of European ships along the Pacific coast.

The ease of making a huge profit in the fur trade brought two powerful companies to the shores of the Pacific. One, the Hudson's Bay Company, was the most important fur-trading company in the world. The other was a relative upstart owned by a German American named John Jacob Astor. Astor had come to the United States at the age of 21 in 1784, and while en route, he had met a fellow German passenger who convinced him that he could make a lot of money in the fur trade. It proved to be an auspicious meeting (Stark 2015, 10).

By the mid-1780s, Astor had opened a business that sent furs that he had purchased from the North West Company in Montreal to New York and then on to England and brought back musical instruments to America, a trade that reflected the economic and manufacturing differences between the two continents, with the New World providing raw materials and the Old World returning finished products. As Astor's business grew, so did his ambition. To realize it, he looked West.

In 1808, Astor decided to put his plan for a global business empire in motion with the incorporation of his American Fur Company. His ships had already opened a trade with China for tea; an outpost in the Pacific Northwest that could store furs for sale in China would make the trips even more profitable. With encouragement from President Jefferson, Astor laid out his plan. In 1809, his ship, the *Enterprise*, would collect furs in the Pacific Northwest and then carry them to China. The following year, he would send two parties to meet at the mouth of the Columbia River. One party would go overland, roughly following the route of Lewis and Clark, and the other would round Cape Horn and arrive by ship. They would build an outpost near the mouth of the Columbia that would function as the linchpin of a global trading network. The first step would be to collect manufactured goods from New York or London to trade with Indians, the usual assortment of knives, iron tools, pots, beads, and such. These trade goods would be exchanged for pelts, the trade extending deep into the interior of the continent. From smaller collection points, the furs would be transported down the Columbia in canoes to Astor's coastal fort. The cargo of furs would be taken by ship across the Pacific and sold at tremendous markup in China, and then, finally, his ships would load up on porcelain, silk, and tea and transport these back to New York and London. The profits, Astor predicted, would be enormous.

Eventually, both the overland and the sea-born parties arrived at the mouth of the Columbia and established Fort Astoria there in 1811. Unfortunately, global politics played havoc with his plans for a global business empire. One problem lay with the Indians. Trade had long been an important part of Northwest Indian life, and coastal Indians were increasingly driving a hard bargain for otter pelts. Worse, many tribes had grown distrustful of the English and Americans who brought disease and sometimes violence. One such tribe, the Clayoquot had recently been betrayed by an American vessel that had taken some of their men on a trip down the West Coast only to abandon them on islands off California. The handful that survived the long and dangerous journey north had few good things to say about the Americans. As fate would have it, Astor's ship the *Tonquin* would visit the Clayoquot on Vancouver Island shortly after completing the fort.

Loaded with trade goods, the ship's headstrong and imperious captain, Jonathan Thorn, set out to acquire furs as rapidly as possible. Thorn had distinguished himself as a naval officer, but he lacked any experience dealing with the shrewd coastal Indians. This would soon prove fatal in his dealings with the Clayoquot.

The negotiations began when a delegation of Clayoquot clambered from their cedar canoes onto the deck of the *Tonquin*. Captain Thorn opened the proceedings by offering two blankets and some smaller items, like fishhooks and beads, for each otter pelt. Nookamis, a village elder and chief negotiator, rejected the offer as much too low and countered with five blankets per otter skin. Thorn did not care much for Indians and certainly did not want to haggle with them. Bargaining, however, had long been a part of Northwest Indian culture, and no doubt Nookamis expected Thorn to make a counteroffer. Instead, Thorn grew angry and waved Nookamis's packet of otter pelts in the aged man's face before finally grabbing him and flinging him into the sea. When confronted for his egregious lack of decorum by the more experienced trader Alexander McKay, Thorn reportedly replied, "You pretend to know a great deal about the Indian character. You know nothing at all. . . . They'll not be so saucy now" (Stark 2015, 203). McKay, cognizant of the great offense Thorn had committed, advised the captain to weigh anchor and leave immediately. Thorn insisted that he had taught the Indians a lesson and that they would soon be back and more amenable to the prices he offered. Thorn would not have long to wait to see the results of his impetuous actions.

Thorn, captain of a ship bristling with cannons, had underestimated the Indians, seeing them as grossly inferior. His arrogance would prove fatal. Early on the morning of June 15, 1811, a canoe of Clayoquot approached the ship, holding up furs and indicating their willingness to trade. The watch allowed the Indians on deck and summoned the captain from his cabin. Thorn may have felt vindicated that his strong-arm tactics seemed to be paying off as more canoes pulled alongside and Clayoquot climbed on deck with furs in hand. McKay and Joseachal, an Indian interpreter, had warned Thorn about the security risk of having too many Indians on deck at any time, but in the midst of the chaos and the apparently fortunate turn of events, all rules were forgotten. The Clayoquot were particularly eager to trade their furs for steel knives, handing over packs of furs in exchange for the sharp new knives.

Finally, realizing the danger, Thorn ordered the Indians off the ship and gave the order to weigh anchor. As several crewmen climbed the rigging to unfurl the sails, a Clayoquot warrior gave a shriek, and all the Indians on deck suddenly produced knives and *pogamoggans*, war clubs made from whalebone and stone. In such close quarters, the cannons were useless, and even single-shot firearms proved less effective than the knives and clubs of the Indians. The surprise was total. James Lewis, the clerk overseeing the trading, took a knife to the back. Alexander McKay, the only crew member wise enough to arm himself, managed to kill one warrior, but others fell upon him with clubs. Captain Thorn, armed only with a pocketknife, fought in vain against numerous assassins, but to no avail. Beaten and stabbed, the Clayoquot flung his body into the sea. The rest of the crew fared no better. They were butchered by the very knives they had so recently traded.

Five or six survivors, all below deck when the attack started, managed to get to the armory and barricade themselves inside. From there, they could withstand any assault. Overmatched, the Indians fled, returning to their canoes under fire from the *Tonquin's* cannons. Unable to sail a ship with only four able-bodied crewmen, the survivors decided to slip out in the longboat under cover of darkness. One or two wounded men stayed behind: the clerk Lewis and possibly Stephen Weeks.

The following morning, the Clayoquot cautiously approached in their canoes. A single and apparently wounded figure appeared on deck and made signs that he wanted to surrender before disappearing below deck. Realizing the ship was theirs, the Clayoquot climbed aboard, eager to see all the treasures their attack had won them. Several hundred Indians, men, women, and children, toured the ship, unaware of what the wounded man had in store for them. Suddenly, a massive explosion tore the ship apart, for below deck in the powder magazine, the lone survivor had detonated some 9,000 pounds of gunpowder. No one on board the *Tonquin* survived. Joseachal, the translator who had been captured by the Clayoquot (and would later report the event), later confirmed that body parts washed ashore for days after the detonation. The four men who escaped in the longboat were later blown ashore and recaptured. The angry and grieving Clayoquot took great pleasure in slowly torturing them to death (Stark 2015, 207–216).

Thorn's ignorance and arrogance had cost his crew dearly, but it cost Astor as well. His vision of a global trade network would not be so easy to accomplish. However, hostilities between his men and the native population paled in comparison to hostilities elsewhere that would eventually undo his efforts. Half a world away from his fledgling settlement of Astoria, a variety of circumstances (trade policy, violations of maritime law, and other factors) had compelled the United States to declare war on Great Britain in June 1812. For the most part, the war would go badly for the United States, and even Astor's tiny outpost would not be spared. After all, the British were also in the Pacific Northwest, with the Hudson's Bay Company active in the area.

The subsequent invasion must surely be unique in the annals of U.S. and British relations, as the British attack force came via canoe. John McTavish, of the North West Company (a subsidiary of the Hudson's Bay Company), commanded roughly 75 men in 10 canoes. He carried with him a letter for Astoria's de facto commander, Duncan McDougall, from Angus Shaw, who, as fate would have it, was McDougall's uncle—Scotsmen, as the names suggest, played an outsized role in the fur trade. The letter warned that in addition to this canoe flotilla, a British warship, the *Phoebe*, and the *Isaac Todd* of the North West Company were sailing for Astoria with instructions to destroy the outpost if it did not surrender. Rather than fight, McTavish offered to buy out the company and let the employees go free. Needless to say, the negotiation, under duress as it was, greatly favored the North West Company.

The offer amounted to 30 cents on the dollar for the American Fur Company's assets. McDougall agreed to these terms on October 23, 1813, much to the outrage of many of the other Astorians, who preferred to defend the colony instead. McDougall, for his part, promptly switched to the North West Company, and John Jacob Astor's colony changed hands.

The transfer, it turned out, would not be permanent, as the 1814 Treaty of Ghent, which ended the war, required a return of everything to its prewar state. This meant that the fort at Astoria would revert to American control, but the enterprise had already proven to be a failure. Astor would recover, of course, and go on to become one of the nation's richest men and an archetype of the self-made man so prominent in American mythology. The founding of Astoria also supported American claims to the Pacific Northwest, and Astor's overland party would be the first whites to cross the Rockies at the South Pass, which would become the preferred route for wagons to creak and crawl their way across the West. Fur traders, for their part, would continue on as well—maybe not as part of a grandiose global scheme but certainly as part of lucrative international trade. Indeed, even before Astor's plan, trappers had begun to ascend up the Missouri River in search of pelts.

The Lewis and Clark Expedition (1804–1806) found an overland route to the Pacific, helped sketch out the map of the West, and solidified U.S. claims on the Pacific Northwest, which were all advantageous to the fur traders—perhaps no other group so benefited from the expedition. Indeed, John Colter, a member of the expedition, did not return all the way to St. Louis with the rest of the Corps of Discovery, as Lewis and Clark's party was called. After asking for permission to end his enlistment with the expedition, Colter joined a party of trappers heading up the Missouri River. He had seen the potential for the fur trade in the region and sought to get ahead of the hordes of trappers who would follow. However, he would be remembered best for being the first white man to see what would one day become Yellowstone National Park, though his tales of bubbling mud pits, geysers, and boiling pools of water mostly elicited jeers and accusations of tall tales about "Colter's Hell." Years would pass before his discoveries were confirmed.

Colter and the men who followed in his footsteps soon gained the name "mountain men." These mountain men relied on Indian assistance and often cemented social ties by taking Indian wives. Such marriages, though typically not consecrated in a church, provided companionship, labor (women continued to process most of the skins), and help from the wife's people. Thus, these mostly forgotten women played vital roles as mediators between two worlds, and their sons often continued to walk in both worlds, typically finding employment in the fur trade or as scouts.

By the 1820s, a flourishing trade connected Spanish (and later Mexican) territory in the Rockies with the United States, and furs played a major role in the development of this trade. Trappers set up a base of operations in Taos, New Mexico, radiating from there across the Rockies, and trapped beaver in the high mountain valleys. Rather than cross over the plains twice every year, which was decidedly dangerous, one company head, William Ashley, proposed a system whereby trappers would remain in the Rockies permanently, and then, once a year, all the various trappers would converge at a predetermined location, or rendezvous. Ashley would send supply wagons to the rendezvous to provide trappers with everything they needed for the coming year, and the trappers, both white and Indian, would supply the furs they had collected, which would then be carried back across the plains and finally to markets in the East.

The trappers fell into one of three categories: the *engages*, who were salaried by the large fur-trading companies; the skin trappers, who were paid by the pelt and often borrowed supplies from the companies and therefore often fell deep into debt; and the free trappers, who worked only for themselves and sold their furs to the highest bidders. Life for all three was exceptionally hard, and many had little to show for their efforts. The rendezvous at least offered the chance for camaraderie and a great deal of heavy drinking and celebration. This system of trapping would last until the 1840s, when the trappers, as they had done in the East, effectively eradicated the beaver on which their trade depended (White 1991, 47).

The ties the Taos trappers had made, however, would be but the first economic penetration by the United States into Spain and later Mexico. And northern Mexico, both New Mexico and California, would soon be visited by increasing numbers of Americans. Some came by ship from Eastern ports like Boston, trading American manufactured goods like tools and cloth for cattle hides from the great ranches of the region. One British resident in Monterey, California declared, "There is not a yard of tape, a pin, or a piece of domestic cotton or even thread that does not come from the United States" (White 1991, 49).

In New Mexico, traders in wagons made their way from Missouri along the Santa Fe Trail, a route made dangerous by the presence of the Comanche. William Becknell opened the trade with an 1821 trip to Santa Fe, benefiting from Mexico's independence. When Becknell returned to Missouri the following year, he had turned a tidy profit. Others soon joined the trade, including New Mexicans who started on the opposite end but likewise profited. Indeed, many New Mexican merchants resold the items they had purchased deeper into Mexico itself, where a market for American products was rapidly developing in the early years of independence. American economic influence thus grew tremendously in Northern Mexico in the 1820s and 1830s, paving the way for later American military and political intrusion in the 1840s as part of the Mexican-American War.

The homely beaver had been the catalyst for all of this, but no animal would prove more important for Indians and white traders than the bison.

THE DESTRUCTION OF THE BISON

The bison is one of the iconic animals of the United States, and at one time, they could be found from Mexico to northern Canada and from the Rockies to the Appalachian Mountains. The animal's primary habitat, however, lay within the Great Plains. The largest animal in North America, a fully grown male could tip the scales at more than 2,000 pounds, and yet these powerful creatures could run at speeds in excess of 30 miles an hour for as long as they desired. At one time, at least 30–40 million bison called the Great Plains home. Of course, so much meat had long attracted Indian peoples, but the arrival of the horse enabled them to hunt these fleet animals year-round. Entire cultures developed that relied on the bison as their primary source of food. Yet, between 1840 and 1880, the number of bison declined so dramatically that they were pushed to the edge of extinction. Until recent decades, the blame for this environmental disaster had been put squarely on the shoulders of professional hunters who arrived on the plains in the 1860s and 1870s and slaughtered these herds with industrial efficiency. Certainly, professional hunters contributed to the bison herds' collapse, but there is a much more complex story that scholars have only recently come to understand. This story involves multiple actors and a vast but fragile ecosystem.

A number of Indian peoples had moved onto the plains in the 18th and 19th centuries. Some, like the Comanche, came out from the Rockies, and others, like the Lakota, moved onto the plains from the east. All came because of the bison, and the bison provided. Food, clothing, shelter, tools, religious objects, and even toys were derived from the shaggy beasts. To be sure, Plains Indian peoples continued to gather plants, but bison formed the basis of their survival and became central to their culture. The seemingly limitless profusion of bison allowed for a rapidly growing population of Indian peoples on the plains. Perhaps as many as 50,000 Indians, from dozens of tribes, called the plains home at least some of the time. Such abundance also led to rising populations. Yet, the bison could not provide everything, especially as manufactured goods began to find their way onto the grasslands.

White traders were happy to provide the Plains Indians with these goods, and outposts appeared at places like Bent's Fort on the Arkansas River in today's southeastern Colorado. In 1857, two traders, John Smith and Nicholas Janis, bought from Elbridge Gerry, whose trading post at Fort Laramie became one of the most profitable, "dozens of blankets, hundreds of bundles of beads, much tobacco, several dozen 'cocoa' and 'ebony' knives, hundreds of yards of cloth . . . coffee mills, combs, a gross of awls, teakettles, and a few hundred hair pipes" (West 1995, 59). Several months later, after doing a vigorous business with Plains peoples, the pair returned with some 213 buffalo robes and the pelts of many other animals, a tidy profit all in all. Traders also lubricated transactions with alcohol, which proved a popular item of trade. For traders, alcohol had major advantages over exchanging more durable trade goods like knives or iron tools. Being both addictive and rapidly consumed, the market for alcohol could never be satiated, requiring Indians to hunt more to satisfy their cravings. Cheap and often watered-down whiskey could thus increase a trader's profit margins immensely. The explorer John C. Frémont noted that Indians would trade fine buffalo robes for watered-down whiskey, writing, "A keg of it will purchase from an Indian every thing he possesses—his furs, his lodge, his horses, even his wife and children" (quoted in West 1995, 67). Frémont felt such actions demonstrated the inferior nature of Indians, but such destructive behavior is a key symptom of drug addiction. Traders on the plains, however, were happy to provide a steady supply. Bison indirectly made these purchases possible, enabling Plains Indians to acquire goods that made their lives easier and more pleasant, but it came at a cost, as acquiring alcohol or less insidious trade goods meant hunting more bison than Indians needed for subsistence.

Just how many more they hunted is difficult to estimate. In 1855, J. W. Whitfield, a U.S. Indian agent on the upper Arkansas, estimated that the 11,470 Indians in his jurisdiction killed approximately 112,000 bison a year, roughly 10 bison per person. The Southern Cheyenne and Arapaho killed perhaps 13 for every member of their respective tribes. All of these figures were well above the roughly 6 bison per person required for subsistence. Increased harvesting of bison must surely have been because of a need to supply bison hides to traders for goods they could not produce themselves. This increased hunting put more stress on the bison population, but Indians were not solely responsible for the rapidly declining bison herds in the first half of the 19th century.

To understand the diverse pressures being applied to the bison herds of the Great Plains, one must understand the animals' habits. Bison do not migrate like birds or butterflies, as once believed, but they do move around to exploit resources in various habitats. The plains might seem a vast and uniform grassland, but there are important environmental differences, most especially between the higher open plains and the river valleys or riparian zones that generally run east from the Rockies to the Mississippi River. The plains are a landscape of extremes, hot and dry in the summer and brutally cold in the winter. Temperatures can plummet to incredibly low levels in the winter, with brutal arctic winds sweeping southward with nothing to staunch their assault. Even the thickly furred bison could not stand such tremendously cold snaps in the open plains. Thus, they often found shelter in the river valleys below the strongest of the bitter winds and where the blizzards did not bury the dried grasses on which they could survive. Springtime found them still in the river valleys, eating grasses that emerged there first. By June, however, the herds had left behind the riparian zones for the short grasses, like buffalo grass, on the open plains that reached their peak in the summer months. Spreading out over the plains in herds of thousands, the bison did not exhaust the resources in any of their environments, and as the seasons turned again, they made their way back to the riverine environment that would protect them from the harshest blasts of winter.

However, by the 1840s, those riverine environments were increasingly being used by others. Indians, for their part, relied on them for many of the same reasons as the bison. River valleys provided them with shelter and firewood to stave off the coldest of nights.

They also provided shelter and forage for their increasingly larger horse herds, animals that directly competed with bison.

Other humans and their animals also used the riparian zones. White emigrants bound for California, Oregon, or Santa Fe passed through in the summer months. Using rivers to navigate the trackless plains, emigrant trains invariably stayed near streams, grazing their animals and using the riparian zone's fragile ecosystem with little concern for its long-term stability: after all, what did it matter if they burned up the wood or let their hardworking animals graze the riverine grass to nubs when they would be safely to Oregon or California before the snows came? Too many animals using the same limited ecosystem had disastrous consequences for the bison. Female bison emerged from the winter thinner than before and were therefore less able to successfully carry calves to term.

These newcomers also brought with them cattle, oxen, horses, and sheep, and with them came new diseases that would devastate bison herds. Anthrax had been introduced by the early 1800s, but *brucellosis*, a parasitic bacterial infection that was common in cattle, was perhaps the worst. Infected animals could die from the disease, but even if death did not occur, one common effect of infection was the spontaneous abortion of unborn calves, which only served to lower bison birth rates at the same time predation by humans was increasing.

All of these factors conspired to put pressure on bison populations, and the capricious natural environment of the Great Plains, which so easily lured people into a false sense of security, would test the resiliency of Indian societies. Nomadic tribes moved onto the plains in pursuit of the bison, but their societies would only last for a century and a half. If given more time, they would have perhaps reached a more sustainable strategy, but given the growing numbers of mouths to feed and the desire to benefit from the acquisition of more material goods, they may have continued on a destructive path. In the end, they would not get the chance to adapt because the tide of white settlers was about to overwhelm them, bringing about the final collapse of the bison population.

Professional hunters that moved onto the plains in the 1870s finally pushed the bison population to the brink of collapse. These professional hunters came for the bison, but for markedly different reasons than the earlier robe trade. Bison robes made by Indian women though a laborious process were luxury items worn by the fashionable in some of the world's largest cities. Professional hunters, however, came to feed America's rising industrial desires.

The United States had become an industrial nation, with most factories scattered around the former Union states of the North. These factories produced a dizzying array of materials, including textiles in massive quantities. Workers risked their health and sometimes lives inside great brick halls filled with thundering machines. Water and steam powered these gargantuan monuments of industrial development, and belts connected their various pulleys, gears, and flywheels. The belts were composed of leather, as the more durable rubber and synthetic rubber would not be developed for decades.

Leather could be effectively employed for such a task, but it had its limitations. Leather belts could snap or stretch, especially given the constant friction and heat, and thus had to be frequently replaced. Naturally, factories wanted to spend as little as possible on these belts given how quickly they wore out, and so the cheaper the source of leather, the cheaper the belt. The cheapest source of leather, it turned out, could be found on the Great Plains among the seemingly limitless herds of bison.

Several factors, besides cost, attracted the leather industry to bison hides. The price of cowhides had more than doubled between 1850 and 1870, and domestic supplies could not keep pace with demand, requiring tanneries to source hides from Latin American countries. Bison offered a cheaper alternative, if they could be brought to market effectively, but several challenges had to be addressed to make this happen. Tanneries had to figure out how best to process the leather, which was markedly different from cattle leather. More porous and elastic than cattle leather, bison leather was perfect for industrial belt applications, but it required a different process to tan the hides. In the early 1870s, tanneries learned to soak the bison hides in a lime solution to make them suitable for industrial use.

Firearm technology had also improved greatly during the Civil War, including the standard issue .50-caliber Springfield Armory rifled musket, which was more powerful and accurate than earlier weapons. In 1872, the Sharps Rifle Manufacturing Company released a new large-bore .50-caliber rifle nicknamed the "Big Fifty" that could launch a one-pound lead slug over 1,500 yards thanks to a massive load of 90 grains of black powder (Isenberg 2000, 131).

It was with just such a rifle that buffalo hunter Billy Dixon allegedly wounded a hostile Indian from nine-tenths of mile at the end of the 1874 Second Battle of Adobe Walls in the Texas Panhandle. Although the veracity of Dixon's claim has been debated for over a century, modern tests have shown the rifle could launch a projectile that far (Spangenberger 2016). Regardless of the legitimacy of Dixon's shot, the Big Fifty became the preferred rifle for professional hunters due to its range, accuracy, and power.

Hunting with these new rifles put professional marksmen at a huge advantage over mounted Indian hunters. Mounted hunters would dive into herds and carefully cull a target from the rest of the herd in a display of skill and bravery that awed those who witnessed it. Professional hunters, on the other hand, set up shop near a herd, preferably on a small rise or hill, and then opened fire. As the largest land animals in North America, bison had little to fear, and the distant pop of a rifle from several hundred yards away did not disturb them in their grazing. Thus, a professional hunter could systematically pick off members of a large herd one by one without causing the animals to flee. A single hunter could kill dozens of bison without moving from his perch.

Improved firearms and new tannery processes enabled the development of the hide industry, but the arrival of railroads onto the plains in the 1860s and 1870s was just as important. The Union Pacific–Central Pacific completed the first transcontinental line in 1869, effectively splitting the bison population into northern and southern herds. The Kansas Pacific reached Denver in 1870. The Atchison, Topeka and Santa Fe arrived at Dodge City, Kansas, in 1872. And the Northern Pacific laid track to Bismarck, Dakota Territory, just prior to its 1873 bankruptcy. All of these lines made the transportation of hides quick and efficient. Professional hunters, after several days or weeks of hunting and stripping the hides off their kills, drove wagons loaded with their bounty to the nearest railhead for transportation to Eastern tanneries. Dodge City became one the main depots for the hide trade. One early resident remembered, "The streets of Dodge were lined with wagons, bringing in hides and meat and getting supplies from early morning to late at night" (Isenberg 2000, 134). The company of Robert Wright and Charles Rath shipped some 200,000 hides from Dodge City in the winter of 1872–1873, and their competitors shipped another 200,000. The transformation had been quick. Colonel Dodge, for whom the city is named, noted that in 1872 bison could be found in multitudes just outside of the town, but by the following fall, he wrote, "Where there were myriads of buffalo the year before, there were now myriads of carcasses. The air was foul with the sickening stench, and the vast plain which only a short twelve months before teemed with animal life, was a dead, solitary, putrid desert" (Isenberg 2000, 134).

A cargo of bison hides awaits shipment via railroad to the east at Dodge City, Kansas. While bison populations began to decline earlier in the nineteenth century, the arrival of professional hide hunters in the 1870s drove the animals to the brink of extinction. (National Archives)

With hundreds of hunting and skinning operations at work on the Great Plains in the early 1870s, the numbers of bison taken soared to numbers previously unimaginable. W. S. Glenn, a professional hunter operating in Texas, estimated that "a remarkably good hunter would kill seventy-five to a hundred [bison] in a day, an average hunter about fifty, and a common one twenty-five, some hardly enough to run a camp. It was just like any other business" (Isenberg 2000, 136). Colonel Dodge estimated that from 1872 to 1874, the hide hunters killed at least 3,158,730 bison.

The rate of killing, compounded by the other problems affecting the bison herds—drought, disease, and the loss of the important riparian forage—led to a population crash. William Hornaday, who would champion the conservation effort for the bison, toured the West in 1889 looking for bison. He found them: "twenty-five in the Texas Panhandle, twenty in the foothills of Colorado, ten between the Yellowstone and Missouri rivers, twenty-six near the Big Horn Mountains, and two hundred in Yellowstone National Park" (Isenberg 2000, 142). Counting those in the Bronx Zoo and elsewhere, less than 500 bison remained from herds that once numbered in the tens of millions. Environmental degradation, technology, and greed nearly doomed the bison, and with the loss of the bison, the

Indians of the Great Plains would also see their independence disappear, but not before they made a brave but futile stand to maintain their control of the Great Plains and their way of life.

THE RISE AND FALL OF THE CATTLE INDUSTRY

The near extermination of the bison opened an ecological niche on the Great Plains that was eagerly filled by Texas cattlemen. Cattle ranching had a long history in Texas that dated back to the first Spanish settlements. Herds of cattle had been brought up from Mexico, and like the rest of the Spanish and Mexican settlement in Texas, the cattle industry remained in the greener country from the lower Rio Grande through San Antonio and northeast toward the Louisiana border. The Great Plains, and whatever potential they offered, remained forbidden territory for cattlemen so long as the Comanche, Kiowa, and Apache remained powerful.

Successfully raising cattle also required access to markets, and most Texas cattle ranching remained for regional consumption. Three factors would help change this: the elimination of the bison, the confinement of Indian peoples to reservations, and the arrival of the railroads. By the 1850s, these forces were starting to assert themselves. A few forward-thinking cattlemen anticipated these changes and looked for ways to bring cattle to beef-starved Easterners. Just as the industry seemed to be taking off, however, the Civil War intervened, isolating Texas from Northern markets. Most able-bodied cowboys also ended up in the ranks of the Confederate Army, leaving ranches undermanned. In their absence, cattle were often left to fend for themselves. Herds of unbranded cattle multiplied across south and central Texas, becoming nearly as wild and hard to catch as deer. These unbranded cattle came to be known as *mavericks*, apparently in honor of Samuel Augustus Maverick, who had abandoned a small herd of cattle on the Matagorda Peninsula in 1847. In 1854, with the help of his two eldest sons, he rounded up the now larger herd and drove them to his Conquista Ranch (Marks 2015). The Texas cattleman Charles Siringo put the origin of the term closer to the Civil War and argued it came about because Maverick had been too lazy to brand his cattle, leaving it to his neighbors to do the hard work. Thus, whatever cow did not have a brand came to be considered one of Maverick's animals. Siringo explained, "Hence the term 'Mavrick.' At first people used to say: 'Yonder goes one of Mr. Mavrick's animals!' Now they say: 'Yonder goes a Mavrick!'" (Siringo 2000, 38).

Whatever the exact origin of the term, maverick cattle were free for the taking and could quickly become the basis of an individual cowboy's cattle empire. Indeed, cowboys working for larger Texas ranches sometimes amassed a small herd of their own composed from their employer's unbranded cattle, which they siphoned off for themselves. Conversely, larger cattle operations also happily rounded up and branded these cattle for themselves, hiring crews of cowboys to venture out into the scrubby timberlands in search of the nearly feral bovine.

Siringo described the difficulty inherent in catching these four-legged fugitives. He and his fellow cowboys would rise before dawn, eat breakfast, and head out into the open country where the cattle thrived. Although eager grazers of open grasslands, the skittish cattle always kept close to scrubby Texas trees and the dense underbrush, so they could make a quick escape through the brambles if approached. Catching these clever cattle required finding them while in the open and getting between them and their protective cover. With the cowboys, lassos in hand, between them and protection, the herd would charge. As Siringo deadpanned, "Then the fun would begin—the whole bunch, may be a thousand head, would stampede and come right towards us. They never were known to run in the opposite direction from the nearest point of timber" (Siringo 2000, 44). The cowboys roped as many as they could as the rest thundered by them into the safety of the trees. They tied these down and awaited the arrival of other cowboys with the main herd of animals they had captured in previous days. They then untied the snared cow, "letting him up so he couldn't help from running into the herd, where he would generally stay contented. Once in a while though, we would strike an old steer that couldn't be made to stay in the herd. Just as soon as he was untied and let up he would go right through the herd and strike for the brush, fighting his way" (Siringo 2000, 44).

One particular breed of cattle played an important role in the development of the Texas cattle industry. The Texas longhorn, initially the preferred breed, descended from the cattle brought by the Spanish with a heavy mix of English longhorn brought by Anglo settlers. Although a lean cow compared to other breeds, the longhorn had a reputation for hardiness and self-reliance, not unlike the reputation of the cowboys themselves. With their long horns, they could fight off wolves that still lingered in the wilds of Texas, and they could tolerate heat and drought better than most other breeds. These strengths offset their rather slim build. But what the longhorn offered in toughness, it lacked in delectability and mass. One angry butcher is alleged to have called a longhorn little more than "eight pounds of hamburger on 800 pounds of bone and horn" (quoted in White 1991, 220). While certainly an exaggeration, the longhorn was not an ideal cow from a productivity standpoint. It was, however, vital to the development of the cattle kingdom in the West.

Unfortunately, Texas longhorns carried, buried in their tough hides, a small tick that transmitted a disease called *splenic fever*, or, more commonly, Texas fever. Longhorns were largely immune to the disease, but other breeds of cattle, like dairy cattle, were not. Once infected, most died. Farmers in more settled environs, like Missouri, soon made the connection between the appearance of Texas longhorns and the devastating disease that killed their livestock and threatened their livelihoods. As a result, farmers pushed for laws to keep Texas cattle away from settled areas, forcing Texas ranching companies to drive their herds farther west into less settled areas. Eventually, those isolated railheads became larger towns, and the cycle started again, with cowboys driving herds even farther west.

The post–Civil War cattle drives became one of the most iconic events of the entire 19th-century West, later immortalized in films such as *Red River* (1948) and *Chisum* (1970), both starring the inimitable John Wayne, and the Pulitzer Prize–winning novel *Lonesome Dove* (1985), by Larry McMurtry (which was almost immediately adapted into an award-wining miniseries starring Robert Duvall and Tommy Lee Jones). In reality, cattle drives offered more grime than glamour and proved to be dusty and dangerous treks across miles of open land to railheads far to the north, in places like Abilene, Ellsworth, Wichita, and Dodge City—all in Kansas. These overland treks were only necessary because railroads had not yet reached Texas.

Driving these herds, of course, were mostly young men who collectively would become famous the world over as cowboys. Beholden to no one, the cowboy is mythologized as a solitary figure in the expansive nothingness of the Great Plains, embodying the very idea of freedom and limitless possibility. His image has sold nearly every product imaginable, perhaps most famously Marlboro cigarettes. The real cowboy, however, was a decidedly different character than his imaginary counterpart. Certainly, the job offered romance and freedom of a sort in the cattle drives, but the cowboy was a relatively low-wage worker, paid only during the drives north and then (unless bringing a herd back to winter in Texas) on their own. When Charles Siringo signed on to take a herd up the famous Chisholm Trail in 1874, he recalled, "My wages were thirty-five dollars per month and all expenses" (Siringo 2000, 52). That was not a princely sum but not bad for few months' work. Financial stability, ultimately, came not from working as a hired hand but in establishing one's own herd and going into business for oneself.

As a group, cowboys were also among the most racially diverse workforces in the United States at the time. Certainly, Anglo-Texans became the most famous cattlemen, and entrepreneurs such as Charlie Goodnight and Richard King became wealthy and powerful men. But their cowboys might have been white, African American, or Mexican American. Bose Ikard, likely the most famous African American cowboy, worked for Oliver Loving and Charles Goodnight. He and Goodnight became lifelong friends, both living until the 1929. Goodnight even purchased a gravestone for his old friend that read, "Bose Ikard served with me four years on the Goodnight-Loving Trail, never shirked a duty or disobeyed an order, rode with me in many stampedes, participated in three engagements with Comanches, splendid behavior" (Blackman 2020). The highest percentage of African American cowboys could be found in Texas and New Mexico. Indeed, in the heyday of the cattle trails just after the Civil War, cowboying would have offered a good job for former slaves that likely kept them away from the worst of the racism endemic in more settled areas.

Mexicans and Tejanos also frequented the cattle trails, and, indeed, most of the techniques required for successful cowboying on the open plains originated in the Mexican cattle industry. Mexican cowboys were vital in the establishment of longhorn herds, as the cunning cattle often kept close to the timber and brambles that protected them. In Texas, even the vegetation is well armed; chasing cattle into the brush meant contending with cat claw, mesquite, and cacti—all bristling with thorns. Yet, Mexican *vaqueros* (cowboys) could pursue the beasts into their sheltered haunts. One Anglo cowboy marveled at their skills, writing, "It took courage, skill and endurance to bring these cattle out of the thickets where they hid by day. Often we worked by moonlight—when they would come out into the open to feed. Then the band of vaqueros (Mexican cowboys) would burst upon the herd with lariats twirling" (quoted in De Léon 2014). Once rounded up, these Mexican cowboys drove their apprehended cattle to collection spots in Texas towns like

Victoria, Goliad, or San Antonio. From there, the herds would be driven north to Kansas.

Mexican and Tejano cowboys certainly accompanied herds north as part of larger cattle drives. Despite their typically superior experience, Mexican vaqueros made less money than their Anglo counterparts. Most made between $10 and $12 a month, though south Texas rancher Richard King paid his vaqueros between $25 and $30 a month while on cattle drives, but still less than his Anglo cowboys (De Léon 2014). Little acknowledged at the time, Mexicans and Tejanos certainly played important roles in the development of the cattle industry.

Every summer, for almost two decades, Texas cowboys drove herds north to railheads, a journey that took several months given the need to allow the cattle time to graze and add bulk as they ambled north. For cowboys, daily life on the trail fell quickly into a routine—usually. Driving cattle north meant living weeks in the open. Extra horses (each cowboy rode as many as six different horses during the long trip) and equipment followed in wagons, and each day the herds made slow but inexorable progress north. All decisions fell to the trail boss, who managed the entire operation. The best and most experienced cowboys typically rode at the front of the herd and along the sides. Less experienced hands took up the rear.

Perhaps the chuck wagon, a mobile kitchen, was the most important amenity on the trails—for hungry cowboys at least. To be sure, the fare was simple: coffee, beans, bacon, biscuits, and so on. Better cooks might occasionally include some desserts, like cobblers. Intrepid cattleman Charles Goodnight is credited with inventing the chuck wagon as part of his 1866 drive from Texas along the Pecos River to Fort Sumner, New Mexico Territory, where the government had interred the Navajo and a few hundred Apache. Goodnight's cattle sale to the government proved profitable and opened a new route that came to be known as the Goodnight-Loving Trail.

Workdays began around sunrise and continued until bedding the cattle down at night. With the summer sun beating down, the days could be hot and dull as the cattle grazed northward. The plains, however, are a capricious landscape, and the hot days often generated thunderstorms that swept across the plains with driving rain, hail, and tornadoes. Such storms could make cattle jittery and prone to the thing cowboys feared the most: the stampede. Siringo described just such an incident: "The night began to storm terribly. The herd began to drift early and by midnight we were five or six miles from camp." Despite their efforts to calm the cattle, "about one o'clock they stampeded in grand shape." He continued, "The herd split up in a dozen different bunches—each bunch going in a different direction. Of course, all I could do was to keep in front or in the lead and try to check them up" (Siringo 2000, 52–53).

Other hazards threatened both man and beast. River crossings were among the most dangerous events on the entire trail. Spring melt and thunderstorms could flood rivers, making crossings difficult. In one story, a vaquero and his horse were hit by a floating log while crossing the engorged Red River, which knocked him from his horse and into the water. A companion jumped in after him, but both men drowned (De León 2014).

After weeks on the trail, cattle drives finally ended at one of the towns that had sprung up along the lines of the railroads. Most famous, or perhaps notorious, was Dodge City, Kansas. Dodge City did not come about by accident. The Santa Fe Trail clung to the north bank of the Arkansas River before crossing and heading southwest. A small hill overlooked the crossing with spectacular, unobstructed view for miles in any direction. The army recognized the strategic importance of the site and sent a detachment of soldiers to establish a fort there in 1865. Fort Dodge became a base of operations for the next decade. More importantly, enterprising individuals realized the economic potential of the site once the Atchison, Topeka and the Santa Fe (AT&SF) railroad arrived. With the railroad's arrival imminent by 1872, a group of Fort Dodge officers, local merchants, and government contractors set about creating a townsite. After a year of paperwork and controversy, the group formally took control of the townsite in June 1873. Unlike the Santa Fe Trail, the AT&SF did not cross the river and head southwest, preferring instead a generally westerly course toward the coalfields of southern Colorado. Thus, Dodge City sat at the southernmost tip of rail, and beyond that, all the way to New Mexico, lay open, largely undisturbed prairie.

Buffalo hunters made the town their base of operations. Hide hunters carried their plunder to Dodge City and loaded it onto railcars for the trip east. As the hide trade quickly burned itself out with the eradication of the vast bison herds, city leaders looked for new clients to fill their hotels and saloons. In 1874, a Kansas City newspaper correspondent described the citizenry of Dodge in typically hyperbolic 19th-century terms as "full of vim and pluck that knows no such word as fail, and . . . determined, if genuine energy and enterprise can accomplish an object to make their town the leading city of Western Kansas" (Dykstra 1968, 59). Fortunately, these plucky and vim-filled citizens had another source of potential income that would support their fledgling town and establish its reputation for all time: cattle.

The AT&SF recognized the town's potential as early as its citizens, writing in 1875, "The country about Wichita is becoming so well settled that the tendency will be to drive more cattle to Great Bend; and it may be necessary, the coming season, to prepare a point of shipment still farther West" (Dykstra 1968, 59). Dodge City would become that point farther west. By 1877, settlement and the fear of Texas fever had finally doomed the Chisholm Trail to Wichita, making the Western Trail to Dodge the increasingly popular choice. One Kansas City newspaper declared the town "the great bovine market of the world" (Dykstra 1968, 62). The facts supported such optimistic declarations. In 1877, cattlemen loaded 22,940 head of cattle onto AT&SF cars that season, a full quarter of all cattle shipped over the line and ahead of even the much larger city of Wichita. Dodge City had arrived.

In addition to the tens of thousands of cattle arriving yearly, hundreds of cowboys also made it to the end of the trail. Paid for their services, these cowboys had plenty of money to their names, and most seemed more than happy to part with some of it for pleasures they had been deprived of on the long ride north. All parted with some of their money, but it seems likely that some parted with all of their money in a few days of drunken frivolity. Joe McCoy, a cattle buyer and later mayor of Abilene, Kansas, noted, "The barroom, the theater, the gambling room, the bawdy house, the dance house, each and all come in for their full share of attention. . . . Such is the manner in which the cowboy spends his hard-earned dollars" (Dykstra 1968, 100). Another declared of Dodge City that "the cowboy spends his money recklessly. He is a jovial, careless fellow bent on having a big time regardless of expense. He will make away with the wages of half a year in a few weeks, and then go back to his herds for another six months" (Dykstra 1968, 100).

Certainly, not all cowboys frittered away their money in alcohol-fueled bacchanals; many spent money on necessities. Food, naturally, was in great demand, and grocery stores did big business. Mercantile stores, barbershops, tailors, saddle and tack shops, and boot makers also did good business, replacing items lost or worn out along the trails.

Saloon owners, professional gamblers, and prostitutes all redistributed the wealth of trail-tired cowboys. During the peak of the cattle drives in the early 1870s, Abilene, Kansas, had some 11 saloons; in 1873, the town of Ellsworth had roughly 10; and Wichita, a bit larger, had 15 that year. Dodge City had 14 saloons in 1878. These ranged from rundown shacks to opulent palaces, such as the Long Branch in Dodge City or the Bull's Head Saloon in Abilene, with felt billiards tables, mirrored walls, and brass and mahogany bars. Gambling proved a popular diversion in these establishments, either sponsored by the owner of the saloon or organized by individual gamblers. Prostitutes also frequented saloons and dance halls, often employed by the business itself, though independent prostitutes also operated within the cattle towns. Many of these independent "working girls" appeared during the summer months, when cowboys arrived with their herds, and disappeared when the weather turned cold. One correspondent for the Dodge City *Globe* explained how the dance halls worked, writing that the typical dance hall "was a long frame building, with a hall and bar in front and sleeping rooms in the rear. The hall was nightly used for dancing, and was frequented by prostitutes, who belonged to the house and for the benefit of it solicited male visitors to dance" (Dykstra 1968, 106). The back rooms, of course, served purposes other than dancing.

Alcohol, gambling, and the attentions of women provided the conditions for conflict, and cattle towns developed a notorious reputation for violence. Just how violent is a subject of debate among scholars to this day. The populations of cattle towns and mining camps were extremely male and young. In southwestern Kansas, including Dodge City, there were 768 men for every woman in 1870; by 1880, the number had dropped to a ratio of 124 to 1 (Courtwright 1996, 58). So many men and so many potential sources of conflict could easily lead to violence, and indeed it did. By one estimate, the rate of homicides in Dodge City was 116 per 100,000 residents, and in Fort Griffin, Texas, the rate may have been as high as 229 per 100,000 in the early 1870s. Someone living in or visiting a town like Dodge or Fort Griffin was at least 10 times more likely to be murdered there than in more settled Midwestern or Eastern areas (Courtwright 1996, 96–97).

Containing the violence as much as possible fell to local police forces, who often mandated that visitors turn over their firearms on arrival—laws that were, at best, unevenly enforced. Frontier lawmen developed reputations for courage, which were often inflated by their portrayals in dime novels. Several famous Western gunmen, most notably Wyatt Earp and Wild Bill Hickok, wore the badge of law enforcement at various times in their careers, but on other occasions, they found themselves on the other side of the law.

Wyatt Earp embodies the contradictions of early lawmen and the power of myth to transform a select few into legends. Earp, the fourth of eight children, came into the world in Monmouth, Illinois, in 1848. He was the third of five brothers, with James and Virgil being older and Morgan and Warren younger. After a brief and unsuccessful sojourn in California, the family returned to Illinois in 1868. In Illinois and Missouri, young Wyatt dabbled in law enforcement, even being elected local constable of Lamar, Missouri. But following the death of his wife in 1870, his life took a turn toward the illegal. In 1871, he was arrested for dealing in stolen horses but escaped from jail before trial.

Earp reinvented himself in the cattle towns in Kansas, but he straddled the line between law enforcer and lawbreaker for years. James Earp and his wife, Bessie, ran a brothel in Illinois, but seeing greener pastures in Kansas, they moved operations to Wichita in 1873. Wyatt, by all accounts a handsome and imposing figure, lived in the bordello with James and Bessie (and several working girls who had taken the name "Earp" but were not related by blood or marriage). He most likely worked as a bouncer in his brother's establishment. As part of the Wichita demi-monde, the Earps made no real effort to hide their activities. The 1875 Kansas state census, for example, lists Bessie's occupation as "sporting," a euphemism for prostitution. Court records also show a variety of fines for prostitution for Bessie and other female "Earps." Such fines amounted to taxes. Local officials might have looked the other way when it came to prostitution, but they were not above fines and bribes of various sorts, which was surely the cost of doing business for brothel owners. The fines for the Earp's establishment ended in 1875, however, a few months after Wyatt took a position with the police force—surely not a coincidence.

Wyatt also worked as professional gambler from time to time, both independently and as a dealer for gambling halls. By all accounts, he was a master of the card game faro. Although easy to learn, a complex series of bets and the speed of the hands dealt made for a dizzying array of possibilities. A dealer, often with an assistant, kept track of all the variations of possible bets. An honest dealer had a slight advantage over other players, but frontier casinos were often far from fair. Experienced dealers often "shaved" cards by slightly bending them up or down, which meant that they could tell by feel what cards they were holding even if the bends were not discernible to the eye. Such trickery made the dealer almost unbeatable. Another common scam involved having someone pose as a novice player. This beginner would place a large bet and, predictably, win big. His success then convinced others that winning was easy, and the money would flow. Wyatt Earp, an experienced dealer, almost certainly participated in these and other nefarious schemes.

During his stint on the Wichita police force, from 1875 to 1876, Wyatt began to earn acclaim as a fearless lawman, willing to use his fists and guns to bring in the bad guys—or at least that was how he would later describe his career. While he certainly exaggerated his exploits, there is little doubt that Earp realized that being a "good guy" carried something more valuable than ill-gotten money, namely public adoration and increased social status—rewards coveted by a young man with a checkered past. Yet, after two years on the force, Earp abruptly left Wichita and moved to Dodge City.

Wyatt, his own self-mythologizer, claimed he made the move at the behest of the mayor of Dodge, who personally wrote to him, after having heard of his skills as a lawman, to come to Dodge City to bring law and order to the unruly cattle town. More likely, he fled after severely beating Bill Smith, a political opponent of his boss, Mike Meagher, in a fistfight. His arrest for disturbing the peace and dismissal from the police force meant he needed a job and a new start. Dodge City seemed just the place.

Dodge City's leading citizens relied on the money the cattle trade brought to their town. Indeed, without the annual cattle drives, there did not seem to be any reason for the town to exist. Leading citizens, bankers, lawyers, and cattle dealers, however, did not want their homes, businesses, and churches overrun by drunken, uncouth cowboys. Thus, the vice district existed on the southside of town, squeezed between the Arkansas River and the railroad tracks, and respectable middle-class citizens resided on the northside, protected from the rough and tumble cowboys. Enforcing this line and protecting the respectable classes from the riffraff fell to police officers like Wyatt, and the job certainly offered its hazards.

Despite the town's weapons ban, many cowboys still carried weapons on their persons. Armed, drunk, and quick to answer any affronts to their masculinity or honor, cowboys could be dangerous and unpredictable. Dodge's marshal, Ed Masterson, the older brother of Ford County Sheriff Bat Masterson, died while trying to disarm a drunken cowboy in a Dodge saloon. Shot at close range in the abdomen, Masterson killed his assailant and another cowboy but soon succumbed to his wounds. A few months later, Wyatt or Bat Masterson killed George Hoy as he tried to flee from town over a bridge on the Arkansas River. Wyatt and Masterson were also involved in another shooting during their time in Dodge, wounding James Kennedy after he killed Dora Hand, the woman he apparently loved but who was the "companion" of Dodge's mayor, James "Dog" Kelley. After the killing, Kennedy fled but was pursued, wounded, and captured by a posse led by Masterson. By the time Earp left Dodge City for the mining town of Tombstone, Arizona Territory, he had already become regionally famous. The gunfight in Tombstone would make him world famous (Isenberg 2013, 77–103).

Like mining towns in the Rockies, cattle towns enjoyed seasons of robust commerce and high profits. Unlike those mining towns, many of which simply disappeared when the minerals played out, towns like Dodge City continued after the boom years of the 1870s. The cattle drives ended as cattle operations spread across the West and railroads finally arrived in Texas. The boom years of the 1870s now gone, these towns became sedate and more mature as banking and mercantile centers for the farms and ranches around them, and those on rail lines, like Dodge City and Wichita, continued to prosper.

The cattle industry spread beyond Texas as ranchers took advantage of an open range that extended from Canada to Mexico. Charles Goodnight established a large ranch near Palo Duro Canyon in the Texas Panhandle at a time when the Comanche had not yet fully surrendered. His Goodnight-Loving Trail also drove cattle north into Colorado. John Iliff, who began as a rancher by buying broken down cattle and oxen off overland trail emigrants, soon amassed large herds east of Denver, which he sold to famished miners at high prices. Even larger ranches developed thanks to the arrival of railroads and an influx of investment capital from wealthy Easterners and Europeans. Following the destruction of the Texas State Capitol in 1881, the perennially cash-strapped state decided to sell three million acres of its public domain to Chicago investors to finance the construction of a new state capitol building in Austin. The investors formed the XIT Ranch in the Panhandle, whose borders, north to south, stretched almost 250 miles.

The XIT's well-defined and surveyed borders were the exception to the rule for cattle ranches on the plains. Needing only the grass and water, cattlemen cared little for the land, and only once in competition with other operations did they begin to take pains to assert control over the range. Springs and river access in the semi-arid plains would be the first places cattlemen would try to exert control, and to accomplish this, some turned to a new and controversial technology: barbed wire.

In the arid West, the absence of trees for fencing and the amount of land one would need to fence precluded the extensive fencing of pasturage that had occurred in Eastern states. Barbed wire changed that. Fences would not be composed entirely out of wood, as in the East. Instead, wooden posts would be connected with strands of the durable wire, making it possible to fence large areas relatively easily and cheaply.

Fencing with barbed wire, soon to be common across the West, really took off in central Texas in the early 1880s. The drought year of 1883 browned the grasses and dried up many of the springs and small streams that traversed the area. Cattlemen turned to barbed wire to fence off water holes for their cattle, depriving their neighbor's herds of the precious resource. Fences soon popped up all across the area, cutting off public roads and impeding movement and the delivery of mail. Churches and houses found themselves fenced off. These moves, often by larger operators, particularly galled smaller cattlemen who did not have the land and access to water to continue their operations. In retaliation, clandestine groups, with names like the Owls, Javelinas, and Blue Devils, cut the fences in the dead of night, often leaving threatening signs not to rebuild them. At least three men died in confrontations between fence cutters and fence building ranchers.

The growing violence and turmoil forced the hand of Texas governor John Ireland, who ordered a special legislative session to deal with the crisis in 1884. The legislature made fence cutting a felony punishable by up to five years in prison, but they also required ranchers to build gates on public roads. These measures mostly worked, though fence-cutting cases would continue sporadically for years to come. Barbed wire, however, would hasten the end of the open range (Gard 2019).

With opaque ownership of land and the availability of unbranded cattle that could be siphoned off, cattlemen often had to enforce their rights with violence. Two of the most famous episodes of violence in the West began this way: the Lincoln County War of the 1870s and the Johnson County War of 1889. The former began as a dispute between rival cattle and mercantile operations in eastern New Mexico, and the latter pitted larger cattlemen against smaller ranchers. Both occurred in areas where legal institutions were ineffective or nonexistent and where corruption and business malfeasance were the rules and not the exceptions.

The Lincoln County War was—along with the perhaps the gunfight at the O.K. Corral—the most iconic event in the violent history of gunfighters in the entire Wild West because it featured perhaps the most famous outlaw of all in Henry McCarty, alias William H. Bonney, but known to posterity as Billy the Kid. Henry was born in 1859 in New York City to Catherine McCarty, an Irish immigrant, one of the millions then immigrating to the United States. Supposedly widowed, Catherine moved with Henry and her other son, Joe, to Indianapolis. It was there that she met Bill Antrim. Eventually, Bill, Catherine, and the boys relocated to New Mexico, most likely in search of a climate cure for Catherine's tuberculosis. Bill married Catherine in Santa Fe in 1873, with teenage Henry in attendance at his mother's wedding. Shortly after the exchange of vows, the now official family moved to the mining camp of Silver City. Unfortunately, the fresh dry air of New Mexico did not work its magic on Catherine. After four months of being bedridden, the dreaded "consumption," the common name for tuberculosis, took her on September 16, 1874. This proved a pivotal moment in young Henry's life. Bill left the boys for months at a time, prospecting in Arizona, but Henry did his best to provide for his brother and himself by working at a local butcher shop. Young Henry loved to sing, dance, and read in his spare time, hardly the expected pursuits of an outlaw in training (Utley 1991, 1–6).

Without the stabilizing influence of his mother, Henry now had ample time to get in trouble. His first crime occurred when he stole several pounds of butter. His next illegal activity occurred in the company of a friend, George Shaffer, the pair stealing some clothes from a Chinese-owned laundry. Arrested and thrown into jail (mostly to teach the boy a lesson), the boy resolved to escape, shimmying his way up a chimney and to freedom. While the local newspaper made light of the crime and subsequent escape, young Henry convinced himself that he was now a fugitive from the law, and so he left Silver City (Utley 1991, 7–8).

Fifteen-year-old Henry wandered around southern New Mexico, working as a cowboy and eventually falling in with some cattle rustlers. He learned the intricacies of cowboying and developed a proficiency with firearms. Henry's life would change forever on the night of August 17, 1877. In George Atkins's saloon near Fort Grant, young Henry got into an altercation with "Windy" Cahill, a noted blowhard and bully who had been tormenting the "kid" for some time. That evening, the kid reached his limit, and during a scuffle, he drew his pistol and shot Cahill in the gut. He died the next day. Whether Henry would have been tried for murder given Cahill's behavior is debatable, but he fled before charges could be brought. His short and violent career as a killer had begun.

The Kid made his way to Lincoln County, an expansive county of 30,000 square miles (roughly the size of South Carolina) composed of open, treeless prairie with furrowed ridges of mountains reaching to almost 12,000 feet at the top of Sierra Blanca. The few settlements, including the town of Lincoln, clung to the sparse mountain streams that flowed down to a confluence with the Pecos River to the east. While running with the Evans gang of New Mexico, a band of horse thieves and outlaws, Henry took the name William Bonney, but many still referred to him as the Kid. The Kid would soon be entangled in the disputes of far more powerful men.

Two factions vied for control of the cattle and mercantile trades near Lincoln. The upstart faction consisted of a young English cattleman named John Tunstall, who ran a ranch about 30 miles from Lincoln, and Lincoln attorney Alexander McSween. Tunstall and McSween also owned a store in Lincoln that directly competed with the other more established faction of Lawrence Murphy and Jimmy Dolan. Tunstall and McSween hoped to challenge the monopoly of the Murphy/Dolan faction, which offered credit to ranchers and farmers for a variety of dry goods. In a largely cashless economy, the farmers and ranchers repaid their debts in cattle and produce, which could then be resold to the government, at a hefty markup, at nearby Fort Stanton, where the government fed the defeated Mescalero Apache.

Dolan and Murphy, his mentor, used a variety of tactics to intimidate their competition. Indeed, the criminal activity of Jesse Evans's gang appears to have been orchestrated by the two men. Evans apparently was a member of "the Boys," gunmen that Jimmy Dolan relied on to enforce his designs. When Evans ran afoul of the law, he was, predictably, broken out of jail by a group of gunmen (including William Bonney) in November 1877. Lincoln Sheriff William Brady was friendly to Lawrence Murphy and did nothing to prevent the escape. Young Billy, however, left the gang shortly after the breakout (Utley 1991, 32–35).

Billy soon fell in with Dick Brewer, the foreman of Tunstall's operation, and this friendship would help move him into the Tunstall/McSween group. By the end of 1877, in fact, Billy was on the payroll of Tunstall's ranch. Tunstall had quietly been recruiting his own group of hired gunmen to counter Dolan's Boys. Tunstall's cowboys tended to be in their late teens and early twenties. Tunstall himself was only 24, but his education and relative wealth set him apart.

By 1878, the competition between the two factions had reached a boiling point. Dolan charged that McSween had embezzled a valuable life insurance policy and convinced the court in a civil suit to hold in surety the assets of McSween and Tunstall until the funds from the policy were paid. This effectively closed Tunstall's store. Sheriff Brady also decided to collect Tunstall's cattle and sent out some men to round them up. The posse included Evans and other members of the Boys. After some tense words in front of Tunstall's ranch house, the posse retreated but threatened to return with more men. Both factions prepared for an escalation, which came on February 18, 1878, when gunmen killed Tunstall as he was riding in a wagon. To complicate matters, Alexander McSween turned to John B. Wilson, the justice of the peace, to supply warrants for the arrest of Tunstall's killers, and Tunstall's own men would serve the warrants after being deputized. Thus, both factions could claim to be legitimate enforcers of the law. Following the leadership of Dick Brewer, this group, including Billy, called themselves the "Regulators." What had begun as a commercial dispute had escalated into open war, and for the few remaining years the Kid had left, he would be in the thick of it (Utley 1991, 39–54).

While both sides claimed to be enforcing the law, Dolan, with important connections, could draw support from the most powerful elements in New Mexico, including U.S. District Attorney General Thomas B. Catron. Catron and territorial governor Samuel B. Axtell both sided with Dolan (Catron held a mortgage on Dolan's operations and thus had an economic interest in its success) and removed the justice of the peace, John Wilson, from office. The Regulators lost their veneer of legality and now became outlaws. Their ambush and murder of Sheriff Brady on April 1, 1878, also turned public opinion against them; previously, they had been seen as in the right, but the brazen murder of Brady changed that. By June, Billy and several other Regulators had been indicted for the killing of Sheriff Brady and, a few days later, the murder of Andrew "Buckshot" Roberts (Utley 1991, 84).

The climax of the Lincoln County War occurred with the five-day "battle of Lincoln" in which McSween, with some 60 men, including a substantial number of Hispanic New Mexicans, made their stand against Dolan's forces. For several tense days, the sides traded shots, but the arrival of federal troops under the command of Lt. Colonel Nathan Dudley turned the battle in favor of Dolan's men. Though the federal soldiers did not fight, their clear support for the Dolan faction sent McSween's supporters fleeing after seeing the superior weaponry of the soldiers, which included an artillery piece and a Gatling gun, an early machine gun. The remaining men, including McSween and Billy, made a daring nighttime escape. Billy and four others made it, but McSween died in a chaotic exchange of gunfire in the early morning hours of July 19. The Tunstall/McSween faction was no more, but Dolan fared little better, as the costs of the war drove him into bankruptcy. Many men had paid with their lives for the ambitions of Tunstall, McSween, and Dolan.

Billy and the surviving Regulators fled to the Texas Panhandle; all were now hunted men. By fall, the Regulators had broken up, and most left the area, except Billy and his close friend Tom O'Folliard. For the next three years, the Kid lived on the run, even staging a famous and daring escape from jail, but his luck finally ran out in the predawn hours of July 15, 1881, at Fort Sumner, New Mexico. Stumbling into his room, he came face to face with Pat Garrett, a sometime friend but now sheriff of Lincoln County and a deputy U.S. marshal. Each man, it seems, was surprised by the other's sudden appearance, and in the dark, they drew and fired, Garrett's bullet finding its mark. Later that day, the Kid was laid to rest next to his friends from the Lincoln County War, Tom O'Folliard and Charley Bowdre, both killed by Garrett's posse the previous year (Utley 1991, 192–195). Dead at 21, Billy the Kid would live on in legend.

The trouble in Johnson County began when wealthy ranch owners—known as the cattle barons—organized the Wyoming Stock Growers Association. The barons hoped to use the organization to crowd out smaller cattle operations. The late 1880s had been hard for cattlemen. The terrible winter of 1886–1887, when temperatures plummeted well below zero and blizzards drove cattle before the winds like fallen leaves, had left tens of thousands of cattle dead and entire ranches bankrupt. Declining prices also hurt profitability, and the larger ranchers, desperate to survive these pressures, targeted smaller operators.

At issue was the status of maverick cattle, the unbranded cattle that belonged to whomever successfully branded them first. Large Wyoming ranches rounded up the mavericks along with their other cattle and added them to their herds. Individual cowboys, however, sometimes took these cattle for themselves and branded them under their own brands. Undoubtedly, some of these cattle belonged to their employers. Skimming a few mavericks out of their boss's herds had long been one way a cowboy could begin to amass his own cattle herd, and normally such practices did not attract too much attention. Indeed, many of the smaller ranchers had started out as cowboys themselves, particularly in Johnson County. The larger cattle ranchers, however, decided the time had come to crack down on the practice, which they denounced as cattle rustling.

While some rustling may have occurred, it did not rise to the levels that the larger cattlemen claimed. At first, the barons turned to the courts, but in Johnson County, the courts would not convict any of the smaller ranchers for rustling. When legal measures did not work, the big ranchers decided to turn to extralegal strategies, including intimidation and lynching. In 1889, a group of gunmen lynched James Averell, a small ranch owner, and Ella Watson. Watson, known as Cattle Kate, allegedly worked as a prostitute, exchanging sex for stolen cattle to create her own herd—or at least Cheyenne newspapers (sympathetic to the cattle barons) claimed.

More lynchings and killings followed, and the large operators escalated the situation further by recruiting a private army of two dozen hired guns from Texas. Eager to bring suspected rustlers to "justice," the hired army and their employers took a special train from Cheyenne to Casper on April 5, 1892, and from there, they rode on horseback to the small settlement of Buffalo, the Johnson County seat. The cattle barons asserted that Buffalo was the focal point of a huge rustling operation and a town populated almost entirely by "land pirates," where local authorities turned a blind eye to cattle theft. Buffalo's newspapers denounced these accusations as lies and claimed that large ranchers, branding every cow they came across, were the real villains.

This army of hired guns, ranch owners, and some selected and trusted men (most of the larger ranches' cowboys were not included in this operation, apparently because they could not be trusted) numbered approximately 50 gunmen. Disembarking from the train, they carried with them a hit list of suspected rustlers. They captured and lynched one suspected rustler and made their way toward the cabin of a cowboy named Nate Champion. Champion belonged to the fraternity of small ranchers and ran some 200 head of cattle on the public domain. While no evidence exists proving that Champion built his herd through rustling, it mattered little to the mob of gunmen.

Several gunmen burst into Champion's cabin. They opened fire as he went for his revolver, their shots missing him in the chaos. He, however, did not miss, wounding one and killing another. The rest retreated. One of the would-be assassins soon confessed to participating in the assault to two local ranchers, John A. Tisdale and Orley "Ranger" Jones. Based on this confession, local authorities charged Joe Elliott, a stock detective for the Wyoming Stock Growers' Association, for the attack on Champion. A few weeks later, however, both Tisdale and Jones were murdered before they could testify in court. Local newspapers called for the indictment of the cattle barons, who they alleged were behind the violence. In February 1892, Champion testified against Elliott, and it appeared that the options were running out for the large cattlemen. Thus, they hatched the plan to "invade" Johnson County with an army of gunmen.

Not surprisingly, Champion was at the top of their list as they returned to Johnson County; killing him would end the case against Elliott and cover their tracks. Spies informed the cattle barons that Champion had holed up at the nearby KC Ranch. The army made its way to the KC and ambushed Champion, who fought to the death, trading shots with the gunmen for at least four hours. He wounded three. It was only after setting fire to the ranch house that they were able to drive him into the open and kill him.

By now, word had gotten out, and hundreds of angry cowboys and small ranchers went after the gunmen. The assassins and their masters now found themselves hunted by at least 400 men. They retreated to the nearby T.A. Ranch with a mob, bent on revenge, in hot pursuit. For three days, the besieged gunmen held out against the posse of cowboys and small ranch owners, many of them Civil War veterans.

When the gunmen retreated to the shelter of the ranch house, they left behind several wagons, including one loaded with dynamite. The surrounding forces decided to fortify this wagon, ram it into the ranch house, and detonate the dynamite. Fortunately, soldiers from nearby Fort McKinney arrived and took the "invaders" into custody before the wagon bomb could be used (Davis 2014). Amazingly, the only death in those three days was a Texas gunman who accidentally shot himself in the groin (White 1991, 346).

The cavalry's arrival at the last minute became a common enough trope in later Western films, but their rescue of the besieged barons was not by chance. When news of the siege, involving some of the wealthiest men in Wyoming, reached the governor, Amos Barber, he immediately wired President Harrison for help from federal troops. The soldiers turned their captives over to the governor, a personal friend of many of the accused. Eight months later, the gunmen and their employers stood trial in Cheyenne, and the charges were quickly dropped against them (Davis 2014). The wealthy and powerful had evaded any culpability for the war they had created.

The governor paid for his participation, though, by losing reelection and taking the Wyoming Republican party with him. Realizing they had lost, the Cattle Growers' Association opened up its ranks to the smaller cattlemen, ending much of the rancor between the two groups. Further, in Wyoming and elsewhere, ranchers were also increasingly fencing in their lands and relying less on the public domain, which in turn lessened the opportunities for conflict.

Weather, more than conflict, brought about the greatest changes to the cattle industry. The terrible winter of 1886–1887 brought unprecedented death and destruction to the Great Plains. After a hot and dry summer, cattle went into the winter in poor condition, and the cattlemen, accustomed to letting their animals largely fend for themselves, did nothing to help them get through the lean winter months. Surely, with so much open range, they could find forage and shelter somewhere on the plains; they always had before. But on January 9, 1887, a blizzard of previously unimaginable severity gripped the plains. Temperatures plummeted to 50 degrees below zero, and nearly two feet of snow blanketed the plains and buried the grass. Millions of cattle died from exposure and starvation. Driven before the storm, herds sometimes foundered against fences, and hundreds of animals froze against the barriers.

Millions of cattle died, and numerous ranches collapsed, including Theodore Roosevelt's cattle operation in North Dakota. Those ranchers who remained changed their practices. They would no longer let their cattle roam over huge expanses to fend for themselves. Now they would fence in their range and provide stored hay to feed their cattle in the hard months of winter. Others diversified, some augmenting cattle raising with sheep. The era of the open ranges was effectively over.

RAILROADS, TELEGRAPHS, AND DAILY LIFE IN A SHRINKING WORLD

Far more than hostile Indians or bands of outlaws, the real enemies to the American conquest of the West were space and time. Early explorers in the West struggled to comprehend the distances. Lewis and Clark spent two years getting halfway across the continent, from St. Louis to the Pacific and back. Snow-clad mountains and scorching deserts where rain fell sporadically or not at all—landscapes unfamiliar and terrifying to a people accustomed to the greenery of the East—presented seemingly unconquerable obstacles to Anglo-American agrarian civilization.

Zebulon Pike, reporting back from his 1805 to 1807 expedition across the Great Plains, Rockies, and Mexico, warned that the environments he passed through would never be permanently settled. The plains, he asserted, were characterized by "a barren soil, parched and dried up for eight months in the year. . . . These vast plains of the western hemisphere may become in time as celebrated as the sandy deserts of Africa" (quoted in Pierce 2016, 34).

A decade later, Stephen Harriman Long parroted Pike's concerns about aridity and the wild swings in temperature from midday to nighttime that surely would not be favorable for American settlement. Vast and foreboding, the center of the continent seemed to challenge the prospects of a continental nation. In the heart of the continent, Long believed, lay the "Great American Desert."

The writer Washington Irving, touring Indian Territory in the 1830s, went even further than Pike and Long. He doubted that the center of North America could ever be settled and tamed. Instead, he asserted that it would be a lawless no-man's-land, a place where the worst examples of Anglos, Indians, and Spaniards would breed together and create a new race that survived through raiding, murder, and theft. He wrote, "Here may spring up new and mongrel races, like new formations in geology, the amalgamation of the 'debris' and 'abrasions' of former races, civilized and savage; the remains of broken and almost extinguished tribes; of fugitives from the Spanish and American frontiers; of adventurers and desperadoes of every class and country, yearly ejected from the bosom of society into the wilderness" (quoted in Pierce 2016, 38). These were not optimistic endorsements.

Yet, a thousand miles west of the Mississippi River, the lush Pacific coast beckoned. American sailors had long been extolling the virtues of the coast, particularly California. The American sailor (and Harvard dropout) Richard Henry Dana visited California at roughly the same time Irving wandered around Indian Territory. Dana, engaged in the hide trade, sold American products to Mexican Californians for leather hides. Its natural resources, ports, long growing seasons, and perpetually temperate climate transfixed Dana. Yet, California had not been properly developed, neglected first by the Spanish and now by the Mexicans, he felt. He lamented, "In the hands of an enterprising people what a country this might be" (quoted in Pierce 2016, 52). A decade later, Americans would indeed gain control of California, but what should they do with the vast, harsh landscape between the Mississippi River and the Pacific coast?

Certainly, the distance could be crossed, as hundreds of thousands of overland trail emigrants proved in the 1840s and 1850s, but the hazardous crossing took the better part of six months. To integrate the West and tap into its extensive resources, faster modes of communication and transportation would be necessary. Fortunately, both had been recently developed. The locomotive and the telegraph would together alter the course of world history and make the United States into a truly continental nation.

When the United States officially won its independence from Great Britain in 1783, the treaty stipulated that the new nation extended to the eastern bank of the Mississippi River. There would be some turmoil surrounding the right of American farmers to deposit goods in New Orleans, as that city lay in the hands of Spain (and France again), but that issue was solved with the Louisiana Purchase of 1803. As President Jefferson understood, the Mississippi River was critical to U.S. economic interests. Farmers in the Ohio Valley could use the Ohio River to transport bulky produce at very low cost to the Mississippi and then down the Mississippi to New Orleans, where oceangoing ships could carry it to market in larger cities. River systems (the Ohio, Cumberland, Tennessee, and, of course, the mighty Mississippi) served as highways, allowing for the cheap transportation of a variety of goods.

The West, however, had no such advantages. The few large rivers, such as the Missouri, Columbia, and Colorado, were not suited to river transport. Lewis and Clark had managed to get a relatively large keelboat to the Mandan villages in North Dakota, but at great effort. To be sure, specially designed shallow-draft steamboats would eventually sail up the Missouri as far as North Dakota. The Columbia, meanwhile, could only be navigated safely to Portland, but rapids and waterfalls in the Columbia River Gorge and east made navigation impossible without expensive improvements. The Colorado, meanwhile, traversed a hopelessly desolate country, and for much of its course, it lay locked inside towering sandstone canyons. Relying on the West's rivers for transportation would therefore be impossible. Fortunately, as Americans headed into the region, a new technology offered to solve these impediments: the locomotive.

Although originally built to pump water out of flooded mines in Great Britain, the idea of using a steam engine to propel a vehicle did not take too long to develop. The American inventor Robert Fulton harnessed the steam engine's power in service of propelling a ship in 1807. Steamboats were soon chugging their way up the nation's rivers, and by the late 1830s, they carried passengers across the Atlantic Ocean in record time. The first decades of the 19th century also saw the steam engine fitted to primitive locomotives. In 1830, the locomotive the *Rocket* pulled a train from Liverpool to Manchester in Great Britain. By the 1840s, Great Britain had laid 1,400 miles of railroad track, the rest of Europe had 1,500, and the United States had already completed over 4,600 of track, almost all in the rapidly industrializing Northeast (Crosby 2007, 76). The South had comparatively few miles owing to the milder climate and the many navigable rivers, and the West, of course, had none. By the early 1850s, a few small railroads operated in California, bringing materials to port cities like San Francisco, but the West remained isolated from the rest of the nation. Railroad construction continued, and by the 1850s, lines had connected much of the agricultural Midwest. By midcentury, the technology had proven itself, making a transcontinental line to California feasible. Proposals to do so, however, ran into the sectional acrimony then tearing the nation apart. Put simply, where should a transcontinental line begin and end?

Southern politicians advocated for a route from New Orleans through Texas to California. Such a route, they claimed, would not be affected by terrible winter weather. Yet, most of the existing rail networks lay farther to the north, so Northerners argued the line should be somewhere north. Mired in the sectional divisions of the decade, efforts to create a transcontinental railroad went nowhere, kind of like the railroad itself. The Civil War changed that. With Southern opposition gone, Northern politicians were free to authorize the construction of a railroad on a route they preferred. However, there remained a problem.

In the settled East and Europe, railroads could build through existing towns, connecting them as they went, and these towns could serve as markets for the railroad's services. In the West, however, there were hardly any towns. The railroad would have to offer the supply before any demand for their services existed and hope that the new railroad would encourage settlers to build towns along their tracks, but if that happened, it would take years to develop. Dr. William A. Bell, a promoter for the Denver and Rio Grande Western Railway, a small regional railroad with track mostly in Colorado, examined the problem in his 1870 book *New Tracks in North America*. He explained that the West was a land of tremendous potential and untapped wealth, but it was an expansive region "where continuous settlement is impossible, where, instead of navigable rivers, we find arid deserts, but where, nevertheless, spots of great fertility and the richest prizes of the mineral kingdom tempt men onward into those vast regions." Here, he explained, "Railways become almost a necessity of existence—certainly of development; and the locomotive has to lead instead of follow the population" (quoted in Pierce 2016, 151).

Railroads would be among the most expensive projects ever undertaken, and private companies saw little potential for profit in such an expensive endeavor. Or as one bitter critic of the bankrupt Northern Pacific Railroad put it in 1873, it was no surprise that the line failed given that it was "a wild scheme to build a railroad from Nowhere, through No Man's Land, to No Place" (quoted in Pierce 2016, 152). The critic was not far from the truth. Railroads would be building an infrastructure that might not be fully used for decades. It would therefore fall to the government to encourage the building of transcontinental lines.

Congress understood this challenge of connecting to the Pacific coast and passing through endless miles of seemingly nothing, and they tried to address the lack of an existing market with the passage of the 1862 Pacific Railway Act. The act contained generous subsidies for the builders of the first line, the Central Pacific and Union Pacific, including low-interest loans to finance the construction and, most importantly, extensive land grants that could be sold. The legislation provided railroads "every alternate section of public land, designated by odd numbers, to the amount of five alternate sections per mile on each side of said railroad" (U.S. Congress 1862).

Thus, the railroad received alternating sections (each section containing 640 acres) on either side of their lines and extending outward like an enormous imaginary checkerboard. While the railroads did not have mineral rights in their grants, they did have rights to timber, and for some (like the Northern Pacific), the land and the timber on it would become more lucrative than the actual rail line. Congress justified this largess by explaining that the line would benefit the government by carrying mail, soldiers, and munitions as necessary.

The Pacific Railway Act was almost as transformative as the actual railroad it built. It ended years of debate about the role of government in financing "internal improvements," dramatically augmented the power and authority of the federal government, and the route, roughly following the 32nd parallel, tethered the West to the industrial Northeast. While not all Western railroads would receive grants, many did, and the federal government and some states, most notably Texas, collectively gave 223 million acres of land to railroad companies.

These lands could then be sold to settlers to generate revenue for the line and to create a market for the line's services. Alternatively, land, with physical existence and therefore tangible value, could also be used as collateral to take out additional loans. The scheme would be repeated with similar grants to other lines, though the largest went to the Northern Pacific, building from Minnesota to Washington State, which received, in some areas, alternating sections extending 50 miles on either side of its right of way. Such a massive giveaway of the public domain might seem extravagant, but it did serve as an effective inducement to build railroads where they otherwise would not have been feasible. In the short term, it cost the federal government little to offer land it only controlled on maps.

The Union Pacific and Central Pacific worked quickly, building toward each other at a frenetic pace. The Union Pacific set off from Omaha on December 2, 1863, its 10,000 workers (many of whom were Irish immigrants) toiling to build the grades and lay the track. Meanwhile, the Central Pacific tackled the imposing granite of the Sierra Nevada mountains almost immediately. For the Central Pacific, though, the first obstacle was finding a labor force large enough to build the railroad using little more than hand tools. California's high labor costs and goldfields, still producing in the late 1860s, meant that the Central Pacific could find few workers willing to take on the grueling task of building railroads for the low wages the company wanted to pay. Whites and Mexican Californians proved reluctant to perform the dangerous and backbreaking railroad work. With few options, Central Pacific reluctantly decided to recruit Chinese immigrants. By 1865, 80 percent of Central Pacific's workers were Chinese, some 10,000 or so chipping and blasting their way through some of the most inhospitable terrain on the continent.

Collectively, the workers of the two lines, in a friendly competition against each other, broke record after record for miles of track

Desperate for laborers, the Central Pacific turned to Chinese immigrants to build their line. With little more than picks, shovels, and gunpowder, these men dug a route through the rugged Sierra Nevada mountains. Hundreds died to complete the line. (Library of Congress)

laid, though the Union Pacific clearly had the easier terrain, building mostly across the open plains. Finally, on May 10, 1869, the lines met at Promontory Point, Utah, a little north of Salt Lake City. Company executives and assorted dignitaries gathered between two locomotives to drive several ceremonial railroad spikes into the last tie, signifying the completion of the railroad and, by extension, the connection of the continent. As the first transcontinental railroad ever created, the line became a symbol of American ingenuity and one that had been finished years ahead of schedule and under budget—although a lot of its construction had been slapdash, and many of the bridges and ties would need refurbishment soon after completion.

The other railroads given federal grants did not fare as well. None got anywhere near the Pacific coast, at least not initially. The Atchison, Topeka and Santa Fe hoped to reach the Pacific but had only made it to Albuquerque, New Mexico Territory, by 1879. The Kansas Pacific made it out of Kansas and all the way to Denver, but no farther. The Northern Pacific made it to Bismarck, North Dakota, but the continued presence of the Lakota and the collapse of the elaborate financing scheme on which the railroad had been built (which kick-started the Panic of 1873) meant it would go no farther for some time (White 1991, 250).

Nevertheless, these lines became large and powerful corporations, and the entrepreneurs at their heads, men like Leland Stanford, Collis P. Huntington, and Henry Villard, soon became among the richest men in the United States. Yet, these corporations, which would ostensibly make money by moving goods and people from place to place, were never terribly efficient at doing that, and the prices they charged often outraged their customers. The real money could be found in the more opaque and complicated aspects of building the railroads. The wealth of these financiers lay in "subsidies, the sale of securities, insider companies for the construction of the railroads themselves, and land speculation" (White 2011, xxviii). For example, the heads of the Central Pacific (Stanford, Huntington, Mark Hopkins, and Charlie Crocker) created a separate construction company to build the railroad. The Central Pacific, which they owned, gave over $90 million in contracts to the construction company, which they also owned, for work that only cost $32.2 million. They pocketed the profit, even as their railroad languished under heavy debt (White 1991, 249).

To facilitate these shady operations, railroad companies relied on backroom deals, bribery, and extensive lobbying of government officials. Similar to the Central Pacific, the major stockholders of the Union Pacific created the Crédit Mobilier company to build the line, guaranteeing lucrative contracts to the company, which would ensure that Crédit Mobilier would turn a profit even if the Union Pacific did not. The entire scheme, of course, was backed up by federal government loans. When more loans were needed, the financiers turned to Congress for additional support. To receive such support, the promoters of the Union Pacific created a massive slush fund, which they used to bribe members of Congress. Corruption became so widespread that an investigation revealed the complicity of dozens of congressmen, a secretary of the treasury, and many other lawmakers (White 1991, 249). The railroads helped create the modern infrastructure of the nation as well as a system of close (and sometimes too close) relationships between wealthy corporations and government officials.

Despite their failings, the transcontinental lines did connect the nation, allowing access to the West that transformed the region in a generation. Other regional railroads would soon be built, joining the larger lines like a series of tributary streams flowing into rivers. While man-made, the analogy between rivers and railroads is not so far off in that humid regions used river systems to move goods and people great distances. In the arid West, railroads provided a technological solution to accomplish the same function. By the peak of U.S. rail mileage around 1914, it was possible to go virtually anywhere in the comfort of a train. For mines, ranches, and farms, the arrival of the railroad meant access to global markets.

Yet, the sparsely populated West did not need so many railroads, and without a population to support them, there would not be a market for their services. Realizing this, railroads embarked on elaborate and expensive advertising campaigns to induce settlers to move to the land near their lines, especially on the Great Plains, which railroad promoters imagined would someday be populated by millions of hardworking farmers who would ship their produce to market over their lines and, in turn, order manufactured products from the East, which would be shipped back over the lines—raw materials going east and manufactured products heading west. It was the old colonial model, not unlike John Jacob Astor's scheme, but for the new of era of steam. But it would only work if there were settled societies planted in the West. With immigration onto the plains moving at a snail's pace, railroads realized they would have to build these towns and cities themselves.

First, railroad promoters set out to dismantle the idea of the Great Plains as the "Great American Desert." Railroads churned out publications recasting the plains as a veritable land of milk and honey—not as an inhospitable Sahara in the heart of North America—where a variety of crops would be easily cultivated and, thanks to the absence of trees in many places, much of the hardest work had already been done by the benevolent hand of nature. Under the pens of railroad and town promoters, the Great Plains underwent a profound transformation from desert to garden.

With the negative image of the plains buried under a steady accumulation of florid prose, railroads could then turn their attention to recruiting the perfect kind of settlers. When pondering which groups would make ideal settlers in the 1870s and 1880s, these promoters ignored free African Americans, who were eager to leave the South and start their own farms, and the growing number of Asian immigrants. Instead, they focused exclusively on northern Europeans. Swedes, Norwegians, Germans, and the Irish were leaving their homelands for a variety of reasons, including famines, the enclosure of larger and larger farms by elites that crowded out smaller farmers, and a general lack of arable land for growing populations to share. For these and other reasons, tens of thousands of immigrants entered the United States every year. Channeling as many of these newcomers as possible to the lands along the various rail lines fell to promotional offices. Except for some debate about the desirability of the Irish, perhaps, Americans generally considered these groups to be hardworking, moral, and white. In other words, they were ideal potential settlers.

The Northern Pacific was perhaps the most aggressive of the West's railroads in its efforts to recruit settlers. In 1871, with track to Minnesota completed, the line turned to Frederick Billings to create a land office. Billings chose John S. Loomis to head the new office, as he had done similar work in Kansas with the Kansas Pacific Railroad. Loomis proposed publishing materials in several European languages, establishing connections with ministers who could preach about relocating to their congregations, and staffing offices in England, Holland, Germany, and the Scandinavian countries. The following year, George Hibbard, the Northern Pacific's superintendent of immigration, informed his superiors, "We are sending forward a good stream of first class settlers and I am happy to report that the tide has commenced flowing from Europe every day bringing us a few good emigrants" (quoted in Pierce 2016, 161–162).

A few families at a time, however, would not fill the line's lands quickly enough, so the company turned to recruiting entire colonies of immigrants. Dozens or hundreds at a time could be hauled out to the northern plains, creating entire communities almost overnight. The Northern Pacific was particularly keen to recruit the Mennonites, ethnic German Protestants. Two centuries earlier, the Mennonites had relocated to Russia to avoid mandatory military service in their homeland. On the Russian Steppe, a landscape not dissimilar to the Great Plains, the Mennonites had become some of the world's best wheat farmers. Czar Alexander II, however, revoked the pacifistic Mennonite's exemption from military service, prompting them to find a new territory. As Hibbard explained to Jay Cooke, the financier behind the line, of the Mennonites in May 1873, "I need not say to you that it is of the utmost importance to our Company that we secure the location of this body of men and I hope no stone will be left unturned to accomplish this object" (quoted in Pierce 2016, 163). While the company would successfully relocate colonies, including some Mennonite colonies, to the lands along their lines, it would still not be enough, as the company's bankruptcy later that year would attest. Nevertheless, this effort at social engineering a new population did not entirely fail. Thousands of immigrants from Germany, Russia, and the Scandinavian countries did indeed relocate to Minnesota, the Dakotas, and Montana, and the policies of the Northern Pacific were a major catalyst for that immigration.

Despite these efforts, none of the early transcontinentals would turn a profit in the 19th century, and most would end up falling into bankruptcy, taking the economy with them in the 1870s and again in the 1890s. As the historian Richard White explained, railroad magnates "built railroads that would have been better left unbuilt, and flooded markets with wheat, silver, cattle, and coal for which there was little or no need" (White 2011, xxvi).

Yet, the railroads did, undeniably, suture together the nation with steel threads, seemingly transcending space and time in a way that a few decades earlier had been unimaginable. Railroads also led to the development of great cities such as Denver, Salt Lake, Kansas City, and, most importantly, Chicago. The cattle of Texas made their way by rail to the slaughterhouses of Kansas City and Chicago and from there as meat products to tables around the nation and even across the ocean. Wheat and corn made their way from Iowa and Kansas to Chicago silos, and the forests of Michigan, Wisconsin, and Minnesota (and later Washington) fell before the axe to build houses for a booming nation. Almost as important, large cities sent goods and services back to the areas that produced all these products. Children on the farms of North Dakota and their counterparts in Colorado mining towns could thumb through catalogs from Montgomery Ward or Sears and Roebuck for almost anything they could imagine. Indeed, rural families could order whatever they needed and have it delivered to their doors: bicycles, clothing, watches, cameras, and even entire house kits. Despite their failures and limitations, the railroads made all of these things possible. Much less well known is that the railroads had an ally just as important, but much less heralded, in another new technology.

WORDS WRITTEN ON LIGHTNING

The importance of railroads was well understood at the time and has been recognized by scholars since, but the telegraph, oddly, has not received the same amount of attention. As the historian Elliott West observed, "The telegraph allowed the railroads to do what they did. None of it would have worked without news moving ahead of lumber, plows, cable, and soldiers. More exactly, all the parts—the railroads, the telegraphs, a western economy and its workers—emerged inextricably together, allowing and feeding each other" (West 2012, 84). While railroads could convey people and materials at speeds previously unimagined, the telegraph moved ideas even faster, at close to the speed of light. Trains could carry their passengers and cargo at 10 to 15 times the speed of horses, converting the once arduous crossing of the continent into a few days of travel. The telegraph, however, conveyed ideas some 40 million times faster. "A single dot of Morse code traveled from Kansas City to Denver faster than the click it produced moved from the receiver to the telegrapher's eardrum" (West 2012, 78). News that once took months to share could be instantly transmitted around the globe. One could live in San Francisco and read in the morning paper what had happened the day before in New York, Washington, DC, or London. The world, in a very real sense, became smaller and more connected, at least with the completion of the telegraph network.

While several inventors had similar ideas about using electricity to send messages, most of the early attempts failed due to over-complexity: for example, using electricity to move armatures to point at letters like electrical Ouija boards. Samuel Morse, a Yale-educated artist, however, came up with a more elegant solution: use the electrical impulses themselves to signify letters. Morse and his partner, Albert Vail, set about constructing such a system, both the wires to carry the electrical impulses and the "system of signs by which intelligence could be instantaneously transmitted," as Morse later explained (quoted in West 2012, 80). His "Morse code" enabled telegraphers to rapidly send and receive messages, which he proved in 1843 to a group of congressmen and other dignitaries by sending a message 37 miles, from Washington, DC, to the rail depot in Baltimore, Maryland after Congress had appropriated $30,000 to construct an experimental line.

Following Morse's successful demonstration, small telegraph lines sprang up around the country, but it would not be until 1860 that Congress appropriated money and offered a right of way for the line. The contract to build it went to the Western Union company. Much like the first transcontinental railroad, Western Union would build toward the west, and a California company would build east. They would meet in Salt Lake City. The Pacific Telegraph Act called for the completion of the line by 1862. Western Union planted the first pole near Omaha, Nebraska, on July 4, 1861, and the last on October 24, 1861. What some had said was impossible had been accomplished in less than six months. Thus, people in California could keep up on the profound events shaking the nation: the start of the Civil War, the great Union victories at Gettysburg and Vicksburg, and the assassination of President Lincoln. All of these events and others appeared in local papers mere hours after they happened.

The telegraph also enabled business transactions across great distances. Stock transactions, like those conducted on the San Francisco Mining and Stock Exchange, might come from that city or, as an employee recalled, "wherever the telegraph wire extended, our orders would roll in on us. The Eastern cities also, New York in particular . . . London, Paris, Berlin, and Frankfort sent us orders" (quoted in West 2012, 92). Capital could now flow easily around the globe, enabling the development of mines and companies in previously unheard-of locations. One lovesick couple, telegrapher William Storey stationed in Camp Grant, Arizona, and Clara Choate of San Diego, even used the telegraph to wed in 1876, sharing their vows across the distance in electrical impulses.

FROM FRONTIER TO INDUSTRIAL SOCIETY

At the beginning of the 19th century, the lands west of the Mississippi did not yet belong to the United States. By the end of the century, however, the entire region had been incorporated into the nation, connected by miles of humming telegraph wire and rail lines snaking over mountain passes and across alkaline deserts. The place of the West had been secured. The region would be dedicated to the extraction of its plentiful natural resources. Mines would pour forth wealth in the form of gold, silver, copper, and, less glamorous but no less important, coal. The great forests of the Pacific Northwest would produce lumber for the construction of homes and buildings all across the nation. Salmon canneries and slaughterhouses would package up the fish and meat of the West for consumption around the nation and even beyond. Oranges too would find their way to market, grown in California and the Rio Grande Valley. Only water remained scarce, the region's few great rivers too powerful to be harnessed by individuals and private capital. It would fall to the federal government, increasingly active in developing the West, to bring those to heel.

To be sure, the economic development of the West had not been shared equally. Railroad magnates, mining millionaires, and cattle barons claimed much of this wealth for themselves, while their cowboys, miners, and railroad workers toiled for little gain in often dangerous conditions. Some workers would make efforts to address the problems of poor pay and dangerous working conditions by turning to controversial unions. For Mexican Americans, as well, the U.S. acquisition of Texas, California, and the Southwest could not be considered an unalloyed good. Many wealthy landowners saw their property, often extensive ranches, stolen from them by a variety of unscrupulous newcomers who often used the labyrinthian U.S. legal system to their advantage. Undoubtedly, the group that lost the most would be the American Indian peoples. At the beginning of the century, the majority of tribes of the West still held sway over their territories. Certainly, their lifestyles had been influenced by the arrival of Europeans. Horses, for example, transformed Indian culture, opening up for some tribes a world of resources that had been previously unexploitable. Over time, however, the negative aspects of this cultural contact would become painfully apparent.

5

POLITICAL LIFE IN THE AMERICAN WEST

POLITICAL EXPANSION

The 19th century brought dynamic and unprecedented changes to the West. The first hints of a new social and political order began on the Pacific coast with the arrival of American fur traders. The acquisition of the Louisiana Territory in 1803, however, would be the catalyst for transformation, giving a young, expansionistic nation control over a tremendously vast territory. The 1804–1806 Lewis and Clark Expedition marked the first contact between this new nation and numerous Indian peoples across the northern swath of the West. But others would come soon after: fur traders, missionaries, more explorers, and finally miners, ranchers, and agrarian settlers.

The 19th century also provided the federal government with an opportunity to increase its power and influence. Indeed, as the nation grew, so did the reach of the federal government. Texas, California, and Oregon would be admitted to the Union before the Civil War; their admittance to the nation, however, also sparked a final reckoning with the institution of slavery and its expansion into Western territories. Yet, as the nation fought its bloodiest war, the four years in the 1860s presented the federal government (now controlled solely by Northerners) with an opportunity to extend its influence even further. Congress, with the passage of the Pacific Railway Act, chose a route from Nebraska to California for the nation's first transcontinental railroad line, inextricably linking the West with the industrial Northeast. Congress also bestowed upon most railroads extensive land grants to help subsidize their construction across the expansive but seemingly empty region.

The Homestead Act in 1862 stamped the mark of free labor on the West, creating, Congress hoped, a nation of small farmers. These would be but a few of the great changes. In following decades, Congress enacted the 1872 Mining Law, allowing for the easy transfer of federal land into the hands of private mining companies and made similarly generous provisions for lumber companies and other extractive industries. Only at the dawn of the 20th century would the federal government realize the costs of such generosity and begin to embrace some conservation practices. Still, the West and the federal government, in many ways, developed together.

LEWIS AND CLARK, THE FUR TRADE, AND THE COMING OF THE UNITED STATES

While the Spanish contented themselves with building missions in New Mexico, Texas, and California with the hope of saving souls and putting Indians to work, the French, British, and Dutch pursued more earthly goals: furs. Among the first industries to develop in North America, the fur trade predated the settlement of the first English colonies, as European ships had sailed along the coast of what would one day be eastern Canada and the United States. Fur trappers pushed inland, with the French, in particular, building up a wealthy trade along the St. Lawrence River and the Great Lakes, a water highway that probed deep into the North American continent. In time, the trade pushed all the way to the Pacific coast. The French officially lost control of their North American possessions with the Treaty of Paris in 1763, at the conclusion of the French and Indian War, but many Frenchmen remained in North America as trappers. Frenchmen, Englishmen, and eventually Americans all made money in the fur trade, but Indians proved the most important people for the industry's success.

In the late 1700s, European and American ships began to ply the waters of the Pacific coast of North America. Russian ships made their way from Siberia and south along the coast of Alaska, and in 1778, the English captain James Cook stopped at Nootka Sound, on

Vancouver Island, and acquired 1,500 otter skins. The British had intended to use the skins on board the ship, but they eventually discovered that such pelts fetched a high price in China—and thus began a flourishing coastal fur trade. American ships increasingly got involved in the trade. These primarily economic enterprises also had political ramifications. Captain Robert Gray's 1792 discovery of the Columbia River, for example, strengthened America's political claims to the Pacific Northwest. Between the Pacific coast and the Mississippi River, however, lay a vast territory, much of it claimed by the Spanish and the French.

By the 1790s, Americans had begun to settle over the Appalachian Mountains and especially along the fertile banks of the Ohio River. Roads over the mountains were mostly roads in name only, and shipping anything overland proved to be costly and difficult. It was far better to load one's produce onto boats or barges and float them down the Ohio River to the Mississippi River and then south to New Orleans. At the "crescent city," named for the shape of a bend in the river on which the settlement had been built, these barges could be off-loaded and the cargo then put on larger ocean-going ships, which could then transport the produce to market on the East Coast or beyond. Unfortunately for American farmers, New Orleans belonged to the Spanish and then again (briefly) to the French.

Thomas Jefferson, the newly elected president, decided to make an offer to purchase New Orleans, and thus, in 1802, he instructed Robert Livingston, the U.S. minister to France, to open negotiations. That same year, Spain (still ostensibly in control of Louisiana but in reality doing the bidding of France) suspended the "right of deposit," preventing American farmers from off-loading their cargo in New Orleans. Spain restored the right the following year, but it proved to be a shrewd negotiating tactic in that it exposed America's reliance on a foreign power. As Jefferson said, New Orleans was the spot "through which the produce of three-eighths of our territory must pass to market" (quoted in Meinig 1995, 10).

Despite driving a hard bargain, France was in truth a motivated seller. Napoleon's effort to hold on to the lucrative sugar-producing island nation of Haiti had proven fruitless, costing the lives of thousands of French soldiers, victims of the Haitian rebels and disease. Louisiana supplied food to the slaves on Haiti, and with Haiti earning its independence, Napoleon had little need for Louisiana. He did, however, need money for yet another war in the seemingly endless series of conflicts between France and its archrival Great

Britain. Thus, when Livingston and the rest of the American delegation arrived in Paris in April 1803, the French foreign minister offered up not just the city of New Orleans but all of Louisiana, a territory so vast that no white man had ever seen it all; its boundaries far outdistanced the known and bumped against the blurry margins of the unknown. Although not authorized to make such an extravagant purchase, the American delegation nevertheless agreed to the terms and returned in July with a treaty that included the entire Louisiana Territory. The official announcement on July 4, 1803, struck Americans as almost divinely inspired.

President Jefferson's enthusiasm for the purchase overwhelmed all opposition, and the Senate quickly ratified the treaty. The United States now had an empire, but an empire, Jefferson hoped, for liberty that Americans could settle for generations, building small farms that would nurture both crops and American democracy. First, however, Jefferson needed to know what he had purchased. To replace the blurry margins of the unknown with the known, he would need to send explorers into the wilderness.

The exploration of such a vast territory necessitated the creation of two expeditions. One (the famous one) would venture up the Missouri River, over the Continental Divide, and arrive at the mouth of the Columbia River. Jefferson hoped a successful expedition would discover an easily navigable route between the Missouri and Columbia Rivers and potentially create a serviceable Northwest Passage that would make shipping possible between the Atlantic and Pacific Oceans. Further, the expedition could solidify American claims to the Pacific Northwest, which was also claimed by Great Britain. The second (largely forgotten) expedition would ascertain the southern boundary of the Louisiana Territory between the United States and Spain, ascending to the headwaters of the Red River.

Jefferson, very much a man of the Enlightenment, proposed that these expeditions make detailed and accurate maps, establish friendly relations with the various Indian tribes they encountered, note important geological features, and catalog the unique plants and animals they discovered. In other words, Jefferson wanted to know everything.

To probe the territory between the Missouri and the Columbia Rivers, Jefferson turned to his personal secretary, Meriwether Lewis. A Virginian, like Jefferson, Lewis had earned the president's admiration and trust. Jefferson wanted someone with intelligence and a willingness to learn as much as possible about botany, natural history, mineralogy, and myriad other subjects. But he also wanted someone with "the firmness of constitution & character, prudence, habits adapted to the woods, & a familiarity with the Indian manners & character, requisite for this undertaking. All the latter qualifications Capt. Lewis has" (quoted in Ambrose 1996b, 77). Lewis, nevertheless, still embarked on a crash course in a university's worth of subjects as he planned and prepared the expedition. He soon realized the need for another officer and approached William Clark about joining the expedition. Both would hold the rank of captain and share command. Clark agreed, and an expedition with a just a few dozen men, almost all experienced frontiersmen, prepared to leave in the spring of 1804.

One of Jefferson's most important goals for the expedition was to develop friendly relations with the Indians. Certainly, this would serve political objectives, but most importantly, Jefferson wanted friendly relations with the Indians to undercut British fur traders by convincing the Indians to supply furs to American companies. To grease the wheels of commerce, Lewis and Clark took with them a wealth of trade goods—metal tools, beads, and the like—but the Indians they encountered wanted firearms above all, something Jefferson did not want to provide. Instead, Lewis and Clark eagerly handed out "peace medals," brass tokens with Jefferson's face on one side and the hand of an Indian shaking the hand of a white man on the other. These peace medals symbolized the peaceful intentions of the United States and its desire to forge beneficial relationships with the Indians, or so the captains explained, but surely these were disappointing trinkets for Indians hoping to acquire guns.

For the most part, the Indians along the Missouri River appeared interested in the offer of friendship with the United States, with the exception of the Lakota Sioux, who saw themselves (somewhat accurately) as the real power on the northern plains. Fortunately, Lewis and Clark managed to avoid a violent confrontation with the Lakota and made their way to the Mandan villages on the banks of the Missouri. It was among the friendly Mandan that the Corps of Discovery would make their winter camp.

The Mandan, a sedentary people surrounded by more nomadic tribes, had carved out an important niche for themselves as a trading people. Other Indians as well as European fur traders converged on their villages to swap manufactured goods for furs. During the winter, the expedition added a French trapper named Toussaint Charbonneau to the expedition along with his young Shoshone wife, Sacagawea. With her newborn baby in a cradleboard on her back, Sacagawea shepherded the expedition up the Missouri River and into the Rockies, the land of her people, and eventually all the way to the Pacific Ocean.

After wintering on the Oregon coast in 1805–1806, the expedition returned the following year to St. Louis, having succeeded in accomplishing nearly all of Jefferson's goals. Certainly, American claims to the Pacific Northwest had been strengthened, and Clark's careful observations would generate the first map of the uncharted territories. The boundaries of scientific knowledge also increased with descriptions of new animals and plants. On other counts, the expedition had been less successful. Jefferson's plan for an easy, mostly water route between St. Louis and the mouth of the Columbia was undone by geographic reality. Most of the year, the Missouri River would be too shallow for ships, and the Snake and Columbia Rivers were too wild, with rapids and waterfalls marking their descent to the ocean. And then there were the mountains. Jefferson had hoped for a range of low hills, not unlike the Appalachian Mountains. Instead, the route Lewis and Clark chose from the headwaters of the Missouri River over the Continental Divide took them through a series of rugged ranges of serrated peaks, each more imposing than the last (there was an easier route over the South Pass, south of where they had crossed, but it was as yet unknown to Americans). There would be no Northwest Passage.

Nor had the expedition been entirely successful in its negotiations with the Indians. There had been an encounter with the Teton Sioux, which nearly ended in violence, but Lewis had been responsible for an even worse diplomatic disaster during the return trip. Hoping to explore more territory, rather than merely retracing their footsteps from the previous year, the captains decided to split up the expedition. Captain Clark explored the Yellowstone River, while Lewis took a party and traveled up the Marias River. Lewis's men encountered a party of Blackfeet in late July 1806, which friendlier tribes, like the Nez Percé, had described as dangerous and violent. Perhaps these negative assessments colored his view, for Lewis was instantly wary of these Indians. To make matters worse, they were one of the only tribes armed with guns, which they had acquired from British trappers, and this monopoly gave them power over other tribes.

The night of July 26, Lewis posted guards and went to sleep, but in the darkness of the early morning, he was awakened by the shout of George Drouillard as he wrestled with a Blackfoot man over his rifle. Realizing his own rifle had been stolen, and spying the thief sprinting into the darkness, Lewis grabbed a pistol and set off in pursuit. Although he retrieved his rifle, more armed Blackfeet began to materialize. Lewis, seeing one aiming in his direction, fired and critically wounded the man. He returned to camp and ordered his men to saddle their horses and retreat. As they collected their belongings and prepared to depart, Lewis noticed the body of an Indian his companions had killed. Angered at the insolence and bravado of the Blackfeet, Lewis placed a peace medal around the neck of the dead warrior so that the Blackfeet "might be informed who we were" (Ambrose 1996b, 391). Lewis's action was more than ironic; it was the action of a tired, rash, and angry man, and with that stroke, Lewis turned the Blackfeet into an enemy. Mostly, however, the Lewis and Clark Expedition had proven successful, and it represented the arrival of the Americans and the federal government into the West.

The other major, but largely forgotten, expedition of the Louisiana Purchase began in April 1806 and was led by Peter Custis and Thomas Freeman. Freeman had worked as a surveyor in Pennsylvania, and Custis was a medical student from the University of Pennsylvania. Another two dozen men accompanied them. In May, they began their ascent of the Red River from Louisiana but found their path blocked by a roughly 80-mile logjam that would become known as the Red River Raft. What should have been a few days of easy paddling became weeks of portages around the massive jumble of logs. Finally, clear of the obstacle they resumed their ascent upriver. However, on July 18, they encountered a Spanish force that had been dispatched to apprehend them. In the face of a well-armed and superior force, the expedition had no choice but to return to Natchitoches, in American territory. Although Freeman and Custis did describe some new plants and animals, the expedition had been a marked failure, and the source of the Red River would elude Americans until the 1870s. The Spanish, meanwhile, continued to stymie American exploration in the coming years, eager to keep the expansionistic nation at bay for as long as possible.

While government explorers sketched out the map and contacted the Indians, private individuals, the rugged fur trappers, accomplished much more in terms of exploration and served as de facto diplomats to the Indians in ways that were far more effective than the government had been. For example, the best route over the Rockies was not through the crenellated geography of the

Bitterroot Mountains of Montana and Idaho but over the comparatively gentle grades at South Pass in modern Wyoming.

Fur trappers also often lived with particular tribes, and often
married into those tribes to leverage their positions to collect furs
with the help of Indian friends and family. Learning the native
languages made trappers vitally important translators, and they
benefited from the Indians' knowledge of the best routes and the
resources of the environment more generally. Conversely, trappers
also represented the first stirrings of a great transformation in the
Indian way of life.

Expansionistic Americans, however, had found their match in
the equally expansionistic Plains Indian tribes, most especially
the powerful Comanche on the Southern Plains and the fearsome,
imperialistic Lakota on the northern plains.

POLITICAL LIFE FOR PLAINS INDIANS AND
THE CHALLENGE OF AMERICAN EXPANSION

The U.S. government in the 19th century imagined Indians as
primitive monarchies, a people who obey the dictates of a chief,
and in many ways, this misconception has endured. Political life for
American Indian peoples, especially the tribes of the Great Plains,
was far more complicated than outsiders realized and with political
power much more diffuse. Independent clans made political decisions, and even individuals could decide what course of action they
were willing to undertake. To be sure, Plains Indians respected and
followed leaders of renown, but even the most powerful leader
could only make decisions if his people supported his course of
action. Further, leadership could change depending on the circumstances. In times of war, a war chief would be called to lead, such
as Looking Glass, who led the Nez Percé on their attempted escape
to Canada in 1877. At other times, however, diplomatic or religious
leaders determined the course of action, such as "Chief" Joseph,
whose respected role as a diplomatic and religious leader made
him at times a major leader of his Nez Percé people.

Large-scale tribal organization was often rare. The Sioux Tribe,
for example, contained three distantly related groups: the Dakota,
the Nakota (also called the Yankton and Yanktonai), and the
Lakota, or Western Sioux. Spread from Minnesota to Montana, the
three major divisions had little to do with one another and never
functioned as a unified tribe, despite having similar languages and
a distant shared history.

Of the three Sioux groups, the Lakota nation presented the greatest obstacle to the expansion of the United States, facing the invasion of the *Wasichus* (the Lakota word for white peoples) as a unified people, but a variety of social and political institutions were brought to bear to create unification.

The Lakota themselves divided into seven interrelated but independent bands: the Hunkpapa, Oglala, Minneconjou, Two Kettles, Brulé, Sans Arc, and Blackfoot Sioux (not to be confused with their enemies the Blackfeet). These seven bands joined together socially, politically, and militarily. They fought their enemies together, discussed their political problems in counsels, and intermarried between their various bands. Working cooperatively, the bands created a formidable and powerful united front, but the social organization of the Lakota was further divided into even smaller groups. Each of the seven bands was composed of large groups of related families, known as a *tiospaye*. At times, especially during the cold winter months, when providing for a large village was difficult, the *tiospayes* broke down into smaller groups of closely related extended families. These smallest groups of immediate relations formed a *wicotipi*. Individuals were always in the presence of their *wicotipi*, surrounded by their close family members, but as the spring warmed, these disparate groups often joined with other *wicotipis* to form *tiospayes*. Then, especially at the height of summer and coinciding with the sacred Sun Dance, the various bands would join together into villages that numbered in the thousands, becoming as close to an entire nation as possible.

The men in the *wicotipi* made political decisions for their families. This meant the selection of a hereditary chief, or "hair coat wearer," for the distinctive coat the chief wore, who helped make daily political decisions. A different respected warrior was typically chosen to be a war chief, or *blotaunka*. Individuals could aspire to this rank, but only if he had proven himself in both hunting and warfare.

The Hunkpapa medicine man, warrior, and leader Sitting Bull went on his first war party at 14, an unusually early age for his people. Even more amazing, he successfully engaged a Crow warrior, felling him with his tomahawk. Killing, wounding, or even simply touching an adversary allowed one to "count coup." Indeed, touching an enemy and escaping unharmed was often seen as the ultimate demonstration of military acumen. In Sitting Bull's case, when he returned to the village, he was presented with a single eagle feather. Over the course of a life of exceptional valor, Sitting Bull eventually had the right to wear 30 such feathers in his headdress.

Warfare occurred every year as groups of young men sought out their enemies. Anyone could lead a war party against one's enemies, and young men were always eager to participate. A successful war party earned respect and prestige, but an unsuccessful one, especially one in which the losses were high, could effectively end a warrior's career. Typically, few casualties occurred in these encounters—a loss of more than one or two warriors on either side was unusual. But if several friends were killed, it was unlikely that the leader of the party would be able to convince others to follow him again. Nevertheless, casualties did happen, and few families were untouched by tragedy. Sitting Bull, for example, saw both his father and uncle fall to the hated Crow.

Back in the village, women found the constant warfare to be less a source of romance and glory and much more the cause of heartbreak and sorrow. Pretty-shield of the Crow recalled, "Always there was some man missing [killed in combat], and always some woman was having to go live with her relatives, because women are not hunters. They had to be cared for by somebody. You see that when we women lost our men we lost our own, and our children's living. I am glad war has gone forever. It was no good" (Linderman 1978, 168–169).

Nevertheless, warfare and participation in secret male-only societies conveyed power and prestige. The Crow leader Plenty-coups, for example, belonged to the Foxes, and for a time, he carried the coup stick of the Foxes. Under no circumstances could he surrender the stick to any enemy, and he was expected to die to defend it. "But I was lucky," he told the anthropologist Frank Bird Linderman. "Nothing happened when I carried the straight [coup] stick of the Foxes" (Linderman 2002, 30).

Sitting Bull became a member of several important Lakota societies, including the Strong Hearts (who provided policing and defense for the village) and the Silent Eaters, a society of respected warriors who helped determine, along with the hereditary chiefs, what to do about the invasion of white Americans into Lakota territory. By 1867, Sitting Bull had risen to the status of *blotaunka*, or war chief, among the Fox Society. But there were other *blotaunkas* among the Fox Society, including his bitter rivals No Neck and Gall. In 1868, Sitting Bull became *wakiconza*, a position that previously had not been found among his band, the Hunkpapa. A *wakiconza* functioned as a something of a judge and a leader, and he exerted a great deal of power in deciding issues of peace and war among his people. However, he was not in a position to dictate or command the bands to follow. His authority lasted only so long as the bands agreed to follow him. Nevertheless, his appointment as the first *wakiconza* in Hunkpapa history helped make him a major figure in the resistance to American expansion until 1877. Indeed, he and Crazy Horse, a younger Ogalla *blotaunka*, became the faces of resistance in the final stages of the Lakota campaign against American expansion, when the Lakota nation faced its gravest political challenge.

MANIFEST DESTINY

By the 1840s, Americans had come to see themselves as the New Israelites, the chosen people of God. Confident in the belief that God wanted Americans to spread across the continent, bringing American democracy, civilization, Christianity, and progress with them, they looked West with great anticipation. The only institution Americans seemed divided on was the question of expanding slavery into new territories. In time, this would tear the nation apart, but in the heady days of the 1840s, as the American eagle stretched his wings for the first time, slavery did not yet seem so divisive.

It all began with Texas. The Republic of Texas had never intended to be an independent country when it won its independence from Mexico in 1836. Sam Houston, the nation's first president, had been particularly keen on having the United States annex this ragtag, virtually bankrupt republic as soon as possible. After all, Mexico disputed the legality of the Treaty of Velasco (which granted Texas its independence) on the grounds that Mexican dictator and prisoner of war Antonio López de Santa Anna had been coerced into signing it, which of course he had. The prospect of Mexico coming to reclaim its wayward state loomed large in the decade between 1836 and 1845.

The other roadblock to annexation was slavery. The Republic of Texas had been founded as a slave nation, and in its settled eastern portion, cotton agriculture had taken root. Texas would, without question, join the United States as a slave state. However, it attempted to do so just as the issue was becoming more divisive. A series of presidents, beginning with Houston's friend Andrew Jackson, had been unable to bring in Texas. Finally, in the waning days of the John Tyler administration, with an expansionistic Democrat president-elect waiting in the wings, Texas received its annexation into the United States.

A staunch believer in what would come to be called "Manifest Destiny," president James K. Polk promised to expand the United States, and in his one-term in office he completed the acquisition of the Oregon Country and provoked a war with Mexico to conquer the Southwest. (Naci Yavuz/ Dreamstime.com)

Although the treaty between Texas and the United States had been signed in 1844, it would take until 1846 to complete the annexation of the independent republic. The new president, a Tennessean named James K. Polk, had campaigned on expansion and vowed to bring America's borders to edge of the Pacific. He would soon keep his promise.

Polk made his plans explicit in his inaugural address: "The Republic of Texas has made known her desire to come into our Union, to form a part of our Confederacy and enjoy with us the blessings of liberty secured and guaranteed by our Constitution." Polk warned foreign powers (meaning Mexico and Great Britain, though he did not mention either by name) from interfering in the annexation, and he addressed concerns that such expansion would be detrimental to the harmony of the union. For these critics, he reminded them that the same concerns had been levied against the Louisiana Purchase and then "the opinion prevailed with some that our system of confederated States could not operate successfully over an extended territory. . . . Experience has shown that [such concerns] were not well founded" (Polk 1845).

Texas, however, was only part of Polk's grander vision. He also looked to the Oregon Country. "Nor will it become less . . . my duty to assert and maintain by all Constitutional means the right of the United States to that portion of our territory which lies beyond the Rocky Mountains. Our title," he explained, "to the country of the Oregon is 'clear and unquestionable,' and already our people are preparing to perfect that title by occupying it with their wives and children." American institutions and government would follow the American people into new lands. He reminded his listeners that Americans had already been engaged in a mission of expansion. "Eighty years ago, our population was confined on the west by the ridge of the Alleghanies. Within that period . . . our people, increasing to many millions, have filled the eastern valley of the Mississippi, adventurously ascended the Missouri to its headsprings, and are already engaged in establishing the blessing of self-government in valleys of which the rivers flow to the Pacific" (Polk 1845).

The annexation of Texas and the zeal with which the new president promoted America's seemingly divine mission prompted one widely read columnist to coin a term that would be forever associated with American expansion: "Manifest Destiny." That columnist, John O'Sullivan, in the pages of the *United States Magazine and Democratic Review*, wrote about the annexation of Texas, but his thoughts already gazed farther west. He wrote that other nations sought to restrain America's greatness to prevent it from fulfilling its destiny. Great Britain, in particular, attempted to stifle American expansion "in a spirit of hostile interference against us, for the avowed object of thwarting our policy and hampering our power, limiting our greatness and checking the fulfillment of our manifest destiny to overspread the continent allotted by Providence for the free development of our yearly multiplying millions" (O'Sullivan 1845). A few months later, as the dispute over the Oregon Country grew more vociferous, O'Sullivan again invoked Manifest Destiny in the pages of the *New York Morning News*, cementing the phrase forever into the American memory. God approved America's expansionistic mission, O'Sullivan claimed, and no nation, not even Great Britain, could stop it.

Early in Polk's presidency, the prospect of a third war with Great Britain over the Oregon Country loomed large. A faction of expansionistic Americans demanded the United States draw its border with Canada at the 54th parallel, coining the slogan "Fifty-four forty or fight." That imaginary line, incidentally, marked the southernmost boundary of Alaska (still in Russian hands) and would have given British Columbia to the United States. British interests in the region, however, mostly revolved around the Hudson's Bay Company, and while the company wanted to maintain control of

Oregon and Washington, the British government did not relish waging a war for the company's benefit. Moreover, the British public cared little about a boundary dispute half a world away and instead wanted better political and economic relations with the United States.

Despite his bellicose rhetoric, Polk also wanted to avoid leading the United States into war with the most powerful nation on the planet. Thus, cooler heads prevailed in the dispute over the Oregon Country. Great Britain offered the United States all of Oregon, Washington, and Idaho, including the entirety of Puget Sound, in exchange for British Columbia and the right of the Hudson's Bay Company to navigate the Columbia River, since its headwaters began in Canada. The Polk administration quickly agreed to these terms, and the Senate ratified the agreement in July 1846. There would be no third war with Great Britain, and now the United States truly extended to the Pacific.

While the Oregon Country made a nice addition, Polk coveted, above all, California. Once again, O'Sullivan had perhaps articulated this desire most forcefully in his annexation essay, writing, "California will, probably, next fall away from the loose adhesion which, in such a country as Mexico, holds a remote province in a slight equivocal kind of dependence on the metropolis." He scoffed at the Mexican nation describing Mexico as imbecilic, distracted, impotent, and incapable of developing the bounty of California. Salvation, however, lay near at hand, for "the Anglo-Saxon foot is already on its borders. Already the advance guard of the irresistible army of Anglo-Saxon emigration has begun to pour down upon it, armed with the plough and the rifle, and marking its trail with schools and colleges, courts and representative halls, mills and meeting-houses" (O'Sullivan 1845). In other words, what had happened in Texas would happen again in California.

At first, Polk attempted to acquire California through diplomacy. In 1845, he dispatched John Slidell to Mexico with an offer to purchase the land between Texas and California, including, most importantly, the port city of San Francisco. The total offer, Polk instructed, could amount to $30 million. Mexican officials, however, refused to meet with Slidell or hear his offer. With the door of diplomacy closed, Polk would have to take by conquest what he could not acquire through purchase. All that was needed was an excuse to unleash O'Sullivan's army of vigorous Anglo-Saxons upon Mexico. Polk would soon have his excuse, but it came not from California but rather from Texas.

The location of the southern boundary of Texas, now a U.S. state, had grown into a controversy. The United States argued that the boundary was the Rio Grande River, but Mexico claimed the boundary to be, in fact, the Nueces River, a bit farther north. Between these two rivers lay a strip of disputed land. In an intentionally provocative gesture, Polk ordered General Zachary Taylor into the disputed area, and on April 25, 1846, a skirmish between Mexican and American forces ended with 11 Americans dead and the excuse Polk needed to justify his war of conquest.

Polk addressed Congress to ask for a declaration of war on May 11, 1846, claiming that all efforts at peaceful coexistence had been exhausted and the events of April 25 made war necessary. He declared, "The cup of forbearance had been exhausted even before the recent information from the frontier of the Del Norte [Rio Grande]. But now, after reiterated menaces, Mexico has passed the boundary of the United States, has invaded our territory and shed American blood upon the American soil. She has proclaimed that hostilities have commenced, and that the two nations are now at war" (Polk 1846).

While a few politicians, such as Illinois congressman Abraham Lincoln, denounced Polk for provoking a war, most Americans seemed enthusiastic about our nation's first foreign war. Although the conflict would last for two years and be hard-fought on both sides, the United States eventually dominated, conquering the capital of Mexico City and winning all the decisive battles. It also provided practical experience for a generation of young officers, such as Ulysses S. Grant and Robert E. Lee. With the United States firmly in command, Polk only had to decide how much of Mexico he wanted. While a few leaders called for swallowing the entirety of Mexico (after all, much of it was suited to cotton agriculture), Polk instead decided to carve off the sparsely populated northern half, taking the Southwest and California along the 32nd parallel (although the maps used were rough at best, and the United States, looking for a southern railroad route, soon came back to Mexico and purchased a strip of land south of the Gila River in 1853). In the end, the United States agreed to pay Mexico $15 million for the territory it had conquered, half the amount Slidell had offered two years earlier.

The Treaty of Guadalupe Hidalgo had been signed on February 2, 1848, and the U.S. Senate had quickly ratified it. However, it still awaited approval by the Mexican legislature. Word finally reached Polk on the afternoon of July 4, 1848 (mere hours after the dedication of the new Washington Monument), that Mexico had agreed to the terms. Polk, and others certainly, saw the date as a portent of great things to come, and he wrote in his diary that night, "I desired to sign it on the anniversary of Independence" (quoted in Johannsen 1985, 6).

The bay of San Francisco, indeed all of Alta California, Texas north of the Rio Grande, Arizona, New Mexico, and bits of what would become Colorado, Nevada, and Utah now belonged to the United States. The acquisition of so much territory, however, had grave consequences for the debate over slavery. This did not catch American leaders by surprise. In fact, Polk's actions had been criticized by some northern politicians for playing into the expansionistic designs of slave owners.

Northern Democrats sought ways to inoculate themselves from angry voters' retribution by trying to distance themselves from the proslavery expansionist zeal of their party's leader. Among them was David Wilmont, a fairly obscure Pennsylvania congressman, who offered up a proviso to the declaration of war stipulating that any territory conquered in the conflict not be open to slavery. While the proviso made it through the House, it died at the hands of Southern senators in the Senate. The "Wilmont Proviso" would return in future legislative sessions, only to suffer the same fate. However, the question of the expansion of slavery into these new territories remained unresolved.

Congress debated several options: outlawing slavery everywhere, as Wilmont wanted; extending the old Missouri Compromise line across to California (thus reserving half of California and the future states of New Mexico and Arizona as slave territory); or settling the issue through popular sovereignty (essentially letting voters decide the issue of slavery for themselves on a case-by-case basis). However, none of these solutions could garner enough support, and each had its vociferous detractors. Ralph Waldo Emerson, the transcendental philosopher and towering intellectual, lamented the war and clearly saw the outcome, declaring, "The United States will conquer Mexico, but it will be as the man swallows the arsenic, which brings him down in turn. Mexico will poison us" (quoted in McPherson 2003, 51).

At first, the acquisition of Mexican territory seemed propitious, proving the naysayers like Emerson wrong. On January 24, 1848, a bit more than a week before the official signing of the Treaty of Guadalupe Hidalgo, James Marshall discovered gold in the mill-race of the new sawmill he had just completed for Johan (John)

Sutter. Despite their efforts to keep the news quiet, word of the discovery spread over the next few months and reverberated around the world in the fall and winter of 1848. One year later, more than a hundred thousand "forty-niners" flocked to the goldfields, and California found itself ready for statehood. The gold rush changed California, the nation, and the world in indelible ways, and one such way was political.

Politically, the admission of California acted like a snowball at the top of a steep hill, growing and accelerating the crisis over slavery. Californians hoped to avoid both slavery and the presence of free African Americans in the state. Nevertheless, a few slave owners did appear in the goldfields of California. William Manney's four slaves, for example, extracted $4,000 in gold in one week alone. Other miners did not have the advantage in manpower that slave owners could exploit, and suddenly the abstract debates about free labor versus slave labor came into sharp focus for forty-niners. Walter Colton noted that he and his fellow miners cared little about "slavery in the abstract, or as it exists in other communities; not one in ten cares a button for its abolition, nor the Wilmont Proviso either: all they look at is their own position; they must themselves swing the pick and they won't do it by the side of negro slaves" (quoted in Pierce 2016, 128).

The 1849 state constitution settled the issue, stating "neither slavery, nor involuntary servitude . . . shall ever be tolerated in this State." What remained, however, was ratification by the Senate to bring California into the Union as a free state. Its admission would disrupt the precarious balance of power in that body, which had been delicately maintained since the 1820 Missouri Compromise. No potential slave state, however, could be carved out of the new territories. Moreover, since there were more people in the North, the free states would control both the House (since representation was based on population) and the Senate with the admission of California, a prospect that was anathema to the South. Something had to be done, however, because California had already demonstrated its economic potential and a rapidly growing population necessitated its admission as quickly as possible.

That something was a Frankenstein's monster of a compromise, cobbled together by the aging statesman Senator Henry Clay. Clay introduced eight resolutions, the first six in pairs that would give something to both the North and South. Clay's plan brought in California as a free state but opened up the rest of the Mexican cession to slavery. It also settled the simmering dispute between Texas and New Mexico as to their border, carving off a good chunk of land Texas claimed on the east bank of the Rio Grande and giving it to New Mexico (Texas's considerable debt, however, would be assumed by the federal government). Clay called for the abolition of the slave trade in Washington, DC (a source of shame for abolitionists), but protected slavery in the capital as a legal institution. Finally, Clay proposed that Congress stay out of regulating the interstate slave trade and enforce the fugitive slave clause of the Constitution more ardently. After long debate, and expert maneuvering by Illinois Senator Stephen Douglas, most of these provisions became law.

The Compromise of 1850 proved to be less a compromise than a "series of separately enacted measures each of which became law with a majority of congressmen from one section voting against the majority of those from the other," in the words of the historian James McPherson (McPherson 2003, 71). While the compromise did bring California into the Union, it did not solve the issue of the expansion of slavery, and, worse, the increased enforcement of the fugitive slave clause caused widespread indignation among Black and white abolitionists in the North.

One other issue of Western land settlement exposed the sectional divide and catalyzed the political collapse that would bring about the Civil War. In 1854, Stephen Douglas introduced the Kansas-Nebraska Act. Douglas, a Democrat, had his sights fixed on the White House, but to do so, he needed the support of both Northern and Southern Democrats. The Kansas-Nebraska Act, he hoped, would win him acclaim from both sides and catapult him into the White House.

The act called for the organization of two new territories directly west of two existing states, the free state of Iowa and the slave state of Missouri. Invariably, Douglas assumed, immigration would flow directly west, with "Free-Soilers" moving into Nebraska and proslavery elements moving into Kansas. With a slave state and a free state to, once again, balance each other out, everyone would be happy, and Douglas would add another skillful compromise to his name. Surely voters would rally around him, and the "Little Giant," as he was called, would become president. His plan hinged on the concept of popular sovereignty, in other words, letting the people vote on the issue of slavery for themselves. Douglas assumed Kansas would vote in favor of slavery (its residents composed, he imagined, of Missourians who had moved west) and Nebraska against the institution.

Unfortunately, the Kansas-Nebraska Act would be a disaster for Douglas's ambitions, dooming his chances of becoming president. First, it set off a rancorous national debate; second, it alienated Northerners, who rallied behind the new Republican party; and finally, it led to two factions, one proslavery and one antislavery, vying for control of Kansas. Soon these factions had declared competing capital cities (a proslavery one in Lecompton and its antislavery counterpart in Topeka), and each had written competing constitutions, one outlawing slavery and the other, predictably, protecting it.

While the rhetoric of politicians grew louder and angrier by the day, on the ground, the situation devolved even further. On May 21, 1865, several hundred armed gunmen descended on the city of Lawrence, a stronghold of the abolition movement. These armed men had been officially deputized by the proslavery government and entered the town on the pretense of arresting several abolitionists. Knowing that any resistance could be used to justify an attack, the residents complied with the posse. The mob then turned on the abolitionist newspapers in town. T. M. Gladstone, an English visitor, watched the sacking of Lawrence. He wrote, "The newspaper offices were the first objects of attack. First that of the *Free State*, then that of the *Herald of Freedom*, underwent a thorough demolition. The presses were in each case broken to pieces, and the offending type carried away to the river." The mob plundered several houses and businesses and put to the torch both the Free State Hotel and the governor's house, until finally "the army of desperadoes, now wild with plunder and excesses, and maddened with drink, retired from the pillaged city" (Gladstone 2008).

Such attacks could not go unanswered, and militant abolitionists promised to repay violence with violence. Among the most recklessly vengeful was a 56-year-old radical abolitionist named John Brown. Brown's anger and zeal made him a terrifying prospect to behold. Following the attack on Lawrence, he declared, "Something must be done to show these barbarians that we, too, have rights" (quoted in McPherson 2003, 152). Recounting the sacking of Lawrence and other recent acts perpetuated by the proslavery faction, Brown calculated that at least five abolitionists had been murdered by proslavery partisans. He vowed to kill an equal number of proslavery men. With four of his adult sons and three other followers, Brown abducted five proslavery men from their homes on the night of May 24–25 near the town of Pottawatomie. He then executed them with a broadsword. Popular sovereignty, which seemed like a democratic solution to the complex problem of slavery, had violently failed, leaving Kansas a chaotic and bloody mess. Soon that bloodshed would spill across the nation with Southern secession and the Civil War, but it was Western settlement that spurred this terrible reckoning.

NORTHERNERS AND THE SHAPING OF THE WEST

For decades, the South and North had debated the future of the West, each hoping to impose their vision on the region, and a stalemate had resulted. Southern secession ended that stalemate and allowed the North to impose its vision on the West. It is unsurprising, then, that the Civil War years saw the passage of several landmark bills that shaped the future of the West. Three bills in particular would leave an indelible impression on the region. One would attract free settlers in search of a better life, another would plan for the future of the region, and the last would unify the continent.

The Republicans in Congress made 1862 a banner year for the future of the West by passing the Homestead Act, the Morrill Act, and the Pacific Railway Act. These three acts articulated a vision for the future of the region. Land would be given to small independent landowners to build productive farms and communities, with the railroads tying these communities to the larger nation and the world, and land grants would be used to support a public education system for the betterment of these fledgling towns and future states. Liberated from the shadow of slavery, the West would blossom under the hard work of these landholders. The famous newspaper editor Horace Greeley declared the Homestead Act to be "one of the most beneficent and vital reforms ever attempted in any age or clime—a reform calculated to diminish sensibly the number of paupers and idlers and increase the proportion of working, independent, self-subsisting farmers in the land evermore" (quoted in White 1991, 143). Together, these bills offered a radical, almost utopian vision for the West, but utopian dreams rarely work out the way their visionaries imagine.

The Homestead Act provided 160 acres (a quarter section) from the public domain to any settlers (including immigrants) for a small filing fee if they resided on and improved the land in five years, a process called "proving up" their claim. Alternatively, would-be settlers with greater financial means could purchase the land outright for $1.25 an acre. The plan harkened back to older ideas, such as Thomas Jefferson's Land Ordinance of 1785 and his agrarian dream of creating a nation of farmers, and thus the law's framers hoped to draw a new generation of Americans back to the land and away from cities to be farmers, not factory workers.

A century of economic development, however, had changed the United States into an industrial nation. Some would come in search of land and opportunity, but not enough to turn back time to an earlier age. Worse, 160 acres might have been enough land in Ohio to start up a small farm, but in much of the arid West, 160 acres, especially without irrigation water, would neither support a farm nor a ranching operation. Nevertheless, between 1862 and 1890, settlers filed some 372,659 claims, bringing over 2 million people into the West, especially to the Great Plains. It was a large number but small compared to the 45 million new people who were added to the nation's population in the same period, most of whom would stay in the more populated states of the Northeast and Midwest. Despite the proclamations of Greeley and others, the West was not the safety valve to divert people back to the soil and lessen the problems of industrialization as many had hoped it would be.

The Homestead Act, however, was not the only way to acquire land in the West. Congress also gave states land from the public domain that they could resell. Under the Morrill Act, for example, states received 30,000 acres of land for every senator or congressman they had, and Eastern states (which did not have any federal landholdings) received scrips that could be redeemed for land in other Western territories. The federal government also turned over millions of acres to private railroad companies in the form of land grants, which many railroads received when they agreed to build a line into the West. This practice began with the very first transcontinental railroad line, the Union Pacific–Central Pacific.

The Morrill Act was the last of the trio of acts passed in 1862. Sponsored by Vermont senator Justin Morrill, the act allowed states to claim land from the public domain to finance the construction "of at least one college where the leading object shall be . . . to teach such branches of learning as are related to agriculture and the mechanic arts . . . in order to promote the liberal and practical education of the industrial classes in the several pursuits and professions of life" (U.S. Congress 1862a). Many states did, in fact, use this to fund the creation of colleges and universities. Taken together, the three 1862 laws offered a road map to the future of a capitalistic society with a growing, free, and educated population—all overseen by an active federal government. While none of the acts would be entirely successful, they nevertheless did encourage widespread settlement and development in the West.

The limitations of the Homestead Act became apparent when settlers actually moved onto the land. Much of the best land had been set aside for railroads as part of their grants (steam engines, after all, needed water, so railroads followed rivers when possible and thus gained ownership of land near streams), and the remaining alternate sections of nonrailroad land within the bounds of the grants quickly increased in price. The remaining areas open to homesteaders were often miles from the closest rail lines, making it difficult to bring produce to market. Other available areas were on arid tracts of land that made it impossible for a family to survive. Hot, dry, cold, isolated, high, and rocky, so much of the West presented challenges American farmers had never encountered. Unsurprisingly, only one-third of the homesteaders successfully completed the requirements to prove up their claims and take full possession of the land. The other two-thirds gave up and abandoned their land in search of easier and better opportunities elsewhere.

Many settlers and politicians failed to see the limitations of the West, and some even offered up optimistic theories that "rain follows the plow," meaning that the mere presence of settlers would fundamentally transform the arid environment of the West. Congress agreed, at least to a degree, with these prognostications. In 1873, for example, Congress passed the Timber Culture Act, which encouraged the planting of trees on the Great Plains in the belief that doing so would transform the climate of the West, essentially making it more like the forested East—that Mother Nature herself had reasons for not planting trees on the plains apparently did not occur to them. Baseless but optimistic theories, of course, proved worthless in the face of the region's environmental limitations. As the writer Wallace Stegner put it, "The inflexible fact of aridity lay like a fence along the 100th meridian. From approximately that line on, more than individual initiative was needed to break the wilderness" (Stegner 1992, xix). A nation that had successfully conquered a continent could not imagine that its conquest could be incomplete, that a nature that had always been beneficent could turn hostile.

One government official took on these assumptions and argued that instead of trying to impose Eastern settlement models on the West that the solution should be to learn to adapt to the conditions of the region, changing how people lived. This official, a former Union officer named John Wesley Powell, proposed a radical reinvention of the relationship between Americans and their land.

Powell, an irascible one-armed former Union major, had become a professor of natural history at Illinois Wesleyan University. In 1868, he led the first expedition down the Green and Colorado Rivers, a land of distant mountains, deep canyons, and inaccessible plateaus that was unlike anything Americans had encountered before. He led a second expedition down the Colorado in 1871–1872, completing the first map of the rugged lands of the Southwest.

As Powell and his men explored the region, they took careful notes about the suitability of the areas they visited for settlement. Certainly, not all of it was desert. Mountains, sitting like island archipelagos above the surrounding deserts, pulled rain and snow from passing clouds. All the West's rivers began this way, with snow collecting on the backs of mountains, melting in the spring, and rushing inexorably to the sea or, in some cases, into the Great Basin. These rivers, Powell realized, would be the arteries for what settlement was possible, diverting them to irrigate a small fraction of the West's land. A bit more land would be suitable for grazing. Valuable mineral lands would also be productive in their own way, and some places in the West, particularly along the Pacific coast, had extensive stands of timber. But the rest of the region, an area so vast as to seem almost beyond comprehension, offered little for settlers. The total population of the region, he believed, would have to be small of necessity. Powell's realization that Americans had to adapt to the reality of aridity proved to be his great insight and the source of his unpopularity with those who did not want to concede the reality of dry West.

By the 1880s, Powell had been put in charge of the U.S. Geological Survey (USGS), and he used his position to counter the beliefs of promoters, officials, and others who felt that the West could be developed in the same way as the humid East. Powell set out his vision for the region, and for a new way of living on the land, in his 1879 report to Congress: *Report on the Lands of the Arid Region of the United States*. If lawmakers had any doubt as to Powell's intentions, he buried those in his opening paragraph: "The object of the volume was to give the extent and character of the lands yet belonging to the Government of the United States. Compared with the whole extent of these lands, but a very small fraction is immediately available for agriculture; in general, they require drainage or irrigation for their redemption" (Powell 1879, vii).

Powell proposed that the old one-size-fits-all system of land distribution, the 160-acre quarter section, be dispensed with in the West. Instead, he felt that 80 acres of irrigated bottomland would produce plenty of food for a single family; 160 acres of irrigated land was too much for a single family to operate. Rangeland, however, was another issue altogether. Cattle, sheep, and horses would have to wander over a much larger area to find enough forage to survive. The standard quarter section could not support more than a few animals. Instead, pasturage for domesticated animals should be at least 2,506 acres (four entire sections and 16 times larger than the standard claim under the Homestead Act). In both cases, the landowners would retain water rights so that their land would be productive for as long as the rivers flowed. Such proposals stunned the orthodoxy, but Powell had only just begun.

Rugged individualism, a hallmark of American culture, could not meet the challenge of settling the arid West. Instead, collective action would be necessary. Powell wrote, "To a great extent, the redemption of these lands will require extensive and comprehensive plans, for the execution of which aggregated capital or cooperative labor will be necessary. Here, individual farmers, being poor men, cannot undertake the task" (Powell 1879, viii). He had seen among the Mormon settlers of Utah an example of the benefits of cooperation. These early settlers had constructed irrigation canals and ditches that brought water to their fields, and they had done this not by competing with each other but by cooperating. The Mormon model, on a grander scale, could solve the riddle of settlement in the West. Powell proclaimed, "It was my purpose not only to consider the character of the lands themselves, but also the engineering problems involved in their redemption, and further to make suggestions for the legislative action necessary to inaugurate the enterprises by which these lands may eventually be rescued from the present worthless state" (Powell 1879, viii).

To make the moribund wheels of democracy move a little quicker, Powell included in his report several proposed pieces of legislation for Congress to adopt. Congress, however, would never take up his proposals, and the system of disposing of the public domain would not change: what had worked in the East would be replicated in the West, or so lawmakers believed. Small landowners would pay the price for this arrogance and struggle to make it in the region. Large corporations, however, would make the West suit their designs, and they had a powerful ally in the federal government.

In addition to attracting farmers, Congress promoted the development of the West by making it easy and profitable for corporations to exploit the region's natural resources. With millions of mouths to feed, cities to build, and factories to support, the demand for Western beef, lumber, and minerals was inexhaustible. The East might be the home of this industrial economy, but the resources to create the industrial nation lay mostly in the West.

Congress passed two laws in the early 1870s designed to convert the natural resources of the region into commodities as efficiently as possible. The 1872 Mining Law focused on mineral wealth. As the California gold rush and subsequent discoveries illustrated, the West had mineral wealth to rival any nation on the globe. Deciding who owned and could exploit those resources, however, had been difficult to determine. Mining laws in the California gold rush developed of necessity, and for the most part, they worked well in the placer diggings. For the mining industry to continue to develop, Congress felt it necessary to create a standardized system to allow for the rapid extraction of valuable minerals. The 1872 Mining Law resulted. The law stated, "All valuable mineral deposits in the lands belonging to the United States, both surveyed and unsurveyed, are hereby declared to be free and open to exploration and purchase, by citizens of the United States and those who have declared their intention to become such" (U.S. Congress 1872).

When Congress said "free," it meant free; despite the billions and billions of dollars in gold, silver, and other metals extracted from the earth, mining companies paid nothing in taxes or royalties to the U.S. government. The act was not intended to make money for the government but rather to encourage corporations to extract that wealth as quickly as possible. Acquiring, or *patenting*, the claim was a straightforward process. The claimant had to mark the boundaries of the claim clearly, file their patent in the land office, and prove that they had completed $500 in development on that claim. Holding onto claims was as easy as proving that the owner had performed "not less than one hundred dollars' worth of labor" per year. The law achieved its purpose in making the West a desirable place for mining, but this development came with economic and environmental consequences, both of which did not become apparent until years or even decades after the law's passage. Amazingly, the law is still on the books, and little has changed since its 1872 creation.

While Congress would never follow up on Powell's proposals, it did at least acknowledge the difficulties of settling the West with the 1877 Desert Land Act. Under the act, a person could claim 640 acres of land at the price of $1.25 per acre if they agreed to irrigate it within three years. A single farmer, however, could never hope to build the required infrastructure to irrigate that much acreage in so short a time. Instead, speculators swooped in, putting a down payment of 0.25 cents an acre on the land, claiming they had completed "adequate" irrigation, and then reselling their claims at a profit a few years later.

By the 1880s and 1890s, the government's efforts to promote the West had largely succeeded. New states had been added: Colorado in 1876; North Dakota, South Dakota, Montana, and Washington in 1889; Idaho and Wyoming in 1890; and Utah in 1896. The early 20th century would see the admission of Oklahoma in 1907 and New Mexico and Arizona in 1912. Alaska and Hawaii would finally gain statehood in 1959.

Despite its wide-open spaces, the West's political power lay in its cities, which had grown dramatically in the late 19th century. San Francisco, the West's largest city in 1880 with a population of 234,000, had already cracked into the nation's top 10 largest cities. Powerful corporations, especially in the railroad and mining industries, exerted tremendous influence on the West and, of course, increasingly so too did the federal government.

Indeed, the federal government decided to remain in the region, keeping control of the public domain rather than, as had previously been the case, trying to extinguish its landownership as fast as possible. New bureaucracies arose to control and manage these extensive landholdings. The Bureau of Indian Affairs ran the reservations that almost exclusively had been created in the West. National parks were set aside, first with Yellowstone and others soon following. Powell's USGS also asserted an important role for government scientists in mapping and measuring the region. Other bureaucracies also developed or made their way out West. The Bureau of Reclamation and the Army Corps of Engineers would soon jockey for primacy in the building of dams on the West's rivers, both great and small. The West's forests were to be administered by the new National Forest Service. Non-forestlands fell mostly under the jurisdiction of the Bureau of Land Management, and whatever was left often went to the U.S. military. Instead of a land of utopian small farmers, the West became the land with the heaviest federal presence, much to the dismay and chagrin of the states and Westerners themselves, who had assumed the federal government's landholdings would be liquidated at fire-sale prices.

In many ways, the prospect of turning the public domain over to Westerners compelled federal authorities to hold on to the public domain. Certainly, had the gates been thrown open (as they always had), the unbridled exploitation of the West's public lands would have continued apace. Leveled forests, polluted watersheds, and unrestrained capitalism had long been the law of the land, quite literally. After all, Westerners were only doing what Easterners had done before them. Development and expansion had always been the goals of "progress" and "civilization." A new, and mostly Eastern, generation of Americans, however, had come to a different conclusion by the 1890s. Unregulated development had been acceptable when an always moving Western frontier offered new promise and limitless resources, but in the 1890s, some Americans realized that the nation's land and resources were, in fact, not limitless.

CONSERVATION AND PRESERVATION

The first stirrings of this new perspective came as a result of the 1890 census. The Census Bureau announced that the frontier line would be removed from its report, as every place had now effectively been settled to a point where one could easily differentiate between civilization and undeveloped wilderness. In other words, the frontier was no more. The nation had completed its great task, expanding across a continent in three centuries. This line on a map, however, had profound cultural significance for a nation that believed expansion was its divinely ordained mission. Fear and uncertainty permeated American culture, finding expression in a wide variety of outlets, including political.

If what we had was all we had, if the forests and rivers and plants and animals were all that would ever be, perhaps it made sense to protect those, to manage them in a way that would preserve those resources in perpetuity. While thousands of Americans would come to advocate for these protections, three men in particular became leaders of this movement. Two were wealthy Easterners, and one was a rather odd Scotsman whose formative years had been spent in the wilds of Wisconsin. All three believed Americans could do better when it came to managing their lands, but they nevertheless had some major ideological differences.

Eleven-year-old John Muir moved with his family from Scotland to Wisconsin in 1849, arriving first in New York at the peak of the gold rush fever, but his father, Daniel, had less worldly concerns in mind as a follower of the Campbellites, a religious sect that sought to return to a simpler form of Christianity. The family settled first at Fountain Lake, northwest of Milwaukee, on a farm on the very edge of the frontier. Their land included a small glacial lake and acres of woodlands. John and his brother, when not working on the farm, had ample time to explore the surrounding woods. Muir reflected late in life, "This sudden splash in pure wildness—baptism in Nature's warm heart—how utterly happy it made us!" (quoted in Wilkins 1995, 16). Daniel ruled over his family like an Old Testament patriarch, forcing his children to work so long as they could stand. Hard unremitting labor and large doses of fire and brimstone theology, he believed, would temper his sons into pious and self-reliant men. Daniel predicted, John remembered later, "that when I was fairly out in the wicked world making my own way I would soon learn that although I might have thought him a hard taskmaster," it was only to prepare him for the reality of life (quoted in Wilkins 1995, 16).

Young John Muir had no intention of spending his life on a farm like his father. A child of the industrial age, he had a penchant for inventing and tinkering with machinery. In 1860, at age 22, he left home with only a few dollars in his pocket to make his way in the world as an inventor. He enrolled at the University of Wisconsin in Madison, choosing the classes that interested him in a variety of fields but never actually advancing to the point of earning a degree. Here, among his varied interests, he developed a passion for botany. The Civil War had now torn the country asunder, and Muir had, fortunately, avoided the draft several times before deciding his luck could not hold indefinitely. As a strong pacifist, he decided, as he put it, to "skedaddle" to Canada and join his brother, Daniel.

The pair eventually found themselves working at a sawmill, where Muir's mechanical skills earned praise from the owners. He returned to the states after the war and continued as a mechanic, this time in Indianapolis. As a mechanic for a carriage parts company, his career seemed to be taking off, but on the evening of March 6, 1867, a metal file he was holding slipped and pierced his eye. He lost sight in his right eye, and within hours, his left eye also shut down. While his sight would gradually return, the accident caused Muir to reevaluate the direction of his life.

For a man who spent all his free time wandering the woods and cataloging new plants, working in a sawmill seemed hypocritical. The sawmill owners offered him a job as head of a new mill, a lucrative position to be sure, but Muir turned them down and decided to embrace nature. He later wrote, "I could have become a millionaire, but I chose to become a tramp" (quoted in Wilkins 1995, 45). Henceforth, Muir decided he would live as he might and always in celebration of God's creation. His life had changed forever, and in the process, he would give voice to a new American attitude about the natural world.

Muir left Indianapolis on foot, deciding to walk to the Gulf of Mexico via a winding route through Kentucky, Tennessee, Georgia, and finally to Cedar Key, Florida. Thus, he wrote, "I bade adieu to all my mechanical inventions, determined to devote the rest of my life to the study of the inventions of God" (quoted in Wilkins 1995, 48).

In the Sierra Nevada mountains of California, however, Muir found his muse. He arrived in the Yosemite Valley in 1869 and found a job as a millwright working for an Englishman named James M. Hutchings, who had already built a hotel in the valley and was working hard to promote the valley to tourists. A keen observer of nature, Muir published an essay proving that glaciation shaped the Yosemite Valley. He argued that gradual processes, like the relentless grinding of glaciers against rock, explained the visage of the planet more than cataclysms such as floods. His insights helped to establish the belief in uniformitarianism, the theory that the processes shaping the earth now are the same processes that shaped it in the past.

By the mid-1870s, Muir was already worried about the fate of his beloved Sierras, particularly the region's spectacular redwood and sequoia trees. Early tourists had scattered among the mountains, destroying everything in their path, it seemed to Muir. Sheep also damaged valleys by overgrazing the fragile grasses, and the shepherds themselves set fires to burn trees and promote pasturage. Finally, lumber companies wanted nothing more than to cut down these largest (and therefore most lucrative) trees on the planet. Muir came out in favor of the preservation of these stands of arboreal giants in a lecture published in the *Sacramento Record-Union* in 1876, titled "God's First Temples." Muir argued that California's extraordinary forests were its most perishable resource, writing, "Our forest belts are being burned and cut down and wasted like a field of unprotected grain, and once destroyed can never be wholly restored even by centuries of persistent and painstaking cultivation" (Muir 1997, 629). More than just trees, Muir warned, the forests helped temper the climate of the state, holding and releasing water for lower elevations. Without forests, the entirety of California would become a desert. He called for government intervention to protect these stands of timber before it was too late, but he doubted "whether our loose-jointed Government is really able or willing to do anything in the matter" (Muir 1997, 633).

By the late 19th century, some Americans began to advocate for government oversight of the West as a way to protect its land and resources. John Muir (right) advocated for preservation of Western lands in their natural state. President Theodore Roosevelt (left) would set aside millions of acres of Western land for both preservation and conservation uses. Here the pair overlook Bridal Veil Falls in Yosemite National Park. (Wellcome Collection)

Increasingly, Muir espoused the idea of federal government protection. Already in his time, there was so little left. Settlers had come to North America with the conviction that everything belonged to them, and "claiming Heaven as their guide, regarded God's trees as only a larger kind of pernicious weeds" (Muir 1997, 703). He concluded another essay, "American Forests," with a call to protect what remained, writing, "Through all the wonderful, eventful centuries since Christ's time—and long before that—God has cared for these trees, saved them from drought, disease, avalanches, and a thousand straining, leveling tempests and floods; but he cannot save them from fools—only Uncle Same can do that" (Muir 1997, 720). Unsurprisingly, he advocated for Yosemite to become a national park, instead of the poorly managed state park it already was, and he wanted as much land set aside as possible throughout the Sierras and beyond. What Muir wanted, above all, was preservation, keeping the wilderness unsullied by the hand of man. Fortunately, Muir's belief in the power of government to protect valuable resources and beautiful places was about to find a powerful champion in a younger generation of American leaders, most notably Theodore Roosevelt.

Indeed, a profound cultural change rumbled to life in the 1890s as Americans realized the end of the frontier era had come. Frederick Jackson Turner's famous 1893 essay "The Significance of the Frontier in American History," while a lament for the passing of the heroic age of American history, helped awaken in Americans a sense that they needed to protect what aspects of the passing age they could. Culturally, this meant celebrating pioneer skills by creating institutions such as the Boy Scouts of America to help teach children woodcraft skills and attendant attributes like self-reliance, resourcefulness, and tenacity. Turner's thesis also could be used to encourage the preservation and conservation of the rugged landscape that settlers had once struggled to conquer. Wielding the power of the federal government, this new generation sought to preserve and manage, rather than conquer and exhaust, the spectacular landscapes of the West. One such proposal called for the establishment of a forest reserve system. These forests would be managed by professionals with an eye to long-term lumber production and sustainability.

After decades of doing everything possible to promote the development of the West, the change toward the federal government limiting the exploitation of resources stunned and angered many Westerners who wanted to continue the unfettered exploitation of the region's resources. The fact that many of the leaders advocating for these changes hailed not from the West but from the East only increased their ire. Detractors, especially Western lawmakers, saw the creation of the national forest reserve system as an attempt by the federal government to lock up the forests from use by average citizens, denying residents access to vitally important timber and grazing land. The bureaucrats in charge of the rapidly expanding federal agencies, however, saw their role as championing the scientific and efficient use of resources, and foremost among these new bureaucrats was Gifford Pinchot.

Gifford Pinchot's father, James, had been successful in both his business dealings and in his choice of wife, for Mary Jane Eno, his new bride, brought with her a large dowry. So successful had James been, in fact, that he retired at the age of 44 to his stately manor house in Milford, Pennsylvania, with the predictably regal name of Grey Towers. As expected of a wealthy gentleman, James dabbled in many different activities, including forestry. The professional management of forests developed in France, Germany, and other European nations decades before Americans, accustomed to seemingly limitless resources, confronted the reality of forest depletion.

The creation of the American Forestry Association in 1875 was a step in the right direction, but the association, like forestry in general, fell to enthusiastic amateurs like James Pinchot. Gifford, born in 1865, would change that.

Gifford Pinchot's early life certainly did not lack for comforts, and he never had to toil as John Muir had on his family's farm. Instead, Pinchot's upbringing was that of an American elite: private tutors, the exclusive Phillips Exeter Academy preparatory school, and finally Yale. Summers, however, gave Pinchot the freedom to explore the grounds around one of his family's numerous estates, and wandering the forests around Grey Towers, in particular, inspired his love of wild places.

Resting on a fortune of several million dollars, Pinchot had the ability to essentially not do anything, to live a life of ease, comfort, and glamour. He, however, had other plans. As he told a friend in 1914, "My own money came from unearned increment on land in New York held by my grandfather, who willed the money, not the land to me. Having got my wages in advance in that way, I am now trying to work them out" (quoted in McGeary 2016, 3). He had decided on a career in forestry before completing his Yale education, but that avocation did not yet exist in the United States. Thus, he set off for Europe, with stops in England, Germany, and the French Forest School at Nancy. Affable, charming, and fluent in French, Pinchot easily insinuated himself into the good graces of the French foresters.

The professionalism of European foresters astonished him. German and French foresters had been managing their woods for centuries, ensuring that every scrap was used, and the forests were protected from fire and illegal harvesting by strict and severe laws. Pinchot returned to the United States in 1889 armed with the latest in woodland management techniques and set up a forestry consulting firm in New York City, an incongruent place for such a business given its ever-growing labyrinth of cement and steel canyons. New York, of course, was also the seat of American economic power, and so his choice was perhaps not as incongruent as it seemed. Indeed, his contact with Frederick Law Olmsted, the nation's foremost landscape architect and the designer of Central Park, led to a chance to implement his plans on the summer estate of George Vanderbilt in 1892.

One of the richest men in the United States, Vanderbilt erected a palatial estate, christened Biltmore, on 8,000 acres in the mountains near Asheville, North Carolina. Always the businessman, however,

Vanderbilt wanted his estate to be profitable. It would be a model farm, a game preserve, and a sustainable lumber operation, with Pinchot in charge of the latter. Pinchot marched across the estate carefully marking which trees would be harvested, leaving the younger trees that would one day grow to maturity. Local lumbermen scoffed at the idea, accustomed as they were to simply felling everything, regardless of size, in their path.

With profits from the lumber sales in hand, Pinchot persuaded Vanderbilt to purchase another 80,000 acres of land adjoining the estate. Vanderbilt agreed, and Pinchot now had a laboratory to experiment with his concept of sustainable forestry. Pinchot's consulting business had attracted other wealthy clients, and his desire to do great things already had him looking beyond being the forester of Biltmore. Indeed, at the first opportunity, he stepped back from the daily management of the estate's forests. With no trained American foresters yet, Pinchot was forced to import one from Germany, a man named Carl Alvin Schenck. Schenck would manage the forests of Biltmore, with Pinchot as a consultant, freeing him up to promote forestry practices on a grander scale.

Pinchot would soon have his chance, for attitudes in the United States were finally changing thanks to men like President Rutherford B. Hayes's secretary of the interior, Carl Schurz (in office from 1877 to 1881). Schurz, a German by birth, saw the need for the United States to emulate European management practices, and he felt the federal government should be in charge of the effort to protect public forests from overharvesting and fires. Perhaps the most important moment in efforts to create federal oversight of the forests came with the passage of the Forest Reserve Act of 1891. Astonishingly, the act slipped through Congress with little opposition or fanfare, but it offered a powerful new tool for the president to wield. Under the act, the president could create forest reserves, withdrawing sections of the public domain from potential sale. Shortly after passage of the act, President Benjamin Harrison set aside 13 million acres in the West as forest reserves. However, the act did not stipulate what use these lands would serve. Indeed, among these early environmentalists, two schools of thought emerged, which were embodied by Muir and Pinchot.

Pinchot, for his part, saw forests as useful. They should be managed in what we today would call a sustainable manner so that water quality would be protected and lumber production carefully controlled. His was a utilitarian view of nature as useful to humanity. A forest whose trees died and rotted into dirt was almost as bad as a forest felled before the clear-cutter's wasteful axe. Forest resources should be "conserved," that is, managed carefully but ultimately used.

Muir, on the other hand, advocated for the preservation of land in its primal state, free from interference from humanity. In truth, as Muir himself recognized, the hand of man, especially that of Native Americans, had indelibly shaped the landscape, but he regarded their use of fire, for example, as beneficial and natural. The distinctions between the two perspectives were not always so fine, and even Muir acknowledged that some extraction of resources would be necessary in some parts of the forest. But he hoped that most of these new reserves would be protected as national parks, prohibiting mining, grazing, and lumber operations from existing in these areas. Once roads were built and trees harvested, the wild grandeur of the place would be forever altered.

Pinchot saw forest reserves as Biltmore estates on a monumental scale, vast tracts of land that would produce lumber for generations to come in a managed and scientific way. In 1896, Congress created a National Forestry Commission to survey and make recommendations for the forestlands of the nation. Pinchot and Muir found themselves members of the commission. Sparring over their conflicting views, the publication of the report languished as the members of the committee splintered into preservationists and proponents of conservation, the former led by Muir and Harvard botany professor Charles Sargent and the latter led by Pinchot. President Cleveland, with no plan coming from the commission, decided to set aside some 21 million acres of land as forest reserves shortly before leaving office in 1897. At the time, once lands had been set aside, the public could not even enter them legally. Most of the land Cleveland set aside lay in Washington, Montana, and California, and lawmakers from these states complained about the government "locking up" this land from the people in the name of the people. Clearly, something would have to be done.

Cleveland's actions enraged Westerners, and many lawmakers called for the repeal of the law and the abolishment of the existing reserves. Preservationists continued to argue that the reserves should prohibit any logging or similar economic activities. Pinchot, however, asserted that the reserves should remain, but they should be used for logging and other commercial uses under the careful stewardship of the professional foresters of the federal government. He lobbied members of Congress, including Westerners, and in the end managed to get enough support for his viewpoint to get the Forest Management Act passed in June 1897. With the exception of national parks, most of the forestlands of the West still controlled by the federal government would be open for development, but development in accordance with Pinchot's principles of conservation.

The following year, in 1898, the new secretary of the interior in Republican William McKinley's administration, Cornelius N. Bliss, offered Pinchot the job of special forest agent to survey the state of the forest reserves and to offer recommendations for the creation of a professional forest service. Pinchot set off filled with optimism and enthusiasm to complete the task, refusing a regular salary and instead working for $10 a day plus expenses.

Oddly, as is often the case of government bureaucracies, it was uncertain which department would best manage the forests. The Department of the Interior had control of the forest reserves, but it had no professional foresters. Conversely, the Department of Agriculture had some foresters on staff but no actual forests to manage. Agriculture would win the struggle to control the forests, in part because the secretary of agriculture decided to offer the head of the Division of Forestry to Pinchot. All that remained was to effect the transfer of the reserves from Interior to Agriculture, a task Pinchot devoted himself to tirelessly throughout the duration of the McKinley administration, and while McKinley liked the idea, the president proved unwilling to push forward with the proposal. The next president, however, would be more willing to fight about the forests, or anything else for that matter.

Truth be told, the Republican party never wanted Theodore Roosevelt to be president. As governor of his home state of New York, the bombastic, energetic, and crusading Roosevelt had rankled the establishment, and his selection as McKinley's vice president in the 1900 election had been made, in part, to sideline him. That plan backfired on September 6, 1901, when McKinley was assassinated in Buffalo, New York (fatally wounded, McKinley would not die until September 14), catapulting Roosevelt into the presidency. With his usual verve and charm, Roosevelt set out to reinvent the presidency and the American system of government. He would advocate for a stronger federal government to regulate private corporations, champion the rights of workers, manage the nation's resources, and preserve its most awe-inspiring natural places. In short, Roosevelt embodied the beliefs of the Progressive reform movement of the era in which government would employ professional experts to make American society cleaner, safer, and more just than it had ever been, and one of those professionals would be his friend Gifford Pinchot.

Roosevelt and Pinchot came from the same elite backgrounds, and each believed that wealthy and powerful figures needed to give back to society. They had become friends in the 1890s when both found themselves in Washington, DC, at the same time. Given their common backgrounds and political views, it is unsurprising that they become friends and close political allies. Indeed, in Roosevelt's first address to Congress following the assassination of McKinley, he made his view clear: "Wise forest protection does not mean the withdrawal of forest resources, whether of wood, water, or grass, from contributing their full share to the welfare of the people, but, on the contrary, gives the assurance of larger and more certain supplies" (Roosevelt 1901). Such a statement sounded exactly like something Pinchot would write, and in fact, it was in large part written by Pinchot. He went on to endorse the transfer of the Forestry Bureau to the Department of Agriculture. The transfer, unsurprisingly, would be mired in bureaucratic squabbles for the next several years, but with Roosevelt's support, Pinchot finally managed to get a bill through Congress, transferring the forest reserves to the Department of Agriculture in 1905. The old Bureau of Forestry became the new United States Forest Service, with Pinchot, predictably, as its head. Despite the complaints of many Westerners, the age of the professional management of the forest reserves (renamed national forests) had arrived.

Westerners expressed far more enthusiasm about federal support for the development of the West's most precious resource: water. Even before the pessimistic reports of Powell, lawmakers had been aware that the scarcity of water would be the West's greatest challenge. Whereas Powell had advocated for adapting to this lack of water through careful collective management and the promotion of a limited population where water could be harnessed, lawmakers envisioned bringing vast tracts of land under cultivation thanks to expensive and expansive resource development: massive dams, complicated canals, and irrigation ditches could make the deserts of the West bloom. Even Teddy Roosevelt endorsed this vision of the West made verdant through the efforts of the federal government.

Before he had moved into the White House, Roosevelt set out to advocate for the West's land and water. Preparing for his first address to Congress, he met with Pinchot and F. H. Newell, from the USGS. Newell asked the president to bring up the issue of irrigation as well as the forest reserves as part of a comprehensive effort to bring lawmakers' attention to the West. Roosevelt proposed a powerful role for the federal government. Given the sporadic nature of the West's rivers, "great storage works are necessary to equalize the flow of streams and to save the flood waters. Their construction has been conclusively shown to be an undertaking too vast for private effort. Nor can it be best accomplished by the individual States acting alone. . . . It is properly a national function," Roosevelt proclaimed in his address (Roosevelt 1901). Roosevelt went on to argue in favor of building canals to send water to areas that could be productive if irrigated. Further, he argued, these lands should be sold by the government to "actual settlers" rather than speculators.

Francis Newlands, a congressman from the desert state of Nevada, offered up a bill that sounded a lot like what Roosevelt was proposing. Under the National Reclamation Act (or Newlands Act, which was a tribute to the author and a convenient description of its purpose), the government would create the irrigation infrastructure to "reclaim" desolate lands and make them productive. This irrigated land would then be sold in 160-acre tracts to settlers, and the profits from the sales would finance the construction of more projects to make more lands productive in a seemingly endless cycle. All of this would fall under the purview of another infant federal bureaucracy, the Bureau of Reclamation, as it would be renamed in 1923. The act never functioned as well as Newlands envisioned; few projects ever made it to fruition, and the acreage irrigated remained modest. The Bureau of Reclamation, however, would see its power and prestige rise dramatically with the construction of new, massive dams in the 1930s and beyond.

CONCLUSION: POLITICAL LIFE AND THE RISE OF THE FEDERAL GOVERNMENT

The image of the Westerner as the laconic, independent cowboy, surveying a range of limitless potential and unbridled freedom, is indelibly etched into the public consciousness, but over the course of the 19th century, that vision proved more and more evanescent, a mirage on the desert air. Large corporations claimed much of the West, most notably the railroads, and a great deal of the region's resources went to lumber, railroad, and mining companies. Time and again, a region that allegedly belonged to all Americans ended up in the hands of comparatively few.

The only counter to this lay in the growing power of the federal government, which after decades of doing everything it could to promote the development of the West by offering up its valuable land, water, minerals, and timber for nothing, or next to nothing, suddenly had a change of heart. At the turn of the last century, a new generation of bureaucrats, like Pinchot and Roosevelt, advocated for federal management of the West's land and resources, and mostly they would be successful. Meanwhile, preservationists like John Muir would win some of their own battles as the nation, especially during Roosevelt's presidency, added to the national park and monument system scores of new parks, most of which could be found in the West.

At the beginning of the 19th century, Meriwether Lewis could look west and exclaim, "We were now about to penetrate a country at least two thousand miles in width, on which the foot of civilized man had never trodden" (quoted in Bergon 1995). A century later, Lewis would have seen the shiny streaks of railroads arcing to the horizon, the curling smoke of growing cities, rows of wheat and corn, and herds of cattle milling about in fenced-off pastures. What would he have thought of this, having seen the West as it was before, is impossible to say, and indeed he himself had represented the first stirrings of a new order, of the coming world. It is impossible to know what he would think, but for most Americans at the time, it seemed the very essence of progress.

One American, in particular, seemed to capture the spirit of the age as she gazed out on the Great Plains from the summit of Pikes Peak, in Colorado. Kathy Lee Bates was an English professor by trade, and thus, unsurprisingly, she put her thoughts to verse in a poem (and later song) called "America the Beautiful." Her poem sings the praises of America's agricultural and industrial development. In it, she describes "amber waves of grain" lorded over by "purple mountain majesties" and intrepid pioneers "whose stern, impassioned stress; A thoroughfare for free beat; Across the wilderness!" Settled now, America's "alabaster cities gleam." Such progress reflected God's divine plan for the nation, as "God shed His grace on thee." The decades-old conquest of the continent had ended, and now America, and the American system of government, truly stretched "from sea to shining sea!" (Bates 1911).

6

RELIGIOUS LIFE IN THE AMERICAN WEST

Religion is an often overlooked motivation for settlement. Certainly, students of American history are versed in the struggle of the Pilgrims in the 17th century to find a place to nourish their spiritual lives without fear of persecution, but how many know the story of the Mormon exodus to Utah or the role spirituality played in American Indians' resistance to expansion? Nevertheless, religion and religious life have played an important role in the story of the American West.

AMERICAN INDIAN SPIRITUALITY

Europeans and Anglo-Americans typically misunderstood Indian spirituality, if they tried to understand it at all. More likely, they simply denounced it as pagan and proof of Indian savagery. Father Atanasio Domínguez captured the frustration of generations of missionaries, writing of his visit to the pueblos of New Mexico in 1776 that "even at the end of so many years since their reconquest the specious title or name of neophytes is still applied to them [Pueblo peoples]. This is the reason their condition now is almost the same as it was in the beginning, for generally speaking they have preserved some very indecent, and perhaps superstitious customs" (quoted in Gutiérrez 1991, 307). In other words, while accepting some of the new practices of the Catholic missionaries, the Pueblos continued to also practice their ancestral traditions. Similarly, Marcus Whitman, the American Methodist missionary sent to the Cayuse Indians of eastern Washington, wrote dismissively that "many of their traditions are evidences of . . . worship of some Animals & Birds" (Jeffrey 1994, 116). Such comments revealed far more about the frustrations and ignorance of missionaries than they did an understanding of the people they had come to convert.

Certainly, much of this misunderstanding stemmed from the ethnocentrism (the belief that their own culture was superior) of the missionaries themselves, but some of it also originated from the profoundly different ways Indian peoples conceived of spirituality. Christianity, whether Protestant or Roman Catholic, offered a world where God stood apart from everyday existence. To be sure, God's presence, believers argued, could be felt, but God himself did not appear in the ordinary lives of believers. Moreover, the supernatural existence of heaven or hell separated those realms from earthly existence. It was only after death that the soul would venture to either of those places. To be sure, supernatural events did occur in the pages of the Bible, such as Moses and the burning bush, but they had been relegated to the distant past for most Christian groups. This distance from God and the supernatural differed greatly from the belief system of American Indian peoples.

Indian spirituality, like languages, customs, and other practices, varied widely from group to group, but certain similarities can be identified. First, for Indian peoples, the supernatural was not separate from daily life. Powerful supernatural entities, both good and bad, could be encountered at any time. The Lakota elder Black Elk recounted to the anthropologist John G. Neihardt that he had his first vision when he was but five years old. He explained, "I was riding into the woods along a creek, there was a kingbird sitting on a limb. This was not a dream, it happened. And I was going to shoot at the kingbird . . . when the bird spoke and said: 'The clouds all over are one-sided.'" Black Elk looked to the sky and saw two men descending toward him while singing a sacred song. When they had almost reached the boy, they "wheeled about toward where the sun goes down, and suddenly they were geese" (Neihardt 1979, 14–15). This would be the first of many visions over the course of Black Elk's life. Such visions connected humanity to the ineffable powers of the cosmos, often providing insight and assistance to people.

Animals, as well, played important roles. In the European worldview, animals were inferior creatures to humanity. In the book of Genesis, God created mankind to be above all other creatures: "Let us make man in our image, after our likeness: and let them have dominion over the fish of the sea, and over the foul of the air, and over the cattle, and over all the earth, and over every creeping thing that creepeth upon the earth" (King James Bible Online n.d.). How different, then, was this from the Okanogan people's story of the creation of the animal people. The world began when Old One, after transforming a woman into the earth, fashioned balls of clay into the ancient peoples. "The ancients were people, yet also animals. In form some looked human while some walked on all fours like animals. Some could fly like birds; other could swim like fishes. All had the gift of speech" (Erdoes and Ortiz 1984, 14–15). Rather than separate and superior to the rest of the natural world, humans were just one of the many and varied kinds of people in existence.

For some Indian peoples, animals provided vital support. The Crow believed animal helpers could bestow their attributes on people or provide connection between the supernatural world and the human world. Pretty-shield told the story of Little-face, a Crow woman, who opened her food pouch, where she kept pemmican to eat, and saw inside a mother mouse and her small children sleeping. Rather than squealing in anger or revulsion, she instead left the mouse and her children to doze in the warm pouch. That night, as the village slept, the mouse crept up to the woman's ear and said, "My friend! My friend . . . in four days your people will be attacked by the Lacota [Lakota]. Can you make the men believe this, get them to go back to the place that you came from?" (Linderman 1978, 120). Explaining to her people what the mouse had told her, the Crow decided to pack up and move before the attack came.

On another occasion, a Crow woman was attacked by a grizzly bear while picking berries. As the terrified woman, severely wounded and bleeding profusely, fled from the bear, an aptly named man called Crazy-brave attacked it with only a knife. Singing his special song that he had learned from the dragonfly, he declared, "The bear will not see me. I am the dragon-fly." Indeed, the bear did not notice the man as he walked up on it. Pretty-shield explained, "This was because he looked like a dragon-fly, and because he was singing his song. Crazy-brave did not stop his attack until he drove his knife into the bear's throat" (Linderman 1978, 101).

172 *Daily Life in the American West*

Such power as that wielded by Crazy-brave came from one's medicine. The somewhat awkward term *medicine* encapsulates an individual's spiritual power, their ability to move from the ordinary world into the world of ineffable powers that control the universe, or *Wakantanka* in Lakota. *Wakantanka* was not a god in the anthropomorphized way of the Christian God but the great, mysterious creative force of the universe. Interceding between this force and the Lakota people required the skills of a highly trained medicine man, or *wicasa wakan*. Often this intercession would take the form of premonitions, visions, or messages conveyed by animals to the shaman. Only those with special training, who had purified themselves in sacred sweat baths and who knew the sacred songs and prayers, could engage in such activities. Many medicine men charged for their services, and when people fell ill, they would often be called to deal with the ailment, which was often believed to have a spiritual cause that manifested in physical symptoms.

Such was the case with Black Elk. Following another vision and out-of-body experience, Black Elk regained consciousness, and his father sent for the medicine man. The shaman, Whirlwind Chaser, told Black Elk's father, "Your boy there is sitting in a sacred manner. I do not know what it is, but there is something special for him to do, for just as I came in I could see a power like a light all through his body" (Neihardt 1979, 38). Such power could be used to help the people, to encourage them to action or to console them in times of uncertainty.

Sitting Bull, the great Lakota leader, gained his considerable influence in part from his spiritual power. Like Black Elk, he had many visions as a child, and as he grew older, his power only shone brighter. He would have two great visions later in life, the first in 1876 and the other sometime around 1890, and both would come to pass. But throughout his life, he repeatedly demonstrated a connection to the ineffable power of the universe.

On his first buffalo hunt, at roughly the age of 14, Sitting Bull proved to be an excellent hunter, partly due to his skill with both his horse and his bow and arrow but also because of his connection to the natural world, most especially with the bison. The bison figured prominently in the economic life of Plains Indian peoples like Sitting Bull's Lakota. Finding bison and successfully hunting them was perhaps the most desirable skill a man could possess, and Sitting Bull proved to be uncommonly gifted at finding the shaggy beasts in even the most difficult of circumstances. His uncanny success depended on his special relationship with the bison.

It was said that Sitting Bull attained his name when he was six years old. While tending to a herd of horses outside of his village, the young boy, then known as *Hunkesni* (translated as "Slow" in English), encountered a large bull bison that was sitting on its haunches. The Indian youth and the majestic creature locked eyes for a moment, and the bison said, "Sitting Bull you've pitied me—thank you—I respect you." Returning to the village, he told his father of the encounter. Knowing that this was an event of great significance, Sitting Bull's father took him to the medicine man to recount the experience. The wise *wicasa wakan* explained that he had shown the bison respect, and in return, the bison would always return that respect by offering themselves up to Sitting Bull in the hunt. Further, the boy would now be known by the name Sitting Bull that the bison had given him (Anderson 2007, 43–44).

Sitting Bull demonstrated his great medicine during a small skirmish between the Lakota and the U.S. Army on Arrow Creek, a tributary of the Yellowstone River. The soldiers were protecting the Northern Pacific Railroad survey as it made its way through the very heart of Lakota territory. The two groups stumbled into each other on a warm August day in 1872. Outnumbered, the soldiers managed to get into a strong defensive position on the riverbank, their concentrated firepower enough to keep the Lakota at bay. Some young men raced their horses within range of the soldier's rifles to prove their bravery, but only one man, Plenty Lice, was killed by the fusillades.

Bored and disgusted with both sides, Sitting Bull announced that he was going for a smoke, and whoever "wishes to smoke with me, come." His nephew White Bull, two Cheyenne, and another Hunkpapa Lakota followed the older man, who, much to their surprise, descended from the hill overlooking the soldier's position into the open field between the two opposing factions. Sitting Bull took a seat in the meadow, well within range of the soldiers' rifles. Here he began to calmly load and smoke his pipe, passing it around with nonchalance to his stunned companions as bullets zipped through the air and thudded dully into the dirt around them. Another young man decided to join this brazen display of bravery, and just as he reached the seated smokers, a bullet struck and killed him. Sitting Bull finished his pipe, cleaned it, and returned it to his pouch (Anderson 2007, 85). This demonstration of his great power amazed the Lakota and Cheyenne and no doubt caused some consternation among the soldiers who had witnessed it. While Sitting Bull remained calm throughout the demonstration, his nephew recalled that he had never smoked a pipe so quickly in his life.

Powerful Lakota figures, like Sitting Bull, also carried with them a *Wotawe*, or medicine bag, which included objects of great power and significance. It was the power inside the *Wotawe* that protected Sitting Bull from the soldiers' bullets. His medicine bag, for example, contained a small white stone, several small balls of human hair, and a few bits of wood or shell, simple items that belied their importance (Anderson 2007, 59). His friend and fellow Lakota leader, Crazy Horse, had a similar charm: a small white stone with a hole bored through it that he wore on a buckskin cord. The stone charm had been given to him in 1862 or 1863 by a medicine man named Chips. Decades later, Red Feather, a friend of Crazy Horse, swore that before he wore the charm he had been wounded on a few occasions, but once the charm came into his possession, he was never again harmed in battle (Ambrose 1996a, 133).

For Plains Indian peoples, like the Lakota and their enemies the Crow, religion was not separate from daily existence. The great mystery, the power of the universe, or *Wakantanka* in Lakota, could be found everywhere and within all things. It fell to medicine men to understand and channel this power.

While one could encounter the mysterious, ineffable force of creation anywhere, some places radiated great spiritual power. These could be any number of physical sites: mountain peaks, rock formations, caves, streams, and lakes. Many of these commemorated great events in time immemorial: for example, the Heart of the Monster butte in Idaho, where coyote defeated a world-devouring monster and created the Nez Percé peoples from its blood, and Devil's Tower, where seven Kiowa girls escaped their brother who had been transformed into a monstrous bear by ascending into the sky to become the Pleiades.

The Lakota, again, provide an interesting case study of how sacred landscapes can be found everywhere. The arrival of the horse pulled Indian peoples onto the plains in larger numbers, including the Lakota. In time, the Lakota came to dominate the northern plains, including the Black Hills of modern South Dakota. The Black Hills became their most sacred landscape, unsurprising, perhaps, given their grandeur and uniqueness as a mountain range surrounded for hundreds of square miles by the *obleyaya dosho*, the Lakota phrase that means "the wideness of the world." Rising up out of this wideness, the Black Hills climb to 7,242 feet at the summit of Black Elk Peak (formerly Harney Peak), the highest point between the Rockies and the Appalachian Mountains. In summer, thunderheads form around them as the hot air rises and cools, accentuating their sense of power and mystery.

Called the Black Hills for the cloak of darker pine trees that cover them, in stark contrast to the browns and tans of the surrounding plains, the hills have attracted humans for tens of thousands of years. Here humans could find water, shelter, wood, and food, as the hills also host deer, elk, and, of course, bison. Such an oasis invariably attracted numerous Indian tribes over the centuries. The Comanche named them the "Red Fir Place," the Kiowa called them the "Black Rock Mountains," the Cheyenne people knew them as the "Island Hills," and to the Sioux, including the Lakota, they were the Paha Sapa, the "Black Hills," but they gave them other names too: the "Meat Pack," for the presence of game, and the "Place of Shelter," for the hills offered shelter from even the harshest of winter storms (Nabakov 2006, 207).

As sacred landscapes go, an odd cloud-cloaked mountain range rising from the vastness of the plains seems appropriate. Throughout human history, people have been ascending peaks to rise toward knowledge and put one in the state of mind to understand the majesty of creation. Indeed, the current name of the Black Hills' tallest peak is a reference to the famous Lakota medicine man, Black Elk, whose greatest vision he claimed occurred on the summit of the peak. About 1872, and then a boy of nine, Black Elk had fallen ill and lost the use of his legs. While convalescing, he had a vision. A great horse came to carry him to the heavens to meet the Six Grandfathers, who told him of the sorrow and suffering that would come to his people, but also how Black Elk could help them endure. The horse sped to the east. "I looked ahead and saw the mountains there," he explained, "with rocks and forests on them, and from the mountains flashed all the colors upward to the heavens. Then I was standing on the highest mountain of them all, and around about beneath me was the whole hoop of the world" (Neihardt 1979, 33). He explained that this was Harney Peak, the tallest mountain at the center of the Lakota world.

The Grandfathers placed Black Elk on the top of the peak so he could behold everything and understand. While Black Elk's vision proved particularly important, such experiences were traditional among Plains peoples as a way for a man or woman to gain insight into themselves or to solve a problem. In the words of Richard

Erdoes and Alfonso Ortiz, a vision quest "may mean staying on top of a hill or inside a vision pit, alone, without food or water, for as long as four days and nights. It is hard, but if the spirit voices reveal or confer a vision that shapes a person's life, then the quest is worth the suffering" (Erdoes and Ortiz 1984, 69).

While the peaks certainly held sacred power, other significant sites were scattered around what is now southwestern South Dakota and eastern Wyoming. An Oglala Lakota man, from the Pine Ridge Reservation near the Black Hills, began to record his people's sacred places when he was in his thirties. His name was Amos Bad Heart Bull. Born in 1859, he lived through the U.S. Army's campaign against his people and the beginning of the reservation period. He completed more than 400 drawings of Lakota sacred places by the time of his death in 1913. Taken together, these amounted to a pictorial map of Lakota culture, history, and sacred spaces. Although the original drawings were buried with his sister, Dollie Pretty Cloud, in 1947, photographs of the drawings and his map had been taken (Nabakov 2006, 212). On his map, Bad Heart Bull included places like the "Race Track," where in time immemorial the two-legged and four-legged creatures raced to see which was the fleetest; the nearby Buffalo Gate; the Old Woman's Hill; and the Bear's Lodge Medicine Pipe Mountain. Other locations described their celestial importance and symbolic ties to constellations. One of the most sacred was *Washu Niya*, or "The Breathing Place." Known now as Wind Cave, for the sound of wind, not unlike breath, emanating from its mouth, the cavern marked the Lakota place "where First Man emerged from the underworld, the place where the Sacred White Buffalo originated and the outlet from which buffalo and other animals emerged to provide sustenance for human beings" (Nabakov 2006, 213–214).

Since the sacred comingled with the ordinary, important events could occur at any time, but there were certainly times when ceremonies should occur, especially ceremonies related to the solstices and equinoxes. The most important of all for many Plains Indian peoples occurred near the summer solstice: the Sun Dance.

The Sun Dance served, in a general way, as a time to thank the sun as the bringer of light and life to earth, for without the sun, there could be no life. It also provided an opportunity for participants to honor the creative force of the universe and ask for help with a variety of problems that could be remedied with supernatural assistance. To win such help, participants danced, prayed, and often offered up their own blood and flesh as sacrificial offerings—at least among the Arapaho, Cheyenne, Blackfeet, and Sioux nations. Tribes that did not perform ritualistic sacrifice nevertheless showed their reverence for the sun by fasting for as many as four days and nights. Among the Lakota, the Sun Dance was called *Wi wanyang wacipi*, which means the "sun gazing dance," because dancers chanted and prayed while staring at the sun for long periods of time. The dance took place in a circular arena called a *hocoka*. At the center of the arena, a sacred cottonwood limb, cut by virgin girls and carried by the sons of important men, presided over the ceremony. Other Plains peoples created enclosed spaces called medicine lodges, but the overall intention of seeking the assistance of supernatural entities remained the same.

The dancers performed with the accompaniment of singing, drumming, and a flute for hours on end, with the ceremony lasting all day and into the night (Stover 2011). Just after sunrise, the Lakota dancers filed into the arena, led by a *wicasa wakan*. All had been fasting and purified in sweat lodges to make them worthy of seeking divine assistance, but those seeking more, those seeking a vision, were separated from the rest of the dancers so that they could prepare for the greater suffering and sacrifice necessary to win the favor of a sacred vision. These men lay on their backs while the medicine man sliced into the skin of their chests to insert a Cherrywood peg that would be tied to a rope and fastened to the center pole. They would lean back, pulling their flesh as they prayed. Their weight pulled against the pegs stretching and tearing at their flesh, causing excruciating pain. Eventually, the dancers collapsed or their skin tore free of the pegs. During the peak of their suffering, the fortunate participants received a vision.

During the Lakota Sun Dance of 1876, Sitting Bull had his most famous vision, and it was unlikely to have been his first participation in the dance. As a young man in the 1850s, he most certainly participated in the ceremony, but only once did he apparently dance around the pole with his body tethered to it. Now in his mid-forties, Sitting Bull had grown too old for the physical challenge of the Sun Dance, so instead of piercing his chest, he sat in the arena, stared at the sun, and chanted while his adopted brother Jumping Bull sliced his back and chest and arms with a sharp knife, offering up bloody pieces to the Great Spirit as payment for a vision (Anderson 2007, 59). With blood streaming from his wounds, Sitting Bull danced and stared at the sun. For hours and hours, he danced, until in the dark of night he finally collapsed. Carried out of the arena, he was brought to Black Moon, the medicine man in charge of the ceremony. At first, no sign of life was apparent; Sitting Bull appeared dead, but eventually Black Moon revived him.

Sitting Bull could not see on account of the damage to his eyes from the hours of staring at the sun. His voice and body were weak from exhaustion and blood loss, but it had all been worth it: Sitting Bull returned with a vision. He explained that in his vision, he had seen the coming of the white soldiers. Most everyone in the large village of Sioux and Cheyenne knew soldiers hunted them in the summer of 1876, so this was not news. But what Sitting Bull said next certainly caught their attention. In his vision, the soldiers fell from the sky like grasshoppers. They sat upon their falling horses upside down, and it appeared that their ears had been cut off. This meant a battle would be coming soon but that the Indians would win. This news renewed their hopes, giving everyone courage for the coming war, and indeed his vision would come to pass a few days later on the banks of the Greasy Grass River (Ambrose 1996a, 416–417).

Visions, spirits, bloody ceremonies, and sacred places all seemed like savage superstitions to Indian agents and missionaries, and, indeed, when the reservation period began, many sacred ceremonies were forbidden, including the Sun Dance. It was not until a change in policy in the 1930s that some of these ceremonies and dances began to return to reservations across the West. Activities that to outsiders appeared as savagery and idolatry were, in fact, exceptionally complicated interactions between mundane existence and the extraordinary, the individual and the cosmos. To Indian peoples, the very land itself was sacred and filled with thick layers of myth, legend, and memory.

CHRISTIAN MISSIONARIES AND CONVERSION EFFORTS

The first efforts to convert Indians in the West, of course, began with the Catholic priests who accompanied expeditions and eventually established missions in the Southwest. Certainly, Álvar Núñez Cabeza de Vaca and his fellow survivors of the failed Narváez expedition relied on their Christian beliefs to help cement their status as healers, but after they disappeared, so too did their beliefs. Father Marcos de Niza's 1539 expedition represented the first formal effort at introducing Catholicism among the Indians, but he returned bereft of wealth and converts. Francisco Vázquez de Coronado, heading up a much larger force, came north the following year, in 1540. Although priests came with him, the expedition's primary goal lay with finding riches, not harvesting souls. He would return to Mexico in 1542 having sown only hatred for the Spanish among the Pueblo peoples and disappointment for Spanish authorities hoping for another Tenochtitlán to plunder.

Finally, the 1598 arrival of Juan de Oñate, with Franciscan monks in tow, heralded the coming religious transformation of the Southwest. Spanish conquest and colonization did not take the piecemeal approach of the British. Spanish settlers arrived along with administrators, soldiers, and priests. This top-down model of colonization promised a rapid and total transformation of the Indigenous world into an outpost of the Spanish empire. Key to this were the presidios, or military bases, and the church.

In New Mexico, this colonization took the form of the *encomienda* system. Control over the various pueblos was given to landlord, an *encomendero* (similar to a European-style nobleman) as a reward for his participation in the conquest of Indian peoples and the expansion of the empire. These Indian subjects would then perform labor to enrich their Spanish Lord, but in exchange, the *encomendero* would protect them and convert them to Christianity (Anderson 1985). Such a system easily and quickly became exploitative, with *encomenderos* taking far more than their supposed share and offering little in the way of protection from attacks by hostile Indian groups like the Ute and Comanche.

The conversion of the Pueblo peoples also proved more difficult. Franciscan monks oversaw the operation of the churches that soon rose in the middle of the pueblos, but traditional religious practices also endured. As the decades passed, this tension grew. The 1675 arrest of several religious leaders eventually led to the Pueblo Revolt of 1680. Following the 1692 Reconquest of New Mexico, the Spanish abandoned the encomienda system but kept the larger political and religious structure intact.

This mission system, however, spread from Texas to California and provided the primary unit of Spanish political and economic power in these areas. Isolated and often vulnerable, the missions in Texas generally struggled, with the exception of the Mission San Antonio de Valero and the nearby Presidio San Antonio de Béxar, founded in 1718. The missions in Arizona and California fared better, but only a little.

While Texas missions were exposed to outside invaders, hostile tribes that pillaged the cattle herds and threatened attacks at any moment, the worst threats to the missions in Arizona and California came from invaders within, more specifically the various diseases the missionaries brought with them. Encouraging Indians who lived in dispersed hunting and gathering societies to instead congregate in close quarters near a mission proved calamitous. Over the course of the mission period in California (from 1771 to 1830), the population of Indian peoples between San Diego and San Francisco declined from 72,000 to 18,000 individuals. Started with the best of intentions, the California missions ultimately caused far more harm than good, and Indian peoples, even after the mission system was abandoned due to Mexican independence and social reforms, remained impoverished and exploited.

The mission system had helped advance both Spanish imperial plans and Catholic conversion efforts, but with Spain gone from North America following Mexican independence, the Catholic Church changed strategy to rely on less expensive conversion strategies.

As early as 1789, Catholic priests had made tentative efforts to reach Indians in the Pacific Northwest, but it would be the fur trade (somewhat ironically, given the allegedly intemperate and immoral character of the stereotypical trapper) that would introduce Christianity to much of the West. In 1824, the British government instructed the powerful Hudson's Bay Company to support missionary work in its vast territory. The company decided to bring potential converts to its settlement at the Red River (of the north). Two Pacific Northwest Indians, a Kootenai and a Spokane, made their way over the Rockies to the settlement. Christened Pelly and Garry, respectively, they immersed themselves in the theology of the Church of England. Completing their studies by 1829, they returned to proselytize among their own peoples. They may have preached to the Nez Percé peoples, prompting the decision to send four men to St. Louis to learn more about the white man's spiritual power. Another six young Indian men began their studies in 1830 and 1831 (Dodds 1986, 51). Clearly, some fragments of Christianity then reached Indian peoples in the Pacific Northwest by the early 1830s.

While the Hudson's Bay Company's efforts had come about because of pressure by British congregations to do something to help the Indians, American religious groups also began to preach for the need to spread the gospel to native peoples in places such as Hawaii and the distant West. In 1810, several Protestant denominations (i.e., Presbyterians, Congregationalists, and Dutch Reformed Church) joined forces to form the American Board of Commissioners for Foreign Missions (ABCFM). Missionaries considered

Hawaii, which was regularly being visited by American and European ships, as the most fertile location for the harvesting of souls. A flourishing trade between Hawaii and outposts in the Pacific Northwest, however, prompted talk of establishing missions there as well.

In 1829, the ABCFM sent Jonathan Green to inspect the Pacific Northwest for possible locations for the establishment of missions on the Oregon coast. As he penned his report, in 1831, the arrival of four Nez Percé in St. Louis set off calls for missionaries to make their way to these people who seemed so desperate for salvation. Coinciding with the religious zeal of the Second Great Awakening, it became almost inevitable that missionaries would hasten over the mountains as quickly as possible. In addition, the fear of Catholic and British influence in the Pacific Northwest stirred American patriots and Protestants to action (as both national pride and religious salvation were at stake).

The appearance of the Nez Percé in St. Louis stunned American religious leaders, but enraptured by the idea of bringing the word of God to heathens in search of salvation, they failed to comprehend the complex reasons for their arduous journey. Religion certainly played a role, but there were other possible purposes for their visit. As early as the Lewis and Clark Expedition, the Nez Percé had hoped to establish a friendship with the United States as a way of gaining access to weapons they could use against their Blackfeet enemies (who had acquired firearms from British trappers). Acquiring another outlet for manufactured goods (besides the Hudson's Bay Company) also played a role. They arrived in St. Louis on a religious, economic, and diplomatic mission, but Americans only seemed moved by the religious motivations.

The Indian peoples of the Pacific Northwest did not seek to replace their traditional beliefs with Christianity. Instead, they recognized that the whites had tremendous power as reflected in the wondrous items they possessed: iron tools, blankets, and guns. Such items reflected powerful "medicine," which was something that Indian peoples coveted. Rather than replacing their religious views, they instead hoped to learn from the whites and incorporate beneficial beliefs into their own in a kind of hybridization of native and Christian beliefs. The fur trader and explorer Benjamin Bonneville noted that many Nez Percé kept the Sabbath "like a nation of saints" but yet worshipped a religion that was "a strange medley; civilized and barbarous" (quoted in West 2009, 38). In time, their willingness to borrow and modify Christian beliefs, rather than abandoning their traditional ways, became a source of contention between Indian peoples and missionaries.

The Methodists arrived first, reaching Fort Vancouver, the Hudson's Bay Company's outpost across the river from modern Portland, Oregon, in September 1834. Led by the imposing figure of Jason Lee, the Methodists opted to settle south of the fort on the banks of the Willamette River. From this first settlement, the well-funded and well-equipped Methodists fanned out across the Pacific Northwest to Fort Nisqually; Clatsop, at the mouth of the Columbia River; the falls of the Willamette; and finally at The Dalles, on the eastern edge of the Columbia River Gorge. Despite years of effort and expense, Lee groused that they had not won over a single Indian convert (Dodds 1986, 51–53). Much of this stemmed from his own failings, the lack of proper training for missionaries, and the insistence that Indians had to learn English before learning the gospel. Protestants stressed a personal relationship with God that depended on reading the gospel for oneself, but this belief made English literacy a substantial obstacle to Indians' adoption of Christianity.

In 1836, the ABCFM sent two couples overland to take up residence among the Nez Percé at Lapwai (in modern Idaho) and the Cayuse at Wiilatpu in today's central Washington. Henry and Eliza Spalding settled among the former, and the newlyweds Dr. Marcus and Narcissa Whitman settled among the latter. Of the two, the Lapwai mission fared better, with the Nez Percé proving more eager to hear about the white man's religion than the Cayuse, but both missions soon established houses, barns, and gristmills that made the settlements largely self-sufficient. Indeed, in time, the Whitman mission became a stopping point for many footsore and exhausted travelers as they neared the end of the Oregon Trail. The Whitmans' conversion efforts, however, bore far less fruit than the fields they cultivated.

For the Whitmans, the Cayuse seemed stubbornly reluctant to embrace Christianity and give up their traditional ways. Narcissa wrote that as she read from the book of Matthew to one Cayuse man, "it seemed to sink deep into his heart; and O may it prove a savior of life to his soul." However, the fact that the man held to many of his traditional beliefs, including keeping two wives, testified to his inability to walk "in the ways of truth and holiness." She concluded, "He thinks he is a Christian, but we fear to the contrary" (quoted in Jeffrey 1994, 164). Narcissa, like the other missionaries, believed that there could only be one way of becoming a Christian: mainly by emulating all the beliefs and practices of the missionaries. The missionaries decried any hybridization between the religious world of the Cayuse and the Christian world as unacceptable.

The Whitmans also courted disaster by being largely ignorant of Indian customs and beliefs. They refused to allow the Cayuse into their home, for example, a practice that struck many potential converts as rude, but fit with the Whitmans' desire to maintain middle-class values and a sense of privacy. The Whitmans also refused to distribute gifts as benefiting someone of their station. Gift giving showed respect and established closer ties between the giver and the receiver, but the Whitmans would only part with blankets, food, and other items in exchange for work. This idea of working for a reward, of course, fit with Christian beliefs about the importance of effort and striving toward a goal, but it ran afoul of Indian customs and thus represented another example of the gaping cultural divide that separated the Indians from the missionaries.

Disease provided another source of distrust. Buffeted by strange diseases, the Cayuse had welcomed Dr. Whitman for his knowledge of the deadly ailments that often preceded the whites. American doctors, like Whitman, had few effective tools to deal with epidemic diseases, as the arrival of the highly contagious disease of measles in 1844 demonstrated. A common disease among European populations, the illness had lost much of its potency over the centuries, but among Indians, with no innate resistance, the disease proved devastating. The contrast between the races was stark: the white children at the Whitman mission contracted the virus but soon recovered. The Cayuse, however, did not fare as well. Deaths climbed steadily, with five or six dying every day. Most of the dead were children. Marcus did all he could, but his efforts proved remarkably unsuccessful, so unsuccessful, in fact, that the Cayuse began to wonder if he was in fact causing the infections. Certainly, a doctor or medicine man like Whitman could heal, but it stood to reason that he could also use his powers to make people ill and even kill them. An eastern mixed-blood Indian resident of the mission even told the Cayuse that he had heard Whitman and Henry Spalding discussing plans to poison the Cayuse and take their valuable horses (West 2009, 50). The real poisoning, however, was that occurring between the missionaries and their Indian charges.

By 1847, the Whitman's mission had clearly failed—at least in its purpose of converting Indians. By this time, Narcissa had become convinced that God's real purpose had been to set up an outpost that could help emigrants make their way to Oregon and Washington, bringing Christians and Americans into lands once set aside for heathens. Indeed, the rising number of American settlers would successfully chase away Indians, Catholics, and the British, serving both nationalistic and spiritual purposes. Her adoption of the orphaned Sager children reified these abstract notions and gave Narcissa a makeshift family to lavish her time and attention on instead of the Indians. In a letter to her mother, she wrote, "My hands and heart are usefully employed, not so much for the Indians directly, as my own family. When my health failed, I was obliged to withhold my efforts for the natives, but the Lord has since filled my hands with other labors, and I have no reason to complain" (quoted in Jeffrey 1994, 196–197).

Clearly, however, the Whitmans had overstayed their welcome, and several incidents suggest that the Cayuse wanted them to leave. Marcus ended up in a shouting match with a Cayuse headman, Tilokaikt, who claimed that the mission lands and livestock did not belong to the Whitmans but instead to everyone in the tribe. In October 1847, a more disturbing incident occurred. Tilokaikt and several other men burst into the Whitmans' house, a space that Narcissa and Marcus had stressed was forbidden for Indians to enter uninvited. One man smashed the door with an axe, and another, Sakiaph, even produced a gun, which he pointed at Marcus. Narcissa called for help, and several friendly Indians intervened and defused the situation. Although the incident did not escalate, it certainly should have served as a warning to the Whitmans. Harassment continued for the next several weeks, but Marcus and Narcissa dismissed these problems as minor and the work of Catholic agitators bent on stirring up trouble.

Finally, on November 29, 1847, a bitterly cold afternoon, the years of pent-up anger and resentment erupted. Several Cayuse men broke into the Whitmans' house and shot and stabbed Marcus and his adopted son John Sager. The other whites at the mission were simultaneously attacked. Narcissa, realizing the danger, tried to collect her adopted children and hide them in the house. Surrounded by an angry mob, she and the others trapped inside were promised safe passage if they came out of the house. As they stepped out the front door, however, they met a volley of shots. Narcissa, wounded, fell in front of the door. An angry Cayuse charged, fell upon her, and began to beat her with a club. The Whitmans and another dozen whites perished in the attack. The Cayuse dismembered the bodies, especially those of Marcus and Narcissa, with both eventually being beheaded. Forty-six others were taken prisoner but released a month later, thanks to the efforts of Father J. B. A. Brouillet and Peter Skene Ogden of the Hudson's Bay Company.

Two years after the founding of the missions at Lapwai and among the Cayuse at Wiilatpu, Catholic missionaries also arrived in the Pacific Northwest. The Hudson's Bay Company had encouraged them in an effort to convince some of their former fur trappers (many of whom were Catholic) to permanently remain in the area and become farmers on lands the company owned near the Puget Sound. In addition, a substantial French-Canadian settlement had already sprouted up in the Willamette Valley. The bishop of Quebec sent two priests, Fathers Francois Norbert Blanchet and Modeste Demers, to set up a mission on the Cowlitz River and another among the French-Canadians along the Willamette River. Other missions would soon be founded that extended over the Cascade mountains and onto the Columbia Plateau (Dodds 1986, 57–58).

The Methodists ceased their efforts in 1844, and Lee was reassigned. Following the murder of the Whitmans in 1847, the remaining missions also closed. The missionaries had little to show for years of effort. Few Indians had accepted their message and become true converts, and in this respect, the missions proved a dismal failure. However, by the mid-1840s, many of the missionaries, including Narcissa Whitman, had concluded that God, omnipotent and mysterious, had actually sent them west to serve the ever-increasing number of travelers coming to the Pacific Northwest to establish American civilization.

New people were also coming to the West, and they imposed their own sense of place and a profound new religious vision of their own upon the landscape of the West.

THE MORMONS

At the dawn of the 19th century, the success of the American Revolution and the wealth generated by a rapidly developing economy had made Americans proud of all they had accomplished and all that would inevitably come for a nation whose rise to greatness seemed assured. This pride extended to the nation's emerging democratic institutions. No nation on earth had so successfully taken political power from the hands of the few and given it to so many. To be sure, there were limits to American democracy, as only white men could participate, but even with those limitations, the United States represented the most democratic nation on earth in the 1830s. These ideal American voters possessed both independence and a belief in equality.

Unsurprisingly, these traits found their way into American views on religion, with a focus on individual salvation and innovation in theology. Americans had created new technologies and unleashed the power of the "common man," so creating new religious ideas certainly seemed within the realm of American innovation.

Upstate New York became the focal point of a series of religious movements in the first decades of the 1800s. Most likely, these movements developed in response to great changes sweeping across what, until recently, had been isolated farmsteads only a few decades removed from being the territory of the Iroquois Confederation. The great stirrings of change, however, had brought capitalism into areas where farming had largely been for subsistence. Most especially, the desire of New York to link the Hudson River to the Great Lakes led to the first large-scale building project in American history: the construction of a canal to connect the Hudson River to Lake Erie. The Erie Canal would do many things: develop the Great Lakes region, including fledgling towns like Chicago; allow New York to rise to unquestioned prominence over rivals like Philadelphia and Boston; and bring thousands of new people into previously isolated areas. While this certainly benefited businesses and farms, it also meant that armies of construction workers and, soon after, canal laborers and boat operators would also make their homes in the area. Fears about these changes, most especially the morality of the low-wage canal laborers, prompted calls for religious reform as a salve. Ironically, the ease of transportation along the canal, which was operated by allegedly immoral wageworkers, made transportation quick and affordable, allowing a steady stream of religious leaders to preach at religious revivals in towns along the canal, among them Charles Finney.

Finney preached a doctrine of individual responsibility, for "God has made man a moral free agent" (quoted in Johnson 2004, 3). Free will would determine whether an individual was saved or damned, which stood in sharp contrast to the early Calvinist idea of predestination that still held sway over many congregations in the Northeast, a doctrine that often led to a fatalistic acceptance of the capricious mystery of God's will. For Finney, though, salvation was the ultimate do-it-yourself project, an idea very much in line with the American beliefs of individual freedom and equality. Finney found an audience along the canal, most especially the burgeoning town of Rochester, New York, eager to listen to his ideas. Self-control, Finney believed, would be the key to salvation. Ordered, rule following, moral, abstemious, and pious—the individual who lived according to these principles could control his or her darker impulses and live a good and moral life.

Unsurprisingly, the adherents to Finney's message came from the middle classes, the shop owners and businessmen of towns like Rochester. These were the very men and women concerned about wage laborers, especially those who worked on the canals, as well as the very people who relied on the canal to connect them to larger markets. They claimed the canal workers were boisterous, prone to consuming alcohol, and quick to fight. Worst of all, they did not keep the Sabbath. Imposing order on them became an important goal of these newly inspired middle-class revivalists. Indeed, bringing more people into the fold would, many believed, perfect society and bring about the millennium, a thousand year epoch of peace on earth that would begin with the Second Coming of Jesus. Raising boatmen, canal workers, and female cabin attendants (who many reformers believed doubled as prostitutes) out of moral depravity was necessary to bring about such lofty religious goals. Benevolent organizations, such as the Boatmen's Friend Society, founded in 1830, established churches in towns along the Erie Canal, in Troy, Albany, Utica, Rochester, and Buffalo, and thus began a large-scale effort to reach these wayward souls. Finney himself referred to the area as the "burned over district" because of the frequency of revivals that swept through the area like raging grass fires.

Other more theologically radical organizations emerged, including the Oneida Community. Established by John Humphrey Noyes in Putney, Vermont, in 1841, the community moved to Oneida, New York, in 1847. Noyes's own conversion occurred at a revival in the seminal year of 1831, prompting him to give up law school and preach the doctrine of perfectionism, which he claimed would bring about the Second Coming. The group's belief that all of their members were married to each other, and therefore able to change sexual partners at will, scandalized the public, as did their proclamation of communal socialism. Nevertheless, the Oneida Community endured for decades and became economically self-sufficient through the production of silverware and other products.

Other spiritual and religious groups called the district home. The Millerites, founded by William Miller in 1834, also believed the Second Coming of Christ was imminent, even predicting His return on October 22, 1844. Sadly, for Miller and his followers, the day passed without incident. Then there were the Campbellites, who became one of the more successful new denominations and endure today as the Church of Christ. Less a religion than an elaborate scam, the Fox sisters of Hydesville, New York, introduced the concept of séances to the public in the 1848 and soon came to national prominence. All of this is to say that no place in the United States, and perhaps nowhere else in the world at the time, was better suited to starting a new religion than upstate New York. While most of the efforts at religious innovation would sputter and flame out in a few years, one would endure to become a major religious denomination. It is known worldwide as the Church of Jesus Christ of Latter-day Saints and more informally as the Mormon Church. Although growing to become an international religion, Mormonism's identity has long been indelibly tied to the 19th-century American West in much the same way that the Bible is tied to the Holy Land.

The story of Mormonism began in a field near Palmyra, New York. Unsure of which of the numerous sects then calling upstate New York home he should follow, a teenager named Joseph Smith prayed for guidance. While struggling with this problem, Smith claimed to have a vision in which God the Father and Jesus Christ came to him and told him not to follow any existing religion but to instead form his own. A few years later, in 1823, the angel Moroni appeared to Smith as he worked in a field. Moroni revealed to Smith the location of several golden plates on which were written a new story of the lost tribe of Israel's arrival in the New World and the later appearance of Jesus Christ in the Americas after his death and resurrection in Jerusalem. Three years after his alleged encounter with Moroni, Smith removed the plates and began to translate the strange language written on them. With the help of a magical "seer stone" and possibly some other wondrous tools, Smith deciphered the strange writings and revealed what came to be known and the Book of Mormon. With his translation in hand, Smith published the first edition of the Book of Mormon in 1830, the same year he began his formal effort at establishing his new church.

Unlike the other new theologies in circulation, Smith stressed that his religious insights, rather than being new inventions, actually represented the restoration of a long-forgotten tale of the rise of Christianity in the Americas. Over time, the descendants of Noah scattered around the globe, and some of these made their way to the

New World. Other groups followed in the centuries after, including, "the Jaredites, who were led away at the time of the Tower of Babel and were, therefore, a part of the earliest dissemination of the descendants of Noah; the Lehi colony, led out of Jerusalem during the reign of Zedekiah, just prior to the captivity of Judah by Nebuchadnezzar; and the colony of Mulek, the youngest son of Zedekiah, who departed Jerusalem eleven years after Lehi" (Johnson 1975). Together, these groups came to be known as the Lamanites, for Laman, the eldest son of Lehi.

According to Mormon doctrine, Lehi migrated from Jerusalem to the New World around 600 BC. Leadership, however, went to Nephi, causing Laman and his other brothers to rebel against Nephi's authority. Failing in their rebellion, they were cursed and literally marked with a darker skin tone. These cursed Lamanites and their descendants became the American Indians of the New World. For a time, peace reigned between the Nephites and Lamanites, thanks to the appearance of Jesus among them. In AD 231, however, a war broke out between the two groups. The darker-skinned Lamanites gained the upper hand and exterminated the Nephites, and with them went Christianity in the New World, as retold on the golden plates Smith would later claim to have found. Smith hoped to bring the gospel back to the Indians, as they were, he believed, part of the nation of Israel. Converting them could help with the creation of Smith's vision of a New Jerusalem being founded in the United States.

Thus, the Latter-day Saints began conversion efforts of Indians, what they called the Lamanite mission, from the very dawn of the church. Unfortunately, most Indian peoples proved indifferent to the message, but later Mormon missionaries would find a more receptive audience among a new group of Lamanites: the peoples of the Pacific Islands. Smith considered the participation of the Indians so critical that the subtitle of the Book of Mormon reads, "[The book] is an abridgement of the record of the people of Nephi, and also of the Lamanites—Written to the Lamanites, who are a remnant of the house of Israel; and also to Jew and Gentile" (Church of Jesus Christ of Latter-day Saints 1981). All three of these groups could have the blood of Israel in them and, therefore, could become part of the chosen people.

In addition to its profoundly original theology, Smith's church also embraced many of the new ideas that had emerged in New York's burned over district. For example, Mormonism, in the words of author Wallace Stegner, embraced "everything the other

[new] religions had, and more: not only total immersion, seizures, the gift of tongues and other aspects of the Holy Ghost, baptism for remission of sins, and the promise or threat of the imminent Second Coming, but also the true apostolic succession and the renewal of the ancient personal communication with God" (Stegner 1981, 18). These last two aspects, as Stegner noted, separated Mormonism from the other sects being established. Mormonism claimed that the descendants of Abraham (and therefore of Israel, with their heritage as God's chosen people) lived among all the peoples of the world. Since the Israelites had a special relationship to God, their descendants, it stood to reason, inherited that mantle as well. But how could one know whether one was a descendant of Abraham? The answer for Smith was simple: if you converted to Mormonism, you had the blood of Abraham in your veins. This notion gave Mormons a unique identity that tied them to the Old Testament idea of a chosen people, and it allowed them to simultaneously proselytize all over the globe.

Smith's claim to have received direct revelations from God also elevated his church about the numerous competitors. As the leader of the church, Smith drew his inspiration from direct communication with God and his messengers. This made Smith more like Moses or the other ancient patriarchs than modern religious leaders. Claiming direct revelation also made Smith's position unassailable, which is a handy card to play when starting a new religion and dealing with doubters.

Such a radical theology, unsurprisingly, courted controversy, something Smith was no stranger to, having been arrested for practicing folk magic on two previous occasions. New York, however, became too tough of an environment for the new church, as its acolytes came under suspicion and persecution there. Smith began to preach that the Latter-day Saints needed to find a new homeland for themselves, a place where they could gather up the disparate pieces of Israel and create their own New Jerusalem. Doing so required land, space, and distance away from hostile nonbelievers, or "Gentiles," as Mormons called them.

Surely, the New Jerusalem could not be in New York or anywhere in the settled East. It had to be somewhere out west. Kirtland, Ohio, became headquarters of the church in early 1831, but already Smith was pondering a move farther West. Within six months, the faithful moved to Zion, in Jackson County, Missouri, near the fledgling town of Independence (Stegner 1981, 18). However, they received a hostile welcome and were soon driven out of Jackson County. Next they settled in Caldwell and Daviess Counties in Missouri and erected the city of Enoch (also known as Far West) on the site Smith believed had once been the location of the Garden of Eden. Missourians, however, opposed the settlement of these strange believers, and rumors began to circulate that a secret force of murderous Mormons known as the Sons of Dan, or Danites, intended to cause their non-Mormon neighbors great harm.

Open conflict began in October 1838 with the so-called Battle of Crooked River, and three days after that, on October 29, a force of armed Missourians fell upon a caravan of Mormons near Haun's Mill, killing over 17 Mormon men and boys. Meanwhile, Missouri governor Lilburn Boggs ordered all Mormons out of the state, and he dispatched nearly 3,000 militiamen under General Samuel Lucas to arrest the Mormon leaders. Surrounding the town of Far West, the militia negotiated the surrender of the Mormon leaders, including Joseph Smith and his brother, Hyrum. Exhausted and bedraggled, the Mormons fled again, this time eastward across the Mississippi and into Illinois.

For a time, it seemed that Illinois would finally be the site of the Mormons' New Jerusalem. Overlooking the Mississippi River, the always industrious Mormons soon erected the city of Nauvoo, Illinois. Within five years, over 20,000 of the faithful had collected, and an imposing temple rose on a bluff overlooking the river. In those five years, the Mormons had flourished, and Smith had become so prominent that he announced a run for presidency in 1844. To protect themselves, the city boasted a 4,000-man militia, dubbed the Nauvoo Legion, with Smith as its commander. Gradually, however, popular sentiment in Illinois turned against the Mormons, as it had in Missouri.

Salacious tales of Mormon practices, especially polygamy, shocked the nation. Disenchanted former Mormons led the charge, publishing exposés of Mormon practices. Among these was John C. Bennett, who had been expelled from Nauvoo in June 1842. For the next several months, he published articles with lurid (and often untrue) descriptions of Mormon practices in a local paper, the *Sangamo Journal*, that soon reappeared in papers across the nation to the delight of scandalized readers.

William Law, however, proved to be more of a threat to Smith's control of the church. Law, a devout Mormon and true believer in Mormonism and Smith's status as prophet and head of the church, nevertheless felt that power was going to the prophet's head. He objected to Smith's use of church funds for his own personal real

estate ventures, but more shockingly, Smith proposed a plural marriage to Law's wife, Jane (something he had done with other leading men of Nauvoo, perhaps as a demonstration of his superior
position). Law and his wife objected and, along with several others,
found themselves excommunicated from the church. Law, however,
refused to leave and began a campaign against Smith that culmi-
nated in the founding of the critical *Nauvoo Expositor* newspaper in
1844. The paper excoriated Smith's behavior, especially his political
revelations and the practice of "spiritual marriage." Within hours of
the printing of the paper's first (and it turned out only) issue, Smith
struck back. His Nauvoo Legion ransacked the office of the *Expositor*
and destroyed the printing press. The Laws fled Nauvoo for nearby
Carthage, bringing with them the stories of their experiences in the
New Jerusalem, which would inflame an already volatile situation.
Non-Mormons in Carthage called for the formation of a militia to
destroy Nauvoo and capture the leader of the church.

With tensions growing, Smith briefly fled the area, but he agreed
to return after Governor Thomas Ford of Illinois promised him
safe passage to Carthage and a fair trial. On June 24, 1844, Smith
rode into Carthage with his brother Hyrum and two other companions and surrendered himself to the governor. Three days later,
the governor journeyed to Nauvoo, leaving the imprisoned Joseph
Smith in jail and guarded by a local militia, the Carthage Greys.
With the governor absent, the Greys and militia from the town of
Warsaw decided to take the law into their own hands. The governor's absence had perhaps been intentional, allowing the militia
to proceed without official oversight. Though imprisoned, friends
had smuggled the accused Mormons a revolver, two canes, and a
single-shot pistol into their cells—scant protection against a mob
bent on murder.

The inflamed militia broke into the cell, and a volley of shots
struck down Hyrum and John Taylor. Smith emptied his revolver
into the crowd, but the militiamen pushed into the cell anyway.
Throwing his empty pistol at his enemies, Smith turned and flung
himself from a second-story window. Accounts differ as to what, if
anything, the prophet said as he fell to his death, but the collected
mob made sure to finish him, shooting him at least four times as he
lay in the dirt. Once the deed was done, and perhaps because of a
"beam of accusing sun that broke through the clouds and touched
Joseph's body," the mob scattered, leaving the fourth Mormon,
William Richards, who had survived the violence unharmed, to tell
the tale (Stegner 1981, 30).

With Smith dead and a growing body of enemies surrounding them, it appeared inevitable that the Latter-day Saints would be forced from their homes again. Still, for nearly a year and a half, Nauvoo continued on, and its residents tried to live with the specter of possible attack by hostile Gentiles.

Even before Joseph Smith's death, the Mormons had been pondering a move farther west, away from persecution. They had pondered several possible destinations: Texas, Oregon, or perhaps California. Smith, of course, would never see the exodus unfold. Instead, leadership and the decision to move again in search of the real Zion fell on Brigham Young, who assumed leadership not as prophet but as president of the Quorum of the Twelve Apostles. Nevertheless, his rule would remain unchallenged and his edicts made law.

With pressure from state officials (and rumors of mob violence circulating), Young decided the time had come to leave Illinois. In January 1846, the Saints headed for the West. The Mormons harbored a profound sense of themselves as historical actors, their actions mimicking those of other persecuted peoples of the past: the Pilgrims coming to the New World or, most especially, the Old Testament Israelites. As Stegner notes, "They were the tribe of Joseph, of the seed of Jacob, this was their flight out of Egypt, Brother Brigham was their Moses, the Mississippi was their Red Sea, Governor Ford was a reasonable facsimile of Pharaoh" (Stegner 1981, 44). They had some advantages on the ancient Israelites, however, in that they had a trail to follow and some sense of a destination thanks to explorers such as John C. Frémont, whose reports painted a glowing picture of the isolated lands on the shores of the Great Salt Lake—one of several possible destinations.

The exodus tried the Mormons. Deaths were a common occurrence from accidents and illness. Progress also proved horribly slow across Iowa. Oregon, one possible destination, must have seemed more like a dream than a real place. Desperate, Young asked Iowa's governor for permission to settle his flock temporarily, allowing the scattered Saints to collect for the journey to come and allow time to repair their wagons and recover their health. The governor agreed in September. That same month, the last Mormons in Nauvoo abandoned the city as a mob descended upon them, beating people and setting fire to the structures. Within a few years, all that remained were impressive ruins.

Young set up the government of the church at Winter Quarters in Nebraska Territory (near modern Omaha), and from there, plans

After years of religious persecution, the Mormons found a home between the Great Salt Lake and the Wasatch Mountains. A belief in collective effort and religious zeal enabled them to build a prosperous city in an arid environment. (Library of Congress)

were made for the move across the plains in the spring of 1847. He was assisted in this by his first, and only, revelation from God that laid out the organization of the wagon companies in great and quite practical detail. While slower family groups would make their way across the plains, Young instructed a group of unmarried men to hurry west and find a suitable location where they could plant crops that would provide for the masses of emigrants who would arrive too late in the year to plant. This group set out at the beginning of April, with the other groups leaving over the following days.

The advance party reached the Great Salt Lake by early summer—although it was still not clear whether this was to be the New Jerusalem or merely another winter camp on the way to somewhere else. The last 30 miles down to the valley proved to be the toughest of the entire trip, as if the Wasatch Mountains were trying to keep people away from the Salt Lake Valley. The wagon road down what came to be Emigrant Canyon tested the mettle of man, wagon, and beast. Settled, at least for now, the advance party wasted no time in setting about their tasks. By the time the main body arrived later that summer, they had already built numerous cabins, dammed a stream for irrigation water, and plowed several fields.

As the main body of Mormon emigrants made their final approach, Brigham Young fell ill. They paused for a few days to see whether his health would improve enough to make the final push. They pressed on, and Young, still convalescing, finally saw the valley for himself on July 24, 1847, from the back of a wagon. Scanning the tawny valley with the shimmering lake in the distance, Young is supposed to have said, "It is enough. This is the right place, drive on" (Stegner 1981, 168). Within a few weeks, Young and his followers had decided to permanently settle on the shore of the Great Salt Lake.

It proved a fortuitous decision. At the time of their arrival, control of the Rocky Mountains was very much in dispute as part of the ongoing war with Mexico, which still held claim to California and much of the West, including the land on which the Mormons had chosen to build their new city. Even if the United States acquired this land, it seemed likely that the president and Congress would simply leave the Mormons alone in their city on the shores of a salty sea in the heart of a desert. To be sure, the Oregon and California Trails passed only a bit to the north, but few would be tempted to lose precious time by descending to Salt Lake City. If they did, they would certainly need provisions that the Mormons could sell them. The seasonal wagon trains, however, represented a comparative trickle of humanity and so were of little concern. As busy and collective as bees, industrious creatures that became symbols of Mormon hard work and industry, the Saints soon had the beginnings of a true city, with irrigation ditches and orderly streets, laid out and emerging from the dirt.

With a new homeland rising between the Great Salt Lake and the towering Wasatch Mountains, it now became feasible to gather all the Saints into one great city, the New Jerusalem of the Mormon faith. Indeed, converts came by the thousands—mostly from the British Isles. There were probably several reasons for this success. Certainly, the tradition of Protestantism allowed people to question religious authority and create new denominations from internal disputes over theology. This helped account for the florescence of new denominations that emerged from the Protestant Reformation, so what, after all, was one more? Moreover, the Mormons offered a new and compelling story. Why simply read about the exploits of the ancient Israelites when one could participate in the reenactment of these Old Testament parallels as the new chosen people of God? Add to these religious parallels the already world-famous romance of Western settlement and the possibility of a better financial life by immigrating to the United States and the prospect of conversion and immigration became undeniable.

And immigrate they did. Thousands of newly minted Saints sold everything they could to book passage to the United States. Once arrived, immigrants made their way across the plains, generally following the Oregon Trail before turning south and heading to Salt Lake. Wealthier Mormons, already settled in Salt Lake, contributed what they could to fund these journeys through the Perpetual Emigration Fund. However, the number of immigrants greatly outstripped the money available; many of the new converts had little more than what they could carry and no money to afford the exorbitant costs of transport to the United States and across the plains.

Mormon leaders devised a plan that would enable these less affluent believers to make the passage across the plains. Rather than come across in a large, heavy, and expensive wagon drawn by costly draft animals like oxen, individual families could pull small lightweight carts with only the necessities of food, clothing, and perhaps a few pounds of personal items. Brigham Young asserted that these families should "make handcarts, and let the emigration foot it and draw upon them [the carts] the necessary supplies, having a cow or two for every 10 [emigrants]." Selling the idea as even better than wagons, Young declared, "They can come just as quick, if not quicker, and much cheaper—can start earlier and escape the prevailing sickness which annually lays so many of our brethren in the dust. A great majority of them walk now, even with the teams which are provided" (Moulton n.d.). Indeed, contrary to popular belief, many able-bodied people walked along the trail, sparing their animals the extra weight of human passengers. Nevertheless, the prospect of entire trains of people pulling what amounted to really large wheelbarrows seems reckless and even slightly insane, but faith is a powerful thing. Therefore, the cart brigades set out in the spring of 1856 from their jumping-off point in Iowa.

Young estimated that the carts could cover the distance from Winter Quarters to Salt Lake in 70 days, averaging roughly 25 miles per day, but to be safe, each cart would contain provisions for 90 days. The newspaper the *Mormon*, advocating for this plan, admitted, "There is nothing very pleasing nor inviting about this journey; but we think, after all, it is better to go there among friends, poor, than to endure the buffetings of a cold, heartless world in poverty" (Moulton n.d.)

Three companies, each numbering 200 or 300 people, arrived in Salt Lake by September, tired and, one imagines, thinner but otherwise healthy. Unbeknownst to Young and the rest of the Mormon leadership, two additional companies had set off astonishingly late. The Fourth Company, led by James Grey Willie, with 500 emigrants, did not set out from Winter Quarters until early August. The Fifth Company, under the command of Edward Martin, finally set off on August 25, 1856. Martin's company had 146 handcarts, 7 wagons, a heavy freight wagon, some 50 cows, and 576 souls.

Already exhausted, Martin's party reached Fort Laramie on October 8, but they did not rest for a few days as most travelers did for fear that the weather could turn at any time. The passage became a slog. The brigades often continued on until almost midnight. Invariably, children and even adults became so weak they could not walk and so became burdens for the rest to carry.

Inevitably, the weather turned. Martin's Fifth Company had managed to make it as far as the modern town of Casper, Wyoming, on the North Platte River, when the first snowstorm hit. The Fourth Company had made it roughly 100 miles farther up the trail along the Sweetwater River when they too became stranded. Then the true suffering began as rations ran short.

Brigham Young finally learned of the existence of these companies when a party of Mormon missionaries (traveling faster on horseback) arrived in Salt Lake in early October and reported passing them along the trail. Within a few days, a rescue party had been organized to find the trapped Saints. Hoping to encounter them making progress toward Salt Lake, the rescuers disappointedly crossed the Continental Divide at South Pass without seeing any sign of the parties. Descending down the eastern side of the divide and along the Sweetwater River, they finally encountered the Fourth Company. Reinvigorated by the food and aid, the Fourth Company began to move again, but the Fifth Company remained lost to the east.

The rescuers pressed on and finally located the party not far from the last crossing of the North Platte. Reinvigorated by food, fresh blankets, warm clothing, and new shoes, the exhausted pioneers once again took up their carts and made their way past Independence Rock (typically passed, as the name suggests, in early July), the Devil's Gate, and on to the Rattlesnake Mountains, where the weather again turned, forcing them to stop in a sheltered area they called Martin's Cove. The rations provided by the rescuers were already running short, and any attempt to winter over in Martin's Cove would mean starvation and certain death. The beleaguered party decided to make one last desperate push for Salt Lake. The

sickest and weakest would be loaded into the few wagons the rescuers had brought, and those who still had strength would carry
what they could on their backs and walk, leaving their handcarts
and whatever they could not carry behind.

The Fourth Company finally arrived in Salt Lake on November
9, but over 70 had died in the crossing. The Fifth Company fared
even worse. Of the 576 people in the company, 174 did not make
it to Salt Lake City. Even for a people accustomed to suffering and
sacrifice, the experience was unforgettable. The handcart tragedy
became ingrained in the Mormon collective consciousness, but not
as a story of human folly. Rather, it was a story of endurance, faith,
and community. Indeed, despite this tragedy, the handcart brigades continued for the next several years, with another five companies arriving in Salt Lake City between 1857 and 1860.

The United States did, in fact, gain claim to the land the Mormons
had settled with the 1848 Treaty of Guadalupe Hidalgo. Barely
more than a week before the signing of the treaty, James Marshall
discovered gold in California. Suddenly, the Saint's New Jerusalem was no longer so isolated, as one of the world's greatest mass
migrations passed just to the north.

The influx of people to California also threatened Brigham
Young's vision for his colony. He had hoped to expand the Mormon's control beyond Utah. In 1849, he outlined plans for a Mormon homeland that he christened the territory of Deseret, stretching
from Salt Lake City southwest across the modern states of Utah,
Nevada, and Arizona to the Pacific coast at San Diego. Ostensibly
a territory of the United States, it did not take much imagination
to see Deseret as effectively an independent Mormon nation, complete with oceanfront access on the Pacific Ocean.

Young's grandiose vision was largely ignored by another expansionistic institution: the government of the United States. Congress
had set about organizing the West into territories. One of these territories, the territory of Utah, included Salt Lake City. Congress
recognized the realities of Mormon settlement and control, so
the president duly appointed Young as governor of the new territory. Still, a power struggle ensued between the Mormons, led
by Young, who appointed his supporters to federal positions, and
federal officials sent to the territory. Indeed, these officials discovered that Utah Territory, in every meaningful way, was a theocracy
with Young at its head. Church leaders controlled all aspects of the
territory, even running a separate court system that ignored the
required federal system completely.

To make matters worse, Young decided to publicly reveal the practice of polygamy as an official church doctrine. Scandalized Americans denounced the practice. Many people compared the institution to slavery in the South, including Harriet Beecher Stowe, the author of *Uncle Tom's Cabin*, who declared polygamy "a slavery which debases and degrades womanhood, motherhood, and family" (quoted in Jeffrey 1994, 181). Young and other Mormon leaders stood behind polygamy and employed the doctrines of states' rights and popular sovereignty to defend it, arguing that they had the right to make their own laws and decisions. Popular sovereignty, of course, had been trotted out by Senator Stephen Douglas as the solution to the question of expanding slavery into the unorganized territories of the West. In effect, Douglas suggested that local settlers should have the authority to decide such things for themselves. It is likely that he never conceived of popular sovereignty being used to justify a practice like polygamy.

By the mid-1850s, the power struggle had exploded into open violence. A gang of Mormon miscreants, for example, broke into the office of federal judge George Stiles and burned the court records. Rumors circulated that the Danites were murdering Gentiles and federal officials under Young's orders, prompting many officials to flee the territory. In 1857, with the nation in the midst of self-destruction, President Buchanan had had enough of this alleged Mormon insurrection and made the decision to send out roughly one-sixth of the U.S. Army (a paltry 2,500 men) to quell the rebellion in faraway Utah Territory

Far to the east, Parley Pratt, an original member of the Quorum of the Twelve Apostles and leading figure of the church, was murdered on May 13, 1857, near Fort Smith, Arkansas, by Hector McLean. McLean's ire had been ignited when his estranged wife, Eleanor, decided to convert to Mormonism and marry Pratt, becoming his 12th wife. Pratt, apparently in an attempt to meet up with Eleanor, was instead ambushed by McLean.

Several months later, a wagon train bound for the goldfields of southern California crossed through inhospitable southern Utah. The train consisted of emigrants from Missouri and Arkansas. Passing a few poor Mormon settlements, the members of the wagon train may have said derogatory things about the Mormons and perhaps even engaged in some minor theft of goods. Or perhaps they had done nothing at all to inflame local hatred, save for hailing from the state that had just murdered a leading patriarch of the church. Whatever the exact cause, the outcome of this antipathy would be tragedy.

The wagon train climbed above the desert heat into the relative cool of a high-altitude meadow. While camped there, they came under attack by Paiute Indians (and some Mormons pretending to be Indians). Surrounded and in dire circumstances, the leaders of the wagon train were grateful for a cease-fire orchestrated by a local Mormon, John D. Lee. Lee explained to the leaders of the wagon train that he had persuaded the Indians to let them pass if they surrendered their weapons. Seeing little alternative, the leaders agreed. No sooner had they done so, however, than the Indians and hostile Mormons set upon them, slaughtering all the men, women, and older children in the party. Some 120 people perished, with only 17 younger children spared. The Mountain Meadows Massacre, as it came to be known, would eventually be exposed, and Lee would take the fall for it, though rumors circulated that Young himself had authorized the attack as revenge for Pratt's murder. At the very least, the massacre reflected an increasingly dangerous and tense environment, perhaps a prelude to more bloodshed to come.

Among the 2,500 soldiers making their way slowly toward Utah were newly appointed federal officials, including a new territorial governor to replace Young. Buchanan had decided that Young's loyalty lay with the church and not the nation. Young, for his part, declared Utah under threat from an external foe and prepared a defense of the territory by calling up the Nauvoo Legion. An alleged insurrection, it appeared, had blossomed into a full-scale revolution. As the army made its way along the Oregon Trail, the situation continued to unravel.

Fortunately for everyone involved, Utah was a long way from anywhere, giving all sides time to cool their rhetoric. Bad weather hampered the army's advance, and Mormon volunteers burned much of the available feed for the military's animals. These problems forced the army to stop for the winter on the Green River and await the arrival of spring before they could finally march on Salt Lake City. The delay, however, created room to negotiate. Brigham Young no longer made pronouncements that seemed like revolutionary decrees. Striking a more conciliatory tone, Young would step down as governor but be absolved of any wrongdoing.

The army finally arrived in the spring of 1858 and remained a presence until the turmoil of the Civil War necessitated a redistribution of troops, but the violence that could have occurred, fortunately, did not. Buchanan's appointees, including new governor

Alfred Cumming, did wrest control of the territorial apparatus from Young upon their arrival in the territory. Young, however, unquestionably remained the most powerful man in Utah.

Mormonism remained controversial throughout the 19th century, stained as it was in the popular mind with the issue of polygamy. Conflict between the Latter-day Saints and federal officials continued for decades. The passage of the Edmunds-Tucker Act in 1887 proved to be one of the last salvos launched by the federal government against the practice. Under the act, polygamist men could be sentenced to six months in prison and a $300 fine, but the bigger issue was that a church that promoted such practices would be forced to pay a much larger fine and forfeit its property. Mormons leaders fought the Edmunds-Tucker Act in court (as they had earlier efforts to curtail the practice of their religion), but when the U.S. Supreme Court upheld the constitutionality of the law, the church had few openings left.

In addition, the church hoped to get statehood for Utah, which would allow Utah residents to elect their own governor and representatives instead of having a governor appointed by the president. Thus, being admitted to the Union would remove some federal oversight and allow the Mormons, the vast majority in Utah, to exercise more power over the state, but the Senate would only ratify a possible constitution if polygamy was abandoned. In September 1890, Mormon president Wilford Woodruff announced that he had received a revelation to end plural marriage among the Mormon faithful. The "manifesto," as it came to be called, received the approval of the Quorum of the Twelve Apostles and the general conference the following month. Officially, polygamy had ended, though some families continued to practice it in secret for years to come (Church of Jesus Christ of Latter-day Saints n.d.).

With the thorny issue of polygamy now resolved, Utah residents could move forward on statehood. President Grover Cleveland's signing of the Enabling Act authorized the creation of a constitutional convention for Utah Territory on July 16, 1894. The convention worked on the drafting of a state constitution over the spring of 1895. The proposed constitution included provisions banning polygamy, protecting the separation of church and state, and (perhaps most controversially) the enfranchisement of women, making Utah only the third place (behind Wyoming and Colorado) to grant women the right to vote. Since most women in Utah were Mormon, their enfranchisement also helped protect Mormon political power. On Saturday, January 4, 1896, President Cleveland signed the Utah

Statehood Proclamation, making the Beehive State the 45th in the nation (Ellsworth n.d.).

Statehood represented the end of the first chapter of Mormon history, a chapter of great struggle, sorrow, and romance. After 1895, Mormonism would slowly gain more acceptance as a legitimate religion, and Mormons celebrated their American citizenship, volunteering in large numbers, for example, in the Spanish-American War of 1898. Salt Lake City, in a way, did indeed become the New Jerusalem for the millions of Mormon followers around the world, and though the kingdom of Deseret would never materialize, in many ways, the Mormons became the most influential religious group in Utah, western Colorado, Idaho, and northern Arizona. Mormon settlers radiated out from the valley of the Great Salt Lake throughout the Intermountain West, building scattered towns and establishing a unique religious culture in the process.

RELIGION IN THE 19TH-CENTURY AMERICAN WEST

Religious ideas left an indelible impression on the West. Perhaps it was in the names Mormons bestowed on mountains and other locations in the areas they controlled, places with names like Lehi, Nebo, and Heber. Or perhaps the places were given English names that had older sacred names in native languages that only they remembered, places where great mythical deeds once occurred, such as Heart of the Monster butte or Devil's Tower.

More obvious signs of the influence of religion exist too. The steeples of churches rise above the tree canopy of most Western towns, but religion never really became quite the focal point of life in the West as it did in other regions. Perhaps this was due to the great distances between places or the stubbornly independent nature of residents in the region. Yet, there have always been exceptions to this. Catholicism remains important in the Southwest, both among native-born Latinos and the more recent arrivals from Central America, and thus the boundaries of New Spain remain, in some very important ways, more than 200 years later.

Today, as many Americans leave organized religion, the West remains at the forefront of the shift in perspective. According to the Pew Trust's survey of religion, 35 percent of Westerners report that they never go to church, more than the 32 percent attend weekly, and 33 percent go a few times per year. A full 60 percent of Westerners report that they never attend religious education groups or

Bible study. Conversely, the South, which remains the most religious part of the nation, sees 41 percent of its population attend church services weekly, and 30 percent report being members of a religious educational group. Only the Northeast rivals the West in these categories, with 35 percent of people reporting that they seldom or never attend church services and 67 percent saying they do not attend religious education groups (Pew Research Center 2014).

On the other hand, Westerners seem to be gravitating toward more independent forms of spirituality in the 21st century. Forty-one percent of Westerners report meditating at least once a week, and 58 percent report feeling spiritual peace. Again, only the Northeast compares to the West, with 37 percent reporting that they meditate at least once a week and 52 percent feeling spiritual peace. For a region as tied to the concept of individualism as the West, such do-it-yourself spirituality is not surprising (Pew Research Center 2014).

Of course, there is Utah and the exceptional nature of the Mormon faith. In 2020, despite decades of increasing non-Mormon immigration into the state, a full 55 percent of the population identifies as Mormon. In the Beehive State, 58 percent believe religion is very important to their lives, and 53 percent attend church services weekly—both substantially higher than the average for the region (Pew Research Center 2014).

Despite these changes, however, the West, like the rest of the nation, remains overwhelmingly Christian, with a smattering of other religious beliefs, like Judaism and Islam, found as well. The presence of Jews, in particular, in the West is as old as the settlement of the region. Typically, as Western towns developed, a few Jewish merchants would open stores catering to the needs of the new community. In larger cities, like Portland and San Francisco, the numbers of Jews grew large enough to support synagogues and community organizations such as B'nai B'rith, a sort of Jewish answer to the Masons. These religious and cultural organizations helped encourage a common ethnic identity that allowed for integration into American society while still maintaining their unique cultural and religious identities (White 1991, 451–453).

Indeed, one of America's wealthiest and most influential Jewish families got its start in the American West. At only 19 years of age, Meyer Guggenheim immigrated to the United States from Switzerland in the late 1840s. Starting out as traveling salesman, he profited as a commission merchant during the Civil War, but his real success came in the 1870s in the West. In 1879, he bought the A.Y.

and Minnie properties in the silver-mining boomtown of Leadville, Colorado, with a partner, R. B. Graham. This alone proved to be a good investment, as the properties were valued a decade later at $14 million, but Guggenheim had bigger plans. With profits from his mercantile operations, he invested in silver mines, and at the behest of his son Benjamin, the Guggenheims shifted their focus from mining (which was unpredictable) to smelting, which was a much safer bet. Their company, the American Smelting and Refining Corporation, grew to become one of the most powerful companies in the mining industry, and the Guggenheims soon amassed one the greatest fortunes in 19th-century America (Ubbelohde, Benson, and Smith 1995, 161).

Christianity's influence also spread among Indian peoples. Despite the frustrations and disappointments expressed by missionaries like the Whitmans and Spaldings, Christianity did, in fact, take hold among some groups, such as the Nez Percé. Decades later, the federal government gave different Christian denominations exclusive access to individual Indian reservations, essentially providing these groups with a captive audience for their conversion efforts, and the results appeared impressive. Not all was at it seemed, however, for while missionaries continued to believe that they could eradicate native beliefs and replace them with a new religious vision, the truth remained more complicated. Christian ideas intermingled with traditional beliefs among a people who, by the 1880s, had seemingly lost everything. Out of this religious milieu emerged a new and desperate religious movement known as the Ghost Dance.

7

THE INDIAN WARS AND THE TRANSFORMATION OF DAILY LIFE FOR AMERICAN INDIANS

Despite the later portrayal of the overland trail experience in movies, violence between emigrants and American Indian peoples was rare. Indian peoples often helped travelers, but violence did occur on occasion. Some of this stemmed from cultural misunderstandings—Indian resentment about the number of people passing through each summer, using, and often abusing, the fragile riparian ecosystem on which they depended in the winter months—and a feeling on the part of emigrants that Indians had become nuisances by begging for food, tobacco, and other goods. From the perspective of Plains Indians along the Oregon Trail, what whites considered begging was in their view a form of tribute for passing through their territory.

Emigrants also complained about the seemingly random theft of objects by Indians in the night. The theft of these items also had an explanation: young Indian boys and men would demonstrate their stealth and bravery by sneaking into an encampment to steal whatever caught their eye. Tools, combs, frying pans, and other small items vanished in this way, much to the consternation of campers waking up the following morning. Cattle and horses also disappeared from time to time, having been stolen or merely wandering off, and a wandering cow falling into Indian hands seemed to them a modicum of compensation for the loss of the bison. Tragically, however, conditions were developing that would lead to more serious confrontations, and it all began with a cow.

THE GRATTAN "MASSACRE"

Many of the Mormon emigrants making their way over the Oregon Trail to Salt Lake were desperately poor, as illustrated by the famous handcart brigades. One such emigrant, a member of a Mormon train, passed near a camp of Brulé (one of the bands of the Lakota) on August 17, 1854. En route to nearby Fort Laramie, the man led an emaciated and lame cow. Despite the animal's poor health, which almost certainly doomed it to death along the trail, it represented the owner's most prized possession. The Lakota laughed as the cow passed, and one, High Forehead, felled it with an arrow—perhaps on a dare, just for sport, or to put it out of its misery. The terrified Mormons fled to Fort Laramie, and the incident grew in the telling and retelling until it became a brazen attack.

The killing of the scrawny cow technically violated the terms of an 1851 treaty negotiated between the Lakota and the U.S. government, in which the Indians had promised to leave travelers alone. Nevertheless, the death of a lame cow should not have escalated into a crisis, and cooler heads should have prevailed. Unfortunately, they did not.

The commander at Fort Laramie, a 28-year-old officer named Hugh Fleming, sent a message to Conquering Bear, the "chief" of the entire Lakota people. Conquering Bear had essentially been appointed to his position by the U.S. government, giving him gifts that he in turn dispensed as he saw fit to other Lakota, which vastly increased his influence and prestige. Conquering Bear, therefore, had an enviable position that depended on good relations with the whites. Thus, he found himself in an awkward predicament when Fleming's messenger arrived demanding that the Indian responsible for the death of the cow be turned over to military authorities immediately. Hoping to defuse the situation, Conquering Bear offered to let the cow's owner choose a horse from his herd as compensation, but Fleming insisted that High Forehead be turned over to him. Conquering Bear explained that High Forehead belonged to the Miniconjou band of Lakota and therefore was not under his authority. Fleming, ignorant of Lakota customs, would not listen to these explanations and the next day decided to send out a detachment of soldiers to arrest the culprit under the command of Lieutenant John L. Grattan, a 24-year-old recent graduate of West Point who was eager to see action.

Grattan belonged to the school of thought that discounted tales of Indian martial acumen and believed the Indians to be essentially cowards who could be easily overawed by the professionalism and skill of U.S. Army soldiers. Like many young soldiers consigned to dusty remote frontier outposts, he had plenty of time to talk and drink, building himself up in his own mind into a great hero.

With 31 men and two small artillery pieces, Grattan rode for Conquering Bear's village, passing other Lakota camps along the way. Seeing the movement of the soldiers certainly raised some concerns. In total, some 1,000 or so Lakota warriors, belonging to several different bands, milled about near Fort Laramie awaiting the annual distribution of goods promised by the 1851 treaty. They represented a more powerful force than any the army could muster, but Grattan did not notice the large number of warriors, painted for war, that loitered near Conquering Bear's village.

When Grattan arrived, Conquering Bear came out of his lodge and tried to placate the officer. After 30 minutes of increasingly tense discussion, Grattan's patience wore out, and he ordered his men to fire. The soldiers fired their rifles, and the mountain howitzer, one of the artillery pieces, roared to life with a volley of grapeshot. Grapeshot, as the name suggests, was a thin metal canister filled with multiple lead balls that when fired turned a cannon into a giant shotgun, spraying multiple shots over a wide area. It was particularly deadly to concentrated groups of people. But on this occasion, the soldiers aimed too high, and the shots did little damage. However, Conquering Bear, directly in the line of fire, stood no chance and was pierced by at least nine balls. He would linger for hours before finally dying from his wounds. Hundreds of enraged Lakota fell upon Grattan and his men, who stood no chance against the onslaught. All of Grattan's men fell in a few moments, but the forces of war once unleashed would not be so easily contained (Ambrose 1996a, 61–65).

The deaths of any soldiers—even though their commanders had clearly been at fault—demanded retaliation, and the following year, General W. S. Harney set out with 600 men to punish the Lakota.

Had the Lakota been able to organize, they could have annihilated Harney's force, but coordinated operations proved difficult for fiercely independent bands to conduct. As a result, Harney's men passed along the trail to Fort Laramie and then northeastward through the heart of Lakota country toward Fort Pierre, on the Missouri River. Harney's orders were simple: terrorize any Lakota they found and demonstrate the ability of the U.S. Army to strike the heart of their territory.

Harney's men located and targeted a village of Brulé led by Little Thunder. Although Little Thunder had been warned about the pending arrival of the soldiers by the trader James Bordeaux, he apparently did not seem alarmed. Likely, he did not comprehend the damage a force of 600 infantry, cavalry, and artillery could inflict, and neither did he understand the idea of "total war" as increasingly practiced by the United States. The fighting would not be the kind of low-scale affair conducted between the Lakota and their Crow enemies, where only a handful of men might die on either side. Harney had been ordered to destroy any village he came across and to kill or capture as many Indians as possible.

At dawn on September 3, 1855, Harney attacked Little Thunder's people. Little Thunder rode out to the American general under a white flag, hoping to stall long enough for the women and children to flee. Harney, meanwhile, had dispatched his cavalry to sneak behind the village and attack from the rear. He launched the attack as soon as his cavalry were in position, catching the Lakota off guard. More massacre than battle, at least 86 Lakota perished, many children and women among them. At least another 70, mostly women and children, were taken prisoner. Before leaving, the soldiers burned the village (Ambrose 1996a, 70–73).

One teenage Lakota, a member of the village, returned after the battle from a buffalo hunt to find the bodies of the dead strewn about, many, including the women, scalped and dismembered. The young man's name was Curly. Like all who witnessed the carnage, young Curly was stunned by the nature of this new warfare, its indiscriminate brutality and scale. He would reach maturity in his people's desperate struggle against this new style of warfare and the people who wielded it as a tool of conquest, and he would be remembered forever by his adult name: Crazy Horse.

Harney's attack did little to degrade the power of the Lakota, but it escalated tensions and ended a period of relative peace and coexistence, poisoning the relationship between the two nations. A few years would pass, however, before the Lakota's eastern cousins, the Dakotas, faced the full brunt of settler invasion that led to the Dakota War in frontier Minnesota, an event that would have profound ramifications for the northern plains.

THE BLOODY TEXAS FRONTIER

Violence on the Southern Plains, or more specifically on the Texas frontier, ebbed and flowed. A frontier of competing empires, Texas had a bloody genesis. The Spanish tangled with the Comanche and their Kiowa allies on many occasions, and once Mexico asserted its independence, it inherited the same tensions and conflicts. By the time of Mexican independence in the early 1820s, Anglo-Americans had also begun to nose about the eastern flanks of Texas, coveting the fertile land and eager to exploit the Mexican government's tenuous hold on it. Somewhat begrudgingly, Mexico honored an agreement between the American Moses Austin and Spain, providing Moses' son, Stephen F. Austin, an extensive land grant in exchange for Anglo-American settlers taking up lands and building settlements in the distant northern province. Mexico's desultory attitude and suspicion of these newcomers would eventually be proven correct when many of these same settlers fomented a rebellion against the Mexican government in 1835–1836.

Anglo-American settlers, however, saw something in long-neglected Texas, and soon guidebooks and travelers' accounts extolled it as a veritable land of milk and honey. The anonymous author of *Texas in 1840: Or the Emigrant's Guide to the New Republic* declared, "The extended landscape furnishes such a view as to a yankee [*sic*] would seem the perfection of beauty in hill and dale, and excited in us a propensity to possess some portion of land destined, at some future day, to rival in wealth and beauty the fairest portions of the world." The author continued, "[Texas] with its extensive limits, [contains], a greater amount . . . of productive and valuable land than any portion of equal extent in the known world" (An Emigrant 1840, 81). Such books, filled with pages of breathless prose, celebrated the opportunities Texas offered, but they neglected to answer the question as to why such a beneficent land had never been extensively settled. To be sure, for Spaniards and Mexicans, Texas did not compare to Central Mexico, with its arable lands, temperate climate, and rich mines. But there was another reason for its sparse settlement: Texas was dangerous.

Anglo-American settlers, of course, knew that Texas could be dangerous, that Spain and Mexico had struggled against invasion from the Comanche and other occasionally hostile groups, but having defeated Eastern Indian peoples, it seems likely that these newcomers underestimated the power of the mounted Indians they now faced. For some, it would prove to be a fatal mistake.

Among these would be the Parkers, emigrants to Texas from Illinois. Attracted by the offer of thousands of acres of land for nearly nothing, in 1833, the Parker clan moved to Texas in a caravan of over 30 oxcarts. In total, the extended family amassed some 16,100 acres of land in east central Texas near the modern town of Mexia (about halfway between the modern cities of Dallas and Houston). Such a spread challenged the imagination, for nowhere in the United States could a family of middling settlers ever dream of acquiring so much land, and good land at that: fertile prairie land with copses of oak, ash, and walnut trees, all of it bisected by spring-fed creeks.

The main drawback to their claim was that it lay on the ragged edge of the frontier with no settlements to their west. The Parkers were not foolish enough to live in such a precarious place without some protection, and in 1835, six of the families (about two dozen people in total) enclosed their cabins within an extensive wooden palisade 15 feet high with four fortified blockhouses that acted as towers and fallback positions in case of attack—a layout that in one form or another had been used by settlers in the East going back to the 1600s. So long as the gates remained closed, the Parker's believed they could withstand any assault (Gwynne 2010, 13–14).

Security, however, is difficult to maintain indefinitely, and the tedium of routine tends to make people relax. Such was indeed the case on a lovely morning on May 19, 1836. Most of the men spent the early hours in their cornfields, while in the fort, the women and children went about their own chores. The cumbersome gate had been left open, no doubt because the men would return for a midday meal. Such laxity, however, proved to be their undoing.

At around 10:00 a.m., a force of well over a hundred mounted Indians suddenly appeared at the open gate, waving a white flag. With the Indians now between the men in the fields and the open gate, the Parkers had lost the protection their fort afforded. Hoping their intentions were peaceful, Benjamin Parker had no choice but to meet the Indians in front of the fort. The Indians indicated they wanted a cow to slaughter, which Parker declined. He promised, though, to give them some food and returned inside the fort. As Benjamin returned, his arms loaded with food, several members of the family left through a small doorway in the back of the fort, hoping to escape before the attack. It proved to be a wise choice, but other family members remained inside.

As Benjamin approached the mounted warriors, one Indian raised his lance and ran it through his chest. The attack had begun. Several warriors rode into the fort, killing Silas Parker, Samuel Frost, and Robert Frost. John Parker and his wife, Sallie, both elderly, managed to make it outside of the fort with Elizabeth Kellogg, but all three were caught. The band tortured, scalped, and finally killed John. They impaled Sallie on a lance, pinning her to the ground, and left her for dead. Amazingly, she would survive. They took Elizabeth captive. Joining her in captivity was Rachel Plummer, about 20 years old, with her 14-month-old son in her arms; Silas and Lucy Parker's 7-year-old son, John Richard; and their 9-year-old daughter, Cynthia Ann (Gwynne 2010, 15–18). Just as quickly as they appeared, the attackers vanished, their captives in tow.

James Parker, Rachel's father, spent much of the next 10 years attempting to locate and purchase the release of the captives. The Comanche needed captives for several reasons: first, women's reproductive capacity could offset population losses from disease epidemics; second, children could be integrated into the tribe more easily than adults; and third, at the very least, captives represented valuable commodities who could be ransomed for desirable goods. John quickly found his sister-in-law Elizabeth in August 1836, for she had been purchased by some Delaware Indians (friendly Indians who had been relocated from the East). They in turn sold her to Parker for $150, which Parker's friend Sam Houston paid. Rachel regained her freedom in 1837, after being purchased by Comancheros, Mexican traders who dealt with the Comanche and other tribes. She arrived first in Santa Fe and then made the passage across the plains over the Santa Fe Trail to Kansas City. She returned to Texas in February 1838. Having been subjected to torture and sexual assault, both her physical and mental health were failing. She died a year later. The two young boys taken captive, Rachel's son James Pratt Plummer and John Richard Parker, were brought to Fort Gibson, in Indian Territory, in 1842, leaving only Cynthia Ann still among the Comanche. Despite the attempts of James Parker, and periodic sightings of her, she remained with them as she grew from a child into a woman (Gwynne 2010, 120–125).

Attacks like the one on Fort Parker occurred with terrible frequency on the Texas frontier from the 1830s through the 1870s, and, indeed, nowhere else in the West was the frontier so bloody or so long-lasting. As an independent nation, Texas had been born in tremendous debt and with enemies on three sides. Without the money to fund an army strong enough to resist Indians, to say nothing of the vastly more powerful Mexican army, Texans had to largely rely on volunteer rangers for their defense. At first amateurish and poorly organized, the Texas Rangers eventually became a formidable force capable of taking the fight to the Comanche.

Technology aided the rangers in their efforts. Before the 1840s, the Comanche had a distinct advantage over Anglos, Spaniards, and Mexicans in that they could fight from horseback. The preferred method of attack for mounted Indians was to overwhelm their enemies with speed and power. Bearing down upon their foes from within a storm of dust and thundering hooves, they unleashed arrow after arrow to devastating effect. Heavy and cumbersome single-shot firearms could not match the lethal speed of arrows launched from the bowstrings of skilled archers. When confronted by these terrifying warriors, one's survival lay in finding a strong defensive position (like a rock field or arroyo) and hopefully making the assault too costly for the attackers. The horses' and their riders' uncanny knack for navigating the seemingly endless, trackless plains meant that they could attack and just as quickly vanish. It is little wonder, then, that they had remained unchallenged for so many decades. In the 1840s, however, that would begin to change with the arrival of the revolver on the Texas frontier.

The revolver, so called because it had a rotating cylinder filled with five or six bullets that rotated with each shot, putting a new round in position to fire, proved so vastly superior to a single-shot pistol that its success seems obvious in retrospect, but the truth seemed otherwise for a long time. The revolver was the invention of a young man with a passion for mechanics named Samuel Colt. Colt had been experimenting with the idea of a pistol with more than one shot since his teens, and in 1838, he established the Colt Firearms Company. His new company began producing a .36-caliber five-shot revolver. Sales, however, proved disappointing. The U.S. Army rejected the weapon, and the public seemed equally apathetic judging by the company's sluggish sales. With the company teetering on the edge of bankruptcy, Colt looked at his list of orders and noted that the company had made only one large sale: an 1839 order from the Republic of Texas for use by its navy (Gwynne 2010, 145).

Eventually, Colt's revolvers found their way into the hands of the Texas Rangers. The rangers, like everyone else, had been overmatched by mounted Indians. The revolver changed that. Small enough to be wielded with one hand while on horseback and capable of blasting five shots at a target before needing to be reloaded, the weapon gave the rangers a chance to fight on roughly equal terms with their Indian foes.

Captain Jack Hays, with roughly fifteen rangers, demonstrated the utility of these new pistols while patrolling through rugged Texas Hill County in June 1844. The patrol decided to rest their horses on Walker's Creek, a tributary of the Guadalupe River. While stopped, they faced an attack from some 75 Penateka Comanche. Surrounded by the fearsome warriors, Hays and his men appeared to be in an unwinnable situation, but as the Comanche approached, his men let loose with their pistols. Shot after shot brought warriors down, prompting the Comanche to turn and flee. Hays and his rangers, however, pursued, much to the shock and surprise of the Comanche. Nothing like this had ever happened before. The minor skirmish at Walker's Creek marked a change in the balance of power on the Southern Plains (Gwynne 2010, 145–147).

As important as the new technology of the revolver may have been, even greater changes emanated from the tectonic rumblings of international politics. The first major change occurred with the annexation of Texas by the United States in 1845. In truth, the majority of Texans had never really wanted to be an independent nation, having voted for annexation at the very beginning of their independence. The problem lay with the United States. Texas independence occurred at the same time that slavery had grown into a more divisive issue, and as a nation with an economy built on cotton and slavery, Texas would unquestionably be brought in as a slave state. Several previous attempts at annexation had foundered over this issue, but by the early 1840s, Americans were also increasingly enthusiastic about westward expansion, finally making the annexation of Texas acceptable.

Admission to the United States may have been good for Texans, but it proved unquestionably bad for the Comanche. An independent Texas could not adequately defend itself from outside invaders, essentially allowing the Comanche to continue their customary raids. Unlike Texas, the United States had enough military power to threaten Comanche domination, and it took little time before the U.S. Army began to erect military outposts all along the Texas frontier. Spaced dozens of miles apart, these forts could not prevent raids, but they could at least make raiding a more difficult and dangerous task for the Comanche and other Indian tribes.

The second political earthquake came soon after annexation. Mexico considered Texas to be a breakaway province, and its annexation by the United States poisoned the relationship between the two nations. Indeed, only a year after Texas's admission to the Union, the United States provoked a war with Mexico, ostensibly over the location of the border between the two nations. The two-year and largely one-sided war dealt a major blow to the nation of Mexico, with the 1848 Treaty of Guadalupe Hidalgo peeling away over half of Mexico's territory. For the Comanche, long adept at exploiting the spaces between competing American and European nations, the treaty put their large and powerful empire inside of a larger, more powerful, and more expansionistic nation. To be sure, the Comanche and their allies continued their raids in both American territory and Mexico, but now they found themselves enveloped by the United States on all sides.

Before the Americans could fully exploit this advantage and perhaps achieve what no other nation had done by defeating the Comanche, the American Civil War intervened. With Northerners and Southerners bent on killing each other, the Comanche suddenly found themselves with space to operate and in a strong position to attack Texans. Most of the Texas Rangers, at least the ones with experience and courage, found themselves in the service of the Confederacy. Meanwhile, the United States turned over the Texas frontier forts to Confederate forces. These outposts, either abandoned or staffed with untrained volunteers, proved incapable of slowing Comanche incursions. Without the Texas Rangers and soldiers to protect the frontier, the Comanche (as well as white outlaw bands) had free rein to brazenly attack settlements all along the frontier. Meanwhile, the U.S. Army, still in control of Kansas and New Mexico Territory, urged the Comanche to leave the Santa Fe Trail alone and attack Texas, something they were happy to do. The resulting four years brought abject terror and chaos to the Texas frontier, forcing hundreds of settlers to abandon their homesteads and retreat east to larger settlements such as Fort Worth for protection.

Shortly before Texas seceded and joined the Confederacy, one of the most noteworthy events in the state's history occurred at a small Comanche village along the Pease River in the northern part of the state. A minor skirmish, that came to be called the Battle of Pease River, had profound consequences. A small detachment of Texas Rangers, commanded by Lawrence Sullivan "Sul" Ross, had ridden north in search of some Comanche who had been raiding settlements in the area.

On the morning of December 18, 1860, in freezing temperatures and whiteout conditions, the rangers located and attacked a small collection of Comanche lodges on Mule Creek, a tributary of the Pease River. As the rangers approached, the Comanche ran for cover, some grabbing their mounts and vanishing into the snow, including two young boys sharing a horse. During the short conflict, Ross pursued two fleeing Indians on horseback. The first he shot in the back, knocking the rider from the fleeing horse. It turned out to be a teenage girl, which Ross claimed he did not know at the time. He chased another rider who was vanishing into the fog ahead of him. This rider was the headman of the village, and his name was Peta Nocona. Nocona and Ross exchanged shots, but Ross's aim proved truer and. The wounded man fell from his horse and crawled into the underbrush before dying.

The rangers took several Indians prisoner, among them Cynthia Ann Parker, the lost white girl from the 1836 Fort Parker raid. In her arms, she clutched a young daughter she had named Prairie Flower. Peta Nocona had been her husband, and together they had had three children: Prairie Flower and the two boys who had fled into the snow, Peanut and Quanah.

Cynthia Ann's "redemption" from "savagery" dominated headlines for a few days in the midst of the ongoing debate over secession. She toured Fort Worth and Austin before being returned to family members. Her real family, however, had been shattered that cold December day. Her husband had been killed, and she would never learn the whereabouts of her orphaned sons. Even her beloved daughter would perish from illness soon after their capture, leaving her distraught and isolated. She died in 1871 as a stranger among her former people.

THE SAND CREEK MASSACRE

While Texans struggled to protect their frontier during the Civil War years, forces in Union territory escalated conflicts with Indians peoples. Why this escalation occurred when it did is a difficult to ascertain. Perhaps it occurred because, despite the war, western expansion continued apace—indeed, many fled to the West to avoid serving on either side of the conflict. Perhaps it occurred because conflict on the frontier meant that local men would not have to serve in the bloody battles back east. Or perhaps the carnage in the east made attacks on Indian peoples in the Far West less newsworthy. Whatever the exact motivations, it is unquestionable that the

1860s, as a decade, set the stage for the final confrontation between Indian peoples and the U.S. military, and while Abraham Lincoln deserves a great deal of credit for holding the Union together during its darkest hours, his Indian policy proved an abject failure, with his tenure in office marred by some of the worst atrocities and miscarriages of justice in the 19th century.

The trouble began in Minnesota. Settlers moved into Minnesota beginning in the 1840s, pushing out a variety of Indians peoples, including the Ojibwa, Winnebago, and Dakota, or Eastern Sioux. The U.S. government negotiated two treaties in 1851 that exchanged lands for yearly annuity payments. Congress, however, rarely appropriated the money for the purchase of the agreed-upon goods, and when it did, the goods were distributed by the local Indian agent. Indian agents typically had few qualifications for the job and often received their appointments as a patronage positions. Most agents had no understanding of Indian peoples or their customs, and in the worst cases, they used their positions to enrich themselves by embezzling payments and goods intended for the Indians.

Thomas Galbraith, the agent for Minnesota, fit this profile perfectly. Galbraith resold the goods intended for the Indians to white settlers, embezzled money, and subsequently turned a tidy profit. When confronted by leaders from the tribes about this corruption and the desperate plight of their famished peoples, Galbraith apparently said that any starving Indians could eat grass. Galbraith's intransigence and hostility only added to growing Indian resentment, which finally erupted into violence in the late summer of 1862.

After some debate, several groups of Dakota decided the time had come to fight back, and they chose Little Crow to lead the campaign against the whites. For the next several weeks, the Dakotas unleashed a campaign of terror and violence against settlers of unprecedented magnitude. They burned homes all along the frontier and left few survivors in their wake. Some 500 settlers died in a few bloody, terrifying weeks, among them was Agent Galbraith, whose corpse was found stuffed with grass. Settlers fled to larger towns for protection, but even there, they faced the prospect of attack. The relatively large town of New Ulm, for example, endured several assaults in late August, with the Dakota able to set fire to several buildings.

Volunteer militias and regular U.S. Army soldiers attempted to retaliate. The arrival of General John Pope with several regiments of soldiers finally turned the tide in the conflict in early September. The roughly three weeks of terror for settlers had ended, but for the Indians of Minnesota, the violence marked only the beginning of their suffering.

The fact that most Dakota and other tribes, like the Ojibwa, had stayed out of the violence mattered little to settlers and U.S. officials. All Indians would pay for the uprising. First, soldiers arrested several hundred Indians (not all of them Dakota) and held hasty trials. Over 300 were convicted on the flimsiest of evidence and sentenced to death. Undoubtedly, some of them had participated in the uprising, but it was equally true that many, perhaps most, were innocent of any wrongdoing and guilty only of being Indians. President Lincoln, hoping to avoid another explosion of violence in the midst of a losing war against the Confederacy, quickly pardoned all but 38.

On December 26, 1862, all 38 were hanged simultaneously in Mankato, Minnesota, in front of a large crowd that had gathered to watch the spectacle. The grim event still holds the record for the largest single-day mass execution in American history. The government also rounded up roughly 1,500 other Dakota and put them into a prison camp built on an island in the Mississippi River. They would remain there for the next several years. Some Dakota fled west, where they shared news of the conflict with their cousins, the Nakota and Lakota. What had happened to the Dakota, they warned, would soon happen to Indians farther west.

The violence along the Minnesota frontier alarmed settlers elsewhere as well. The discovery of gold in Colorado in 1858 set off a rush for the front range of the Rockies. The following year, over 10,000 prospectors crossed the plains to search for gold. Denver quickly became the supply hub for the mining camps in the mountains. Vital supply lines stretched across the Central Plains— through the heart of Cheyenne territory—keeping the thousands of miners fed and clothed. Any disruption to those supply lines would prove fatal to miners in the Colorado goldfields. This realization made Coloradans nervous.

Tensions ran high in the late summer and fall of 1864 on the Central Plains. The massive invasion of gold seekers to Colorado had disrupted life for the Cheyenne, Arapaho, and Lakota, and anger and fear on the part of Indians over the Dakota War comingled with anger and fear on the part of Colorado miners and settlers. Sporadic attacks along the Platte River Road, the main supply line between Denver and the East, only added to the tension. Colorado territorial governor John Evans declared that assaults on the supply lines would "be destruction and death to Colorado" (quoted in West 1998, 290). Evans's rhetoric and that of other politicians and newsmen added fuel to the roiling cauldron of fear and rage in the territory. In such a context, a single event could trigger an explosion of violence. That event occurred in early August 1864.

Ranchers had quickly taken up land east of Denver on the plains. With scores of hungry miners to feed, the local market for beef meant high profits. Among these new ranching families were the Hungates, Ward, his wife, and two young daughters. Ward managed a ranch just outside of Denver. A group of warriors (by some accounts Arapaho who had a grudge against the ranch owner) brutally murdered the family. Their scalped and mutilated bodies were brought to town and placed in coffins in front of a Denver mercantile store, a macabre display designed to inflame passions. Governor Evans declared the situation a crisis, and on August 10, he ordered that all friendly Indians move to designated "safe" locations to be monitored. Meanwhile, soldiers would seek out and kill any hostile Indians, meaning Indians not located in these designated "safe zones." The governor declared, "The conflict is upon us, and all good citizens are called upon to do their duty for the defense of their homes and families" (quoted in West 1998, 291).

Evans's declaration put Plains Indians in a difficult position. The scant resources of the plains made it difficult to concentrate large populations, especially near forts, where soldiers and their stock used up the available grass and water. Moreover, the summer months offered the best opportunities for hunting. Spending them tethered to islands of supposed refuge near forts but without food rations only replaced the threat of a violent death with a slow death by starvation. Evans promised the distribution of food would be enough to support these population concentrations, but the Indians rightfully doubted such promises; most continued their summer hunts. Perhaps they might take up the governor's offer in the colder months.

One such gathering place was Fort Lyon, on the Arkansas River, in southeastern Colorado, and indeed, as the days grew colder, a large band of roughly 500 Cheyenne and Arapaho did set up camp about 30 miles from the fort on Sand Creek under the leadership of Black Kettle. Black Kettle had once been a more warlike leader, but he had since opted to pursue a course of conciliation and peace. Symbolic of his intentions, he flew an American flag from the poles of his tipi that he had been given a few years earlier at a peace treaty conference. Although Black Kettle called for peace, he was an old man, and war was the occupation of younger men. He could not force young warriors, eager to make their mark and increase their status, to idle their time away near the fort. Many of them continued to hunt through October and November, and some certainly could have participated in the sporadic raids that continued unabated. Black Kettle's village, therefore, contained mostly women, old men, and children.

Governor Evans, sending alarmist letter after alarmist letter to federal authorities, received permission from the U.S. government to form the Third Volunteer Cavalry. Colorado already had the First and Second Volunteer Cavalries, regiments composed of generally well-disciplined and experienced troops (Colorado soldiers had participated in the 1862 Battle of Glorieta Pass against Confederate soldiers in New Mexico, for example). The Third, authorized to operate for only 100 days, had a clear purpose: kill Indians. Bloodthirsty Denverites eagerly filled the ranks of the regiment, and when not enough of them could be found, they emptied the bars of anyone willing to sign on for 100 days. The resulting regiment, composed of untrained and undisciplined men, hungered for glory.

Command of the regiment went to John M. Chivington, a sometime Methodist minister with less of an interest in God than in his own elevation to prominence. He had commanded troops against the Confederacy at Glorieta Pass, and now a crushing victory over the Indians would assure him a place among Colorado's emerging political elite. When Colorado achieved statehood, Chivington hoped he would be elected representative or even senator. Leaving Denver on November 14, with his men in tow, Chivington had every intention of returning a conquering hero.

Meanwhile, the commander of Fort Lyon, Major Scott Anthony, demanded more than assurances of peace from the Arapaho and Cheyenne encamped near the fort. Any guns should be surrendered, and the Indians had to promise to keep near the post. They did their best to honor these terms, handing over some antiquated guns with which they "could make but a feeble fight if they desired war," Scott concluded (quoted in West 1998, 299). Food for both men and beasts was scarce near the fort, however. Sand Creek the best place to locate a village with enough forage for their horses that was still close to the fort. Anthony promised Black Kettle that "no war would be waged against them" so long as they remained peaceful. With Anthony's promise in hand, Black Kettle settled his people and waited out the coming winter. Several of the young men in the village set out to find buffalo to bring back and would be absent on the fateful day that was to come.

Chivington, with 700 soldiers of the Third Volunteer Cavalry and some members of the First, arrived at Fort Lyon on the evening of November 28, 1864. They brought with them four mountain howitzers. Chivington and Anthony conferred on strategy, and apparently Anthony agreed with Chivington's plan to attack the village, despite the promise he had made to Black Kettle. Captain Silas Soule and Lt. Joseph Cramer tried to convince Anthony to change his mind, but to no avail. After a short rest and resupply, Chivington's men set out to cover the 30 miles to Black Kettle's village under a clear and cold November night.

Stretched out along the creek, Black Kettle's camp of roughly 120 lodges squatted at the foot of sheltering bluffs to protect from the cold north winds. The creek offered enough water for both horses and people, and firewood collected from a copse of cottonwood trees would keep winter's chill away. The village slumbered in the gray twilight before dawn as Chivington's soldiers thundered in from the south.

At first, the people in the village mistook the rumble of hooves for a miraculous herd of bison, but as people poked their heads out to see the cause of the commotion, they were met by the report of gunfire. Chivington shouted, as the massacre began, "Remember the murdered women and children on the Platte" (quoted in West 1998, 304). It was not a battle but a slaughter. With few warriors to defend them and hardly any guns, Black Kettle's people stood no chance. George Bent, half-white and half-Cheyenne, the son of trader William Bent and Owl Woman, was in the village and recalled the attack. He looked toward Black Kettle's lodge and saw the old man standing in front of it, waving his American flag. "I heard him call to the people not to be afraid," Bent later wrote, "that the soldiers would not hurt them; then the troops opened fire from two sides of the camp" (quoted in West 1998, 304).

Gunfire and explosive rounds from the howitzers tore through the tents as soldiers cut down anyone who emerged from a tipi. Women and children ran for cover near the creek, burying themselves in pits hastily dug in the sand, while the few men there fought back as best they could. Chivington's men rode up on the people huddled in the sand and fired indiscriminately into the mounds until they stopped moving. In total, some 150 Indians were murdered, almost all women, children, and the elderly, but Chivington would claim to have killed more than 500 warriors in a grand and glorious victory over a hostile force.

After the battle, as the wounded lay groaning and dying, some soldiers picked over the bodies, stealing rings and other valuables. Several soldiers took scalps and other body parts as grisly trophies. Finally, on December 7, Chivington's men left and rode north for Denver.

Just as Chivington hoped, he and his men returned as victorious heroes, and the bars offered participants free drinks. Fortified by copious amounts of liquor, several men clambered onto music stages to recount their exploits and show off their trophies. Local newspapers rhapsodized about their bravery and daring, with the *Rocky Mountain News* declaring that Chivington's campaign would be remembered as one of "the brilliant feats of arms in Indian warfare" (quoted in West 1998, 306). Only later, thanks to survivors such as George Bent, would the truth slowly start to emerge. Congress eventually investigated the massacre and denounced the soldiers' actions. In the end, however, official blame fell on the victims, the Cheyenne, for not being on designated reservations in Indian Territory, where they would supposedly be safe. None of the men who participated in the massacre were charged with any crime. Chivington, for his part, did not entirely avoid the taint of his actions; his association with the massacre eventually doomed his political career, sending him skulking back to his native Ohio.

More immediately, the aggrieved Cheyenne vowed revenge and sent riders out to their allies, both north and south, with calls to strike back at the treacherous whites who had broken the peace. What the people of Denver most feared, an unrestrained war on the plains, was exactly what they created with the Sand Creek Massacre. War parties burned isolated ranches, stole livestock, and killed any whites they encountered. Venturing east of Denver meant taking one's life in one's hands. The stage stop at Julesberg, an important waypoint on the road to Denver, was completely destroyed (West 1998, 307).

To the north, the Lakota, allies of the Cheyenne, had their own simmering dispute with the whites encroaching on their lands. This encroachment began, as most did in the West, with the discovery of gold. This time, the new California would be in Montana, where the discovery of gold in 1862 on Grasshopper Creek, near the modern town of Bannack, set off a predictable frenzy, as it had in California, Oregon, and Colorado before. Montana, however, proved more difficult to reach than Colorado, so prospectors had two options: move along the Missouri River, a long and circuitous route, or take the Oregon Trail to Fort Laramie before breaking off and heading northwest to the goldfields. John Bozeman, a former prospector who had decided it was more profitable to go into the freighting and guiding business, proclaimed that his new trail offered numerous advantages over the longer Missouri River route. As was often the case, the Bozeman Trail followed a route Indians had been using for thousands of years. While still some 500 hundred miles long, it did offer a more direct route, with easy travel over open plains and plenty of grass and water for animals. However, prospectors would pass through the Wind River Country, in the heart of territory promised to the Lakota in the 1851 Fort Laramie Treaty. Great herds of buffalo called the area home, which the Lakota considered their own, and whenever whites moved through an area, as the Lakota knew, the buffalo herds soon diminished. With Lakota eager to dissuade the whites from using it, the Bozeman Trail, unsurprisingly, soon became the most dangerous of passages.

In 1864, a year after Bozeman had opened the trail, four wagon trains, a total of 450 wagons and 1,500 people, made the trip along the trail, mostly without incident. The Townshend party, however, would not be so lucky. The Townshend wagon train, with a 150 wagons, encountered a group of Lakota and Cheyenne. After the death of one traveler, the previously peaceful relations broke down, and the two sides exchanged shots. Armed with new repeating rifles, the emigrants managed to chase off the Indians, killing 13 before the fight ended (Drew 2014).

In response to increasing attacks, the army set up three outposts along the trail: Fort Reno, Fort Phil Kearny, and Fort C. F. Smith. The increasing military presence did little to deter the attacks. After all, the Lakota could range over a huge area and avoid the forts and occasional patrols. But the presence of soldiers infuriated the Lakota even more. Led by Red Cloud, they exacted a terrible toll on any who dared make the passage north. Traffic along the road dwindled, but the military presence remained, though the soldiers increasingly found themselves under siege.

Certainly, the Lakota would never attack the concentrated firepower of a fort, but soldiers could not remain inside at all times. At the very least, they had to leave the comfort and safety of the forts to cut firewood to feed the stoves that would keep the bitter Wyoming winter at bay. Largely confined to the forts with little to do on a daily basis, the soldiers complained. Major William J. Fetterman, stationed at Fort Phil Kearny, the central fort in the chain, carped about the lack of initiative on the part of the fort's commanding officer. Arguing that Indians were essentially cowards, he boasted that with only 75 men he could whip the entire Lakota nation. As fate would have it, he would get his chance.

Running low on firewood, the commanding officer, Colonel Henry Carrington, dispatched a party of woodcutters. To protect them from the Indians that always seemed to appear whenever someone left the post, he authorized Fetterman to take 80 men. His orders were clear: do not engage the Indians, and do not abandon the woodcutters. Such a show of force, he reasoned, would deter the Lakota from attacking. On the bitterly cold morning of December 21, 1866, the wagons and their escort moved out of the fort and headed for a stand of pine trees a few miles away. As they moved along the trail, Lakota warriors appeared on the hills above them, taunting the soldiers with war cries but vanishing whenever the soldiers threatened them. Such cowardice, Fetterman may have thought, proved his point about Indians. Finally, Fetterman, tempted by a small group of warriors just out of rifle range, abandoned the woodcutters and set off with his men after the roughly dozen or so mounted warriors. Leading this small party of Lakota was a young man who had already earned esteem among his own people, but he was unknown to the whites. They would soon learn his name: Crazy Horse.

Crazy Horse and the other members of his party kept just in front of Fetterman's charging men, leading them over the ridge, down into a bowl-shaped valley, and into a trap. As Fetterman and his 80 men reached the bottom of the valley, Lakota, Cheyenne, and Arapaho warriors materialized, seemingly rising out of the ground and from behind every scraggly sagebrush. By some accounts, as many as 2,000 Indians now surrounded Fetterman's patrol. Fetterman's men stood no chance. They held out for as long as they could, but the clouds of arrows were so thick and the closing ranks of Indians so close that some warriors were being wounded by friendly fire. As ammunition ran out, the soldiers could only swing their rifles as clubs. Fetterman and Captain Fred Brown, by previous agreement apparently, turned their pistols on each other, each pressing the barrel to the other's head. They counted to three and then killed themselves, a death preferable to one at the hands of the enraged Lakota. A few of the besieged soldiers managed to get into some rocks and poured out deadly fire from them, making a desperate last stand, but these too would fall (Brown 1962, 177–183). Fetterman and all the men under his command paid with their lives for his arrogance.

News of the Fetterman disaster reverberated around the nation, stirring up the already vociferous debate over the proper course of action with regard to the Indians of the West. Following the Sand Creek Massacre, many Americans argued that Indians should be treated better and peace be made with them. Others, especially in the West, demanded their subjugation, if not total extermination. General William Tecumseh Sherman, now in charge of the army in the West, spoke for many when he declared, "We must act with vindictive earnestness against the Sioux, even to their extermination, men, women, and children" (quoted in Utley 1984, 105).

Meanwhile, Red Cloud's warriors kept up their offensive with several skirmishes in the summer of 1867. Traffic along the road ceased, and even resupplying the forts with military escorts proved perilous. With few good options, the U.S. government offered to negotiate a cease-fire in the fall of 1867. Red Cloud replied that he was too busy to talk, but perhaps they could the following year. As Red Cloud's haughty reply suggested, the Indians knew full well that they were winning the conflict. When they agreed to meet, they would be in the stronger position. The next year, the government attempted once again to open negotiations. Red Cloud replied, "We are on the mountains looking down on the soldiers and the forts. When we see the soldiers moving away and the forts abandoned, then I will come down to talk" (quoted in Utley 1984, 119).

The signing of the 1868 Treaty of Fort Laramie later that summer ended the hostilities—though most of the hostile bands of Lakota, including those who followed Red Cloud, did not participate in the negotiation. Nevertheless, the soldiers did withdraw from their forts later that summer. No sooner did they leave than the Indians rode in and torched the buildings. Red Cloud's War had been a resounding victory for the Lakota and their allies. In addition, the treaty promised the Lakota would continue to hold sway over a vast area of the Northern Plains (eastern Montana, eastern Wyoming, and the western half of the Dakota Territory) as their homeland.

The government negotiated a similar treaty with the Indians of the Southern Plains in the fall of 1867, the Medicine Lodge Treaty. This treaty established reservations in Indian Territory for the Kiowa, Comanche, and Southern Cheyenne. On reservations, they would receive rations, but they could leave the reservations to hunt bison on the open plains. Under these terms, the Indians could benefit from food and supplies in the winter months and then spend the summer hunting; for the Indian peoples, it appeared to be the best of both worlds. As years wore on, however, bison numbers continued to plummet. Upon leaving the reservations, many Kiowa and Comanche instead headed south and plundered along the Texas frontier, killing people and stealing livestock, which Comancheros would surreptitiously trade for and then resell in Colorado and elsewhere. Texans complained that the government essentially subsidized these raids by feeding and sheltering the Indians in the winter months and then allowing them to leave in the summer, and they were correct.

The Medicine Lodge and Fort Laramie Treaties, seemed fairly clear-cut victories for the Indians of the Great Plains. The Lakota maintained control of their most important territories, including the sacred Black Hills and the Wind River Country. The tribes of the Southern Plains, meanwhile, could count on government assistance in the hard winter months but then spend their summers doing as they pleased. For the administration of President Grant, this "peace policy" also seemed to be working, as the next several years remained relatively peaceful.

General Sherman, however, took a different view, writing to President Grant that "the chief use of the Peace Commission is to kill time which will do more to settle the Indians than anything we can do" (quoted in Utley 1984, 118). With towns popping up all along the Rocky Mountains, farmers pushing onto the plains, and railroads laying track from coast to coast, Sherman knew that time was on his side.

Other tribes also faced the onslaught of expansion and military conquest during the Civil War years. Chief among these would the Navajo, or Diné, of northern New Mexico and Arizona. Over the decades, raids and counterraids occurred between the Navajo and the Mexican American population of New Mexico, but at other times, both sides carried on friendly trade. The United States inherited this complicated relationship when it conquered New Mexico, and now the U.S. military, already embroiled in a Civil War, would have to deal with policing the two groups. The army initially focused its efforts on defeating the Mescalero Apache in eastern New Mexico. Kit Carson, a scout and mountain man, led the army in the field. Once conquered, the army forced the Mescalero onto a new reservation of sorts at Bosque Redondo, a forested area on the edge of the eastern plains, along the Pecos River. To guard these people, the army built Fort Sumner. With the Mescalero threat eliminated, the government turned its attention to the Navajo.

For their part, the Navajo attempted to placate government officials and offer peace, but Navajo leaders, who often had large herds of sheep and spent at least some of the time farming, could not control the elements of their people who depended on raiding to provide for their families. In April 1863, two leading Navajo, Barboncito and Delgadito, met with General James Carleton, the top officer in New Mexico. They promised peace, but Carleton told them that if the Navajo wanted peace, they would have to move to Bosque Redondo, several hundred miles east of their canyon country homeland. The chiefs rejected such a shocking offer. Two months later, Carleton told the commander of the newly built Fort Wingate, located on the edge of Navajo territory, to inform them that "they can have until the twentieth day of July of this year to come in—they and all those who belong to what they call the peace party; that after that day every Navajo that is seen will be considered as hostile and treated accordingly" (quoted in Utley 1984, 82).

The Navajo had done little to deserve such treatment, and their remote territory offered no gold or even much arable land. There was really no justification for a campaign against them. But such concerns mattered not, and war came for them nonetheless. Kit Carson, having effectively beaten the Mescalero, set out to conquer the Navajo. Carson and his forces proved up to the challenge, killing livestock and burning crops in a campaign of brutal terror and efficiency that stunned the relatively peaceful and prosperous Navajo. By the end of 1863, Carson's soldiers had killed at least 78 Navajo and confiscated at least 5,000 head of sheep, goats, horses, and mules. His scorched-earth campaign proved so effective that the surviving Navajo, with what stock they still possessed, had little choice but to surrender and agree to move to Bosque Redondo.

Under military escort, some 6,000 Navajo walked nearly 300 miles from their homeland to their new reservation. The exodus came to be known (and bitterly remembered) as the Long Walk. Like the Trail of Tears, the Long Walk symbolized their defeat and subjugation as a people, and it too proved fatal to many. Unlike the Trail of Tears, however, the exodus made almost no sense. No settlers waited to gobble up Navajo lands the way they had Cherokee farms in Georgia, and few miners believed it worthwhile to prospect in their former haunts. Yet, the military continued to usher groups of several hundred Navajo at a time to Bosque Redondo.

The Bosque Redondo Reservation, however, proved to be a terrible location, lacking in the necessary resources to sustain the

6,000 Navajo and hundreds of Mescalero crowding there. As part of the "civilizing" campaign (and in an effort to save the government money), officials instructed the Navajo to grow crops, but the scrawny Pecos River was no Nile. Most of the time, it had little water to speak of, but then sporadic floods would swell the river's banks and wipe out farmers' fields. Summer hailstorms (common on the high plains) destroyed plants, and clouds of grasshoppers consumed much of the rest. Their livestock devoured what grass could be found and soon starved. Worst of all, their exposure on the edge of the plains, with nothing to protect them, made the Navajo easy targets for raids by Kiowa and Comanche (Utley 1984, 83–85). For the Navajo and Mescalero to survive, the government would have to provide them rations and support indefinitely, something the government simply would not do.

General Carleton saw all of this as a triumph. He had defeated two hostile tribes and made New Mexico, he believed, a safer place. That he had made enemies out of a largely peaceful people did not apparently bother him, and even when it became apparent that the Bosque Redondo reservation was a dismal failure, he refused to concede his error. His superiors, however, eventually came to see things differently. In 1868, as part of the larger effort to make peace with Indians, General Sherman met with the Navajo at Bosque Redondo. At first, he tried to offer them a reservation in Indian Territory, but they refused. Believing the land of their homeland essentially worthless and dealing with the ever-escalating costs to feed them on their current reservation, Sherman finally relented and signed a treaty restoring their lands and allowing them to return home. After four years of unnecessary and pointless suffering and privation, the Navajos accepted the terms and happily returned home. Unlike so many other Indian peoples, they remain on their land today (Utley 1984, 120).

The Navajo avoided any further conflicts with whites, and the northern plains of the late 1860s remained largely peaceful with the Lakota enjoying the promises of the Fort Laramie Treaty. Strife and violence, however, reverberated across the Southern Plains, caused by both by the tribes and white settlers.

THE RED RIVER WAR

The Grant administration had hoped that its peace policy would force Indian peoples onto reservations with less acrimony and be beneficial to both Indians and white settlers, with the latter taking vacated land and the former settling into lives as farmers. Settlers and some members of the military, however, claimed the strategy weakened the position of the United States toward the Indians. Indeed, as practiced on the Southern Plains, the policy did not work. The Comanche and Kiowa left their reservations under the pretense of hunting bison, a right promised them in the Medicine Lodge Treaty. The bison, of course, were mostly gone, and these trips from the reservations targeted settlers. Indian raids garnered cattle that could be resold, captives for ransom, and anything else they wanted to carry away with them. Further, the Texas Rangers were forbidden from pursing the Indians on the reservations, so any plunder was safe once the war parties crossed the Red River.

Texans, led by Republican governor Edmund J. Davis, decried the ineffectiveness of the peace policy and demanded action against the Indians. Despite his status as the Republican Reconstruction-era leader of the state (at a time of unchallenged Republican rule nationally), Davis felt that President Grant and national leaders ignored the suffering of Texans, making his efforts to rebuild the state along official Republican lines more difficult. Events, however, would soon turn in Texans' favor.

The U.S. military, of course, had a strong presence in Texas and Indian Territory. One could draw a line from Fort Clark in the south and connect Fort McKavett, Fort Concho, Fort Griffin and the northernmost post of Fort Richardson. In addition, several other forts protected the road west to El Paso, including Forts Stockton, Davis, and Bliss. These posts, generally spaced 50 miles or so apart, could not fully protect settlers from Indian raids, but they could act as staging points for forays into the territory still held by the Comanche and Kiowa. Indeed, as late as the early 1870s, the Comanche and their allies still held areas where few white men had ever penetrated, most particularly Palo Duro Canyon, a massive canyon east of modern Lubbock and Amarillo. The canyon and the semiarid high plains that surrounded it had long stymied all efforts to penetrate it, making it the last stronghold for the Indians of the Southern Plains.

Surrounded on all sides by a powerful industrial nation and their bison herds shrinking daily, in the early 1870s, the tribes of the Southern Plains were struggling to maintain their independence. The catalyst for a new and more martial response to the Indians in the region came in May 1871. General Sherman toured some of the posts of Texas and made his way toward Fort Sill in Indian Territory. His inspection had been prompted by Texans' demands for the federal government to play a stronger role in controlling Indians. Many federal officials, however, scoffed at the tales of Indian depredations that Texans spread, and it was Sherman's job to see whether these tales contained any truth. The inspection tour started in the south, and Sherman stopped at Forts Concho, Griffin, and Belknap before reaching Fort Richardson. During their entire tour, they had not seen a single Indian, and Sherman concluded that Texans had greatly exaggerated the Indian threat. While en route to Fort Richardson on May 17, Sherman unknowingly passed a party of Comanche and Kiowa who were hidden from view. Only the presence of a strong military escort prevented an attack. The next party on the trail, however, would not be so lucky.

The day after Sherman's entourage had passed, a train of freight wagons made its ponderous way north. Loaded with goods and lacking the firepower of Sherman's escort, the wagons proved an irresistible target. The teamsters driving the wagons were defenseless against a war party of several hundred Kiowa, Comanche, and Cheyenne. The leader of the wagon train, Henry Warren, and six other teamsters perished, some tied to wagon wheels and slowly tortured to death. The Indians released three others, who made their way toward Fort Richardson to report the attack. Realizing that he had traveled over that very road the day before, Sherman revised his view on the threat posed by Indian raids and ordered Colonel Ranald Mackenzie to immediately pursue the war party.

Infuriated, Sherman rode north to Fort Sill, where he demanded the immediate surrender of the leaders of the attack. He personally arrested three Kiowa leaders responsible for the raid, Satank, Satanta, and Big Tree, on May 27 and ordered them sent to Jacksboro, Texas, to stand trial for murder in a civilian court. On June 8, Satank allegedly died in a failed escape attempt. Satanta and Big Tree arrived in Jacksboro, and following a perfunctory trial, they received death sentences from the jury. Pacifistic Quaker activists, however, convinced Governor Davis to commute the sentences to life in prison. Two years later, in October 1873, they were paroled in a gesture of goodwill. Satanta would not live as a free man for long. After being arrested in 1874 for allegedly organizing raids against whites, he returned to the state penitentiary in Huntsville, Texas. In 1878, he committed suicide by leaping from an open window rather than spend the rest of his days confined.

The Warren Wagon Train Raid (also known as the Salt Creek Massacre) proved to be a small affair, but it was the mundane nature of the attack that so alarmed Sherman and convinced him that the peace policy had failed. Of course, settlers bore responsibility for much of the situation with their role in the destruction of the bison and the continued encroachment on Indian lands, but Sherman, like many of his fellow Americans, concluded that only conquest could finally break the Indians. Mackenzie wrote to Sherman, "The Kiowas and Comanches are entirely beyond any control and have been for a time." With free rein to attack and plunder, they would have to be defeated. He continued, "This can only be accomplished by the Army" (quoted in Gwynne 2010, 242). Sherman, one of the chief architects of the total war concept that had crushed the Confederacy, agreed and sought to unleash the American military on the Comanche and Kiowa, and he turned to Mackenzie to do it. Officially, nothing had changed, but unofficially, everything had.

The Indian peoples of the Southern Plains had fought, and often defeated, Spaniards, Mexicans, Texans, and even Confederates. They had never fought an enemy like the U.S. Army. First, the United States had never bothered to unleash a large force against the peoples of the Southern Plains. For decades, ambivalence about the plains had made Americans apathetic toward the area. Second, the intervening Civil War prevented a campaign against the Indians of the region. And finally, the attempted peace policy had worked against large-scale military intervention. All of these factors gave Indians just enough room to operate. By the 1870s, however, the situation had changed, and this new enemy would finally bring its full force to bear. The advantages of the U.S. Army were many: technologically advanced weaponry, inexhaustible supply lines, professional and battle-hardened officers, and a government capable of coordinating all of these into a devastatingly effective campaign. They also had their enemies surrounded on all sides by a much larger society.

In the fall of 1871, Mackenzie and 600 soldiers pierced the eastern edge of the Llano Estacado for the first time. The expedition ended when Comanche, apparently led by Quanah Parker, the son of Peta Nocona and Cynthia Ann Parker, stole over 60 horses in the night, including Mackenzie's personal horse. Mackenzie had much to learn to meet the Comanche on their own terms. Yet, the stunning incursion into Blanco Canyon alarmed the Comanche, forcing them to retreat deeper into their expansive fortress of plains and canyons. The following spring, Mackenzie returned with a larger force and provisions for months. His goal was less to attack the Comanche and Kiowa and more to ascertain the lay of the land, taking the time to make maps that would enable soldiers to navigate the open grasslands and contorted canyons. The increasing pressure of the soldiers' presence disrupted other Comanche activities, such as hunting the increasingly rare bison and pasturing their horses. Still, the Comanche stayed one-step ahead of Mackenzie, always able to outwit or outride his forces, but each time he got better.

In September 1872, the army located and attacked a village of 262 lodges belonging to Kwahada-Kotsoteka Comanche, the most militant of the Comanche clans, along the north fork of the Red River. At least 24 warriors were killed, and more than 100 women and children were captured. The soldiers also captured a large number of horses and mules, and before departing, they set fire to the lodges, burning all the supplies the Comanche had managed save in advance of the winter. The army interred the captive women and children at Fort Concho, and Mackenzie promised they would be returned once the Comanche bands agreed to move to their reservations and remain there permanently. Destitute and anxious to retrieve their loved ones, many agreed (Hämäläinen 2008, 334). Mackenzie had learned his lessons on the cruel effectiveness of total relentless war well.

Not all Comanche, Kiowa, and Southern Cheyenne capitulated, however. The young warrior Quanah and a mysterious medicine man named Isa-tai advocated for a more militant response. Both in their twenties, Quanah and Isa-tai hungered to make their mark and wage war on the whites, even if it must have seemed a hopeless struggle. Isa-tai bragged that his medicine made him, and anyone who followed him, immune to soldiers' bullets. He also claimed to have the ability to vomit up all the bullets that would be needed for the campaign ahead—a magical but repulsive solution to the chronic Indian problem of a shortage of ammunition for sustained military campaigns. In his vision (which predated the similar Ghost Dance by some 15 years), he promised that if the Comanche held to the old ways, performed the sacred Sun Dance, and joined together, they could forestall the collapse of their society and defeat the whites. Large groups of Comanche and allied peoples heard his message and began to congregate at Elk Creek, on the north fork of the Red River. Among the growing village were Comanche from most of the clans as well as Kiowa, Cheyenne, and Arapaho. Internal disputes, however, made any coordinated action difficult, even with Isa-tai's presence. Some advocated attacks on Texans, others argued for attacks on buffalo hunters who were then slaughtering bison in the tens of thousands, and some denounced violence and returned to the reservations.

Finally, enough warriors agreed on a target to make an attack feasible. They chose an isolated outpost of buffalo hunters in the Texas Panhandle called Adobe Walls. At dawn, on June 27, 1874, a force led by Isa-tai and Quanah Parker attacked. Vastly outnumbered, the 28 buffalo hunters and 1 woman had two advantages. First, their outpost, as the name suggests, was composed of thick abode walls that provided cover, and, second, they had superior long-range rifles. Each time the Indians attacked, the hunters unleashed a withering fusillade. Several warriors died in brave but doomed charges, and when Isa-tai's horse was shot from under him, his enthusiasm for the assault evaporated. After a few days of ineffective siege, the Indians left. The reputations of both Isa-tai and Quanah Parker suffered from this embarrassing loss, and any semblance of a united front diminished, as individual bands broke up and went in separate directions.

The Battle of Adobe Walls also hardened the resolve of whites to crush the Indians of the Southern Plains once and for all. The army sent additional troops to Texas to prepare for a massive campaign against the southern tribes. The government issued an order that all the tribes of the Southern Plains should report to their reservations by August 3 or be considered hostile. While many heeded the order, at least 2,000 Comanche, Kiowa, and Cheyenne remained at large. Soldiers from all directions began a final assault on the last Comanche stronghold in Palo Duro Canyon.

Mackenzie, with the help of his Tonkawa Indian scouts, located a large village hidden in the bottom of Palo Duro Canyon. On September 28, 1874, his forces struck, and the surprise was total. Comanche, Kiowa, and Cheyenne men, women, and children scattered before the soldiers' attack, many seeking refuge in the canyon. The soldiers did not pursue the fleeing, terrified people. Instead, they turned their attention to the lodges and everything inside them. They set fire to some 200 tipis, thousands of pounds of dried meat, flour, sugar, blankets, and clothing. They also rounded up some 1,400 horses. In previous assaults, Mackenzie had tried to take these animals with him, but on several occasions, Comanche raids had stolen most of them back. He would not make that mistake again. The horses were rounded up, taken to an arroyo, and shot. Although only three Comanche perished in the assault, the devastation was total. After looking over what they had done, the soldiers left. With their horses dead, their provisions destroyed, and winter coming soon, the survivors of the Battle of Palo Duro Canyon had no choice but to walk the several hundred miles to Fort Sill.

The following year, hungry and hunted, Quanah Parker and a few hundred other Comanche and Kiowa finally rode into Fort Sill and surrendered, ending the Red River War and Indian independence on the Southern Plains. Now the federal government could turn its attention to the northern plains, where tensions had been rising as well.

THE SIOUX WARS OF 1876–1877

Much like on the Southern Plains, the Indians of the northern plains, in particular the Lakota Sioux and the Northern Cheyenne, had also been living with the promises made under the treaties of the 1860s. Increasingly, however, the same problems afflicting the Indians of the Southern Plains also visited the northern plains. Industrial-scale hide hunting decimated bison populations. The recently completed Union Pacific Railroad bisected the Great Plains, and another line, the Northern Pacific, pushed into the northern reaches of Lakota territory. Worst of all, prospectors and settlers poked around the margins of areas promised to the Lakota. All these challenges accelerated when the government decided to send an expedition to the Black Hills to ascertain whether rumors of gold there were true. For the Lakota, the Black Hills offered shelter and food, but more importantly, they were the most sacred and religiously powerful landscape in the Lakota universe. Sending a military expedition into the hills profoundly and brazenly violated the terms of the Fort Laramie Treaty and insulted Lakota sovereignty.

Gold is typically found in mountains, and rumors of gold in the strange Black Hills resonated around the nation following the collapse of the economy in 1873. The Panic of 1873 had been caused by the bankruptcy of the Northern Pacific Railroad, but, somewhat ironically, the railroad helped open the Black Hills because it had already laid track only a little to the north. Unlike the earlier California gold rush (which took some prospective miners six months to reach), the Black Hills rose only a few hundred miles west of Minneapolis and were thus within easy reach. If gold existed in the hills, thousands of down-on-their-luck Americans would undoubtedly converge on them. But rumors alone would not start a rush;

the American people wanted to know whether gold really lay hidden in the Black Hills. To separate fact from rumor, an expedition would have to be sent to probe the mysterious range.

Ostensibly, the expedition's purpose was to locate a site for a potential fort, as the Lakota were not living up to their commitments under the Fort Laramie Treaty, according to General Phil Sheridan. Sheridan's false assertion provided the thinnest of pretenses, but it was enough to justify an expedition. Always eager to take a high-profile position and get his name in the papers, Lt. Colonel George Armstrong Custer applied for command of the expedition.

To dissuade the Lakota from attacking, the expedition packed a tremendous amount of firepower: 10 companies of Custer's Seventh Cavalry and 2 companies of infantry, plenty of artillery pieces, and three Gatling guns (rapid-fire proto–machine guns). In addition, over 100 Indian scouts, from tribes like the Crow, who despised the Lakota, served as guides. The civilian contingent rivaled the military component in size. It featured mining engineers and geologists to look for gold, the naturalist George Bird Grinnell, four newspaper reporters, a photographer, and dozens of mule skinners to drive the wagons of supplies. In total, the expedition numbered at least 1,000 men and nearly 2,000 horses and mules (Ambrose 1996a, 375–376).

After reaching the hills in late July 1874, it took less than a week for the mining engineers to discover gold on French Creek. Custer himself wrote that he had in his possession "40 or 50 small particles of pure gold, in size averaging that of a small pin-head, and most of it obtained today from one panful of earth" (quoted in Ambrose 1996a, 379). By late August, the news of gold in the Black Hills had buzzed around the globe on telegraph wires. Custer's discovery and the subsequent rush to the sacred Black Hills would set off a final confrontation between the Lakota and the U.S. government.

Unsurprisingly, the U.S. government sent representatives to the Lakota to negotiate a treaty for the purchase of the Black Hills. Miners would unquestionably pour into the hills, tearing up the land by building towns, roads, and mines, and the government had no interest in preventing the influx. However, it was important to give the acquisition a veneer of legitimacy that could only come from the signing of a treaty. Many such treaties had been enacted in American history, and even the most dubious ones had Indian signatures on them. In such cases, officials typically found some members of a tribe (or on occasion members of other tribes) willing to part with the land in exchange for goods. The signature of any Indian would be enough to legitimize the process.

The Lakota became divided over the question of the sale. More conciliatory leaders like Red Cloud advocated for selling the Black Hills, but at hefty price. Red Cloud had abandoned his hostile ways after a visit to Washington, DC, where he saw firsthand the size of the United States and the power of its army. He knew that Indian peoples did not have the power to defeat the invaders. Red Cloud and another leader, Spotted Tail, represented the Lakota who had taken up residency near the Indian agencies, living off government rations now that the buffalo had been hunted out of the Dakotas. Being pragmatic, they assumed the government would take the Black Hills regardless of a treaty, but they also knew the value whites put on gold and the eagerness of the government to strike a deal. Thus, they advocated for a sale that would help ensure the survival of their people and their economic independence.

A more militant faction, however, argued that the Black Hills could not be sold for any price because losing the rumpled range meant losing a key part of their identity as Lakota. White man's roads, towns, and mines would irrevocably profane the sacred landscape. This faction had two of the most admired of all the Lakota in Crazy Horse, his reputation now secured after annihilating Fetterman's command, and Sitting Bull. They refused to come anywhere near the agencies, remaining out in Wyoming and the Montana plains.

In 1875, the government suggested a meeting in Washington, DC, to hammer out a deal on the Black Hills. Red Cloud, seen by the whites as the preeminent chief of the Lakota, would attend, but without the support of the more militant faction, no agreement would be seen as legitimate. Thus, Red Cloud attempted to convince Crazy Horse and Black Twin, another leader of the militant faction, to accompany them to see the "Great White Father" in Washington, but both refused. The meeting in Washington ended without a commitment on the part of the Lakota delegation.

Spotted Tail decided the best option would be to have the Lakota and white representatives tour the Black Hills. After the inspection, Spotted Tail argued that the hills were worth $7,000,000 and full rations for all Lakota for seven full generations—an astronomical price to be sure, but as miners washed gold from the creeks, it was hard to argue against the value of the hills. Showing how much the Lakota had learned of the white man's system, Spotted Tail declared that any agreement should be "so large that the interest will support us" (quoted in Ambrose 1996a, 394). The negotiations dragged into the fall, with neither side willing to budge on amounts. Moreover, a clause in the Fort Laramie Treaty required that any new treaties be signed by three-fourths of the tribe, which was an impossibility without the participation of the militant faction, who refused to attend the negotiations. Frustrated with the delay, the government changed tactics.

President Grant issued an order declaring all Lakota and their allies the Cheyenne and Arapaho not on designated reservations as hostile. These hostile factions had until January 31, 1876, to relocate to reservations or feel the brunt of the U.S. Army. Effectively, the United States was declaring war on the hostile faction. President Grant hoped to intimidate the hostile Indians into giving up and moving to the agencies. It had, however, the opposite effect. Everyone, both Indian and white, knew that fighting on the northern plains would commence in the summer of 1876. The Plains Indians, of course, put great stock in martial exploits, and young agency Indians, bored and with few options for winning the glory and respect their elders had obtained in their youth, saw a chance at earning a name for themselves by leaving the agency for the hostile camps of Crazy Horse and Sitting Bull. The militant faction needed every man they could get to mount a defense against the U.S. Army; moreover, these agency Indians were often well armed with new rifles. Thus, as the U.S Army prepared for its summer campaign, the Indians did likewise. When the deadline passed without the appearance of the hostiles, Zachary Chandler, the secretary of the interior (under whose jurisdiction the Indians fell), formally notified Secretary of War William Belknap, writing, "Said Indians are hereby turned over to the War Department for such action on the part of the Army as you may deem proper under the circumstances" (quoted in Ambrose 1996a, 397). Come summer, there would be war.

The army did not know the exact location of Crazy Horse and Sitting Bull's camp (although the scores of young agency Indians had no trouble finding it and joining the cause), but they had a rough idea: north of the transcontinental railroad, east of the Rockies, and west of the Dakotas. The plan, therefore, called for three armies to march into the search area and finally meet together to crush the remaining hostiles. General Alfred Terry (with Custer's Seventh Cavalry included) would head west from Fort Abraham Lincoln in Dakota Territory with the largest force, some 2,700 men. General George Crook, with approximately 1,200 men, would advance from the south along the Bozeman Trail. And Major General John

Gibbon would advance eastward from Montana's Fort Ellis with 450 soldiers in his command.

While the Lakota and Cheyenne had little knowledge of the movements of the armies, they certainly knew that soldiers were looking for them. With strength in numbers, their ranks swelled over the spring and into the summer. So great was the village, and so numerous the warriors, that people took comfort in believing that the soldiers would not dare attack them, and if they did, their warriors would be able to repel them. Many also looked forward to the coming Sun Dance in late June.

The Sun Dance represented the most important religious celebration of the year and a time to ask for the *Wakantanka*'s (Great Spirit's) help with a variety of challenges, and with the presence of soldiers and their way of life increasingly threatened, they could use all the help they could get. In 1876, with the specter of attack looming, the Sun Dance must have had an anxious backdrop. Despite the background of fear, many remarked that it was the largest gathering in years, and a sense of bittersweet excitement pervaded the camp, with feasting and dancing almost constant. Even the bison seemed surprisingly plentiful, with meat enough for all. As participants would recall later, the event marked the last hurrah of a way of life.

Sitting Bull sponsored the Sun Dance, and he himself—despite being well into his forties—participated in the grueling ceremony. After collapsing in the arena, Sitting Bull received the vision he sought. He prophesied that a great battle would soon happen and that the Indians would win, defeating the soldiers and killing them all. The audience cheered at this news, and the prospect of a great victory certainly improved morale. Sitting Bull, however, paid a great price for his vision in blood and suffering; his eyesight would not return for weeks. When the great victory he predicted occurred, he would miss the fight as he convalesced in a dark tipi with his eyes wrapped, for even the slightest light stung his wounded eyes.

The Indians' large mobile city, by some estimates over 10,000 people strong, required frequent relocation so that their horses would not exhaust the available grass. Thus, after the Sun Dance, the village moved again to southeastern Montana and a place they called Greasy Grass River. On the soldiers' maps, it bore the name Little Bighorn.

General Crook's force made contact first near Rosebud Creek. Scouts informed Crazy Horse of the large force of over 1,000 soldiers and another 260 Crow and Shoshone Indians. The village leaders held a council. Some advocated for a retreat away from the soldiers, but the more militant leaders wanted to send every available warrior to meet Crook, or "Three Stars," as the Lakota called him. Crazy Horse argued against both options. Retreating would not work, as the soldiers would simply continue their advance, and leaving the large village unprotected from additional armies would be disastrous. Crazy Horse, instead, advised putting together a force as large or larger than Crook's while leaving enough warriors in reserve to protect the village. Eventually, the gathered men agreed with the wisdom of this approach. On the evening of June 16, Crazy Horse set off with some 1,500 men to confront Three Stars and his army of bluecoats and Indian scouts. At sunrise, having covered over 30 miles in the dark, he allowed his men time to rest their horses and put on their war paint. At roughly 8:30 a.m., they set off to attack Crook's approaching column, waiting for him out of sight behind a ridge.

Crook's Crow and Shoshone scouts were nervous as they approached the ambush. The Shoshone chief Washakie warned Crook that there were too many Lakota ahead, but Crook apparently ignored him. Nevertheless, Crook was convinced to send out some Crow scouts to check the area before moving any farther. These scouts, riding up the ridge, were the first to see the Lakota and Cheyenne waiting for them. They turned and rode back downhill, yelling, "Sioux! Sioux!" The trap now sprung, the Lakota and Cheyenne crested the ridge and thundered down on Crook's force at full gallop.

The ensuing Battle of the Rosebud became a long and chaotic fight, with the Lakota and Cheyenne repeatedly charging into the scattered ranks of the soldiers. The situation resembled Crazy Horse's victory over Fetterman, but with one important difference: the presence of the 260 Crow and Shoshone scouts. Crook's Indian allies comported themselves magnificently against their bitter enemies. Time and again, they fought back against the Lakota and Cheyenne charges, buying time for the soldiers to regroup and preventing a flanking maneuver Crazy Horse had attempted. After hours of fighting, the Lakota and Cheyenne withdrew. Still holding the field of battle, Crook claimed victory.

In reality, the Battle of the Rosebud did not look much like a victory for the army. Crook had lost 41 men (28 soldiers and 13 of the heroic Indian scouts). Crazy Horse later reported that 36 of his men died, a high number for them. Yet, Crook retreated following the battle, accomplishing Crazy Horse's strategic goal of pushing them back out of Lakota territory. Indeed, Crook essentially sat out the rest of the campaign (Ambrose 1996a, 420–423).

Meanwhile, Terry and Gibbon had joined up, augmenting the size of the force heading from the northeast, but they had no idea of the fate of Crook's army or the location of the Indian encampment. Reconnoitering was an essential task of the cavalry, and General Terry tasked Custer's Seventh with locating the village. On June 10, Terry ordered Custer's second in command, Major Marcus Reno, to take half of the Seventh Cavalry and explore the area around the Tongue and Powder Rivers. The rest of the Seventh, under Custer, would advance in front of the larger force and await Reno's return. If Reno did not find an encampment, then the Indians would be south along the Rosebud or Little Bighorn Rivers. Once again at full strength, the Seventh would advance toward those rivers.

Custer protested Terry's plan, fearful that Reno might find the Indians and win glory for himself at Custer's expense, but he had no choice. So, he waited at the mouth of the Tongue River and prepared his men for their turn to search for the hostile village. Ten days later, Reno returned, claiming to have found evidence that the Indians were most likely camped on the Bighorn River. After debating the next steps, Terry gave Custer his orders on June 22, 1876. Custer would ride toward the Little Bighorn River, fol-lowing the signs Reno had spotted. He could engage the Indians if he felt he could carry the day or await the arrival of Terry's larger force.

Eager for glory and perhaps pondering a run as president in the upcoming 1876 election, Custer would never wait and share the glory with his commanding officer. If given the chance, he would attack. As an experienced Indian fighter, he knew that if the Indi-ans detected his presence, the village would scatter in every direc-tion and a make a decisive victory impossible. All of these reasons, perhaps, explain his decision to attack, and, indeed, in all his years as a soldier, in all the battles he had fought, his amazing luck had always held out. One last victory over the Indians, having already defeated other Indians and the Confederates before them, and he would be catapulted into national prominence and perhaps the highest office in the land.

As Custer prepared for his chance at the Lakota, Terry offered him several Gatling guns and some additional companies of the Second Cavalry. Custer demurred, saying the guns would slow him down and the additional men were unnecessary (all the credit and glory would go to the Seventh). Both of these turned out to be fateful decisions. At noon on June 22, Custer and the 611 men under his command rode off to their fate.

Custer's column moved quickly toward the Little Bighorn, covering 60 miles in only two days, and everywhere they saw signs of a large number of Indians nearby: grass mowed down by large horse herds, abandoned campfire rings, and the deserted Sun Dance arena from a few days earlier. On June 24, they reached the point where the massive village had crossed the Rosebud heading toward the Little Bighorn. There were so many travois marks (the poles Plains peoples attached to their horses to transport their possessions) that the ground looked like a plowed field. Custer's Indian scouts grew increasingly apprehensive and advised caution, but Custer, certain that a great victory would soon be his, pressed on toward the Lakota and Cheyenne encampment. That night, he and his men rode on, covering 10 more miles in the dark.

The morning of June 25, Custer's Indian scouts made their way to the bluffs overlooking the Little Bighorn. What they saw stunned them. Although they could not see the entire village because of a curve in the river valley, they saw dozens of lodges hugging the bank and beyond those the largest herd of horses they had ever seen. Bloody Knife, an Arikara scout who had long served with Custer, warned him that there were more Indians in the village than the Seventh had bullets. Custer, again, brushed off the warning. Fearing that the Indians would scatter once they were alerted to his presence, Custer decided not to rest his men while waiting for Terry's larger force to catch up. He would attack immediately.

Custer dusted off a battle plan that had served him well in the past. Back in November 1868, he had won his first great victory over the Indians (Southern Cheyenne, mostly) at the Battle of the Washita in modern Oklahoma. That day, he divided his forces, having his second in command lead a diversionary attack on the village that would draw out the warriors while Custer swept in from behind and rode through the now undefended camp, killing indiscriminately. It had worked well, except for the loss of some 20 troopers, which Custer blamed on his former, now deceased, second in command. Custer decided the same strategy would work again.

His second in command, Major Marcus Reno, would attack the village directly, crossing the river and making a show of his advance. This would draw the warriors out while Custer took his men and moved toward the village from behind the bluffs that overlooked the village, thus obscuring their presence. Finding a place to descend, he would ride down into the village, killing anyone they encountered, and then squeeze the warriors between the two pincers of his army. On that snowy day in 1868, he had faced perhaps 200 warriors. Now he faced no fewer than 2,000—and likely far, far more. Custer advanced with only the vaguest idea of his enemy's position and no idea at all about their strength.

Reno carried out the plan as drawn up. His men rode toward the village with no effort to conceal their presence. Several women, washing clothes in the river, witnessed the soldier's approach and raised the alarm. In truth, however, Custer's presence had long been known, and Crazy Horse and the other leaders had hoped he would attack. They were more than prepared. Rather than charge directly into the village, Reno had his men dismount and form a skirmish line. They fought in small groups of four, one man to hold the horses and three to fight. If they became overwhelmed, Reno wanted his men to be able to remount and retreat quickly. Just as Custer predicted, Reno's presence attracted a large force of warriors. However, this was just a small fraction of the total number of warriors available. Knowing Custer's larger force was still out there, Crazy Horse kept his men in reserve. Though Custer did not know it yet, he was riding into a trap.

Reno, confronted by an ever-growing force of Indians, decided to pull back to a copse of cottonwood trees near the river to provide his men some cover. The scout Bloody Knife stood nearby. A lucky shot from someone struck the scout in the head, splattering chunks of brain and skull over Reno's face. At this moment, Reno wiped the gore from his face and, by most accounts, froze. When he snapped back to reality, he ordered his men to retreat and ride for the nearest high point. If he and his men could reach it, they could get into a defensible position and concentrate their fire in an attempt to hold off Indian attacks. Riding across the river and up to the bluffs, with Indians hot on their heels, Reno and his men reached refuge on the summit of a small hill. He ordered his men to dig in, and some shot their horses and lay down behind them to find cover.

Captain Frederick Benteen's men, who had been attempting to reach Custer, joined Reno after they likewise turned back. Here they would spend the next several days fending off sporadic attacks. They suffered without water in 100-degree heat, all the while within sight of the shimmering Little Bighorn River. Unlike the men with Custer, Reno's men would survive and be rescued by Terry's force a few days later. Nevertheless, his actions that day, particularly his desultory attack, would later lead to his court-martial and make him the scapegoat for what came to be called "Custer's Last Stand."

Custer continued his advance, with no knowledge of Reno and Benteen's predicament. As far as he knew, the plan was working. Crazy Horse, meanwhile, led his men across the river and up the bluffs to confront Custer's force. He rode through the village, exhorting men to join him by promising them that glory would soon be theirs. Eager to join in the combat, warriors mounted their horses and followed him up the bluffs.

Custer never reached the village. Confronted by an overwhelming number of angry warriors as he approached, he realized the danger and ordered his men to ride for the safety of the hills. He intended, like Reno, to concentrate his men on the high ground and use their superior weaponry to keep the Indians at bay. All he had to do was reach the summit first. Both men and horses, exhausted from the frenetic pace of the last several days, pushed hard. With death bearing down on them, they must have summoned what strength they had left to race to the top. Custer's men made it to within sight of the summit, but they did not reach it. Crazy Horse and his men rounded the top first. There would be no refuge for Custer. Swarmed by hundreds of fearsome mounted warriors, Custer's men fought in small, desperate groups. All 225 men directly under his command would perish.

Crazy Horse and Sitting Bull had orchestrated the greatest victory of the Indian Wars of the 19th century and certainly the most famous Indian victory in history. In death, the vainglorious Custer had also attained an unprecedented level of fame. Custer had hoped that news of his success would reach the Eastern press and catapult him into the Democratic nomination for president; instead, papers reported his crushing defeat during the nation's centenary Fourth of July celebrations.

Such disasters, however, galvanized public opinion and motivated the nation's leaders like nothing else. Custer's Last Stand proved a monumental victory for the Plains Indians, but it was a victory that sealed their fate. Unable to sustain such a large village in the leaner winter months, the Lakota, Cheyenne, and Arapaho who had joined together at Little Bighorn had no choice but to break into smaller villages with the coming of winter. The U.S. Army, now greatly reinforced and with resources provided by a willing Congress, pursued these tribes relentlessly. This constant pressure forced the surrender of village after village in the winter of 1876–1877. Even Crazy Horse's village suffered from the absence of bison, the bitter cold, and the constant threat of the soldiers. Realizing they could not continue on, Crazy Horse surrendered in

The death of George Armstrong Custer and his men at the Battle of Little Big Horn shocked the nation and prompted calls for the destruction of the Lakotas and Cheyennes responsible. Indeed, the Indians' success at the battle proved fleeting. In the years following the disaster numerous artists published similar paintings of *Custer's Last Stand*. (Library of Congress)

May at Fort Robinson, Nebraska. As leader, he knew he would be imprisoned, but he asked not to be sent back East. The commander of the fort agreed, but a few months later, while being taken to the railhead to be sent back East, he would make a half-hearted effort to escape. Stabbed by a soldier's bayonet, he died that evening. Sitting Bull, meanwhile, led his people into exile in Canada, where they received better treatment. But with no bison there either, they reluctantly returned to the United States and surrendered. The Lakota had been defeated.

Over the next few years, the military continued its operations against Indians across the West. The friendly Nez Percé, on whose land gold had been found, would be hunted across the Pacific Northwest. For months, they outmaneuvered the army, and their dash for freedom in Canada actually made many Americans sympathetic to their plight. At the Battle of Bear Paw, less than 40 miles from Canadian border, the Nez Percé were captured and forced to surrender in October 1877. Meanwhile, other campaigns continued, with Geronimo and his followers being the last to surrender in 1886 at Skeleton Canyon in southern Arizona. All Indians would now be placed onto reservations, forced to abandon their traditional ways, and compelled to walk "the white man's road."

THE RESERVATION SYSTEM AND THE DAWES ACT

Today, the establishment of Indian reservations seems a foregone conclusion, something that has simply always been. To most Americans, reservations seem distant and almost foreign from the average person's existence. The establishment of reservations, however, was anything but a foregone conclusion. Indeed, their creation resulted from a variety of needs and desires on the part of the dominant society. First, Indian peoples would never be allowed to retain their expansive landholdings and the resources on them. So much land for so few people struck American leaders (and the general public) as inefficient and wasteful. Intensive agriculture, mining, and industrial uses were proper activities, not the dispersed lifestyle of hunting and gathering. Much of this justification, of course, covered for a voracious greed that permeated American society, and when Americans saw lands formerly the domain of Indians become farms, towns, and mines, they invariably equated this with progress. Consigning Indian peoples to small reserves on often marginal land opened the rest to settlement and exploitation.

There were legal and humanitarian reasons for the establishment of reservations as well. Legally, Indian tribes had been declared to be domestic dependent nations by the Supreme Court in the early 1830s. Effectively, Indian tribes (and their homelands) functioned as independent nations inside and dependent on the United States. Thus, the treaty-making process, which negotiated between two nations, dictated the legal relationship between two sovereign nations. Yet, Indian peoples were also considered citizens (though not full voting citizens) of the United States. Not yet at the level of their white brethren, Indian peoples would need time to assimilate, and the establishment of reservations could buy them that time— or so reformers claimed. This idea, in fact, predated the Supreme Court cases of the Jacksonian period and was expressed by Thomas Jefferson, among others, in his support for the establishment of an Indian Territory in the Louisiana Purchase.

From this came the humanitarian justification for reservations. Concentrated on reservations and protected from the worst elements of contact with frontiersmen, Indians could become wards of the government until they were ready for full citizenship. Indian peoples would be safe on reservations, fed and protected by a paternalistic U.S. government, and here they could be Christianized and "civilized." A key part of this would be to convert the nomadic hunter-gatherer cultures into farmers. Hopefully, humanitarians argued, the Indians would learn their lessons quickly, enabling them to effectively integrate into American society and making the reservations obsolete—a transition stage on the path to total integration and assimilation into American society.

To accomplish this assimilation, the government forbade virtually all traditional practices on reservations. They outlawed religious ceremonies, like the Sun Dance, and even traditional arts and crafts, like weaving, would be frowned upon until a change of policy in the 1930s that encouraged Indians to produce beadwork, blankets, and pottery for sale to wealthy white collectors. In place of traditional religious views, the government encouraged conversion to Christianity. Of course, the government could not choose an official denomination to proselytize to the Indians because of the constitutional requirement for a separation of church and state; instead, it gave different tribes to different denominations.

Schools, unsurprisingly, played an important role both on and off reservation in the assimilation policy. More malleable than adults, children adapted to new ways more easily. Like the reservation system itself, boarding schools emerged quite by chance and without official planning. Following the conclusion of the Red River War in 1874, the government attempted to separate the younger and more militant warriors from the more complacent and manageable population of Comanche, Kiowa, Arapaho, and Cheyenne. These militant men became prisoners of war, and 72 of them would be sent away from their people to Fort Marion, a military base in Florida. Captain Richard Henry Pratt received orders to accompany them to their destination.

Unsure of what exactly he was supposed to do with these men, Pratt put them in cast-off military uniforms, cut their hair, and subjected them to the rigor of military discipline. Amazed at the transformation from "savage" to "civilized," he then recruited teachers to give his wards a rudimentary education along the lines of a grammar school. Word of his efforts spread and eventually attracted wealthy patrons who applauded his work as a humane solution to the "Indian problem." Pratt, with backing from wealthy investors, convinced the government to give him an abandoned army base at Carlisle, Pennsylvania, for use as a school. In 1879, his Carlisle Indian Industrial School opened. It would attract Indian children from all over the United States, and Pratt himself recruited many of these students, visiting tribal elders to convince them that sending their children to learn about the white man's society would be the best way to ensure that Indians survived. Reluctantly, many agreed.

At Carlisle (and the other off-reservation schools that followed), students were educated through total assimilation into American society. Children spent years at the school, many not leaving until their early twenties. All native practices and even languages were forbidden. Students wore drab uniforms and short hair, obliterating all semblance of their native identity. In place of their traditional culture and language, teachers instead provided instruction in English, mathematics, civics, and industrial education. Pratt believed an industrial education, preparing students for farm work and other nontechnical occupations, would be the best course of action for students. Believing Indians to be inferior to whites in intelligence, he doubted they could excel in fields like medicine or the law—though some would. Pratt summed up his educational philosophy when he declared, "We must kill the Indian, to save the man." The Indian peoples—remade to be almost exactly like their white counterparts in every way but skin color—might endure, but Indian culture would not.

While these children did learn English and other subjects at the schools, the assimilation program exacted a terrible price; the students endured a traumatic experience they would carry for the rest of their lives. Many also learned occupations that did not exist on their people's reservations, making their skills useless. But far worse was the sense of isolation and alienation from their culture and their loved ones. Unable to speak their native language after years of being forbidden to do so, they could no longer communicate with their parents and grandparents. Amazingly, the boarding schools continued, in some cases until the mid-20th century.

Boarding schools provide a tragic example of self-styled friends of the Indians causing Indian peoples irreparable harm. Another well-meaning attempt to help the Indians adapt that also spectacularly backfired came with the 1887 passage of the Dawes Allotment Act.

At the heart of the Dawes Act lay the belief that reservations prevented the Indian peoples from advancing. On the reservations, as they long had, Indian peoples worked together, sharing what they had equally. Reformers believed these communal and collective efforts actually stymied their progress. Indian peoples could only advance if they became individualistic entrepreneurs, like whites. As one agent for the Yankton Sioux put it in an 1877 report, "As long as Indians live in villages they will retain many of their old and injurious habits." These included, he explained, frequents dances and celebrations where participants shared gifts among themselves. The future, he hoped, would break these traditions and place the Yankton on a better, less communal course, and "I trust that before another year is ended they will generally be located upon individual farms. From that date will begin their real and permanent progress" (quoted in Debo 1970, 299).

Individual landholdings, turned into productive small farms, would instill in Indian peoples a sense of individualism and accomplishment. Ending the collective ownership of reservation land and transforming reservations into small private farms would certainly advance Indians, or so the philanthropists claimed. As a model, the government had only to turn to the 1862 Homestead Act, which allowed settlers to claim 160 acres of the public domain. The fact that many of the homesteaders abandoned their claims within a few years or that the arid West proved ill-suited to intensive farming without the aid of irrigation water did not seem to slow down lawmakers' efforts to create a similar provision for Indian peoples. As an added benefit, some tribes still held extensive landholdings, and once the 160-acre allotments were divvied up to every head of household, there would be "surplus" land that could then be opened to non-Indian settlement.

Bills to create such an act wended their way through the labyrinthine process of legislation, but between humanitarian "friends of the Indians" and avaricious entities eager to get access to Indian lands, the momentum to pass something grew. President Grover Cleveland supported such a bill and made mention of it in both of his Annual Messages in 1885 and 1886. In his 1886 speech, he argued that the era of reservations should end. "The present system of agencies [reservations]," he explained, "is in the present stage of Indian management inadequate, standing alone, for the accomplishment of an object which had become pressing in its importance—the more rapid transition from tribal organizations to citizenship of such portions of the Indians as are capable of civilized life" (Cleveland 1886). Collected on reservations, defeated by the military, and surrounded by American civilization, "it is no longer possible for them to subsist by the chase and the spontaneous productions of the earth." To be sure, Cleveland noted, the government would have to continue to care for Indians, guiding them as a parent would children. Nevertheless, "with an abundance of land, if furnished with the means and implements for profitable husbandry, their life of entire dependence upon Government rations from day to day is no longer defensible. Their inclination . . . is to cling to the habits and customs of their ancestors and struggle with persistence against the change of life which their altered circumstances press upon them. But barbarism and civilization can not live together" (Cleveland 1886). The passage of a bill allowing for the allotment of reservations, the president asserted, would solve these problems, enabling "the more progressive members of the different tribes [to be settled] upon homesteads, and by their example lead others to follow, breaking away from tribal customs and substituting therefor [*sic*] the love of home, the interest of the family, and the rule of the state" (Cleveland 1886). To accomplish this, Cleveland proposed a commission be created to ascertain the suitability of individual tribes for allotment.

Sponsored by Senator Henry L. Dawes of Massachusetts, a self-proclaimed advocate of Indian rights, a bill similar to Cleveland's proposal passed in February 1887. Originally, the so-called Five Civilized Tribes (the Cherokee, Chickasaw, Choctaw, Creek, and Seminole, who all moved to Indian Territory from the east in the 1830s) were spared allotment. The act would be amended in 1891 to give some land to not just male heads of household (since women in many tribes traditionally held property) but to women and children as well. To prevent the land from being swindled by unscrupulous individuals who would offer cash to desperate Indians for their allotments, the land would be held in trust for 25 years. Ironically, but not surprisingly, these provisions would be routinely exploited by whites who managed these trusts. Guardians of the trusts often imposed high management fees, and merchants charged exorbitant interest on goods, driving Indians into debt that could only be erased by handing over allotments. Poor whites often attempted to intermarry into Indian families to claim ownership of land, and, in some cases, these whites even murdered their Indian spouses to gain sole ownership of allotments. These practices were especially common in Oklahoma, where Indians such as the Osages found themselves with allotments that contained sizable reserves of oil.

Full citizenship proved to be one of the strongest inducements used to convince Indian peoples to accept an allotment. Indians would no longer be treated as second-class citizens. Any Indian who took an allotment would be granted citizenship and voting rights. With Indian peoples transformed into small yeoman farmers and made citizens, the government hoped it could get out of the Indian business entirely. Taken as a whole, the Indian problem would finally be solved, and the Indian peoples would be assimilated into the body politic of the United States. Their surplus lands could be resold to non-Indians, and everyone would be happy. The Dawes Act seemed foolproof.

As always, Indian peoples had no input on the drafting or passage of the act, and when tribal leaders voiced opposition to the act, government officials dismissed their concerns as foolish and ignorant. Reservation after reservation was surveyed and allotted in the 1890s, the surplus land then opened for settlement, but nowhere was the opening of lands more spectacular than in Indian Territory (now Oklahoma).

Non-Indians, eager to get good claims for themselves, registered for allotments, which would be disbursed in a literal race. These *land rushes*, which began in 1889 and occurred with the opening of each of the allotted reservations, were spectacular and memorable occurrences. Following the crack of the starter's gun, participants hurtled across the plains on horseback or in wagons to reach the best claims first. A few famously risked arrest or even death by sneaking out under cover of darkness before the day of the opening to locate the most desirable tracts (those with plentiful access to water, mostly) for themselves. These unscrupulous folks who left too soon came to be known as "Sooners" and became part of the romantic mythology of Oklahoma, even giving rise to the nickname for the University of Oklahoma and for the state itself as the Sooner State.

For Indian peoples, however, the Dawes Act proved an unmitigated disaster. Invariably, tribes that faced allotment saw the sizes of their reservations shrink to almost nothing. Millions of acres changed hands this way, further undermining the resource base and independence of tribes. Only the Diné, or Navajo, actually saw the size of their reservation increase through a series of executive actions in the late 19th century, mostly because they occupied land that seemed of no value to anyone else. Other tribes did not fare as well. In addition, the allotments, which were designed to provide for Indian independence, suffered from the same problems as those distributed under the Homestead Act, namely that 160 acres in the West without irrigation was not enough land to successfully farm, and where valuable resources, as in Oklahoma, were found on allotments, these invariably changed hands to whites who understood how to manipulate the economic and legal systems in their favor.

The swindling of Indian land and the betrayal of Indian trust that the Dawes Act represented proved to be but the latest blows to a people who had already lost so much. Daily life on the reservations generally remained bleak. Farming largely proved to be a failure, though Indian peoples tried hard to coax life from arid soil. Survival depended on government rations, and Indian peoples waited outside agency offices for their monthly distribution of goods. Employment also proved difficult to locate. Generally, Indian peoples could not venture away from reservations without permission from government officials, and being off the reservation often proved extremely dangerous anyway. Thus, the only jobs to be found were those on the reservations themselves, but without any industrial or service base to sustain employment, the few opportunities to be found required working for missionaries or as Indian policemen, both reliant on keeping in the good graces of white administrators and authorities. Taking such jobs, however, often put one at odds with other members of the tribe or even one's family members. Being an Indian policeman, for example, meant policing Indians in service to the white reservation agent. As such, traditionalists often derided Indian policemen as traitors and sellouts.

On the reservations, poverty was universal, starvation was only a missed ration distribution away, and depression and alcoholism became endemic. Diseases such as tuberculosis and influenza also burned across reservations. Indeed, the early reservation period marked the lowest point for Indian populations. Many observers lamented this fact, but in a time of rampant Social Darwinism, it seemed likely that Indian peoples would "vanish like snow before the summer sun" in an oft used phrase. The "vanishing Indian" became a common motif of painters like Charlie Russell and photographers like Edward Curtis and a call to action for early ethnologists to learn as much about Indian cultures as possible before they invariably went extinct.

Deprived of their traditional lifeways, dependent on rations to survive, and increasingly forbidden from practicing their traditional ceremonies (medicine men could be arrested under the Indian Bureau's 1883 List of Indian Offenses—not so different, really, from the laws of the Spanish in colonial New Mexico two centuries earlier), daily life became a bleak struggle to survive. Indian peoples grew desperate for something to cling to in the midst of the suffering and change. To fulfill this need for hope, Indian peoples across the West turned to an apocalyptic religious movement that promised to erase the last decades of hardship, warfare, and suffering, a movement known as the Ghost Dance.

THE GHOST DANCE AND THE TRAGEDY OF WOUNDED KNEE

The message came from the Far West. It had been given to a Paiute man named Wovoka (known to the whites in the area as Jack Wilson). Wovoka lived on the eastern edge of the Sierras, not far from Lake Tahoe, and worked on the Wilson ranch as a laborer. On New Year's Day, in 1889, as Wovoka chopped wood, he heard a "great noise" nearby. Putting aside his axe, he went to investigate. Ominously, the sky grew dark and the midday sun began to disappear. And then he died. It was during this "death," which coincided with a total eclipse of the sun in the area, that he had his great vision. He regained consciousness as the eclipse subsided and the sun returned. His people would see this as an illustration of his great power, bringing both himself and the sun back from the dead.

During his vision, Wovoka explained, he had gone to heaven and had spoken directly with God. God showed him a perfect world without suffering, where the dead were alive and happy and young again. He gave Wovoka the power to command the elements of nature, to bring rain to end droughts, and proclaimed that Wovoka would become president of the West while Benjamin Harrison remained president of the East. Further, Wovoka was shown a sacred dance that he would teach his people to perform. This dance, performed over a succession of nights, would bring the dead back to life (Hittman 1997, 63–64).

Like many mystical movements, the exact origins and beginning of the Ghost Dance are difficult to ascertain (another version had Wovoka falling into a state of delirium during a bout of scarlet fever), but from Wovoka's original vision, the great Ghost Dance movement would be born. Wovoka's prophesy, however, had an array of elements that did not come from Indian religious beliefs but from Christianity. The God Wovoka met was not the amorphous concept of the Great Spirit but instead the Christian God, personified as a wise old man, and the great revelation owed both

On an unseasonably warm December morning in 1890, the soldiers of the 7th cavalry opened fire on a peaceful Lakota village. The ensuing "Wounded Knee Massacre" left at least 150 Lakota and 25 soldiers dead. Several days later the army dug a mass grave for the victims. The massacre represented the end of armed conflict between Indian peoples and the U.S. military. (Library of Congress)

to the Christian conception of heaven and the apocalypse in the book of Revelation.

One can only imagine how the meaning of the ceremony changed time and time again as it passed from tribe to tribe and from one language and culture to another across the West. In time, what Wovoka claimed was a peaceful vision (in some accounts his heaven included the whites as well) became darker and more militant. Instead of being about venturing to heaven, it became about reclaiming the earth from the domination of the whites.

Among the defeated Lakota, the more militant interpretation of the Ghost Dance found its greatest adherents. The Lakota had much to lament. Congress had set about shrinking their reservation even more. Already the Black Hills had been taken by force, and the passage of the Dawes Act now put the rest of the enormous Great Sioux Reservation in jeopardy. The Sioux Act of 1888 applied the Dawes Act to the reservation but reversed the procedure: "surplus" lands would be opened for settlement first, and the remaining lands would be used to create six smaller reservations scattered across North and South Dakota, both recently granted statehood.

The 1868 Fort Laramie Treaty, however, stipulated that three-fourths of the male population had to vote on the change. Convincing the Indians that signing was their best option fell to Major General George Crook and the (aptly named) Crook Commission. Crook, though willing to do his part to secure the necessary signatures, harbored some sympathy for the Indians. The government, he told them, would take their land either way, but it would be better to make a deal that preserved at least some of their territory. He told the Lakota, "It strikes me that you are in the position of a person who had his effects in the bed of a dry stream when there was a flood coming down, and instead of finding fault with the Creator for sending it down, you should try and save what you can" (quoted in Utley 1984, 248). Crook, however, also worked to divide the Lakota and marginalize the opponents of the proposal. His tactics worked, and he garnered the three-fourths majority necessary for passage. Many Lakota signed on only so long as the government continued to honor its other treaty provisions, most especially the provisions to continue to provide rations to their people. Crook and the other commissioners repeatedly promised that the land issue would not have any effect on the distribution of food, which would continue as before.

Two weeks after the commission departed with signatures in hand, orders arrived from Washington to reduce the annual beef ration on the Rosebud Reservation by two million pounds, on the Pine Ridge Reservation by a million pounds, and so on across all six Lakota reservations. Once again, the Lakota had been betrayed and could only watch as settlers flooded into their former lands beginning on February 10, 1890. The bitterness of these events added to the growing sense of anger and despair that gripped them. Where could one find hope in a world where all the sureties of the past had disappeared along with the buffalo?

The winter of 1889–1890 brought more suffering. The ration cuts led to starvation on the reservations, and a weakened people suffered epidemics of measles, influenza, and whooping cough. A summer drought baked the crops that were supposed to help the Lakota transition to farming. Worst of all, without their horses, the bison, or the open plains to traverse, many questioned what being a Lakota even meant.

Needless to say, when the Ghost Dance reached the Lakota, it brought the only whisper of hope these demoralized people had heard in a long while. James Mooney, the early ethnologist who interviewed Wovoka shortly after the tragic events in South Dakota, put it thus: "When the race lies crushed and groaning under an alien yoke, how natural is the dream of a redeemer, an Arthur, who shall return from exile or awake from some long sleep to drive out the usurper and win back for his people what they have lost" (quoted in Utley 1984, 252). The vision, as the Lakota learned of it, promised to turn back the clock, and eager to learn more, they decided to send two emissaries by train to find Wovoka. One of these was Kicking Bear, a nephew of Sitting Bull.

After returning from his visit with Wovoka, Kicking Bear began to preach about what he had learned. Sitting Bull (recently returned to the Standing Rock reservation after touring with Buffalo Bill's Wild West show) invited his nephew to come and teach the Ghost Dance to people near his home in October 1890. Kicking Bear said that he had spoken to the Messiah (meaning Jesus, possibly in the form of Wovoka) "who is again upon the earth." The Messiah would wipe away the whites, perhaps in a massive flood, and only spare the Indians who understood the Ghost Dance. Once this destruction was over, the dead would return, the bison would be renewed, and the good times would return. All practitioners of the dance, Kicking Bear explained, needed to wear ghost shirts decorated with images of bison skulls, symbolizing the animal's return; astronomical symbols; and natural phenomena, such as rain and hail. They should also have eagle feathers to help the believers ascend over the flooded waters of the earth. Best of all, these magical shirts made the wearers impervious to bullets. This strange mix of native and Christian beliefs became the Ghost Dance ceremony, and many of the Lakota drifted away from the agencies to perform the ceremony away from the prying eyes of Indian agents (Anderson 2007, 172–173).

Sitting Bull, his prestige greatly diminished in the reservation era, had his doubts about the Ghost Dance, but he likely saw in it an opportunity to increase his declining stature and, more importantly, turn his people back to more traditional ways. So, he embraced it—though not as passionately as some other Lakota. While heavily influenced by Christianity, in practice, the Ghost Dance resembled the now forbidden Sun Dance in the layout of the arena and in the hours and hours of chanting and dancing. In Sitting Bull's camp, his prayer tree became the focal point of an arena created by clearing brush and piling it into a circle. For weeks throughout the fall, dancers gathered and performed the ceremony as instructed.

Individuals danced until they collapsed, often returning to consciousness with a vision confirming that they had communed with their dead relatives who were preparing to return to earth. The pull of the dance and the sliver of hope it offered proved irresistible: children stopped attending reservation schools, churches lay empty, and some of the Lakota policemen abandoned their posts and joined the dancers. In late October, Sitting Bull himself entered the arena and danced. The dance seemed, for a time, to be turning back the current of change, prompting a renewed hope for a return to the old ways.

It is likely that the Ghost Dance among the Lakota would have eventually fizzled out as it did other tribes. After all, no amount of dancing and praying would cause the disappearance of the whites and the resurrection of the dead, both human and animal. Tired and hungry, the Ghost Dancers would inevitably have given up, and life would have returned to normal on the reservations. Unfortunately, the reaction of the Indian agents, most especially Pine Ridge's agent, Daniel Royer, greatly escalated the situation.

Royer represented the worst of the Indian Bureau. A down-on-his luck local politician and physician with ties to South Dakota senator Richard Pettigrew, he had no experience or interest in Indian affairs. Royer simply wanted to follow in the tradition of agents who used their position to line their own pockets. As had often happened when administrations changed hands, Royer owed his position to patronage rather than qualifications, and the Pine Ridge Agency had recently lost a far more capable agent in Valentine T. McGillycuddy. In 1886, McGillycuddy's opponents, including the aging but still powerful Red Cloud, succeeded in getting him dismissed from his position. Royer took over in October 1890, just as the fervor of the Ghost Dance was reaching its pinnacle. His lack of experience and clear dislike of Indians quickly earned him a name among the Lakota as "Young-Man-Afraid-of-Indians."

Royer's ignorance of the culture of his wards created a terrible and volatile situation, and what little Royer and the other agents understood of the Ghost Dance alarmed them. Talk of the disappearance of the whites sounded to the agents like a group of Indians preparing an attack. Royer, in one of his increasingly alarmed letters dated November 12, wrote, "We need protection and we need it now. Indians are dancing in the snow and are wild and crazy. . . . The leaders should be arrested and confined at some military post until the matter is quieted, and this should be done at once" (quoted in *Ken Burns Presents: The West* 1996).

On November 23, 1890, several agents on the plains sent a message to Brigadier General John Rutter Brooke, the army commander of the Department of the Platte, begging for the return of soldiers to reservations, a practice that had ended earlier in the decade with the development of Indian police forces. The letter declared, "As the agents appealed for Protection & Reported they had lost all control over their Indians it became necessary for the military under your orders to assume control" (quoted in Moulton 2011, 248). Worried about the growing threat, General Nelson Miles ordered soldiers back to the Lakota reservations, including Pine Ridge. Miles ordered Brooke to only rely on soldiers and not mix with friendly Indians like the Indian police. Also, Brooke's orders explained, Indian leaders "should be arrested if favorable opportunity offers" (quoted in Moulton 2011, 248).

McGillycuddy, no longer in a position of authority, watched the return of the military with alarm. The Ghost Dance, he believed, would burn itself out, and by spring, it would be over and the crisis past. "I should let the dance continue," he wrote. "If the Seventh-Day Adventists prepare their ascension robes for the second coming of the Saviour [*sic*], the U.S. Army is not put in motion to prevent them. Why should not the Indians have the same privilege?" (quoted in Moulton 2011, 248). Unfortunately, such common sense would not prevail.

Both Indians and non-Indians could feel the increasing tension in the fall of 1890. White settlers appealed for soldiers and more guns to protect themselves against the supposed Indian uprising. Settlers had recently killed three Lakota. South Dakota governor Arthur Mellette wrote to H. M. Day, the head of the South Dakota National Guard in the Black Hills area in early December, cautioning him to "be descreet in kiling [*sic*] the Indians" and not do anything to "precipitate an attack by them upon un-protected settlers" (quoted by Moulton 2011, 249).

Sitting Bull's fame and prestige, both among whites and Indians, made him the highest-profile follower of the new religion (and since Crazy Horse's death in 1877, Sitting Bull was easily the most famous Indian in the world). Standing Rock's agent, James McLaughlin, looked for ways to eliminate his presence among the Ghost Dancers, including arrest or even assassination. On October 22, 1890, McLaughlin sent out the Lakota police force to ambush the aged leader as he drove an acquaintance to the steamboat landing site on the Missouri River. The attempt failed, however, when Sitting Bull took a different route. News of the plot reached him, however, prompting him to remain near his camp in the relative safety of his supporters and friends, and so he ignored McLaughlin's requests for him to meet at the agency.

By early December, the rift between McLaughlin with his Indian police force and Sitting Bull and the Ghost Dancers had grown into a chasm. Word reached the Standing Rock reservation that the Messiah would appear in earthly form at the Pine Ridge Reservation, where a large camp of Ghost Dancers had fled into a terrain of rough canyons nicknamed the "Stronghold." Sitting Bull sent a letter to McLaughlin on December 11 that stressed the peaceful nature of the dance and asked for permission to attend. McLaughlin refused, worried that Sitting Bull and his followers were hoping to join a rumored band of militant Indians preparing for an attack. Spies inside Sitting Bull's camp, however, informed McLaughlin that the great man intended to leave Standing Rock with or without official permission. McLaughlin, working in concert with Colonel Drum, the commander of U.S. soldiers at Standing Rock, decided the time to arrest Sitting Bull had come. The agent stressed that it should be Lakota policemen, not soldiers, tasked with his arrest (but a large detachment of soldiers would be nearby in case of trouble). On December 14, he penned a short order to Bull Head, chief of the Lakota police, to apprehend Sitting Bull.

Camped near Sitting Bull's cabin to observe the Ghost Dancers, the police moved out before dawn on December 15. Bull Head, accompanied by 26 policemen with several hundred soldiers in reserve, knocked on the old man's door and entered the cabin. As they informed Sitting Bull of his arrest, his supporters, camped near his cabin, stirred to life. The crowd swelled in front of the cabin as the increasingly nervous police urged Sitting Bull to dress faster so they could leave on the waiting horses. A policeman shoved Sitting Bull out of the door of his cabin. Just then Catch-the-Bear, an enemy of Bull Head, exclaimed, "You think you are going to take him. You shall not!" Others joined in, and Sitting Bull's teenage son, Crow Foot, exhorted his father to be brave: "You always call yourself a brave chief. Now you are allowing yourself to be taken by the Indian police" (quoted in Anderson 2007, 185–186). At this, Sitting Bull paused, unsure of what to do next.

Catch-the-Bear pulled a Winchester rifle from under his blanket and fired, hitting Bull Head in the side. Bull Head, his revolver drawn already and pointed at the back of Sitting Bull's head fired, killing the revered leader instantly. An open gun battle now erupted, for both the policemen and Sitting Bull's supporters were armed.

Little Eagle, Hawk Man, and Broken Arm, all policemen, fell before the shots, but as they died, they returned fire indiscriminately into the crowd. Catch-the-Bear was killed by Lone Man, and other shots took the lives of Bob Tail Bull's son, Spotted Horn; Brave Thunder; Joe Shield; and Jumping Bull. Bull Head, Shaved Head, and Lone Man retreated into Sitting Bull's cabin, finding Sitting Bull's son cowering inside. Both Bull Head and Shaved Head had been critically wounded. Lone Man grabbed the boy and shoved him out of the cabin, where a hail of bullets tore him apart. The surviving policemen barricaded themselves inside of Sitting Bull's cabin and fought off attacks until the arrival of the U.S. Cavalry just after sunrise. Eight people, including Sitting Bull, lay dead outside of the cabin, and four policemen were dead inside. Shaved Head and Bull Head would make it to the hospital, but they too would succumb to their wounds a few days later. In total, 14 people died as a result of the events that day, a mix of Ghost Dancers and policemen, but all Lakota.

Sitting Bull's death also brought to fruition a grim prophesy he had received earlier. In this vision, he saw that he could die at the hands of his own people, a terrible fate for a man who had lived his life to protect them. Like the vision he had had in 1876 before Custer's attack, this vision also came to pass. Two days after the failed arrest, Sitting Bull's body was placed in a simple wooden coffin, covered with corrosive lye to destroy it and prevent graverobbers from digging it up for grisly trophies, and buried in an unmarked grave on the northeast corner of the Fort Yates's cemetery (Anderson 2007, 186–190).

News of Sitting Bull's murder spread quickly across the Dakotas, and both whites and Indians expected more trouble. Thus, when news reached agent Royer at Pine Ridge on December 28 of the approach of a large number of Indians, he worried that they intended to attack and demanded that the soldiers investigate. A detachment of the Seventh Cavalry, Custer's old command, set out to apprehend them. This band of roughly 350 people were under the leadership of Big Foot, a chief with a reputation for peace. Big Foot had been a strong supporter of the Ghost Dance, but he had grown weary of the ceremony and had lost faith in the new religion when the promises never materialized. His people, cold, hungry, and sick, headed to Pine Ridge in search of food and shelter.

The cavalry found the party and rode toward the ragtag line of people, some in wagons and on horseback but many trudging through the snow on foot. As they approached, Big Foot waved a white flag from a wagon with what strength he had left, stricken as he was with pneumonia. Tentatively, the Seventh rode up on the Indians, who explained to the soldiers that they had no hostile intentions and wanted to make it to the agency. The soldiers agreed to accompany them, but the short December light was failing; they would not make it to the agency headquarters before nightfall. Instead, the soldiers guided the exhausted group to nearby Wounded Knee Creek. The women set about erecting the tipis, as they long had, and the soldiers busied themselves with building their own tents. That night, a larger force of soldiers, under the command of Colonel James W. Forsyth, arrived and took over. On the ridge above the village, Forsyth placed four Hotchkiss guns. These guns, the precursors to modern artillery pieces, could fire exploding shells hundreds of yards. Despite their promises of peace, Forsyth did not trust the Lakota. Lakota and soldiers settled in for the night, unaware of the terrible morning that awaited them.

The next morning, as the weak December sun climbed over the horizon, everyone prepared to pack up and depart. Forsyth decided it would be wise to send a detachment through the village to confiscate any weapons the Indians might still possess as a precaution against a surprise attack. The sight of these soldiers moving through the village alarmed the Indians. A medicine man began to perform the Ghost Dance, throwing handfuls of dirt to disperse in the wind, as the whites were said to do when the Ghost Dance was fulfilled. The medicine man hoped, perhaps, that the Messiah would intervene in this, their most desperate hour. He also reminded the people around him that no harm could come to them if they wore their ghost shirts.

The medicine man's chants and dancing worried the soldiers watching from the ridgeline, who thought his performance was a signal to attack. Meanwhile, the detachment came to a man, by some accounts an old, deaf man still asleep or in others a man who had died in the night, clutching a rifle in his hands. A soldier bent down to pull the weapon out of the man's hands and it went off. A single shot rang out through the cold morning air, followed a moment later by the terrible crackle of hundreds more.

The soldiers fired indiscriminately, and weapons materialized in the hands of some of the Lakota, who returned fire in a desperate attempt to protect their people. The Hotchkiss guns opened up, raining down shells that destroyed tipis in puffs of smoke and fire. Bullets and shrapnel from the shells tore through the village, cutting down anyone who had the ill fortune to be in the way. The shooting lasted for minutes and then longer, for almost an hour, before the last pops of gunfire finally subsided. Now the only sounds to be heard were wailing and the groans of dying people. Nearly two-thirds of Big Foot's people had been killed or wounded, 150 were killed on the field and another 50 wounded, many of whom would also succumb to their wounds in the hours and days that followed. The Lakota, defending their people, had managed to kill 25 soldiers and wound another 39.

Stunned, the survivors, both Indians and soldiers, loaded the wounded into wagons for transport to the agency. There was nothing they could do for the dead. At the agency, the post's single doctor and some of the wives of the officers hastily converted the largest building on the post into a hospital. The hall, still festooned with Christmas decorations, became a makeshift emergency room.

Several days would pass before a party arrived to bury the dead. The dead lay frozen where they fell. Big Foot, reclining on a blanket, was there, and the medicine man, and 150 other men, women, and children. Chipping into the frozen ground, the gravediggers managed to dig a trench long enough to inter the dead. They dragged body after body into the trench, a mass grave. They came to the corpse of a woman, cloaked in a buffalo robe, and as they pulled her into the pit, the cloak snagged and revealed a baby clutched in her cold arms. The baby girl, still alive, was rushed to the hospital. A white officer volunteered to take the orphan and promised to raise her as his own, a strange and, it turned out later, terrible choice. He named her Margaret, but to the Lakota, she became known as the "Lost Bird." The Wounded Knee Massacre, an attack that should have never happened (though given the tense climate at the time it is not surprising that it occurred), symbolized the end of an era. It marked the end of the Indian peoples' attempts to live life on their own terms in their traditional ways. They would have no choice but to navigate the white man's world while somehow attempting to salvage some semblance of what it meant to be an Indian.

The Wounded Knee Massacre marked the end of three centuries of conflict and conquest.

It did not, however, mark the end of Indian peoples' suffering and mistreatment. Indeed, the period from 1890 to 1934 was every bit as dark as the era of the wars in the West. Reservations would be allotted, more Indian land would be taken, rations would continue to be cut, attempts at farming would mostly fail, and Indian children would continue to be taken to boarding schools to trade their culture and identity for the white man's education. Things would improve, a bit, with the passage of the Indian Reorganization Act of 1934, sometimes called the Indian New Deal. The act allowed for more tribal autonomy, the creation of tribal governments, and a return to traditional ceremonies and cultural practices, but the government would continue to rule over Indian peoples through the powerful Bureau of Indian Affairs for decades to come.

8

INTELLECTUAL LIFE AND THE MYTH OF THE WEST

Americans had long felt a sense of mission in their expansion to the West. Lewis and Clark certainly knew their expedition offered more than just the prospect of new territory for the nation, and a generation later, Oregon Trail pioneers felt much the same. Western expansion was not just a physical journey; it was also a psychological and mythical journey, and the West became the crucible of values Americans felt created the American character and made them superior to the more refined and cultivated cultures of Europe. In short, the West, and the long legacy of western expansion, made Americans American: rugged, individualistic, self-reliant, and fearless.

The Western had, rather ironically, been invented before the West itself had been settled. Its genesis flowed from the minds of Easterners. A New Yorker, more than anyone else, gave the Western its heroic outlines. James Fenimore Cooper, born in 1789, became one of the first popular novelists in American history. Inspired by the romantic adventure novels of Sir Walter Scott, Cooper eventually tried his hand at writing similar tales set in North America, beginning with the publication of *The Spy* in 1821, but it was the *Leatherstocking Tales*, a series of novels chronicling the life of Natty

Bumpo, also known as Leatherstocking, that made him famous. Bumpo, a frontiersmen, a distinctly American type, made his first appearance as an aged archetype of American frontier heroism in *The Pioneers* (1823). An eager paying public soon craved more adventures about the earlier life of the scout, Indian fighter, and adventurer, and Cooper complied, writing the character's most famous adventure in *The Last of the Mohicans* in 1826. In total, five novels chronicled Bumpo's life, albeit not in chronological order, over a roughly 20-year period. Close to nature, unfailingly brave, and as comfortable in the woods as the best Indians but still a representative of the culture that was conquering and transforming the West, Bumpo made an ideal American hero. So when Americans began to venture out onto the actual prairies of the Midwest (where Bumpo dies in the 1827 novel *The Prairie*), they took with them the idea of Natty Bumpo, and a few most likely took Cooper's actual books as well. Thus, the myth of the West had been solidly fixed into the minds of Americans before Americans had actually really ventured into the West.

There did exist a few real-life analogues to Cooper's leather-clad hero. Daniel Boone certainly rose above all others as the most famous frontiersman at the dawn of the 19th century. Born in 1734 in Pennsylvania and dying in September 1820, Boone lived an exciting and remarkably long life for such a rugged individual. Over the course of those 86 years, Boone became, in the words of historian and biographer John Mack Faragher, "a hero of a new, democratic type, a man who did not tower above people but rather exemplified their longings and, yes, their limitations" (Faragher 1993, xvi). Boone certainly personified this new type, the American: fearless, filled with wanderlust, ambitious, and always searching for a new opportunity. He had explored from Pennsylvania to Florida and from North Carolina to Missouri. He helped build roads, founded settlements, and, of course, fought Indians, most especially the Shawnee.

Unsurprisingly, generations of Americans found Boone's life inspirational, and fame found him long before his death. Boone's granddaughter Harriet, for example, read him Daniel Bryan's 1813 epic poem *The Mountain Muse: The Adventures of Daniel Boone*. When asked about the work, Boone admitted that it "contained a historical basis" but was far too exaggerated to be taken seriously. The aged frontiersman concluded that "such productions ought to be left until the person was put in the ground" (quoted in Faragher 1993,

320–321). Bryan's work, as Boone probably could have predicted, would not be the last to take inspiration from the frontiersman's life. Indeed, over the next several decades, Boone's story inspired "scores of books, including one of the best-selling biographies of the nineteenth century. He would become the subject of paintings and engravings, great literature and dime novels, poems inspired and insipid" (Faragher 1993, 321). Boone's fame even crossed the Atlantic, with the backwoodsman making a substantial appearance in Lord Bryon's masterpiece *Don Juan*, and back again on American shores, Boone certainly influenced the creation of Cooper's Natty Bumpo. Indeed, Boone's famous rescue of his daughter Jemima and the two Callaway sisters from the clutches of a party of Cherokee and Shawnee inspired much of the plot of Cooper's *The Last of the Mohicans*. Together, Natty Bumpo and Daniel Boone provided a blueprint for the Western hero, and while the setting might change from the primeval forests of the East to the arid Trans-Mississippi West, the hero's silhouette would remain largely unchanged.

Some of these heroes remained fictional only, but allegedly true tales of derring-do by historical figures such as Billy the Kid, Wild Bill Hickok, Calamity Jane, and Kit Carson also inspired readers. Many of these folks made their appearances as larger-than-life figures in the pages of the dime novels that flourished after the American Civil War. New printing technology, including the use of exceedingly inexpensive pulp paper, made it possible to print scores upon scores of novels that could be sold for a nickel or a dime. Gone were the days of books as an expensive diversion only afforded the rich; now everyone could own a book, and with literacy rates in the United States among the highest in the world, reading a book had become a decidedly popular and democratic pastime. Unsurprisingly, dime novels became popular reading for children and teens, much as comic books would be a century later. While the invention of superheroes lay in the future, 19th-century youths found plenty of role models in American history and culture, and most of those heroes swaggered across the West. It mattered not that the writers of these stories tended to be Easterners with little or no knowledge of the West or that they had not done any research into actual events, concocting stories that existed only in their imaginations, because avid readers devoured them as fast as they could roll of the presses.

By the 1890s, the Western genre had matured into a more serious literary form. Owen Wister is usually credited with creating the first literary Western with his 1902 novel *The Virginian*. Wister described his titular character thusly:

> Lounging there at ease against the wall was a slim young giant, more beautiful than pictures. His broad, soft hat was pushed back; a loose-knotted, dull scarlet handkerchief sagged from his throat; and one casual thumb was hooked in the cartridge-belt that slanted across his hips. He had plainly come many miles from somewhere across the vast horizon, as the dust upon him showed. (Wister 1988, 3)

The image of Wister's lean cowboy as narrated by his Eastern newcomer has remained steadfastly affixed to American culture ever since.

Owen Wister shared much in common with his novel's narrator. Hailing from the East and Harvard educated, Wister's first trip to the West came as a 25-year-old in 1885. Like many others, he had gone in search of better health but found much more in the "extraordinary and beautiful . . . valleys we've been going through." For Wister, going West represented a transformative experience, a chance to get in touch with a more authentic self, to, as he put it, "feel I'm something of an animal and not a stinking brain alone" (quoted in Etulain 1996, 6). Wister was certainly not alone in this, as other well-heeled Easterners were doing much the same thing, including the New York artist Frederic Remington (who contributed his iconic illustrations to *The Virginian*) and Theodore Roosevelt, to whom Wister dedicated *The Virginian*. Sojourners rather than settlers, these members of the Eastern establishment could face physical hardship and danger in the West, testing their mettle against the rugged landscape and making themselves better and stronger men in the process.

Theodore Roosevelt, for his part, sunk a fifth of his family fortune into his Dakota cattle operation in 1884, fleeing the expectations of his name and Eastern identity and running away from his grief over the death of his young wife. The Badlands presented a gloomy landscape for a man in the clutches of despair and depression. He wrote, "Nowhere does a man feel more lonely than when riding over the far-reaching seemingly never-ending plains. . . . [N]owhere else does one seem so far off from all mankind" (quoted in White 1968, 80). Upon his arrival in the West, however, Roosevelt was less the brooding Byronic hero, alienated from civilization and human contact, and more the very archetype of an Eastern dandy. One local described him as "a slim, anemic-looking young fellow dressed in the exaggerated style which newcomers on the frontier affected, and which was considered indisputable evidence of the rank tenderfoot" (quoted in White 1968, 83).

Gradually, though, Roosevelt healed, metaphorically reborn and made strong again by facing the inhospitable heat and cold, privation and challenges. There was the incident in a bar when he knocked a drunk gun-toting cowboy out cold and roundups where Teddy had to keep up with the more experienced ranch hands. Hunting also provided Roosevelt the opportunity to test his mettle against nature. A long hunt for mountain goats provided him with the opportunity he sought. His guide, Jack Willis, had his doubts about his client, remarking, "He looked too much like a dude to make any hit with me. He had red cheeks, like those of a brewer's son I knew, and that did not help any." Over the course of the next several days, however, Willis came to appreciate Roosevelt's tenacity and willingness to suffer in the wilderness. His hunting, as well, improved, climaxing with a successful shot of a mountain goat from a quarter of a mile. "It was a lucky shot," Willis noted, "but that didn't alter the fact that he got what he shot at, and I took off my hat to him" (quoted in White 1968, 86–87).

Roosevelt's own transformation from dandy to authentic cowboy appeared in Wister's *Virginian*, with his narrator undergoing a similar process. Other Easterners had come west for similar reasons, but a few would stay, including an acquaintance of Teddy Roosevelt's named Charles Fletcher Lummis. In the fall of 1884, Lummis left his Ohio home behind and took a job at the *Los Angeles Times*. To publicize himself and learn about his new home in the West, Lummis decided to forgo the train and cover the 3,000 miles on foot. Over the next several decades, he transformed himself into an authority on the West, a combination of writer, promoter, ethnologist, and activist. The journey did, indeed, change him, giving him an appreciation for the harsh beauty of the West and the diverse peoples he encountered along the way. Reflecting on this journey near the end of his life, he wrote, "I wasn't born a frontiersman—I Earned [*sic*] it. I was born a little, narrow, prejudiced, intolerant Yankee." He continued, "The real Western Spirit is as much broader, freer, braver, richer, more independent and more tolerant than [Northeastern] Puritanism or Tenderfootedness" (Lummis 1917). It was in the West, he felt, where Americans could reach their highest aspirations and develop the nation into the greatest on earth.

Other real-life (and more authentically Western) figures sought to perpetuate the myths of their own heroism. Some, like Pat Garrett, who had killed Billy the Kid, failed to achieve the fame or fortune they sought, but others would be more successful. None, arguably, were as successful at creating a vision of the Wild West and inserting themselves in the middle of it than William F. "Buffalo Bill" Cody.

Born in 1846, young Cody seemed eager to get out in the world. By the time he was 15, in the words of historian Louis Warren, Cody had "freighted wagons over the plains with rough teamsters, befriended Wild Bill Hickok, was captured by enemy Mormons in the government's abortive war against polygamy, survived a starvation winter at Fort Bridger, skirmished with some Indians and befriended others, prospected for gold in Colorado, and trapped beaver on the Plains" (Warren 2006, 3). At 13, young Will hired on as a rider with the fledgling Pony Express company in 1859 and came back to do an even more dangerous and arduous leg in the Sweetwater Division the following year—or so Cody claimed in his 1879 biography. The truth proved a bit more complicated.

The Cody family had migrated to Kansas just as the territory was being torn apart by the question of slavery. Will's father, Isaac, sided with the Free-Soilers, who wanted neither Blacks nor slavery inside of the territory. As the situation worsened, Isaac had to hide out from proslavery gunmen. It was not Indians but proslavery assassins searching for his father that Cody outran in the summer of 1856, desperate to get a message to his father warning him of their plans. He also did work as a teamster as a teenager, driving a wagon from Leavenworth, Kansas, to the boomtown of Denver, Colorado, in 1860, but he likely was never in the employ of the Pony Express, and certainly not in 1859, as the company did not begin operations until 1860 (Warren 2006, 18).

Cody did serve with the Seventh Kansas Volunteer Cavalry, which saw action in Mississippi and pursued Nathan Bedford Forrest and Sterling Price's Confederate armies in Mississippi and Missouri (Warren 2006, 38). With the Civil War over in 1865, Cody turned his hand to a variety of activities, including working for a railroad, running a hotel, selling alcohol, and even building a town. None of these enterprises panned out, so Cody made money selling buffalo meat on the streets of Hays, Kansas, where locals took to calling him "Buffalo Bill," one of many so-named fellows wandering the plains from Texas to the Dakota Territory (Warren 2006, 46–47).

Professional buffalo hunting soon became his most obvious path to financial stability, and in 1867 and 1868, it provided almost all of his income. Demand for buffalo robes as winter coats drove the market, but in the early 1870s, bison leather began to be used in place of cattle leather. A buffalo hunt, with Cody riding his striding horse into a crowd of tame buffalo, later became a staple of his Wild West show, but the hunting of his professional days proved a far cry from the glorious thrill of the hunt he portrayed in the arena. Professional buffalo hunting was an industrial occupation. After having located a herd, the hunter, using a high-powered rifle, took aim from a great distance away. The single shot, unlike a charging horseman, did not alarm the great woolly beasts, who continued to graze even after one of their own fell. Thus, a hunter could safely and easily eradicate a small herd with very little effort. Next, teams of skinners stripped the hides off the dead animals and loaded them into a wagon. Sometimes the skinners took meat off the bison, but more often than not, they only removed the hide and left the rest of the animal to rot in the sun (Warren 2006, 54). Professional hunters like Cody could kill dozens of animals a day and thousands of animals a year, and with the plains hosting hundreds of such operations, the number of bison in the great herds plummeted catastrophically. The population of an animal that may have been around 60 million in 1800 had declined by the end of the century to a few hundred animals in private herds, Yellowstone National Park, and a few in zoos such as the Bronx Zoo.

His time as professional hunter gave him a name he would use for the rest of his life, and in June 1868, Cody hired on for a brief stint as a detective for the army after several soldiers stole government horses from Fort Hays. To find the horse thieves, he got assistance from the deputy U.S. marshal, a man named James Butler Hickok but already known to many as "Wild Bill." Cody learned much about mythmaking from Hickok and, naturally, embellished his connection to the renowned gunman as necessary (Warren 2006, 58–59).

In 1865, already an experienced horseman and teamster with a litany of tales, both real and imagined, at his disposal, Cody met the author Ned Buntline. Buntline, perhaps more than any other writer of the century, popularized the dime novel, and in Cody, he found the model for a dashing young protagonist. Buntline soon published the first allegedly true story of Cody's life. By 23, Cody had become famous, and he parlayed his dime novel fame into theatrical productions (playing himself, naturally).

As the war with the Lakota came to a climax in 1876, Cody suspended his acting career and returned to the West as a scout for the army. Cody's renown as a scout, however, owed less to his ability to read the subtle signs and tracks and more to the fact that he always rode with Indian trackers and knew enough to trust their judgment when army officers did not; invariably, he took all the credit for their insights (Warren 2006, 118). That summer, while scouting for the Fifth Cavalry, Cody added another chapter to his legend, one that he could exploit for decades to come.

In early July 1876, Cody and the Fifth received orders to intercept several hundred Cheyenne that had left the Fort Robinson agency to join Crazy Horse and Sitting Bull. On July 7, Cody and the rest of the men in the Fifth learned that Custer and most of his command had been killed at Little Bighorn. Ten days later, the Fifth Cavalry encountered a small party of Cheyenne on Warbonnet Creek. The soldiers attacked, and in the small skirmish, perhaps, three Cheyenne perished. The encounter had little significance, save for the fact that Cody, dressed in his black velvet stage costume, ended up in a fight with a Cheyenne named Yellow Hair (though mistranslated and remembered as Yellow Hand). Cody had apparently been in the process of riding out to warn two messengers of an ambush when he accidentally crossed paths with Yellow Hair. Startled by the other's sudden appearance, both men hurriedly drew their weapons and fired. Cody's aim proved truer, felling the warrior. Cody then took the dead man's scalp as a trophy.

It took Cody almost no time to embellish the story and capitalize on public anger over Little Bighorn. That fall, he commissioned a play based on the incident called *The Red Right Hand; or, Buffalo Bill's First Scalp for Custer*, in which Cody again played himself. By the time he told the story three years later, in his 1879 biography, the encounter had become a clash between himself and half a dozen soldiers against 200 angry Cheyenne, with Cody and Yellow Hair engaging in single combat. In this version, with his soldiers riding to his defense, he took the scalp in sight of the enemy, turned and "swung the Indian-chieftain's top-knot and bonnet in the air, and shouted: 'The first scalp for Custer'" (quoted in Warren 2006, 118–119). It is unlikely that any other person could have pulled this off: killing and scalping an actual Indian warrior during a campaign while wearing a costume that was part of a stage show about his fictitious persona, thereby making his fictitious persona less fictitious, but then turning the episode into a play, straining the limits of credulity. Blending fact and fantasy until one was indistinguishable from the other became Cody's stock in trade.

With bison and hostile Indians becoming hard to come by, Cody decided to turn to mythmaking full time. Incorporating everything he had learned about stagecraft and life on the frontier, he created Buffalo Bill Cody's Wild West and Congress of Rough Riders of the World show, easily the most famous and successful Wild West show of all time. Cody founded his show in 1883, but it did not become a roaring success overnight. Indeed, he faced several challenges. Many critics warned that cowboys, Indians, and related Western characters made poor role models for children. Hard-living men from the ragged edges of civilization could not possibly be appropriate heroes for impressionable young Americans. The *Chicago Tribune*, in its review of Cody's show, sneered at the low-class and mixed-race fans of dime novels that crowded around to see their paperback heroes in the flesh. Dime novels, like comic books in the 1950s or video games today, allegedly influenced children to commit all manner of illicit and violent activities. To make the show successful, Cody needed to overcome these prejudices and attract middle-class and wealthy attendees, not bootblacks and newsboys.

Following a somewhat rough first season, Cody turned to a professional theatrical manager named Nate Salsbury for help. Salsbury would play an important role in developing the production, bringing in musicians, giving it a more coherent theme, and, most importantly, attracting the right kind of audience (Warren 2006, 236). Rather than a circus-like production of strange and frightening characters, Cody's Wild West show became a celebration of American expansion and progress as savagery gave way to civilization. Themes of patriotism and the expansion of American values spoke to middle- and upper-class theatergoers—and not just American audiences. Within a few years, the show and its creator had attained international fame with sold-out runs in Paris, London, Berlin, and Milan (Warren 2006, ix).

Wister, Cody, Roosevelt, and scores of others perpetuated the belief that the Western experience made Americans exceptional, but the very process of taming the frontier would ultimately destroy it. Frank Bird Linderman, who lit out for Montana as a teenager in 1885, expressed what many felt when he wrote that he feared "the West of my dreams would fade away before I could reach it" (Linderman 1968, 2). If the West offered a strenuous life, a chance to test oneself against the elements and nature at her wildest and most dangerous, then the arrival of civilization (ironically embodied in its conquerors) would inevitably take the wild out of the Wild West. This irony lay at the heart of the mythology of the fading West. This idea of a vanishing frontier, and the negative effects of its disappearance, found articulation in the most famous historical essay of all time.

That essay was "The Significance of the Frontier in American History," and it was authored by Frederick Jackson Turner, a 32-year-old professor of history from the University of Wisconsin. Delivered in 1893 to an audience at the Chicago World's Fair (who must have grown tired of the Ferris wheel and other diversions to sit through a long historical lecture), Turner's "Frontier Thesis" gave an academic stamp of authority to ideas already in wide circulation. Turner began his remarks by noting that the recent 1890 U.S. Census had dropped the frontier line from its census reports. One could no longer see the location of the frontier on a map. More than a line on a map, however, the disappearance of the frontier meant an end to America's period of conquest and settlement and, therefore, would have grave consequences for the United States, because, in Turner's view, the frontier defined the character of America itself. He intoned in the essay's most famous line, "Up to our own day American history has been in large degree the history of the colonization of the Great West. The existence of an area of free land, its continuous recession, and the advance of American settlement westward, explain American development" (quoted in Faragher 1994, 31).

Turner went on to explain that settlement followed an evolutionary path with stages of progress. The first settlers from Europe, when coming to the New World, confronted a harsh and unforgiving nature and hostile native peoples. Of necessity, these settlers lost some of their cultivated habits and devolved (temporarily) into near savages of their own. He wrote, "The wilderness masters the colonist. It finds him a European in dress, industries, tools, modes of travel, and thought." This encounter, however, "strips off the garments of civilization and arrays him in the hunting shirt and moccasin. It puts him in the log cabin of the Cherokee and Iroquois and runs an Indian palisade around him." The settler became the savage because "at the frontier the environment is at first too strong for the man." Yet, all was not lost, for "little by little he transforms the wilderness, but the outcome is not the old Europe . . . [but instead] here is a new product that is American" (quoted in Faragher 1994, 33–34). With each wave, like an advancing glacier, civilization pushed against the retreating the frontier.

It was there on the frontier where the characteristics of the ideal American took shape. Out of necessity, frontier settlers were independent, resourceful, courageous, and resilient. This process, in turn, transformed the European immigrant into a quasi savage and finally into an American, a character that embodied the best of both European civilization and American wilderness. Successive generations, moving west, repeated the process and likewise benefited from their contact with the frontier. Turner believed this made "the frontier . . . the line of most rapid and effective Americanization" (quoted in Faragher 1994, 33).

Such a civilization, Turner believed, could not help but be democratic, and he claimed that "the most important effect of the frontier has been in the promotion of democracy here and in Europe" (quoted in Faragher 1994, 53). Rejecting outside control and any semblance of social hierarchy or titled nobility, settlers on the frontier expected to be judged only on their abilities and to be treated by their peers as equals.

Taken as a whole, therefore, the frontier experience, the taming of the Wild West into a peaceable land of productive farms and ranches, mines, and towns represented the crowning achievement of a process of settlement that began in 1607 with the founding of Jamestown, a process that also made Europeans into Americans and Americans into the bravest and best of the world's nationalities. The frontier made Americans exceptional.

There was, however, a problem, a fear that ran through Turner's essay from his opening paragraph to his concluding sentence: "And now, four centuries from the discovery of America, at the end of a hundred years of life under the Constitution, the frontier has gone, and with its going has closed the first period of American history" (quoted in Faragher 1994, 60). His essay became an elegy for a passing era.

Truth be told, Americans typically pay little attention to the worries and admonishments of historians, but Turner's essay proved to be the exception. Given the extraordinary importance of the frontier experience on developing the American character, it seemed an obvious question to wonder what would become of American individualism, independence, and ingenuity in a tame world of orderly farms and dense cities. How could the United States continue to grow into an urban and industrial power and yet still retain the characteristics that came from contact with the wild frontier? How could Americans, in their increasingly hectic and safe urban existence, still come into contact with the Western frontier in their daily life? While seemingly a minor concern, this fear of a diminishing American vigor caused a great deal of consternation among Americans at the turn of the last century.

A few years after Turner's essay, Theodore Roosevelt likewise worried about the future of the nation in an address he gave before the Hamilton Club in Chicago on April 10, 1899. This address called on Americans to embrace the rugged life, as he himself had done, most recently in the Spanish-American War. "I wish to preach," he began, "not the doctrine of ignoble ease, but the doctrine of the strenuous life, the life of toil and effort, of labor and strife; to preach that highest form of success which comes, not to the man who desires mere easy peace, but to the man who does not shrink from danger, from hardship, or from bitter toil" (Roosevelt 1900). Men should not aspire to a life of comfortable leisure, and even for those who had attained wealth, it remained a national imperative that they continue to work, if not in factories then in "some kind of non-remunerative work in science, in letters, in art, in exploration, in historical research—work of the type we most need in this country" (Roosevelt 1900). In other words, these men of wealth and leisure should do exactly as he had done. The following year, Roosevelt addressed, more specifically, the youth of America. His "The American Boy" essay extolled the virtues of hard work, studying, and athletics, like the game of "foot-ball" that had recently been gaining in popularity, but the best training still lay in "a good deal of outdoor work or a good deal of what might be called natural outdoor play" (Roosevelt 1900).

Social reformers called for methods to preserve some semblance of the frontier experience or to create alternative experiences (such as attending summer camps or playing football) that could instill the same characteristics in America's youth. The preservation of wild landscapes became, for the first time, a major national concern. Led by men like John Muir, Theodore Roosevelt, and Aldo Leopold, Americans began to see the natural world in a different way. Wilderness, a land supposedly untouched by the hand of humanity, had been viewed for much of the history of Western civilization as a terrible place, home to howling wolves and other fearsome creatures, a place of darkness, fear, and temptation, as in Jesus's 40 days in the wilderness. The wilderness was also a place of savage Indians, who early Americans imagined engaged in a variety of terrible rituals. Mary Rowlandson, who was taken captive in Massachusetts during King Philip's War of the 1670s, spoke of her "mourning and lamenting, leaving farther my own Country, and travelling into the vast and howling wilderness" (quoted in Nash 1982, 28). For Rowlandson and other 17th-century settlers, the wilderness was something to be feared, but ultimately something that had to be confronted and conquered.

This attitude, however, began to change in the 19th century. More and more Americans came to see cities as scary, dehumanizing, polluted, and dangerous, and the wilderness, once the home of savage creatures, became a serene landscape of peace and refuge, a place to go and restore oneself from the hardships of industrial society. Painters like Thomas Moran and Albert Bierstadt made grand canvases showcasing tall mountains, thundering waterfalls, and the beauty of the natural world—mostly based on landscapes in the West.

Contact with the wilderness or a proximate analogue, like a summer camp, could also provide instructive training for young people; at least, that was the belief that underlaid scouting. While the Boy Scouts would officially be founded by the Englishmen Robert S. S. Baden-Powell in 1907, thinkers on this side of the Atlantic had already been toying with similar concepts, most notably the Canadian novelist Ernest Thompson Seton. Seton lamented the condition of the modern world, declaring, "Our system has broken down. Our civilization is a failure. Whenever pushed to its logical conclusion, it makes one millionaire and a million paupers. There is no complete happiness under its blight" (quoted in Deloria 1999, 99). Seton felt that somehow modern people had to reconnect with a more primitive world and a revivifying natural order.

In 1902, Seton proposed what he called the Woodcraft Indians in a series of articles in the *Ladies Home Journal*. The previous year, the author had confronted a gang of troublemaking children on his property and pacified them with some of the Indian legends he knew. Hoping to channel their energy into more productive pursuits, Seton convinced the boys to build a faux-Indian village on his Connecticut estate. He had them create Indian costumes for themselves, and then he set about giving them activities and games, supposedly based on American Indian traditions. Seeing success with this first "tribe" of children, which he named the Sinaways (a name which must surely have been a pun on the goals of the organization, though Seton was no moralist in the conventional sense), he sought to spread his concept nationwide.

A heavily romanticized view of American Indian culture, Seton felt, could influence young people and help them develop skills that they could carry for their entire lives. The Woodcraft Indian experience would stress an outdoor life that "teaches the duty of respecting and perfecting the body" and encourages "character-building forces in the form of recreation." Seton's method "works primarily with Woodcraft in its widest sense, which includes swimming, boating, camping, forestry, nature-study, scouting, photography, etc.," and "counts enormously on the magic of the campfire" (Seton 1915). Many of Seton's activities revolved around dances and supposed American Indian ceremonies like sunbathing (Seton elevated the practice by calling it a "sun healing ceremony"), spear throwing at a burlap bear, or a "Hopi Snake Dance," wherein participants passed around "a snake of some harmless kind." After praising the snake's inspiring attributes, a priest declared, "You are not poisonous, O Brother! You do no harm to me or mine. So, I have no right to harm you. Now, therefore go in peace" (Seton 1915, 44–45). The circle of boys, apparently with a new appreciation for nature, applauded as the snake slithered away, apparently unaware of its starring role in the ceremony. Seton's conception of the Woodcraft Indians was pacifistic, romantic, and not affiliated with any Christian denomination. It was intended to celebrate the uniqueness of American Indian culture and wisdom—though without any input from any actual Indians. Woodcraft, he observed, "accepts the Redman as the great prophet of outdoor life" (Seton 1915, xv).

Even before the advent of the Boy Scouts, Seton had competition in the field of instructional outdoor programs. Daniel C. Beard founded a similar organization in 1905 called the Sons of Daniel Boone and the Boy Pioneers. As the name suggests, Beard looked to white pioneers for inspiration rather than embracing a romantic "Indianness" like Seton. Instead of a tribe, Beard organized the children into "stockades," with a president taking the title of Daniel Boone, the secretary the name Davy Crockett, and the treasurer christened Kit Carson. Here they would mimic the characteristics of American frontiersmen, including acting out combat against Indian foes.

Eventually, both Seton's Woodcraft Indians and Beard's Sons of Daniel Boone were swallowed up by the Boy Scouts of America, and both men played a role in the new organization, at least for a time. Seton quickly grew to dislike the militaristic overtones of the Boy Scouts, with its uniforms and ranks. In his resignation from the Scouts, he declared, "The study of trees, flowers, and nature is giving way to wig-wagging, drills, and other activities of a military nature, thus destroying the symbolism of the organization" (quoted in Deloria 1999, 96). Indeed, his Woodcraft Indians had been "opposed to military terms and methods, especially the military code, which teaches that men may stifle their conscience and commit any or every crime merely because it is announced by their government to be in the interests of their country." He also abhorred "false patriotism which lauds evildoing because it was done by 'our own country.' We should be truer to our country if we were frankly taught to see its faults" (Seton 1915, xviii). He concluded by mentioning the recent atrocities of Wounded Knee and the Boxer Rebellion in China. Needless to say, his view differed greatly from the quasi-military trappings of the Boy Scouts of America, but all three organizations believed that contact

Television brought the myth of the Wild West into almost every home in the nation. A generation of children grew up imagining themselves riding the range with Gene Autry, Roy Rogers, or Fess Parker as Davy Crockett. This 1950s advertisement directed children to purchase a Davy Crockett Flashlight so their adventures could continue after dark. (Digital Comic Museum)

with the natural world would shape the industrial youth of the 20th century into better, stronger men.

Older Americans could also benefit from a different kind of contact with nature, namely hunting. Theodore Roosevelt, unsurprisingly, advocated for hunting as a solution to the problem of American men becoming less vigorous in the industrial age. Hunting, of course, had long been a necessity for many American families, a way to add meat to the diet. For the Lewis and Clark Expedition, a productive hunt meant the difference between success and failure. Meriwether Lewis confided to his journal that "I

sent Drewyer [Drouillard] and Shields before this morning in order
to kill some meat as neither the Indians nor ourselves had any thing
to eat." Fortunately, the pair succeeded in downing a deer, which
the famished expedition and their Shoshone friends ate with rav-
enous desire. The hungry Shoshone, much to Lewis's dismay, fell
upon the deer like "famished dogs each seizing and tearing away
a part of the intestens [sic] which had been previously thrown out
by Drewyer who killed it; the seen [sic] was such when I arrived
that had I not have a had a pretty keen appetite myself I am confident I should not have taisted [sic] any part of the venison shortly"
(Bergon 1995, 235–236). Hunting, therefore, served as a vital source
of nourishment at the beginning of the 19th century, and it would
continue to do so for many in the coming decades. However, by the
end of the 19th century, hunting had become a leisure sport for men
of means and a way to prove their primal masculinity in an increasingly industrialized and alienating world.

William Kent, a California congressman, declared that hunting
allowed modern men to "go out into the wilderness and learn the
endurance of nature which endures" and become, temporarily, "a
barbarian, and you're glad of it. It's good to be a barbarian. . . . [A]
nd you know that if you are a barbarian, you are at any rate a man"
(quoted in Nash 1982, 153). Certainly, Theodore Roosevelt shared
a similar sentiment, which prompted him to form the Boone and
Crockett Club in 1888. Named for the rugged frontiersman of yore,
its founding members represented the highest stratum of American society: Roosevelt, the author and prominent eugenicist Madison Grant, and two future U.S. senators in Elihu Root and Henry
Cabot Lodge. To attain membership, a hunter had to have the trophies of at least three big game animals. The hunter, Roosevelt and
the naturalist George Bird Grinnell exclaimed in an article for the
club, "Must be sound of body and firm of mind, and must possess
energy, resolution, manliness, self-reliance, and a capacity for self-
help" (quoted in Nash 1982, 152).

Hunting provided one of the best ways for the soft and flabby
modern man to achieve these valuable characteristics, and for
wealthy elites like Roosevelt and his companions in the Boone and
Crockett Club, it served an important cultural function as well.
Certainly, more authentic Westerners, like Roosevelt's guide Jack
Willis, found a good deal of humor (and profit) in leading buckskin-
clad rich kids into the wilderness in search of big game, but what
did men like Roosevelt find? Buckskin duds like those Roosevelt
and others would be photographed wearing (often in a New York

studio complete with fake plants and a painted alpine background) were not so different, after all, from the costumes of children playing Indian in Seton's faux-Indian villages. Indeed, these grown men acting like Boone and Crockett participated in a very similar ritual of self-affirmation.

Industrial society, on both sides of the Atlantic, created tremendous new sources of wealth. Titans of industry like Andrew Carnegie and John D. Rockefeller amassed fortunes previously only attainable by legendary ancient kings, fortunes that cared not for titles of rank or nobility. The spread of democratic values around the Western world also challenged established hierarchies. How could elite young men continue to be confident in their birthright to rule over society given these myriad economic and cultural changes? The positive attributes of courage, self-reliance, and confidence— in short, masculinity—gained by ritualistically participating in the hunt in distant mountains or jungles could then be transferred to the concrete jungles of cities and boardrooms. Contact with nature, red in tooth and claw, could therefore alleviate the anxiety these men felt in the changes occurring in society, and their fitness in the hunt could translate to their fitness to lead in industrial society as well.

Dressing in buckskin, hoisting a rifle, and heading out in search of big game enabled these men to claim masculinity for themselves. This was not something women could do, after all, and, moreover, it was not something for the masses or men of color. Poor people or people of color might hunt for subsistence (although game laws increasingly restricted such practices), but they could never be seen as real "sportsmen" who valued the thrill of the hunt and the trophy above mere considerations of sustenance and survival. To spend weeks in such fashion invariably meant that one needed both wealth and leisure time. Thus, being a member of a club like the Boone and Crockett Club conveyed to the member rank, privilege, and genuine masculinity, the kind of masculinity necessary to lead armies, corporations, or even nations.

Trophy hunting by elites such as Donald Trump Jr., as promoted by sportsmen like Teddy Roosevelt, remains part of our culture today. But as American attitudes have changed, these hunts no longer seem like heroic displays of masculinity to many and instead are denounced as unnecessary animal cruelty. For example, in 2015, American dentist Walter Palmer faced death threats and protests for killing Cecil the lion, a protected animal that had been lured out of Zimbabwe's Hwange National Park by Palmer's guides (Sehmer 2015). Trophy hunting of the kind Teddy Roosevelt once pursued is increasingly frowned upon in our own time, but many in our society remain obsessed with demonstrating masculinity.

Even in the 19th century, some Americans steered clear of such bloody displays, seeking a less sanguinary encounter with the natural world. Certainly, Americans had come to gradually see the wilderness as a place not of conflict but of contact with a more authentic and beautiful natural world. Across the 19th century and into the 20th, philosophers and naturalists like Henry David Thoreau, John Muir, and Aldo Leopold worked to convince Americans that the natural beauty of North America gave the United States an inheritance that eclipsed anything on offer in Europe. Culturally, the United States could not hope to compete with Europe's long history, its composers and artists, its writers and scholars, and its centuries of architectural beauty. In its snowcapped mountains, yawning canyons, endless caverns, and geysers, the United States had natural beauty unrivaled in the world. Rather than cross the ocean to see Europe, railroads implored Americans to head out west and "See America First."

Of course, the railroad companies had an ulterior motive: selling more tickets on their lines. Railroads shortened the time to travel across the continent from months to days, and the advent of luxury railroad cars, like those made by the Pullman Company, turned an ordeal into a pleasurable diversion. Railroads just needed attractive destinations. One solution lay in selling the Western climate as healthier and more beneficial than the congested East's, and railroads soon invested in luxury health resorts and hotels to cater to wealthy Easterners who sought to get away from the crowded, filthy, and disease-ridden East. The Denver and Rio Grande Western developed such a resort at Manitou Springs, Colorado, and another at Glenwood Springs, on Colorado's Western Slope. Larger railroads, such as the Atchison, Topeka, and the Santa Fe (AT&SF), also established resorts. The AT&SF built its Montezuma Hotel in Las Vegas, New Mexico, and the Southern Pacific outdid them all in 1880 with its massive Hotel Del Monte on the shores of the Pacific in Monterey, California. Far from roughing it, these hotels offered first-class amenities. As Lewis Morris Iddings observed in *Scribner's Magazine*, "An invalid needs not only good climate, but the best of food and many comforts. Roughing it for sick people has been much-over estimated" (quoted in Pierce 2016, 60). Dry Western air and healthy outside activities were not just beneficial for those suffering from ailments like tuberculosis. All people could benefit from a hike in the mountains, in John Muir's estimation, for "the summer climate of the fir and pine woods of the Sierra Nevada would be found infinitely more reviving [than sanitariums]; but because these woods have not been advertised like patent medicines, few seem to think of the spicy, vivifying influences that pervade their fountain freshness and beauty" (quoted in Pierce 2016, 56–67). Muir may have regretted such pronouncements, as he, perhaps more than anyone of his time, did much to promote the West and its natural beauty to Americans.

Railroads also played a huge role in promoting and even creating national parks. The transcontinental lines, in particular, wanted to carry visitors to these parks. Yellowstone National Park was created in 1872, the first in the nation. Rugged and out of the way, touring Yellowstone was not for the faint of heart, but that changed in 1883 when the Northern Pacific Railroad built a spur line into the park (Rothman 1998, 45–47). Few places exhibited the transformation from obstacle to national treasure quite like the Grand Canyon. The AT&SF, hoping to promote it as one of the wonders of the world, built a spur from Williams, Arizona, north to the rim of the canyon in 1901. To accommodate their discerning upper-class clientele, the railroad and its subsidiary the Fred Harvey Company built the extravagant El Tovar Hotel at a cost of $250,000; it opened in 1905 (and amazingly is still in use). Perched on the very edge of the canyon, the rooms offered visitors spectacular canyon vistas and amenities such as hot and cold running water, steam heat, and electric lighting (Rothman 1998, 58–59).

While train travel put the parks in the national consciousness, it was the automobile that democratized travel and made the national parks accessible. Instead of taking the AT&SF lines to Grand Canyon National Park, postwar tourists could instead journey there along Route 66, which passed just a few miles to the south. Middle-class Americans could now load the family into station wagons and sedans and make the trip themselves to sites across the West, experiencing the freedom of the open road on their own schedule. Gazing at the open chasm of the Grand Canyon, feeding panhandling bears in Yellowstone National Park, or having lunch hundreds of feet underground at Carlsbad Caverns became American rites of passage by the 1960s.

Americans also looked to the West for new forms of recreation. Skiing began to develop in the United States in the 1920s and 1930s, originally brought to the West by immigrants from Norway and Sweden, who used the contraptions for transportation, but it did not really take off until after World War II. Former mining towns, such as Aspen, Telluride, and Breckenridge in Colorado and Park City in Utah, became famous for their powdery snow. These and other mountain towns had been hard hit by the decline in mining and the Great Depression, and they looked to skiing to bring back opportunity. Certainly, opportunity came with affluent skiers, including many celebrities, but so too did rapidly escalating prices that forced older residents to relocate or into jobs in the lower-paying service industry.

Today, the West remains the place to challenge oneself, whether that involves scaling El Capitan in Yosemite, windsurfing in the Columbia River Gorge, skiing down the slopes in Vail or Park City, or mountain biking the trails in Moab, Sedona, or Durango. The West and its spectacular landscapes continue their siren call for current and future generations. The region remains the land of wide-open spaces, fresh starts, physical challenges, and new opportunities. Where railroads once promoted the region with glossy brochures, Instagram "influencers" now post their experiences for all to see.

For Americans who lacked the wealth or leisure time to take a trip west in search of big game animals or the resources for a Western vacation or summer camp, there remained, of course, the Western. Writers such as Zane Grey, B. M. Bower, Clarence Mulford, and Max Brand (the nom de plume of Frederick Faust) churned out Western novels for eager audiences. Grey's most successful work, *Riders of the Purple Sage*, debuted in 1912 and sold over two million copies in his lifetime. Like Wister's *The Virginian*, these novels continued many of the conventions of the dime novels but generally told more sophisticated stories with appreciably better writing. Still, the good guys tended to wear white hats and protect the little guy and American values from the forces of greed and evil. Louis L'Amour and others would continue this tradition, their works found in bookstores as well as grocery stores and gas stations from coast to coast (Etulain 1996, 27). Literary Westerns also provided models for a new form of entertainment: the motion picture.

By the dawn of the 20th century, if you could not go west, Hollywood was sure to bring the West to you. Indeed, the motion picture camera's development in the 1890s opened up a whole new way to appreciate the Western. Filming Westerns with literary source material proved to be comparatively easy. Authentic settings, especially as Hollywood developed, were near at hand, and filmmakers could assume their audiences already understood the basic plot, setting, and cast of characters that any good story would surely employ. There would be plenty of action and very little dialogue (which was a good thing, as "talkies" would not debut until 1927), and good always triumphed over evil. One of the first attempts at a making a coherent film came from Thomas Edison's company, the roughly 10-minute silent movie *The Great Train Robbery* (1903). As the name suggests, the action revolves around a band of dastardly train robbers, who succeed in robbing the train but are ultimately defeated by the posse sent to arrest them. More Westerns followed, despite the limitations of the silent movie format. Western actors such as Gilbert "Broncho Billy" Anderson, Williams S. Hart, and Tom Mix rode and shot their way across the silver screen, enthralling audiences of all ages the way Cody's Wild West show had a generation earlier.

By the 1930s and 1940s, Westerns ranked among the most popular genre of movies. John Ford's *Stagecoach* premiered in 1939, the first major role for a young stuntman turned actor named John Wayne. Errol Flynn fought both Indians and government bureaucracy in 1942's *They Died with Their Boots On*, with the hero's last stand taking on greater significance in the early days of World War II. Alan Ladd played a heroic but also somewhat tragic gunfighter in 1953's *Shane*, and a year earlier, Gary Cooper faced down a gang as Sheriff Will Kane in *High Noon*. Wayne and Ford teamed up again in the 1956 classic *The Searchers*, in which Wayne's character searches for his kidnapped niece, played by Natalie Wood. The story was loosely inspired by the story of James Parker's search to find his niece, Cynthia Ann Parker.

The Western, with its noble heroes and traditional gender roles, could also be adapted into family-friendly fare. The 1930s and 1940s witnessed the proliferation of films with stars like Gene Autry and Roy Rogers, who not only took down the bad guys, saved the town, and got the girl but also found time for some sweet singing on the side. Both Rogers and Autry later transitioned from movies to careers to television.

Westerns remained popular in the 1960s, with the "spaghetti Westerns" (so called because they starred Italian and American actors and were filmed in Spain) attracting large audiences for their brutal realism and violence. Italian director Sergio Leone's trio of spaghetti Westerns featured a character with no name whose actor, Clint Eastwood, became a household name around the world, perhaps the only actor whose credentials as a Western hero rivaled those of John Wayne.

Westerns also made their way to the small screen as an increasingly affluent nation of suburban dwellers put televisions into their homes in the 1950s. Many early Western television shows aimed for the youth audience, such as NBC's sarsaparilla-swilling hero in *Hopalong Cassidy*, which premiered in 1949. Cassidy had been created in 1904 by Clarence Mulford in a series of short stories and novels, but the character made the jump to movies. In total, some 66 films, or "Hoppies," as they were called, were made before the character transitioned to television. *The Lone Ranger*, which began as a radio series in 1933, moved to television in 1949, at the very dawn of the television age, and ran successfully until 1957. The tale of the Lone Ranger and his Indian sidekick, Tonto, continued in various television, movie, comic book, and novel adaptations for decades after the show's cancellation in 1957.

Wagon Train, which ran on NBC and later ABC, tells the story of a wagon train heading from Missouri to California. The series ran from 1957 to 1965, making a pretty slow passage to California. Not as long-lived, but still popular, *Wanted: Dead or Alive* followed Steve McQueen's character, Josh Randall, around the West as a bounty hunter for three seasons, from 1958 to 1961. The two longest-running and most successful Western series, though, were certainly *Gunsmoke* (1955–1975) and *Bonanza* (1959–1973). *Gunsmoke* actually began as a radio show, but it moved to television with James Arness playing the series's hero, Marshal Matt Dillion. Gritty and intended for adults, *Gunsmoke* took the television Western in new directions. *Bonanza*, meanwhile, followed the Cartwright family on adventures near their Ponderosa Ranch in western Nevada. Lorne Greene starred as the family's patriarch, Ben Cartwright, with his three sons, Adam Cartwright (Pernell Roberts), Eric "Hoss" Cartwright (Dan Blocker), and the youngest, Joseph "Little Joe," played by Michael Landon. The Cartwrights tangled with bad guys on a weekly basis, defeating everyone from corrupt businessmen to dangerous outlaws.

Davy Crockett became a television star with Fess Parker playing the role of the dashing frontiersman in a five-part ABC miniseries from 1954 to 1955. Disney then spliced the first three episodes together and released it in the theaters in 1955 as *Davy Crockett: King of the Wild Frontier*. The catchy theme song and popularity of the movie set off a Crockett craze, with young fans buying up toy Kentucky rifles and faux-coonskin caps in the thousands.

Despite its popularity, the Western was not immune to cultural changes, and by the 1970s, the genre seemed headed to the end of the trail. As Americans lost confidence in the Vietnam War and countercultural protestors and civil rights activists denounced the U.S. war effort and institutional racism, the Western, with its simple (and almost always white) heroes seemed out of touch with modern views. Newer Westerns even took the perspective of former villains, like 1970's *Little Big Man*, starring Dustin Hoffman as a white man raised by Cheyenne Indians. *Little Big Man* mocked American pretentions to military righteousness (a thinly veiled swipe at the Vietnam War) and included a major starring role for Dan George, a Coast Salish Indian actor, as Hoffman's surrogate grandfather—a far cry from movies like *The Searchers* that featured white actors portraying Indians in "red face" and speaking in broken English.

By the 1980s and 1990s, Westerns had largely disappeared from the nation's cinemas, with notable exceptions being 1990's *Dances with Wolves* (starring Kevin Costner) and Eastwood's 1992 film *The Unforgiven*, both of which won Best Picture at the Academy Awards. Eastwood intended his film to mark the end of his participation in the genre as both an actor and a director. Set in the twilight of the Wild West and following an aged gunfighter, Eastwood intended the film, quite consciously, to be an elegy on the Western genre.

But maybe the Western is not as dead as Eastwood and others believe. It perhaps replaced its horses with spaceships, as several recent science fiction programs seemed to be decidedly Westerns in space. ABC's *Battlestar Galactica* (1978), which was essentially *Wagon Train* in space, lasted only one season. Joss Whedon's similarly short-lived but much-loved Fox series *Firefly* (2002) had many Western trappings. Most recently, Disney launched its wildly successful new series *The Mandalorian* (2019), with its self-conscious nods to, in particular, Eastwood's Man with No Name character. *Star Trek*, which debuted in the 1960s, when the Western still held sway, was perhaps the first show to make the connection between the Western and science fiction explicit with Captain Kirk (played by William Shatner) intoning over Alexander Courage's ethereal music, "Space, the final frontier."

It is unlikely the myth of the West will ever really die. As long as the United States endures, it seems likely that Americans will still choose to imagine themselves as inheritors of the legacy of the American West (even if that legacy is hopelessly interwoven with mythology). Thus, it is not surprising that former president Donald Trump (a New Yorker with no real ties to the West) chose to mention the mythic West in his Republican National Convention acceptance speech in 2020. After waxing poetic about settlers and the Oregon Trail, he exclaimed,

Ranchers and miners, cowboys and sheriffs, farmers and settlers. They pressed on past the Mississippi to stake a claim in the wild frontier. Legends were born. Wyatt Earp, Annie Oakley, Davy Crockett, and Buffalo Bill. Americans built their beautiful homesteads on the open range. Soon, they had churches and communities, then towns, and with time, great centers of industry and commerce. (Trump 2020)

Here is the old Turnerian ideal of stages of progress, of Roosevelt's taming of the frontier, of Cody's Wild West show, repackaged and recapitulated for a nation not of settlers and farmers but instead city and suburb dwellers. The mythology of the West remains a vital part of American culture, even if its star has diminished.

EPILOGUE: THE FUTURE OF THE WEST

Wyatt Earp, the legendary lawman of the Old West, wrote his friend the actor William Hart in 1923 to encourage him to make a movie about his "true" exploits. Earp explained, "Many wrong impressions of . . . myself have been created. I am not going to live to the age of Methuselah, and any wrong impression, I want to make right before I go away. The screen could do all this" (quoted in Isenberg 2013, 204). Earp, well into his seventies, hoped to solidify his place as a hero in Western lore, and he increasingly turned to the new media of film to ensure that posterity remembered him. He even offered that Hart should direct the film with a younger star like Tom Mix playing him.

By 1923, Earp had taken to life in Los Angeles, acting as a kind of expert and adviser on the numerous Westerns already being cranked out by the fledgling film industry. He even had a walk-on role in the 1916 Western *The Half-Breed*, starring the dashing Douglas Fairbanks. To be sure, Earp had long invented and reinvented himself, but in film, he found a medium that could forever guarantee his memory and heroism. Having a real lawman of the Wild West advising on Western films that traded in the mythology of the West and were filmed on back lots in a rapidly growing urban metropolis illustrates the complicated interaction of the mythology of the West with the reality. The aging heroes of the vanished

past—such as Earp, Buffalo Bill, and Quanah Parker—all understood how myth and reality intertwined to create a new reality, an
imagined West that would continue to play out in the beliefs and
values of a real society.

Still relatively a land of wide-open spaces, the West remains a
place for the imagination, a place for individualism and self-reliance, and a place to experience profound natural beauty in rugged,
silent deserts or icy mountain peaks. Yet, those open places and
scenic vistas where the individual can act out ritualistic behaviors
of exploration (and post to Instagram for likes and follows or You-
Tube for subscribers) only exist because of decisions about how to
use the lands of the region. National parks, for example, are created spaces, lines drawn on maps, with rules and bureaucracies to
enforce how they are used. Often the real people who lived there
(typically native peoples) were removed, their history effaced to
make room for the parks as avatars of sublimity and unaltered
wilderness.

Despite the lingering mythology, the West is no longer an unpeo-
pled frontier. The region boasts some of the nation's most populous
cities, places like Los Angeles, Phoenix, and San Antonio. California grew after World War II into the nation's most populous state,
and Texas ranks second. Similarly, Western cities continue to grow
at phenomenal rates with seemingly total disregard for the region's
environmental limitations. The history of how Western states engi-
neered their societies around the building of massive dams like
Hetch Hetchy and, later, far larger structures on the Columbia,
Colorado, and other rivers rarely troubles the public, despite grave
predictions about climate change, years of ongoing droughts, and
increasingly terrible fire seasons.

Americans have long placed their dreams on the West, and many
have come to fabulous fruition, but the West has also had a way of
reminding us that it is a land of extremes not easily tamed.

BIBLIOGRAPHY

PRIMARY SOURCES

Backus, Harriett Fish. *Tomboy Bride: A Woman's Personal Account of Life in the Mining Camps of the West*. Boulder, CO: Pruett Publishing Co., 1969.

Bates, Katharine Lee. *America the Beautiful and Other Poems*. New York: Thomas Y. Crowell Co., 1911. https://archive.org/details/americabeautiful00baterich

Bergon, Frank, ed. *The Journals of Lewis and Clark*. New York: Penguin Books, 1995.

Bidwell, John. *Echoes of the Past about California*. Chicago: Lakeside Press, 1928. https://tile.loc.gov/storage-services//service/gdc/calbk/141.pdf

Borthwick, J. D. *Three Years in California*. Edinburg and London: William Blackwood and Sons, 1857. https://tile.loc.gov/storage-services//service/gdc/calbk/117.pdf

Cabeza de Vaca, Álvar Núñez. *Chronicle of the Narváez Expedition*. Translated by Fanny Bandelier. New York: Penguin, 2002.

Catlin, George. *Life among the Indians*. London: Gall and Inglis, 1870. https://www.google.com/books/edition/Life_Among_the_Indians/X41TAAAAcAAJ

Church of Jesus Christ of Latter-day Saints. *The Book of Mormon: Another Testament of Jesus Christ*. Salt Lake City, UT: Church of Jesus Christ of Latter-day Saints, 1981.

Cleveland, Grover. "Second Annual Message." December 6, 1886. https://millercenter.org/the-presidency/presidential-speeches/december-6-1886-second-annual-message

Coronado, Francisco Vázquez de. "Vázquez de Coronado's Letter to the King, October 20, 1541." In *Documents of the Coronado Expedition, 1539–1542*, edited and translated by Richard Flint and Shirley Cushing Flint, 319. Dallas: Southern Methodist University Press, 2005.

Crampton, Frank. *Deep Enough: A Working Stiff in the Western Mine Camps*. Norman: University of Oklahoma Press, 1956.

Ebey, Winfield Scott. *The 1854 Oregon Trail Diary of Winfield Scott Ebey*. Independence, MO: Oregon-California Trails Association, 1997.

An Emigrant. *Texas in 1840, or the Emigrant's Guide to the New Republic*. New York: Arno Press, 1973; New York: William A. Allen, 1840.

Flint, Richard, and Shirley Cushing Flint, trans. and eds. *Documents of the Coronado Expedition, 1539–1542*. Dallas: Southern Methodist University Press, 2005.

Frémont, John C. *The Exploring Expedition to the Rocky Mountains, Oregon, and California*. Buffalo: Derby, Orton & Mulligan, 1853. https://www .google.com/books/edition/The_Exploring_Expedition_to_the _Rocky_Mo/rwY1AAAAIAAJ

Gladstone, Thomas H. "The Sack of Lawrence, Kansas, 1856." EyeWitness to History, 2008. http://www.eyewitnesstohistory.com/lawrencesack .htm

Hom, Marlon K. *Songs of Gold Mountain: Cantonese Rhymes from San Francisco Chinatown*. Berkeley: University of California Press, 1992.

Jefferson, Thomas. "Third Annual Message to Congress." October 17, 1803. https://avalon.law.yale.edu/19th_century/jeffmes3.asp

Larkin, Thomas O. "More about the California Gold." *Baltimore Commercial Journal*. Newspapers.com, September 18, 1848. https://www .newspapers.com/clip/23853970/letter_describing_mining_for _gold_and/

Lavender, David. *One Man's West*. New York: Doubleday & Co., 1943.

Lehmann, Hermann. *Nine Years among the Indians, 1870–1879*. Albuquerque: University of New Mexico Press, 1993.

Linderman, Frank B. *Montana Adventure: The Recollections of Frank B. Linderman*. Lincoln: University of Nebraska Press, 1968.

Linderman, Frank B. *Plenty-Coups: Chief of the Crows*. Lincoln: University of Nebraska Press, 2002.

Linderman, Frank B. *Pretty-Shield: Medicine Woman of the Crows*. Lincoln: University of Nebraska Press, 1978.

Lummis, Charles F. "I Guess So." *Los Angeles Times*, September 30, 1917.

Muir, John. *John Muir: Nature Writings*. Edited by William Cronon. New York: Library of America, 1997.

Neihardt, John G. *Black Elk Speaks*. Lincoln: University of Nebraska Press, 1979.

New York Daily Herald. "Continuance of the Gold Excitement: Extraordinary Condition of Affairs." September 27, 1848. https://www.newspapers .com/clip/23854275/1848-gold-rush-news-continuance-of/

O'Sullivan, John. "Annexation." *United States Magazine and Democratic Review* 17 (1845): 5–6, 9–10. https://www.americanyawp.com/reader/manifest-destiny/john-osullivan-declares-americas-manifest-destiny-1845/

Parkman, Francis. *The Oregon Trail: Sketches of Prairie and Rocky-Mountain Life.* Boston: Little, Brown, and Company, 1891. https://www.google.com/books/edition/The_Oregon_Trail_Sketches_of_Prairie_and/KZItAQAAMAAJ

Poetry Foundation. "Robert W. Service." Accessed January 24, 2022. https://www.poetryfoundation.org/poets/robert-w-service

Polk, James K. "Fourth Annual Message to Congress." December 5, 1848. https://millercenter.org/the-presidency/presidential-speeches/december-5-1848-fourth-annual-message-congress

Polk, James K. "Inaugural Address." March 4, 1845. https://avalon.law.yale.edu/19th_century/polk.asp

Polk, James K. "Message of the President." May 11, 1846. https://avalon.law.yale.edu/19th_century/polk01.asp

Powell, John Wesley. *Report on the Lands of the Arid Region of the United States.* Washington, DC: Government Printing Office, 1879. https://www.google.com/books/edition/Report_on_the_Lands_of_the_Arid_Region_o/OToAAAAAQAAJ

Roosevelt, Theodore. "First Annual Message." December 3, 1901. https://millercenter.org/the-presidency/presidential-speeches/december-3-1901-first-annual-message

Roosevelt, Theodore. "The Strenuous Life." 1900. https://www.bartleby.com/58/1.html

Sehmer, Alexander. "Cecil the Lion: Zimbabwe Searches for Hunter Who Killed Iconic Big Cat with Bow and Arrow and Rifle." *The Independent*, July 30, 2015. https://www.independent.co.uk/news/world/africa/cecil-lion-zimbabwe-searches-hunter-who-killed-iconic-big-cat-10416833.html

Seton, Ernest Thompson. *Manual of the Woodcraft Indians.* New York: Doubleday, Page, and Company, 1915. https://www.google.com/books/edition/The_Birch_bark_Roll_of_Woodcraft/BxJZAAAAYAAJ

Shirley, Dame. *The Shirley Letters from California.* San Francisco: Thomas C. Russell, 1922. https://cdn.loc.gov//service/gdc/calbk/146.pdf

Siringo, Charles A. *A Texas Cowboy: Or, Fifteen Years on the Hurricane Deck of a Spanish Pony.* New York: Penguin, 2000.

Tedlock, Barbara. *The Beautiful and the Dangerous: Dialogues with the Zuni Indians.* New York: Viking, 1992.

Thoreau, Henry David. "Eastward I Go Only by Force; but Westward I Go Free." Quote Fancy. Accessed January 24, 2022. https://quotefancy.com/quote/824490/Henry-David-Thoreau-Eastward-I-go-only-by-force-but-westward-I-go-free

Trump, Donald J. "Acceptance Speech, Republican National Conven-
    tion." Transcript from National Public Radio, August 27, 2020.
    https://www.npr.org/2020/08/27/901381398/fact-check
    -trumps-address-to-the-republican-convention-annotated
Twain, Mark. *Roughing It.* New York: Harper and Row, 1962.
U.S. Congress. "General Mining Act of 1872." 17 Stat. 91–96. https://
    www.loc.gov/law/help/statutes-at-large/42nd-congress/session
    -2/c42s2ch152.pdf
U.S. Congress. "Morrill Act (1862)." *Our Documents*, Library of Congress,
    1862a. https://www.ourdocuments.gov/doc.php?flash=false&doc
    =33&page=transcript
U.S. Congress. "Pacific Railway Act (1862)." *Our Documents*, Library of
    Congress, 1862b. https://www.ourdocuments.gov/doc.php?flash
    =false&doc=32&page=transcript
Walker, William. "Letter to G.P. Disoway." *Christian Advocate and Jour-
    nal and Zion's Herald* 7, no. 27 (March 1, 1833). https://brbl-zoom
    .library.yale.edu/viewer/15495314
Wister, Owen. *The Virginian.* New York: Penguin, 1988.
Wyeth, Nathaniel J. *Journal of Captain Nathaniel J. Wyeth.* Ipswich, MA:
    Great Neck Publishing, 1983.

SECONDARY SOURCES

Books

Ambrose, Stephen E. *Crazy Horse and Custer: The Parallel Lives of Two Amer-
    ican Warriors.* New York: Anchor Books, 1996a.
Ambrose, Stephen E. *Undaunted Courage: Meriwether Lewis, Thomas Jeffer-
    son, and the Opening of the American West.* New York: Touchstone,
    1996b.
Anderson, Gary C. *Sitting Bull and the Paradox of Lakota Nationhood.* New
    York: Pearson, 2007.
Andrews, Thomas. *Killing for Coal: America's Deadliest Labor War.* Cam-
    bridge, MA: Harvard University Press, 2008.
Berg, Scott W. *38 Nooses: Lincoln, Little Crow, and the Beginning of the Fron-
    tier's End.* New York: Vintage, 2012.
Betty, Gerald. *Comanche Society before the Reservation.* College Station:
    Texas A&M Press, 2002.
Brown, Dee. *The Fetterman Massacre.* Lincoln: University of Nebraska
    Press, 1962.
Calloway, Colin G. *One Vast Winter Count: The Native American West before
    Lewis and Clark.* Lincoln: University of Nebraska Press, 2003.
Courtwright, David T. *Violent Land: Single Men and Social Disorder from
    the Frontier to the Inner City.* Cambridge, MA: Harvard University
    Press, 1996.

Crosby, Alfred. *Children of the Sun: A History of Humanity's Unappeasable Appetite for Energy.* New York: W. W. Norton, 2007.

Debo, Angie. *A History of the Indians of the United States.* Norman: University of Oklahoma Press, 1970.

Deloria, Philip. *Playing Indian.* New Haven, CT: Yale University Press, 1999.

Dodds, Gordon B. *The American Northwest: A History of Oregon and Washington.* Wheeling, IL: Forum Press, 1986.

Dykstra, Robert R. *The Cattle Towns.* Lincoln: University of Nebraska Press, 1968.

Erdoes, Richard, and Alfonso Ortiz. *American Indian Myths and Legends.* New York: Pantheon, 1984.

Etulain, Richard. *Re-Imagining the Modern American West: A Century of Fiction, History, and Art.* Tucson: University of Arizona Press, 1996.

Faragher, John Mack. *Daniel Boone: The Life and Legend of an American Pioneer.* New York: Holt, 1993.

Faragher, John Mack. *Rereading Frederick Jackson Turner.* New York: Henry Holt and Co., 1994.

Faragher, John Mack. *Women and Men on the Overland Trail.* New Haven, CT: Yale University Press, 1979.

Furtwangler, Albert. *Bringing Indians to the Book.* Seattle: University of Washington Press, 2005.

Gutiérrez, Ramón. *When Jesus Came the Corn Mothers Went Away: Marriage, Sexuality, and Power in New Mexico, 1500–1846.* Stanford, CA: Stanford University Press, 1991.

Gwynne, S. C. *Empire of the Summer Moon: Quanah Parker and the Rise and Fall of the Comanches, the Most Powerful Indian Tribe in American History.* New York: Scribner, 2010.

Hämäläinen, Pekka. *The Comanche Empire.* New Haven, CT: Yale University Press, 2008.

Hittman, Michael. *Wovoka and the Ghost Dance.* Lincoln: University of Nebraska Press, 1997.

Hutton, Paul Andrew. *The Apache Wars.* New York: Broadway Books, 2016.

Isenberg, Andrew C. *The Destruction of the Bison.* New York: Cambridge University Press, 2000.

Isenberg, Andrew C. *Wyatt Earp: A Vigilante Life.* New York: Hill and Wang, 2013.

Jeffrey, Julie Roy. *Converting the West: A Biography of Narcissa Whitman.* Norman: University of Oklahoma Press, 1994.

Johannsen, Robert W. *To the Halls of the Montezumas: The Mexican War in the American Imagination.* New York: Oxford University Press, 1985.

Johnson, Paul E. *A Shopkeeper's Millennium: Society Revivals in Rochester, New York, 1815–1837.* New York: Hill and Wang, 2004.

Johnson, Susan Lee. *Roaring Camp: The Social World of the California Gold Rush.* New York: W. W. Norton, 2000.

McGeary, M. Nelson. *Gifford Pinchot: Forester-Politician*. Princeton, NJ: Princeton University Press, 2016.

McPherson, James. *Battle Cry of Freedom: The Civil War Era*. New York: Oxford University Press, 2003.

Meinig, Donald. *The Shaping of America: A Geographical Perspective on 500 Years of History*. Vol. 2, *Continental America, 1800–1867*. New Haven, CT: Yale University Press, 1995.

Moulton, Candy. *Valentine T. McGillycuddy: Army Surgeon, Agent to the Sioux*. Norman, OK: Arthur H. Clark Company, 2011.

Nabakov, Peter. *Where the Lightning Strikes: The Lives of American Indian Sacred Places*. New York: Viking, 2006.

Nash, Roderick. *Wilderness and the American Mind*. New Haven, CT: Yale University Press, 1982.

Nelson, Megan Kate. *The Three-Cornered War: The Union, the Confederacy, and Native Peoples in the Fight for the West*. New York: Scribner, 2020.

Pierce, Jason E. *Making the White Man's West: Whiteness and the Creation of the American West*. Niwot: University of Colorado Press, 2016.

Rothman, Hal. *Devil's Bargains: Tourism in the Twentieth-Century American West*. Lawrence: University of Kansas Press, 1998.

Schlissel, Lillian. *Women's Diaries of the Westward Journey*. New York: Schocken Books, 1982.

Sheriff, Carol. *The Artificial River: The Erie Canal and the Paradox of Progress, 1817–1862*. New York: Hill and Wang, 1997.

Stark, Peter. *Astoria: Astor and Jefferson's Lost Pacific Empire*. New York: Ecco Books, 2015.

Stegner, Wallace. *Beyond the Hundredth Meridian: John Wesley Powell and the Second Opening of the West*. New York: Penguin, 1992.

Stegner, Wallace. *The Gathering of Zion: The Story of the Mormon Trail*. Lincoln: University of Nebraska Press, 1981.

Ubbelohde, Carl, Maxine Benson, and Duane A. Smith. *A Colorado History*. Boulder, CO: Pruett Publishing Co., 1995.

Unruh, John D., Jr. *The Plains Across: The Overland Emigrants and the Trans-Mississippi West, 1840–60*. Champaign: University of Illinois Press, 1993.

Utley, Robert M. *Billy the Kid: A Short and Violent Life*. Lincoln, NE: Bison Books, 1991.

Utley, Robert M. *Frontier Regulars: The United States Army and the Indian, 1866–1891*. Bloomington: Indiana University Press, 1973.

Utley, Robert M. *The Indian Frontier of the American West, 1846–1890*. Albuquerque: University of New Mexico Press, 1984.

Wallis, Michael. *The Best Land under Heaven: The Donner Party in the Age of Manifest Destiny*. New York: W. W. Norton, 2017.

Warren, Louis S. *Buffalo Bill's America: William Cody and the Wild West Show*. New York: Vintage, 2006.

West, Elliott. *The Contested Plains: Indians, Goldseekers, and the Rush to Colorado*. Lawrence: University of Kansas Press, 1998.

West, Elliott. *The Essential West: Collected Essays*. Norman: University of Oklahoma Press, 2012.

West, Elliott. *Growing Up with the Country: Childhood on the Far Western Frontier*. Albuquerque: University of New Mexico Press, 1989.

West, Elliott. *The Last Indian War: The Nez Perce Story*. New York: Oxford University Press, 2009.

West, Elliott. *The Way to the West: Essays on the Central Plains*. Albuquerque: University of New Mexico Press, 1995.

White, G. Edward. *The Eastern Establishment and the Western Experience: The West of Frederic Remington, Theodore Roosevelt, and Owen Wister*. Austin: University of Texas Press, 1968.

White, Richard. *"It's Your Misfortune and None of My Own": A New History of the American West*. Norman: University of Oklahoma, 1991.

White, Richard. *Railroaded: The Transcontinentals and the Making of Modern America*. New York: W. W. Norton, 2011.

Wilkins, Thurman. *John Muir: Apostle of Nature*. Norman: University of Oklahoma Press, 1995.

Articles

Anderson, H. Allen. "The Encomienda in New Mexico, 1598–1680." *New Mexico Historical Review* 60, no. 4 (1985): 353–377.

De León, Arnoldo. "Vamos Pa' Kaiansis: Tejanos in the Nineteenth-Century Cattle Drives." *Journal of South Texas* 27, no. 2 (Fall 2014): 6–21.

Kohler, Timothy A., Mark D. Varien, Aaron M. Wright, and Kristin A. Kuckelman. "Mesa Verde Migration." *American Scientist* 96, no. 2 (March–April 2008): 146–153.

Romano, Andrea. "You Can Go Glamping in Oregon Trail Style in Yosemite's New Covered Wagons." *Travel + Leisure*, September 4, 2018. https://www.travelandleisure.com/travel-news/yosemite-pines-covered-wagon-glamping

Thoreau, Henry David. "Walking." *The Atlantic*, June 1862. https://www.theatlantic.com/magazine/archive/1862/06/walking/304674/

West, Elliott. "Family Life on the Trail West." *History Today* 42, no. 12 (December 1992): 33–39.

Websites

Blackman, Joseph Andrew. "Ikard, Bose (1843–1929)." *Handbook of Texas*, Texas State Historical Association. Updated: September 16, 2020. https://www.tshaonline.org/handbook/entries/ikard-bose

Church of Jesus Christ of Latter-Day Saints. "The Manifesto and the End of Plural Marriage." Accessed January 24, 2022. https://www.churchofjesuschrist.org/topics/the-manifesto-and-the-end-of-plural-marriage

Cocke, Elizabeth. "The Wilberg Mine Fire." *Utah History Encyclopedia*. Accessed January 24, 2022. https://www.uen.org/utah_history_encyclopedia/w/WILBERG_MINE_FIRE.shtml

Davis, John W. "The Johnson County War: 1892 Invasion of Northern Wyoming." WyoHistory.org, November 8, 2014. https://www.wyohistory.org/encyclopedia/johnson-county-war-1892-invasion-northern-wyoming

Drew, Marilyn J. "A Brief History of the Bozeman Trail." WyoHistory.org, November 20, 2014. https://www.wyohistory.org/encyclopedia/brief-history-bozeman-trailEllsworth, S. George. *Utah's Road to Statehood*. Updated May 29, 2002. https://archives.utah.gov/research/exhibits/Statehood/intronew.htm

Fandom. "Drive." Accessed January 18, 2022. https://x-files.fandom.com/wiki/Drive

Gard, Wayne. "Fence Cutting." *Handbook of Texas*, Texas State Historical Association. Updated September 21, 2019. https://www.tshaonline.org/handbook/entries/fence-cutting

Johnson, Lane. "Who and Where Are the Lamanites." *Ensign* 5, no. 12 (December 1975). https://www.churchofjesuschrist.org/study/ensign/1975/12/who-and-where-are-the-lamanites

Ken Burns Presents: The West, episode 8. Directed and produced by Steven Ives. PBS Home Video and Turner Home Entertainment. 1996. https://www.pbs.org/weta/thewest/program/episodes/eight/likegrass.htm

King James Bible Online. Accessed January 24, 2022. *Genesis*, Chapter 1, verse 26. https://www.kingjamesbibleonline.org/Genesis-1-26/

Marks, Paula Mitchell. "Samuel Augustus Maverick." *Handbook of Texas*, Texas State Historical Association. Updated December 1, 2015. https://www.tshaonline.org/handbook/entries/maverick-samuel-augustus

Moulton, Candy. "Mormon Handcart Horror." Historynet.com. 2014. https://www.historynet.com/mormon-handcart-horrors.htmPew Research Center. "Religious Landscape Study." 2014. https://www.pewforum.org/religious-landscape-study/

Smithsonian, National Museum of the American Indian. "A Blessing for the People: Native Stories of Horse Origins." Accessed January 24, 2022. https://americanindian.si.edu/exhibitions/horsenation/blessing.html

Spangenberger, Phil. "The Shoots Far Gun." *True West Magazine*, August 11, 2016. https://truewestmagazine.com/the-shoots-far-gun/

Stover, Dale. "Sun Dance." *Encyclopedia of the Great Plains*, 2011. http://plainshumanities.unl.edu/encyclopedia/doc/egp.rel.046

Texas beyond History. "Leanne's Burial." Accessed January 24, 2022. https://www.texasbeyondhistory.net/plateaus/prehistory/images/leannes.html

INDEX

About the Author

JASON E. PIERCE is a professor of history at Angelo State University in San Angelo, Texas. His teaching and research interests include American Indian history, the history of the American West, and American Environmental History. His previous published works include *Making the White Man's West: Whiteness and the Creation of the American West* (2016). Like any good Western historian, he enjoys hiking, camping, and mountain biking in the great outdoors.